Postdoctoral Appointments and Disappointments

A Report of the

Committee on a Study of Postdoctorals
in Science and Engineering
in the United States

Commission on Human Resources

National Research Council

NATIONAL ACADEMY PRESS
Washington, D.C.   1981

The work on which this publication is based was performed pursuant to Contract No. SRS-7824661 with the National Science Foundation.

Library of Congress Cataloging in Publication Data

National Research Council. Committee on a Study of
   Postdoctorals in Science and Engineering in the
   United States.
   Postdoctoral appointments and disappointments.

   At head of title: National Research Council, Commis-
sion on Human Resources.
   1. Scientists--United States. 2. Engineers--United
States. I. National Research Council. Commission on
Human Resources. II. Title.
Q149.U5N358 1980   502'.3   80-29104
ISBN 0-309-03132-X

Available from:

National Academy Press
2101 Constitution Ave., N.W.
Washington, D.C. 20418

Printed in the United States of America

COMMITTEE ON A STUDY OF POSTDOCTORALS
IN SCIENCE AND ENGINEERING IN THE UNITED STATES

<u>Chairman</u>
DR. LEE GRODZINS, Department of Physics, Massachusetts Institute of
  Technology
DR. RICHARD D. ANDERSON, Department of Mathematics, Louisiana State
  University
DR. FREDERICK E. BALDERSTON, Center for Research in Management Science,
  University of California-Berkeley
DR. KENNETH E. CLARK, Dean, College of Arts and Sciences, University
  of Rochester
DR. GERHART FRIEDLANDER,* Department of Chemistry, Brookhaven
  National Laboratory
DR. HERBERT FRIEDMAN, Superintendent, Space Science Division, Naval
  Research Laboratory
DR. JOHN C. HANCOCK, Dean of Engineering, Purdue University
DR. DONALD F. HORNIG, Director, Interdisciplinary Programs in Health,
  Harvard School of Public Health
DR. SHIRLEY ANN JACKSON, Scattering and Low Energy Physics, Bell
  Laboratories
DR. ERNEST S. KUH, College of Engineering, University of California-
  Berkeley
DR. WILLIAM F. MILLER, President, SRI International
DR. NICHOLAS C. MULLINS, Department of Sociology, Indiana University
DR. THOMAS A. REICHERT, Department of Medicine, Duke University
  Medical Center
DR. HELEN R. WHITELEY, Department of Microbiology, School of Medicine,
  University of Washington

<u>Study Director</u>
MR. PORTER E. COGGESHALL, Commission on Human Resources, National
  Research Council

<u>Consultant</u>
MR. ROBERT K. WEATHERALL, Director, Career Planning and Placement,
  Massachusetts Institute of Technology

*During the final 3 months of the study Dr. Friedlander served as com-
mittee chairman while Dr. Grodzins was on leave outside the United
States.

iii

ACKNOWLEDGMENTS

This report of the Committee on a Study of Postdoctorals in Science and Engineering in the United States has been prepared for the National Science Foundation under the aegis of the Commission on Human Resources of the National Research Council. The foundation provided the financial support for both the interim and final phases of this 3-year study.

The report has benefited from the assistance of numerous individuals and organizations. The committee first wishes to acknowledge the many scientists and engineers who participated in our surveys, site visits, and other data collection activities. Without the cooperation of these individuals this study would not have been feasible.

John A. Scopino was most helpful throughout the study in his role as project officer for the National Science Foundation. We also appreciate the assistance of Charles E. Falk, Director of Foundation's Division of Science Resources Studies, and other staff members in this division who were involved in the study.

Within the Commission on Human Resources Porter E. Coggeshall directed the activities of the committee, designed the data analyses, and had primary responsibility for drafting this report. Prudence W. Brown supervised the data-gathering efforts and produced the tables and figures used in the report. Ellen Jackson assisted with the project administration and typed draft copies of the report; Imani Ansari typed the final manuscript. The committee is also indebted to George Boyce and Marinus van der Have, who were responsible for data processing, and to Doris Rogowski and her clerical staff, who coded the survey results. Robert K. Weatherall, who served as a consultant, participated in many of the committee's site visits and drafted the second chapter of this report. Dorothy M. Gilford served as the principal investigator during the first 2 years of this study. Harrison Shull, Commission Chairman, and William C. Kelly, Executive Director of the Commission, offered helpful advice throughout the course of the study. The committee especially wishes to thank Herbert B. Pahl, Staff Director for the NRC Study of Biomedical and Behavioral Research Personnel, for the cooperation and assistance that he and his staff have given us.

v

ABSTRACT

This report presents detailed findings on a broad range of issues
concerning the importance of postdoctorals to the nation's research
effort and the value of postdoctoral experience to young scientists
and engineers pursuing careers in research. Although in both respects
the postdoctoral appointment has proven to be an important institution, some serious concerns have arisen in recent years regarding its
present and future role. The report identifies as issues of particular concern:

(1) the lack of prestige and research independence in
    postdoctoral appointments for the most talented
    young people;
(2) the mismatch between the important role that post-
    doctorals play in the nation's research enterprise
    and the lack of opportunities that they find for
    subsequent careers in research;
(3) the lack of recognized status of postdoctoral
    appointments in the academic community; and
(4) the underutilization of women and members of
    minority groups in scientific research.

Four specific recommendations are made in the report:

A. Establishment of 250 federally supported, portable
   postdoctoral fellowships annually, for specially
   qualified young scientists and engineers--with
   2-year stipends competitive with employment
   salaries and with some research expense funds to
   foster innovative research.
B. Establishment of 50 additional fellowships a year,
   similar to those described above, but expressly
   for minority Ph.D. recipients.
C. Establishment, at every university with sizable
   numbers of nonfaculty research personnel, of a
   standing committee on postdoctorals and other nonfaculty doctoral research staff to review the situa-

tions of members of these groups on its campus and to recommend university policies.

D. Expansion of the National Science Foundation's longitudinal data-gathering effort to include a survey specifically focussed on career decisions of young scientists and engineers.

Beyond these specific recommendations, the committee believes that the entire postdoctoral institution is in a state of transition and must be reexamined by federal and university policymakers. This report, which is the first comprehensive study of postdoctorals in science and engineering in more than 10 years, should prove valuable as a primary resource for these reevaluations.

CONTENTS

LIST OF FIGURES

xi

LIST OF TABLES

1. THE STUDY

This report presents the findings and policy recommendations of the Committee on Postdoctorals in Science and Engineering in the United States. The committee was appointed in the late fall of 1977 by the National Research Council to study the changing roles of postdoctorals in research and higher education in the United States and to consider the implications of its findings for federal and institutional policy decisions. During the past 3 years the committee has met a total of 8 full days to plan analyses, review the findings, and formulate its recommendations. The study has been funded by the National Science Foundation and conducted under the aegis of the Commission on Human Resources of the National Research Council.

The motivation for the study may be summarized as follows. For many of the most talented scientists and engineers the postdoctoral appointment has served as an important period of transition between formal education and a career in research. The appointment has provided the recent doctorate recipient with a unique opportunity to devote his or her full energies to research without the encumbrance of formal course work or teaching and administrative responsibilities. Those holding such appointments have made valuable contributions to the quality, creativity, and productivity of ongoing scientific inquiry. While the overall magnitude of these contributions has varied markedly depending on the field of research, postdoctorals have played a significant role in the research effort in virtually every field of science and engineering—even in those fields in which their numbers have been quite small. Whether or not the postdoctoral will play an important role in the future, however, will depend on how universities and the scientific community as a whole adapt to a rapidly changing environment. Already apparent are some significant changes in enrollment levels, faculty hiring patterns, sizes of research budgets, and other factors affecting the supply and utilization of doctoral personnel. The aim of this study is to assess the impact that these changes will have on the postdoctoral role and the implications of this impact for federal and institutional policy decisions.

Preliminary Phase: Policy Issues

The study has been divided into two phases. In the preliminary phase the committee set out to identify the most important policy issues, to examine available information that was relevant to these issues, and to determine what additional information was required to make sound policy recommendations. An interim report[1] describing the findings from this phase of the study was transmitted to the National Science Foundation in June 1978. In that report the committee proposed a study that would consider the following topics:

(1) the character of the contribution of postdoctorals to the research effort of their host departments and laboratories;

(2) their influence on graduate and undergraduate education;

(3) the desirability, from the graduate student's perspective, of taking a postdoctoral appointment;

(4) the responsibilities of host institutions towards their own postdoctorals;

(5) the alternative mechanisms for postdoctoral funding;

(6) the contributions of foreign nationals holding postdoctoral appointments at U.S. universities;

(7) the role of postdoctoral training in the career development of women and minority scientists and engineers; and

(8) the advantages and disadvantages of postdoctoral experience for those pursuing careers outside the academic sector.

Each of these topics is addressed in the present report.

In order to obtain as broad a perspective as possible on these eight topics, the committee initiated several information-gathering activities. At the outset, a total of approximately 280 department chairmen, university deans, and provosts who were actively involved in the administration of postdoctoral appointments at 50 different institutions were invited to comment on each of the eight issues described above.[2] The response to this request was most satisfying; more than 150 university administrators provided thoughtful, and often detailed, comments. Letters were also sent to 50 managers in government and industrial laboratories, soliciting their opinions on the utility of postdoctoral experience for scientists and engineers pursuing careers

---

[1]The interim report also served as a proposal for the second phase of this study. See National Research Council (1978).

[2]A copy of this letter and a list of recipients are included in Appendix A. Recipients were selected to obtain a balance among fields, sizes of postdoctoral programs, and geographical distribution.

outside the academic sector.[3] Approximately 40 responses were received. Excerpts from several of the comments provided by university administrators and government and industrial managers are quoted in Chapters 5 and 6 of this report.

Additional information was gathered from site visits to more than 50 departments at 15 different universities.[4] In these visits committee members and staff talked with university deans, faculty, postdoctorals, and graduate students who were about to receive their doctorates. The discussions afforded an opportunity to probe more deeply into the postdoctoral role in a variety of institutional and departmental settings, and provided much needed input from the postdoctorals and graduate students, who often presented a somewhat different picture from that of their mentors. The site visits were particularly useful in helping us formulate the questions to be included in the surveys conducted in the second phase of the study.

In the preliminary phase the committee and the staff also considered findings from many other relevant studies,[5] and consulted with other groups that at that time were concerned with policy issues pertinent to our own study. Among those consulted were committees under the aegis of professional societies, the National Science Foundation and other federal agencies, and other units of the National Research Council. The findings and recommendations of these groups, too numerous to summarize here, have been helpful to the policy deliberations and planning of our own committee. Particularly valuable were survey activities that had recently been completed by the American Physical Society[6] and the National Research Council.[7] Many of the questions used in these efforts were incorporated into our own survey questionnaires. In addition. the committee analyzed data from three longitudinal surveys[8] sponsored by the National Science

---

[3]Copies of the letters to government and industrial managers are included in Appendix A, along with lists of recipients.

[4]A list of institutions and departments visited is included in Appendix B.

[5]These studies are summarized in Chapter I of the committee's interim report, National Research Council (1978).

[6]The American Physical Society conducted an indepth survey of 1,400 physicists who held postdoctoral appointments in 1973. See B. F. Porter (1979), pp.113-92.

[7]The National Research Council Committee on National Needs for Biomedical and Behavioral Science Research Personnel recently completed a survey of 14,300 biomedical and behavioral scientists who earned doctorates during the FY1971-75 period. A description of this survey is reported in National Research Council (1977), Appendix C.

[8]These include the Survey of Doctorate Recipients and the Survey of Earned Doctorates, conducted by the National Research Council, and the Survey of Graduate Science Student Support and Postdoctorals, conducted by Moshman Associates, Inc.

Foundation in order to determine what additional information was required to address each of the eight topics that had been identified. On the basis of the committee's preliminary review, a study plan was developed for the second and final phase of the study. The plan was reviewed by the National Science Foundation and approved for funding.

Second Phase: Survey Activities

The second phase of this study has been primarily devoted to the collection and analysis of survey data and to the drafting of this report. Under the auspices of our committee national surveys of four groups were carried out:

(1) chairmen of science and engineering departments that hosted one or more postdoctorals in 1977;
(2) U.S. citizens who had received science or engineering doctorates (Ph.D. or equivalent) during FY1972 (July 1, 1971, through June 30, 1972);
(3) U.S. citizens who had received FY1978 doctorates in these fields; and
(4) foreign citizens who held postdoctoral appointments at U.S. universities as of April 1979.

A brief description of the sampling procedures and response rates for each survey follows. Copies of the questionnaires used in this effort and an analysis of the responses to each survey item are presented in Appendixes C, D, E, and F. Also included in the Appendixes is a list of the disciplines subsumed under engineering and each of the eight major fields of science.

In April 1979 survey questionnaires were mailed to a sample of 1,063 chairmen of science and engineering departments. The survey sample was selected from a population of 2,022 departments that, according to the 1977 Survey of Graduate Science Student Support and Postdoctorals,[9] hosted at least one postdoctoral. For purposes of sample selection the departmental population was stratified on major field, institutional control (i.e., public and private institutions), and number of postdoctoral appointees.[10] Disproportionately large samples were chosen from the small population strata. As shown in Table 1.1, a total of 846 chairmen (80 percent) responded to the survey. There were only small differences in the response rates by

---

[9]This survey collects data from essentially all graduate departments in Ph.D.-granting institutions.
[10]Two categories of size were used: departments with 1 or 2 post-doctorals in 1977 and those with more than 2.

Table 1.1

RESPONSE RATES FOR SURVEY OF SCIENCE AND ENGINEERING DEPARTMENT CHAIRMEN

	Popu-lation N	Sample Size N	Survey Response N	%
All Departments	2,022	1,063	846	79.6
Departmental Field				
Mathematical Sciences	41	41	32	78.0
Physics	165	114	97	85.1
Chemistry	170	102	89	87.3
Earth Sciences	95	81	67	82.7
Engineering	320	159	123	77.4
Agricultural Sciences	111	74	63	85.1
Biosciences-Graduate Schools	439	156	126	80.8
Biosciences-Medical Schools	483	166	122	73.5
Psychology	78	73	57	78.1
Social Sciences	120	97	70	72.2
Department Within				
Private Institution	1,347	428	331	77.3
Public Institution	675	635	515	81.1
Department Hosted				
1-2 Postdoctorals in 1977	1,053	499	409	82.0
>2 Postdoctorals in 1977	969	564	437	77.5

field or other stratification variables. A detailed analysis of the survey results is given in Appendix C. Response data have been appropriately weighted to provide population estimates.

In April 1979 survey questionnaires were also sent to 5,536 individuals who had earned science and engineering doctorates in FY1972 and 5,511 individuals who had earned doctorates in this same set of fields in FY1978. The sample of FY1972 graduates was selected from a population of 15,680 respondents to the Survey of Earned Doctorates[11] who held U.S. citizenship at the time they received their doctorates. The FY1978 population included 14,334 respondents. For purposes of sample selection, the two populations were stratified on major field of doctorate, sex, racial/ethnic group,[12] and post-doctoral plans (i.e., those planning postdoctoral study after receipt of their doctorates and other Ph.D. recipients). Samples of more than 60 percent of the doctorate recipients in physics and the biosciences were selected so that analyses of the survey results for several disciplines within these two fields could be made by other committees. In each of the other seven fields a sample of approximately 25 percent was selected. A proportionally large sample of women and minority graduates was chosen so that the sampling errors reported for these groups would be approximately equal to sampling errors for other science and engineering Ph.D. recipients.

A total of 3,680 persons (66 percent) in the FY1972 cohort and 4,231 persons (77 percent) in the FY1978 cohort responded to the surveys, as reported in Tables 1.2 and 1.3. Since the questionnaires and survey procedures used for both groups were very similar, the difference in response rates can be largely attributed to the difficulties encountered in locating FY1972 graduates. For a majority of members of the survey sample, the most recent address available was one that they had provided at the time they received their doctorate-- for FY1972 graduates it was 7 years out of date. The low response rate obtained from social scientists in the FY1978 cohort can be explained by the fact that the sample in this field was augmented after the first survey mailing and those who were added were not contacted as often as other members of the sample. Otherwise the differences in response rates by field or other stratification variables were not large. Copies of the questionnaires sent to FY1972 and FY1978 graduates and an analysis of the responses to each survey item are provided in Appendixes D and E. For both of these surveys

---

[11]This survey is believed to include all research-doctorate (Ph.D. or equivalent) recipients from regionally accredited universities.
[12]The FY1978 cohort was separated into those belonging to racial/ethnic minority groups--blacks, Hispanics, Asians, and American Indians--and other graduates. The FY1972 cohort was not stratified on this variable since information was not available (prior to our survey) on the racial/ethnic group of these graduates.

Table 1.2

RESPONSE RATES FOR SURVEY OF SCIENTISTS AND ENGINEERS,
FY1972 PH.D. RECIPIENTS

	Popu-lation N	Sample Size N	Survey N	Response %
All 1972 Ph.D. Recipients	15,680	5,536	3,680	66.5
Ph.D. Field				
Mathematical Sciences	1,047	279	176	63.1
Physics	1,302	938	639	68.1
Chemistry	1,645	529	326	61.6
Earth Sciences	482	187	127	67.9
Engineering	2,365	347	227	65.4
Agricultural Sciences	642	172	118	68.6
Biosciences	3,318	2,014	1,405	69.8
Psychology	2,148	624	395	63.3
Social Sciences	2,731	446	267	59.9
Sex				
Men	13,836	4,471	2,990	66.9
Women	1,844	1,065	690	64.8

8

Table 1.3

RESPONSE RATES FOR SURVEY OF SCIENTISTS AND ENGINEERS,
FY1978 PH.D. RECIPIENTS

	Popu-lation N	Sample Size N	Survey N	Response %
All 1978 Ph.D. Recipients	14,334	5,511	4,231	76.8
Ph.D. Field				
Mathematical Sciences	726	237	180	75.9
Physics	821	700	543	77.6
Chemistry	1,210	349	255	73.1
Earth Sciences	533	242	194	80.2
Engineering	1,331	358	267	74.6
Agricultural Sciences	637	206	157	76.2
Biosciences	3,377	2,215	1,821	82.2
Psychology	2,935	738	527	71.4
Social Sciences	2,764	466	287	61.6
Sex				
Men	11,246	3,999	3,080	77.0
Women	3,088	1,512	1,151	76.1
Racial/Ethnic Group				
White	13,382	4,682	3,747	80.0
Minority	952	829	484	58.4

response data have been appropriately weighted to provide population estimates. The overall high response rate for these two surveys—72 percent—was gratifying.

The reader should be cautioned that all results reported from the survey of department chairmen and the surveys of FY1972 and FY1978 Ph.D. recipients represent estimates derived from sample surveys and are not precise population statistics. These estimates are subject to both sampling and nonsampling types of errors. Sampling errors occur because the survey results reflect the responses of a sample group and not the entire population. Nonsampling errors can be attributed to a variety of sources including misinterpretation of survey instructions or questions, mistakes in the coding or processing of survey responses, and other errors in the collection and reporting of results.

The sample in each of the three surveys was chosen in a completely random fashion. Other samples of identical size could have been selected, and each would likely yield a somewhat different set of responses. The sampling error associated with a survey estimate is a measure of the precision with which that estimate approximates the average result that might have been derived from all possible samples.[13] Consequently, the sampling error provides a confidence interval for a reported estimate. The probability that the actual population statistic being measured lies within a range of one sampling error of the sample estimate is approximately 0.67—and within a range of twice the sampling error, approximately 0.95.

A discussion of the estimation and interpretation of sampling errors in each of the three surveys is given in Appendix G. Provided in the appendix tables are sampling errors associated with estimates reported on various survey groups. Sampling error, however, does not measure any systematic biases in the data (e.g., the misinterpretation of an ambiguous survey item). The reader should be mindful that the accuracy of a survey result depends on both sampling and nonsampling types of errors.

In order to obtain information about the foreign component of the postdoctoral population at U.S. universities, the department chairmen we surveyed were asked to provide the names of all foreign citizens holding postdoctoral appointments in their departments. From the preliminary responses received from department chairmen, 911 foreign postdoctorals were identified. All of these individuals were sent questionnaires, and 545 (60 percent) responded (Table 1.4). Since the sample was not randomly chosen (because the population of foreign postdoctorals was not known at the time of the survey), no attempt has been made to inflate the response data to population estimates.

---

[13] For a detailed discussion of the measuring of sampling error, the reader may wish to refer to Gonzalez et al. (1975).

Table 1.4

RESPONSE RATES FOR SURVEY OF FOREIGN POSTDOCTORALS
IN SCIENCE AND ENGINEERING DEPARTMENTS

	Sample Size N	Survey Response N	%
All Departments	911	545	59.8
Departmental Field			
Mathematical Sciences	18	7	38.9
Physics	122	79	64.8
Chemistry	311	164	52.7
Earth Sciences	31	24	77.4
Engineering	123	76	61.8
Agricultural Sciences	29	18	62.1
Biosciences-Graduate Schools	137	89	65.0
Biosciences-Medical Schools	116	74	63.8
Psychology	17	12	70.6
Social Sciences	7	2	28.6

Nonetheless, the responses to this survey provide some useful information about the characteristics and employment plans of the group surveyed.

Defining the Postdoctoral Population

For use in all of the data collection activities, the committee adopted the following definition:

> POSTDOCTORAL APPOINTMENT means a temporary appointment the primary purpose of which is to provide for continued education or experience in research usually, though not necessarily, under the supervision of a senior mentor. Included are appointments in government and industrial laboratories which resemble in their character and objectives postdoctoral appointments in universities. Excluded are appointments in residency training programs in the health professions.

In providing this definition the committee has intended to exclude from the postdoctoral population persons holding the following types of positions: (a) junior faculty positions that are understood to be included in the regular series of academic appointments leading to a permanent position within the host institution; (b) visiting or adjunct faculty appointments that fill regular positions in the departmental structure; (c) service-oriented research positions not intended to provide research training; (d) medical internships and residencies not involving research training; and (e) status as a graduate student in a second doctoral or masters program. This definition is consistent with the one used in an earlier study by the National Research Council,[14] except that we have excluded postdoc-torals who held M.D. or other professional doctorates and those who had received their doctorates from foreign institutions.

The committee fully recognizes that the postdoctoral population, as defined above, is by no means a homogeneous group. Doctoral scientists and engineers may take postdoctoral appointments for a variety of reasons and at different stages in their careers. The responsibilities and privileges of this group can also vary widely. Some postdoctorals may be given considerable freedom in selecting and working on a research problem; others may be expected to carry out laboratory tasks under the close supervision of a senior mentor. Some teach courses and advise students; others take courses. Many have no involvement at all in formal programs of education.

The problem of defining the postdoctoral population is largely one of interpretation. The counts of individuals holding postdoctoral

---

[14]For a discussion of the definition used in the earlier study, see National Research Council (1969), pp. 41-5.

appointments in a particular field may vary significantly depending on what definition is used and who is asked to furnish the count. This point is clearly illustrated in Table 1.5, which compares estimates of the 1979 postdoctoral populations in universities, as derived from three separate sources. The data in the first column are based on combined estimates from the Survey of Doctorate Recipients and the Survey of Earned Doctorates, both of which are conducted by the National Research Council with the sponsorship[15] of the National Science Foundation. The estimates represent the numbers of Ph.D. recipients who were employed in academia and who indicated that they held postdoctoral appointments--defined as a "temporary appointment in academia, . . . the primary purpose of which is to provide for continued education or experience in research." The survey response has been appropriately weighted and adjusted to provide population estimates (see footnote 1 in Table 1.5). However, the estimates do not take into account postdoctorals at U.S. universities who had earned their doctorates from foreign institutions.

The data in the second and third columns of Table 1.5 come from our own Survey of Science and Engineering Department Chairmen (described earlier). The second column excludes persons with foreign-earned doctorates; the third column includes this group. Both sets of estimates are based on the committee's own definition of a postdoctoral appointment (quoted above). The data in the fourth column come from the National Science Foundation's Survey of Graduate Science Student Support and Postdoctorals. These counts were also provided by department chairmen. In this survey chairmen were instructed to include "individuals with science and engineering doctorates or M.D.'s (including foreign degrees that are equivalent to U.S. doctorates) who devote FULL TIME TO RESEARCH activities or study in the department under temporary appointments that carry no academic rank."

No one set of estimates is necessarily more reliable than the others. They all are based on subjective categorizations by survey respondents. and responses to the committee's surveys depend on each individual's interpretation of the primary purpose of the appointment. The estimates from the foundation's survey of department chairmen (fourth column) are substantially larger than the others primarily because they include recipients of professional doctorates as well as foreign graduates. The estimates from the surveys of doctoral scientists and engineers (first column) exclude both of these groups. In most of the analyses in the report we have used postdoctoral estimates from the latter source for the following two reasons. First, the surveys of doctoral scientists and engineers provide valuable information about the utilization of the postdoctoral group

---

[15]These survey activities are also sponsored by the National Institutes of Health, the National Endowment for the Humanities, and the Office of Education.

Table 1.5

COMPARISON OF INDEPENDENT ESTIMATES OF THE NUMBERS OF SCIENCE
AND ENGINEERING POSTDOCTORALS IN UNIVERSITIES, 1979

	SDR/DRF (1)	Dept. Survey (2)	(3)	GSSSP (4)
Total S/E Postdoctorals	10,442	8,411	12,051	13,856
Mathematical Sciences	200	122	157	199
Physics	853	989	1,283	1,443
Chemistry	1,454	1,564	2,649	2,616
Earth Sciences	324	181	245	329
Engineering	387	517	914	1,069
Agricultural Sciences	185	175	222	245
Biosciences	6,044	4,474	6,107	7,112
Psychology	565	228	273	446
Social Sciences	430	161	201	397

NOTE: Estimates reported in the first three columns of this table are derived
from sample surveys and are subject to sampling errors of varying sizes.
See the accompanying text and Appendix G for a discussion of the estimation
and interpretation of sampling errors.

SOURCES: (1) Weighted population estimates from the 1979 Survey of Doctorate
Recipients (National Research Council) have been adjusted using
counts from the 1979 Survey of Earned Doctorates. The adjustment
was required since the former survey did not include persons who
had earned research doctorates (Ph.D. or equivalent) between
July, 1978 and February, 1979. The adjustment was made on the
basis of postdoctoral plans reported in the latter survey.

(2) Estimates are from the committee's Survey of Science and Engineering
Department Chairmen and exclude persons who had earned their
doctorates from foreign institutions.

(3) Estimates are from the same survey (2), but include those with
foreign doctotates.

(4) These data are from the 1979 Survey of Graduate Science Student
Support and Postdoctorals (National Science Foundation) and include
both recipients of foreign doctorates and those with professional
doctorates (M.D., D.V.M., D.D.S., etc.).

(e.g., time devoted to research and other work activities). Secondly, these surveys also collect data on other groups in the Ph.D. labor force--including faculty, other academic staff, postdoctorals in industry and government, and other scientists and engineers employed outside the academic sector. Thus, with the use of data from these surveys, comparisons can be made between the full-time equivalent research effort of postdoctorals and other groups (these comparisons are presented in Chapter 6).

The committee has confined itself in this study to postdoctorals with a Ph.D. degree or an equivalent research doctorate. While recognizing that postdoctoral training plays an equally important role in the career development of clinical investigators (i.e., those who hold M.D. or other medical doctorates), the committee has not included this group in its study for the following reasons. First, another committee[16] of the National Research Council has already undertaken a comprehensive study of this group; a report of the findings is expected to be completed by early next year. Secondly, for the clinical investigator the postdoctoral appointment usually represents his or her first formal training in research and consequently may play a markedly different role in the career development of this individual than it does for the Ph.D. scientist who in qualifying for the doctorate has already demonstrated competence in research. Finally, the career options available to the clinical investigator completing postdoctoral apprenticeship are quite different from those available to the Ph.D. scientist. The former may choose to devote part or all of his/her time to clinical service and receive a substantially higher income than that received by most Ph.D. scientists. Preliminary evidence[17] indicates that the number of individuals pursuing careers in clinical research has steadily declined during the past decade. The factors contributing to this decline and the long-term implications for clinical research are now being examined by the other committee referred to above.

Study Prospectus

In the chapters that follow we present a comprehensive examination of the changing character of postdoctoral training and research in each science and engineering field. The report is written with two objectives in mind: to marshal the information required to make sound policy recommendations and to provide an up-to-date statistical picture of the postdoctoral situation in each field. Not all of the

---

[16]The Committee on National Needs for Biomedical and Behavioral Research Personnel is considering a variety of issues pertinent to the training of clinical investigators.
[17]National Research Council (1980), Chapter 2.

topics examined in this report have direct relevance to the four
recommendations made by the committee (Chapter 7), but all, we
believe, contribute to better understanding of the postdoctoral situation. For instance, in Chapter 5 we consider the utility of postdoctoral training for careers outside the academic sector; in Chapter 6
we examine the role of foreign postdoctorals in the research effort
within the U.S. universities. Neither of these topics involve issues
that, in the committee's judgement, require policy action at this
time. Nonetheless, both of these topics should be of considerable
interest to federal and university policymakers as well as to the
scientific community as a whole.

Chapter 2 begins with an account of the development of postdoctoral education since its inception almost a century ago. It is clear
from the history of its development that postdoctoral education has
long played an important part in the universities' mission as centers
of teaching and research. Chapter 3 provides a summary of the changing employment situations of young doctoral scientists and engineers.
During the past decade some important changes have occurred that have
had an impact on the supply and utilization of postdoctorals. Chapter
4 examines the flow of recent Ph.D. recipients into postdoctoral appointments in each major field, with particular attention given to
their purpose in taking these appointments and their subsequent career
employment. Chapter 5 then addresses specific issues related to the
advantages and disadvantages of these appointments, from the perspective of the young scientist. Among the issues considered are the
postdoctoral education and subsequent utilization of women and
minority Ph.D. recipients. Chapter 6 provides a statistical description of the postdoctoral contribution to the national research effort.
Consideration is given to the numbers of postdoctorals involved in
research, the magnitude of the total postdoctoral effort (compared
with other groups of research personnel), and the importance of their
role to the research project. Chapter 7 concludes with a summary of
the study findings and the committee's recommendations.

In the course of the study the committee has compiled extensive
information on the education and utilization of young scientists and
engineers. The analyses presented in this report focus on eight broad
topics (listed earlier) that are directly relevant to postdoctoral
education and research. The information that has been compiled is
relevant to a number of other topics as well. In fact, another
committee of the National Research Council is planning to use the
survey data we have collected from FY1972 and FY1978 graduates to
analyze differences in the utilization of recent doctorate recipients
in the various biomedical disciplines. The survey data might also be
used, for example, in studies of the education and utilization of
young women and minority scientists and engineers, the status of
nonfaculty research staff in universities, and the career objectives of foreign postdoctorals. With this in mind the committee
invites professional societies, federal agencies and their contrac-
tors, and individual investigators to make use of its valuable data
resources.

References

Gonzalez, Maria, Jack L. Ogus, Gary Shapiro, and Benjamin J. Tepping. Standards for Discussion and Presentation of Errors in Survey and Census Data. Journal of the American Statistical Association 70:5-23, September, 1975.

National Research Council. The Invisible University. Washington, D.C.: National Academy of Sciences, 1969.

_____. Personnel Needs and Training in Biomedical and Behavioral Research. Washington, D.C.: National Academy of Sciences, 1977.

_____. Interim Report and Proposal for Continuation of Study of Postdoctorals in Science and Engineering in the United States. Washington, D.C.: National Academy of Sciences, 1978.

_____. Personnel Needs and Training in Biomedical and Behavioral Research. Washington, D.C.: National Academy of Sciences, 1980.

Porter, B. F. Transition-A-Follow-Up Study of 1973 Postdoctorals. In The Transition in Physics Doctoral Employment 1960-1990. New York: American Physical Society, 1979.

2. HISTORICAL OVERVIEW

Beginnings of Postdoctoral Education

The history of the research university in this country is
also the history of the postdoctoral research appointment. In his
plans for Johns Hopkins, the first university with a declared com-
mitment to research, President Gilman included a program of fellowships "to give scholars of promise the opportunity to prosecute
further studies, under favorable circumstances, and likewise to open a
career for those who propose to follow the pursuit of literature or
science. The University expects to be benefitted by their presence
and influence, and by their occasional services; from among the number
it hopes to secure some of its permanent teachers."[1] Ten fellowships were offered initially in 1876, the year the university opened,
but no other university in America offered young scholars a similar
opportunity; and when applications were received from 152 candidates,
of whom more than 100 were regarded as eligible, the number of awards
was increased to 20. Among the first 20 fellows, 4 already held
Ph.D. degrees. One had received his degree in this country (at
Harvard), but the other 3 had gone to Germany (to Heidelberg, Leipzig,
and Gottingen).[2]

From the first the purpose was twofold: to foster the development of young scholars, and to promote research. "What are we aiming
at?" Gilman asked in his inaugural, and answered: "The encouragement
of research; the promotion of young men; and the advancement of
individual scholars who by their excellence will advance the sciences
they pursue and the society where they dwell."[3] On both sides of
the Atlantic there was concern about the need to promote research.
Germany, newly unified as a single nation, was outperforming the rest
of the world in the publication of significant scholarship and in the
application of science in business and industry. A collection of

---

[1]French (1946), p. 40.
[2]French (1946), pp. 40-1.
[3]Gilman (1898), p. 35.

essays published in England in 1876, which made a strong impression on Gilman, gave currency to the phrase "the endowment of research."[4] The very word "research," as Gilman recalled later, was being given a new meaning.[5] In 1877, in an address on "the endowment of research" prepared for the annual meeting of the American Association for the Advancement of Science, the young Harvard astronomer Edward C. Pickering praised the Hopkins fellowships as "an important step in the right direction" and pointed out how much more needed to be done:

> Many other colleges indirectly countenance or mildly en-
> courage research, some actively, but most of them pas-
> sively. Some persons . . . even go so far as to maintain
> that the time and energy of a college professor is paid
> for, that he may teach, and regard original work as out-
> side occupation. Were this view general, small indeed
> would be the growth of science in this country.[6]

Gilman, who kept a file of quotations on the value of fellow-ships, acknowledged in his inaugural the debt he owed to European ideas:

> We shall hope to secure a strong staff of young men,
> appointing them because they have twenty years before
> them; selecting them on evidence of their ability;
> increasing constantly their emoluments; and promoting
> them because of their merit to successive posts, as
> scholars, fellows, assistants, adjuncts, professors,
> and university professors. This plan will give us an
> opportunity to introduce some of the features of the
> English fellowship and the German system of privat-
> docents; or, in other words, to furnish positions
> where young men desirous of a university career may
> have a chance to begin, sure, at least, of a support
> while waiting for promotion.[7]

During the next four decades support for postdoctoral research grew slowly. An increasing cadre of universities organized themselves as centers of research, but funds and facilities were limited. In 1901 the dean of the colleges at the new University of Chicago la-mented that "the number of research fellowships offered to those who have made the doctorate is as yet inconsiderable." He urged the endowment of "a considerable number of research fellowships . . . to

---

[4]Appleton (1876).
[5]Gilman (1906), p. 242
[6]Pickering (1877), p. 6.
[7]Gilman (1898), p. 29.

be granted only to those who have already on foot an investigation which promises results."[8] In 1913 the American Association for the Advancement of Science appointed a Committee of One Hundred, under the chairmanship of Professor Pickering, to consider the state of scientific research in America. At a meeting the following year Pickering noted that a recent study of "men recognized as eminent by the great scientific societies of the world" had identified only six in the United States, "the same as from Saxony. The ratio of the populations is about twenty to one. Of the Americans thus selected no one devoted much, if any, of his time to teaching, and three were born outside of the United States." He continued:

> The universities of the country devote vast sums to the
> diffusion of knowledge, but their contributions to its
> extension are comparatively limited. . . . If a tenth of
> the money used for teaching were employed in research,
> Americans would soon take their proper places among the
> great men of science of the world.[9]

Some universities recognized the need to trade teaching time for research. One was Pickering's own university, Harvard. In 1915, for example, the division of mathematics at Harvard announced that it would appoint two instructors each year--Benjamin Peirce Instructors--who would be offered "every facility towards the prosecution of original scholarly work, the members of the division being ready to give all possible aid and encouragement." The teaching required of the instructors, who must have completed their Ph.D. degrees, was "very moderate": two and one half elementary courses (a "course" at Harvard being "three fifty-five minute periods a week throughout the year"), and "one other course which would ordinarily be of an advanced character." The instructorships, which would be renewable for three years, would be offered in open competition. Candidates were asked to submit such evidence of their ability as their Ph.D. dissertation and "published contributions to mathematical science," as well as certificates of their ability and success as teachers.[10]

These instructorships, since elevated to assistant professorships, still are awarded at Harvard. They have provided a model for similar instructorships at a number of other universities and have played an important role in the development of American mathematics. All was not dark in the landscape the Committee of One Hundred surveyed. What shortly transformed the situation, however, was the impact of the First World War. The resources of German chemistry were suddenly unavailable--indeed were thrown into the war against us--and the nation had to turn to American chemists to fill the void. At the

---

[8]Association of American Universities (1902), pp. 40-1.
[9]Science (February 1915), p. 316.
[10]Science (January 1915), pp. 86-7.

same time, American physicists and engineers were called upon to match
their wits against the ingenuity of German weaponry, particularly the
submarine.

The National Academy of Sciences responded to the challenge by
forming the National Research Council "to bring into cooperation
existing governmental, educational, industrial, and other research
organizations" for the defense effort. A Committee on Organization
under the chairmanship of the astronomer George E. Hale sought the
approval of President Woodrow Wilson, who gave the Council his blessing in a public letter to Hale in July 1916. In a press release the
White House declared: "Preparedness, to be sound and complete, must
be based on science."[11] The council's work during the war showed
that this statement was the honest truth.

The Committee on Organization, which besides Hale included the
biologist Edwin Grant Conklin, the physiologist Simon Flexner, the
physical chemist Arthur A. Noyes, and the physicist Robert A.
Millikan, had recommended that the council's "plan of procedure"
should include "cooperation with educational institutions, by
supporting their efforts to secure larger funds and more favorable
conditions for the pursuit of research and for the training of students in the methods and spirit of investigation." Nothing came of
this plan during the war. In May, 1918, however, President Woodrow
Wilson issued an executive order requesting the Academy to perpetuate
the council as a peacetime institution. During the next several
months Hale and Millikan had discussions with the Rockefeller foundation on the merits of a national program of postdoctoral fellowships
in the physical sciences. In April, 1919, the foundation gave
$500,000 for the support of a fellowship program for 5 years in
physics and chemistry. Thirteen National Research Fellows were
selected before the end of the year.

As with Gilman's fellowships at Johns Hopkins, the purpose of the
National Research Council Fellowships was not only the encouragement
of young investigators "and their more thorough training in research";
it was also to "increase knowledge relating to the fundamental princi-
ples of physics and chemistry," and, through the conditions host
institutions would be required to meet, to create "more favorable
conditions for research in the educational institutions of the
country." The council stated quite clearly what it expected of host
institutions:

> Able investigators, actively engaged in productive re-
> search, are needed to inspire and guide the work of the
> Fellows. Research laboratories, adequately manned with
> assistants and mechanicians, and amply supplied with
> instruments, machine tools, and other facilities, are
> indispensable; and funds to provide supplies and to

---

[11]National Research Council (1932), pp. 5-6; Kevles (1979), p. 115.

satisfy the constantly recurrent demands of research
must be available. Above all, there must exist the
stimulating atmosphere found only in institutions
that have brought together a group of men devoted to the
advancement of science through pursuit of research.[12]

In 1922 the Rockefeller Foundation and the Rockefeller-endowed
General Education Board, working together, pledged another $500,000
for fellowships in the medical sciences, with emphasis on the pre-
clinical sciences, and in 1923 the foundation gave $325,000 for fel-
lowships in the biological sciences. At the same time the original
program in physics and chemistry was broadened to include mathematics.
All three programs were continued when the initial grants ran out, and
received further extensions thereafter, although with reduced funding
after the onset of the Depression.

In 1924 another Rockefeller organization, the International
Education Board, launched a fellowship program in physics, chemistry,
and biology to support "the international migration of select students
to . . . centers of inspiration and training . . . to be trained with
reference to definite service in their own countries after completion
of their studies," and asked the National Research Council to screen
applicants from the United States.[13]

The success of the National Research Council in rallying support
for the natural sciences encouraged representatives of the social
sciences to establish the Social Science Research Council in 1923. It
had the blessing of another Rockefeller charity, the Laura Spelman
Rockefeller Foundation, and in 1925 the foundation provided the funds
for a program of Social Science Fellowships. The purpose of the
program was described as follows:

> Generous as American Universities have been in helping
> students to obtain Doctor's degrees, they have not been
> generous or wise in treating their young instructors. A
> newly fledged doctor, appointed to a junior position in
> one of our departments, is usually assigned a heavy teach-
> ing schedule, when he neither knows thoroughly the subjects
> he has to cover, nor knows how to teach. . . . Some univer-
> sities have established fellowships especially for their
> young instructors. Others have obtained funds for support-
> ing research programs in which young faculty members can
> join. Still others are seeking to cut down the teaching
> schedules of individuals with marked capacity for re-
> search. . . . But the need is far from met. If our few
> research fellowships can give the ablest among the
> hundreds of men who aspire to do scientific work in the

---

[12]National Academy of Sciences (1919), pp. 313-4.
[13]Fosdick (1952), p. 148; Kevles (1979), p. 198.

social field opportunity to develop their powers
while they are still in their flexible years, we
may hope for large results, ultimately if not
immediately.[14]

The Social Science Research Council offered 15 fellowships in
1925. By 1939 it had made awards to 246 individuals, an average of 16
each year. By comparison, 1,146 individuals held National Research
Fellowships between 1919 and 1938. During the 1920's new awards ran
roughly 70 a year. During the 1930's they averaged roughly 40 a
year.[15]

In 1930 the American Council of Learned Societies, with
Rockefeller help, launched a parallel fellowship program in the
humanities. The council characterized its fellowships as "postdoctoral fellowships in the humanities of the type already made
available in other fields by the National Research Council and the
Social Science Research Council."[16] For some reason this program
was unsuccessful. Only 48 candidates applied in the first year and
only 26 the following year. In 1936, after 82 fellows had been
selected, the program was suspended. A spokesman for the American
Council of Learned Societies told the Association of American Universities in 1935 that the Depression was probably to blame; in uncertain
times a temporary fellowship was not so appealing as a regular
university appointment. But this instability cannot be the whole
answer because candidates in the other programs were exposed to the
same uncertainties.[17]

Another program of fellowships open to scholars in the humanities
that did not lack candidates was the Guggenheim Fellowships, established in 1925. Endowed by Senator and Mrs. Simon Guggenheim in
memory of their son, the Guggenheim Fellowships were open, without
restriction as to field, to individuals of "high intellectual and
personal qualifications who have already demonstrated unusual capacity
for productive scholarship or unusual ability in the fine arts." By
1936 fellowships had been awarded to 525 U.S. candidates, of whom 38
were in the social sciences and 186 in the humanities (history, literature, philosophy, languages). One-fourth of the awards were in the
physical and life sciences, mathematics, and engineering. Young faculty members (up to 35 years old) going on sabbatical were eligible
for appointments. This provision may explain why the fellowships were
(and have remained) a continuing success in the humanities as well as
in other fields.[18]

---

[14]Mitchell, (1926), pp. 16-8.
[15]Social Science Research Council (1939), pp. vii-xiii.
[16]National Research Council (1938).
[17]American Council of Learned Societies (1929), pp. 24, 65.
[18]John Simon Guggenheim Memorial Foundation (1936), pp. 14-9.
Today, in different circumstances, older candidates are eligible and
are favored.

23

The Guggenheims, like the National Research Fellowships, were
intended to provide time for research. "It has been my observation,"
Senator Guggenheim wrote, "that just about the time a young man has
finished college and is prepared to do valuable research, he is compelled to spend his whole time in teaching. Salaries are small; so he
is compelled to do this in order to live, and often he loses the im-
pulse for creative work in his subject, which should be preserved in
order to make his teaching of the utmost value, and also for the sake
of the value of the researchers in the carrying on of civilization."[19]

There is no question that these fellowship programs played a
significant role in the development of American Science in the 1920's
and 1930's. During the 1920's nearly one-third of all applicants to
the National Research Fellowship program received an award. Between
1919 and 1932 one in eleven of all Ph.D. recipients in the natural
sciences became National Research Fellows. More than half held their
awards for a second year; others won other fellowships. Linus
Pauling, for example, who won a National Research Fellowship for the
1925-26 academic year, was a Guggenheim Fellow the following year. J.
Robert Oppenheimer won an International Education Board Fellowship for
1928-29 to follow on his National Research Council award for 1927-28.
A number of young Ph.D.'s were supported for 3 years, and some received awards for 4.[20]

A study of 500 scientists newly starred as leaders in research in
the 1937 and 1943 editions of American Men of Science found that more
than half had been postdoctorals, most of them National Research
Fellows. By 1950, 65 former National Research Fellows had been
elected to the National Academy of Sciences and 3 had won Nobel
prizes. More have been so honored since. Looking back on a program
in which he had had no small stake, Millikan ventured the opinion in
1950 that the National Research Fellowships had been "the most
effective agency in the scientific development of American life and
civilization" in his lifetime.[21]

Between 1919 and 1938 about one-fourth of the National Research
Fellows took their fellowships overseas, but the International Education Board program brought large numbers of foreign scholars here. A
student of the development of American physics estimates that in
physics, if not in other fields, "at least as many European scientists
studied in the United States . . . as Americans studied in Europe.
. . . [M]ost of the European visitors were experimentalists attracted
by superior American equipment, while most of the Americans supported
in Europe were theoreticians. All but one of the Americans returned

---

[19]John Simon Guggenheim Memorial Foundation (1925).
[20]National Research Council (1932), p. 18.
[21]Visher (1947), pp. 361, 530; Rand (1951), p. 79; Millikan (1950),
p. 213.

to posts in the United States, but dozens of Europeans were induced to remain in America, including several fine young theoreticians."[22]

As Hale's Committee on Organization had intended, the fellows were attracted to universities and research institutes offering the best environment for work in their field. Five institutions in this country hosted over half of the National Research Fellows during some part of their tenure--Harvard, Princeton, Chicago, the California Institute of Technology, and Johns Hopkins.[23] The head of the General Education Board, Wickliffe Rose, was delighted to "make the peaks higher" in this way. In his view, "the high standards of a strong institution will spread throughout a nation." Under his leadership, the General Education Board concentrated its direct grants to universities at a few select institutions where science departments which were already strong could be brought to the front rank in their field. He singled out Princeton, Chicago, and Caltech for particularly generous support.[24]

At Caltech in the 1920's three of the architects of the National Research Fellowship program, Hale, Noyes, and Millikan, were turning a little-regarded engineering school, known until 1917 as Throop Institute, into a leading center of scientific research. With the help of munificent benefactors who shared their ambitions for American science--"Just imagine," wrote William Röntgen in 1921. "Millikan is said to have a hundred thousand dollars a year for his researches"-- they achieved almost instant success. In the early 1920's, according to one historian, "only Caltech among American universities even remotely resembled the European institutes" where Bohr, Born, and others were in process of creating a new order in physics with the quantum model of the atom.[25] A young American physicist in Germany in 1927 who told a friend "theoretical physics has reached a terrible state . . . new methods have to be learned every week, almost" also wrote: "Caltech--there is something magnetic about that place [for] . . . Europeans."[26] Many National Research Fellows interested in quantum physics went to Germany, but of those who stayed on this side of the Atlantic half went to Caltech. The rest went to Harvard, Berkeley, Princeton, or Chicago.[27] Caltech also shone in biology. The French biologist Jacques Monod, who used a Rockefeller Fellowship in the 1930's to study at Caltech under Thomas Hunt Morgan, recalled the experience in 1965:

> This was a revelation to me--a revelation of what a group
> of scientists could be like when engaged in creative activ-

---

[22]Coben (1971), p. 450.
[23]National Research Council (1938), pp. 1, 2, 81-4.
[24]Coben (1971), p. 451.
[25]Coben (1971), p. 452.
[26]Kevles (1979), pp. 169, 201.
[27]Monod (1966), p. 475.

ity, and sharing in constant exchange of ideas, bold speculation, and strong criticism: it was a revelation of
personalities of great stature such as George Beadle,
Sterling Emerson, Bridges, Sturtevant, Jack Schultz, and
Ephrussi, all of whom were working in Morgan's department.

Morgan already was a Nobel prizewinner; both Monod and Beadle were to
win Nobel prizes later.[28]
   Caltech gave formal recognition to postdoctoral study as a part
of its institutional mission. The Caltech Bulletin, for example,
included a section on research fellowships, listing the fellowships
available to postdoctoral researchers at the institute and welcoming
scientists "who have already received their Doctor's degree and desire
to carry on special investigations." The 1936 Bulletin lists 26
postdoctorals on fellowships at the institute; besides National
Research Fellowships, the Bulletin mentions fellowships provided by
industrial sponsors and fellowships funded by the institute itself.
   Other universities also awarded postdoctoral fellowships of their
own--for example, Columbia gave Isidor I. Rabi a fellowship in 1927 to
allow him to study in Germany--but generally universities reserved
their fellowship money for graduate students.[29] In 1934 a repre-
sentative of the National Research Council reproached the universities
for not playing a more active role in promoting postdoctoral study:

   Contrary to what might have been expected, the universities
   have not been instrumental either in initiating the fellowship experiment or in shaping its course. Their part has
   been the passive one of placing libraries and laboratories
   at the disposal of Fellows.[30]

Two years later a committee of the Association of American
Universities that had been appointed to conduct "a comprehensive study
of postdoctoral education in America" commended those universities
that supported their own postdoctoral fellowships and suggested "that
a larger proportion of the funds now devoted to subsidizing candidates
for advanced degrees could be advantageously allocated to the support
of post-doctoral fellows," but came down in favor of national fellowships over local fellowships:

   University administered post-doctoral fellowships are
   likely to be limited to a smaller group of applicants,
   and often are limited to the institution which awards them.
   Your Committee believes that a need exists for a system

---

[28]Kevles (1979), pp. 200-1; Coben (1979), p. 451.
[29]Kevles (1979), p. 214.
[30]Association of American Universities (1935), pp. 129-36.

of country-wide post-doctoral training fellowships more numerous and broader in range than are now available.[31]

It appears that few doctoral recipients held appointments in the universities as assistants or associates on a senior investigator's research funds. When in 1927 Noyes invited James B. Conant of Harvard to consider an appointment at Caltech as professor of organic chemistry, Conant asked if he could have a research budget that would enable him to hire "two or three men or women who had already received the doctor's degree." Conant recalls: "He did not like the idea at all. Quite apart from the size of the budget, he thought my proposal to carry on research with the aid of research assistants was absurd to the point of madness." The University of Illinois chemist Roger Adams, with whom he discussed Noyes' invitation, also "rejected completely my idea of importing a German practice. . . . He granted my diagnosis of the reasons why some of the German professors had been so productive, but was certain no American professor could successfully imitate the practice. Millikan was even more explicit. He spoke in terms of the best way of expending money. He had been publishing papers of great significance. The experimentation had all been done by graduate students . . . supported by teaching fellowships. What Millikan said, in effect, was that . . . teaching fellowships would yield at least twice as many helping hands as would the same amount used for hiring Ph.D.'s as research assistants. I remained unconvinced. If one planned to tackle the problems in organic chemistry on which the leading German chemists were working, one needed more mature help than any student, however bright, could give." Conant stayed at Harvard, where he was given a research budget which permitted him to hire "some of Roger Adams's recent doctors as research assistants to work on the structure of chlorophyll. They were excellent men, well trained, and they performed as I expected."[32]

Elsewhere other faculty investigators began to use postdoctoral associates, but in the lean times of the Depression this was not easy. In 1932, for example, Ernest O. Lawrence found $1,500 to hire his recent student M. Stanley Livingston to help him in the development of the cyclotron, but two other research associates who joined the Radiation Laboratory that year came initially without pay.[33]

In 1938 it was still possible for a committee, appointed by the Secretary of the Interior, Harold L. Ickes, to consider the relation of the federal government to research, to comment on "the lack of appreciation by great numbers of college executives in various positions of the importance of research in the life of today and of the true responsibility of the colleges relative to this work and to the

---

[31] Association of American Universities (1938), pp. 38-40.
[32] Conant (1970), pp. 74-5.
[33] Childs (1968), p. 176.

preparation of personnel for it." The committee noted the contribution made by the national fellowship programs and went on to say:

> While some of the awards seemingly brought disappointing
> returns, perhaps 20 percent were highly gratifying. There
> is a strong feeling that these postdoctoral fellowships are
> an important factor in the research development of the Na-
> tion and should be maintained as generously as possible.

"Possibly," the committee added, "federal grants for this purpose
should be made."[34]

Enter the Federal Government

It happens that, even as the committee was sitting, the first
steps were being taken towards federal support of postdoctoral work.
In April 1937, a bill was submitted in Congress for the establishment
of a National Cancer Institute in the Public Health Service to conduct
research on cancer and to coordinate the work of other organizations
fighting the disease. Representatives of the American Society for the
Control of Cancer (later to become the American Cancer Society) testi-
fied in favor of the bill, and it was passed in July without a dis-
senting voice.

Among other provisions of the Act, the Surgeon General was
authorized to provide facilities where qualified persons might
receive training in the diagnosis and treatment of cancer, and to pay
such trainees up to $10 a day. He was also authorized to establish
"research fellowships in the institute" and to pay the fellows what he
thought necessary "to procure the assistance of the most brilliant and
promising research fellows from the United States or abroad."[35]

The National Cancer Institute appointed its first trainee in
January 1938, and its first fellows later the same year. The institute contracted with hospitals and universities to carry out the
training provisions of the act. The act's authorization of fellowships "in the institute" was not construed to mean that they had to be
held at the institute, and while many of the early fellows held their
awards at the institute, many went elsewhere. All the early trainees
held M.D. degrees and their training was directed to clinical practice, not research, but several of the fellows were Ph.D. recipients.
Although the act provided for the establishment of a National Advisory
Cancer Council, it did not give the council any responsibility for
overseeing the fellowship and training programs; and the selection of
training centers, trainees, and fellows rested effectively with the

---

[34]U.S. Department of the Interior (1938), pp. 183-6.
[35]U.S. Congress (1937).

institute's professional staff. Between 1938 and 1946 the institute
supported 111 trainees and 43 research fellows.[36]

The machinery of the National Cancer Institute was in place when
the country again found itself at war. If the First World War proved
the importance of physics and chemistry in national defense, the
Second World War, while confirming the lessons of the First, also
demonstated the benefits of medical science. The death rate in the
U.S. Army from all diseases was 0.6 per thousand during the Second
World War, compared with 14.1 per thousand in the First. Penicillin,
the active constituent of which was first isolated between 1940 and
1942, was distributed to Army and Navy doctors in time to save
countless lives. Malaria was held in check among troops in the
tropics. Safe blood transfusions and other operating-room techniques
greatly reduced the death rate from wounds.

In 1944 Congress passed an act reorganizing the Public Health
Service to help it better respond to the medical needs of the country.
The National Cancer Institute was made a branch of a new division of
the Public Health Service called the National Institutes of Health;
and the Surgeon General was authorized to award fellowships from now
on in any field "relating to the causes, diagnosis, treatment,
control, and prevention of physical and mental diseases and impair-
ments of man."[37]

Meanwhile, the federal government enlisted the major research
universities in a massive effort to develop new technologies for the
military. The Manhattan Project was the most ambitious and expensive
among hundreds of other undertakings. Annual federal investment in
research and development shot up from $48 million at the start of the
war to $500 million at the end. Whereas in the First World War the
government had put the scientific community to work mostly in off-
campus locations (for example, at the submarine base at New London,
Connecticut), in the Second much of the work was done at the universities themselves.

In 1944 President Roosevelt asked Vannevar Bush, Director of the
wartime Office of Scientific Research and Development, to prepare a
report on the support of science after the war. In his report,
Science, The Endless Frontier, published in 1945, Bush stressed the
unique role of the universities in promoting basic research and training future research workers. He wrote:

> It is chiefly in these institutions that scientists may
> work in an atmosphere which is relatively free from the
> adverse pressure of convention, prejudice, or commercial
> necessity. . . . Industry is generally inhibited by pre-
> conceived goals, by its own clearly defined standards, and

---

[36]Spencer (1949), pp. 750-6; U.S. Department of Health, Education,
and Welfare (1959), pp. 1-6.
[37]U.S. Congress (1944).

by the constant pressure of commercial necessity. . . .
Although there are some notable exceptions, most research conducted within governmental laboratories is
of an applied nature. This has always been true and
is likely to remain so. Hence, government, like industry, is dependent upon the colleges, universities,
and research institutes to expand the basic scientific
frontiers and to furnish trained scientific investigators.

He urged the establishment of a National Research Foundation that
would support basic research in universities and provide undergraduate
scholarships, graduate fellowships, and "fellowships for advanced
training and fundamental research." He envisaged a research budget of
$25 million in the first year rising to $90 million in 5 years, and a
combined scholarship and fellowship budget of $7 million rising to $29
million.[38]

Long before his proposal for a National Research Foundation became a reality in the shape of the National Science Foundation,
established in 1950, other agencies showed their regard for the
universities as centers of peacetime research and education. One was
NIH. The National Cancer Institute had been joined by a National
Institute of Mental Health in 1946 and by a National Heart Institute
and a National Institute of Dental Research in 1948. Still other
institutes were authorized in 1950. Starting with a National Cancer
Institute appropriation of $45,000 for fellowships (predoctoral and
postdoctoral) in FY1946, the fellowship appropriation of all the
institutes rose quickly to $1,400,000 by FY1950. Appropriations for
training programs rose from $25,000 to $5,415,000. In FY1950 the
several National Institutes of Health awarded 306 postdoctoral fellowships, far more than all the privately funded national programs
together awarded in any year before the war.

At the same time agencies were pouring money into the universities for research. In the 1930's the federal government had given the
universities something like $6 million annually, mostly for agricul-
ture. Total research spending in the universities totalled $31
million in 1940. But by 1949 the Public Health Service, the Defense
Department, and the Atomic Energy Commission together were spending
more than $63 million on campus research.

A decade later, in 1960, the budget of the universities for basic
research alone totalled $433 million, of which $299 million came from
the federal government. The National Institutes of Health were supporting nearly 1,000 postdoctoral fellows and were providing $75
million for predoctoral and postdoctoral training grants. The
National Science Foundation, now a major supporter of university
research, was the patron of 277 postdoctoral research fellows,
selected by the National Research Council, and of another 302 Science

---

[38]Bush (1945).

Faculty Fellows (college faculty awarded fellowships to strengthen their science teaching). Almost as numerous as postdoctoral fellows and trainees, however, were postdoctoral research associates supported on research funds. The program director for physics in the mathematical, physical, and engineering sciences division of the National Science Foundation estimated in 1958 that there were probably 200 such postdoctoral research appointees "scattered throughout physics departments in the nation." In his view they played "an impressive role" in physics research:

> Without them research in universities would lose much of
> its vitality and certainly move at a slower pace. . . .
> The research-associate positions have been a boon to
> fresh young Ph.D.'s wishing to extend their experience
> and obtain post-Ph.D. training. A year or two of ap-
> prenticeship as a research associate is considered the
> best entree to better jobs and an opportunity of doing
> research under burden-free conditions.[39]

Evidence gathered later from chemistry departments suggests that there may have been two or three times as many research associates in chemistry at this time.[40]

In 1960 Bernard Berelson, making a study of graduate education, wrote:

> Today there is so much post-doctoral training that many
> people are becoming perplexed or even alarmed at where
> it is all going to end, or rather, are becoming concerned
> lest it not end any where!

From questionnaires distributed to faculty teaching at the graduate level, he found that 23 percent of such faculty under 35 years old had had postdoctoral appointments. In the physical and biological sciences the percentages were even higher. Furthermore, two-thirds of the faculty in these sciences, including those who had not been postdoctorals as well as those who had, felt that postdoctoral experience was "becoming necessary or highly desirable for proper advancement."

Berelson noted that "many top professors prefer postdoctoral fellows because they are better research assistants," but found many others worrying that the spread of postdoctoral training reflected a failure in graduate education. He quoted a dean who felt that "the present rapid growth of the post-doctoral fellowship idea is, at least in part, a direct result of many of our Ph.D.'s having been trained in too-large groups, in over extended graduate departments, and under "team-research" circumstances. . . . [T]hey are compelled to return to an academic setting to learn what they should have learned before

---

[39]McMillen (1958), p. 14.
[40]National Research Council (1965), p. 179.

their degree was granted." Universities were also concerned, Berelson reported, about the allocation "of so much space, equipment, and faculty time to a group that provides no tuition."[41]

In 1964 the role of postdoctoral appointments in physics and chemistry came under the scrutiny of two distinguished committees appointed by the National Academy of Sciences to survey the state of physics and chemistry and report on the needs and potentials of each. The Physics Survey Committee, which reported in 1966, declared that in many fields of physics postdoctoral training was "rapidly becoming a **sine qua non.**" It attributed the increase in the number of individuals taking postdoctoral appointments to "the explosive growth of scientific knowledge" and to government support of scientific research that had "made it possible for university departments to offer research-associate positions to new Ph.D.'s at salaries comparable to those paid men beginning their teaching careers. . . . The academic climate is thus such that the new Ph.D. feels the need for further study, and funds for such study are available to him." The committee went on to say that postdoctorals were "essential to the present research effort in physics" and that "without the assistance of postdoctoral associates, it would not be possible in many fields to train the number of graduate students presently engaged in research."

> [Postdoctorals] contribute to a vital and exciting intellectual environment for both faculty and students and toward accelerating the progress of research. . . . We conclude that postdoctoral personnel make an essential contribution to both teaching and research in physics. . . . We underline this point because today there is a real possibility that the opportunities for postdoctoral study may be curtailed, or may not be expanded in proper proportion to the over-all growth in physics. This possibility exists for two reasons. First, . . . a cutback in research support . . . is most easily applied to those funds allotted for postdoctoral research positions. Second, it has been argued that any action that delays the entrance of a new Ph.D. into the teaching profession raises grave hardships. . . . We do not agree with this view; the additional training for both research and teaching that a new Ph.D. received abundantly justifies the time spent on postdoctoral study.[42]

The Chemistry Survey Committee, which reported in 1965, was less categorical. It agreed that a postdoctoral appointment provided valuable further experience in both research and teaching:

---

[41]Berelson (1960), pp. 190-4, 315.
[42]National Research Council (1966), pp. 17-9.

At this level, a student achieves his greatest personal
boost toward a professional career; he is usually in a
stimulating environment, at a time in his life when he
has great energy and motivation, when he is reasonably
free to exercise his own professional judgement, and when
he is least burdened by additional responsibilities. The
momentum he achieves in this period is likely to determine
the direction and extent of his future career, and hence
this period is one of the most important for advanced education. . . . [A]s chemistry becomes more complicated, a more
varied apprenticeship becomes desirable. The increase in
numbers [of postdoctoral appointments] has been beneficial
in terms both of increased research productivity for the
universities, and of increased opportunities for the students.

But, the committee added:

It has been unplanned. Some universities regard postdoctoral training as a natural extension of doctoral work,
others have incorporated the post-doctorals practical-
ly as junior members of their teaching staffs, while
still others have taken almost no official notice of the
large number of young Ph.D.'s in residence. The Committee is not entirely agreed on the nature and purpose--and
therefore on the proper limits, if any--of post-doctoral
research at the universities. Despite the advantages of
a post-doctoral program, university administrators and
faculty members must decide whether the program should
be expanded when funds for research are limited. . . .
Should the post-doctoral program be officially recognized,
and perhaps formalized? Or should it be left to the
discretion of each individual recipient of a federal grant
to carry on his research as best he can, using graduate
students, postdoctorals, technicians, or whatever personnel he believes are most suitable. . . . Fortunately, the
growth in numbers of post-doctorals so far has generally
strengthened chemical research at the universities.
In any event, a study of the role of post-doctorals in
the university in all aspects would be highly desirable. . . .[43]

The Invisible University

Questions such as these, coming from many sides, prompted the National
Research Council in 1966 to undertake the first truly comprehensive

---

[43]National Research Council (1966), p. 147.

study of postdoctoral education in the United States. Financial
support for the study came from five separate agencies of the federal
government as well as the Alfred P. Sloan Foundation. The study was
published in 1969 under the title The Invisible University.

Questionnaires were received from a total 10,740 individuals who
considered that they held postdoctoral appointments according to the
study committee's definition--an appointment of a temporary nature at
the postdoctoral level which is intended to offer an opportunity for
continued education and experience in research, usually, though not
necessarily, under the supervision of a senior mentor. Assuming a 65
percent rate of return, the committee estimated that "in the spring of
1967 there were approximately 16,000 postdoctorals including U.S.
citizens either in this country or abroad and foreign nationals in
this country."[44] Since this estimate includes both postdoctorals
with foreign-earned doctorates and those who held M.D. or other
professional doctorates, the estimate cannot be compared with the data
presented in Table 1.5 of the previous chapter.

The 10,740 postdoctorals who completed questionnaires gave the
following information about themselves:

- Many of them did not know for sure whether they held a
  fellowship, a traineeship, or an appointment paid out of
  research funds. It appeared that somewhat less than half
  held fellowships, nearly a third were research associates,
  and a quarter held other appointments, including
  traineeships.[45]
- The agency whose funds for training and research supported
  the largest number of postdoctorals was the Public Health
  Service, responsible for 40 percent, followed by the
  National Science Foundation (over 8 percent). The Department of Defense, the Atomic Energy Commission, and the
  National Aeronautics and Space Administration together
  supported another 15 percent. Host institutions supported
  8 percent and private foundations approximately 6
  percent.[46]
- Roughly two-thirds held Ph.D. degrees (or equivalent)
  and one-third medical doctorates.[47]
- The postdoctorals were distributed as follows by
  field:[48]

---

[44]National Research Council (1969), p. 49.
[45]National Research Council (1969), p. 90.
[46]National Research Council (1969), p. 234.
[47]National Research Council (1969), p. 51.
[48]National Research Council (1969), p. 54.

Physics and astronomy	13%
Chemistry	16%
Mathematics, engineering, earth sciences	7%
Biochemistry and other basic life sciences	22%
Other biosciences	8%
Agricultural sciences	1%
Medical sciences	25%
Social sciences	4%
Arts and humanities	2%
Other fields	3%
	100%

- Eighty percent were at institutions of higher education in the United States. Eight percent or so were at nonprofit institutions (hospitals, research institutes, etc.), a slightly smaller percentage were at government laboratories and government-supported laboratories like the Los Alamos Scientific Laboratory, some were abroad, and a small fraction were in industry.[49]
- The distribution of postdoctorals in the universities was "highly skewed." Fifty percent were at 17 institutions. If time taken to get the Ph.D. was a measure of quality (the shorter the time the better), the best postdoctorals were at the leading universities.[50]
- Most postdoctorals were anticipating academic careers. Seventy-seven percent of those who had received Ph.D. degrees within the previous two years--"immediate postdoctorals"--said that they would probably be employed in a university or college. Only 8 percent expected to work in industry and only 5 percent in government.[51]
- Forty-five percent were foreign. Only one-fifth of those with Ph.D.'s received the degrees in this country. Four-fifths came after receiving doctorates abroad. Seventeen percent of the foreign postdoctorals thought that they would be staying in this country.[52]

On the basis of questionnaire returns from deans, department chairmen, individual faculty, and former postdoctorals, as well as the questionnaires received from current postdoctorals and visits to campuses, the National Research Council committee concluded that postdoctoral education was a "useful and basically healthy development. . . . Its major purpose . . . is to accelerate the development of an independent investigator capable of training others in research."

[49]National Research Council (1969), pp. 54, 115.
[50]National Research Council (1969), pp. 57, 78.
[51]National Research Council (1969), pp. 61-2.
[52]National Research Council (1969), pp. 54, 209, 221.

The committee found no evidence that postdoctoral education had resulted "from a failure of graduate education to fulfill its function." And it welcomed the foreign postdoctorals:

> In addition to the contribution to international educa-
> tion, the presence of foreign postdoctorals has enriched
> our science and has stressed the international nature of
> research."[53]

Recent Developments

Since 1969 the climate in the universities has changed considerably. For one thing, real expenditures for basic research in the
universities, which had been rising rapidly for 20 years, have grown
at a considerably slower pace since the time The Invisible University
was written. At the same time, partly for demographic reasons and
partly for lack of funds, hiring of new faculty has also slowed during
the past decade. Between 1969 and 1977, for example, the total number
of faculty increased by only 3 percent a year; for the 8 years earlier
the faculty was expanding at a rate of more than 10 percent
annually.[54]

In the face of these changes, the already high percentage of new
Ph.D. recipients in the physical and biosciences taking postdoctoral appointments increased markedly. In chemistry the percentage
spurted between 1970 and 1973, but has since fallen back a little; in
physics and the biosciences the increase has been steady through the
decade (Table 2.1).

Since the late 1960's the National Science Foundation has collected statistics each year on the total number of postdoctorals in
university departments. Changes in the survey population prior to
1974 obscure the postdoctoral growth trends prior to that time. Since
1974 it appears that the postdoctoral population--including U.S. and
foreign citizens with either Ph.D., M.D., or other doctorates--has
grown significantly in U.S. universities, but that the rates of growth
have been quite different in the major fields of science and engineering (Table 2.2).

In 1973 a national sample of postdoctorals was asked a question
that had not been asked in the study for The Invisible University:
"What was the MOST important reason for taking the appointment?" The
answer was striking. While the majority of respondents said that they
were seeking additional research experience, nearly one-fourth of
those who had received the doctorate during the previous year indicated that they had taken a postdoctoral appointment because an

---

[53]National Research Council (1969), pp. 242, 254-5.
[54]National Research Council (1979), Table 1.

Table 2.1

PERCENT OF PH.D. RECIPIENTS IN SELECTED FIELDS WHO PLANNED TO TAKE
POSTDOCTORAL APPOINTMENTS AFTER COMPLETION OF THEIR DOCTORATES,
1970-79

	FY70-1	FY72-3	FY74-5	FY76-7	FY78-9
All Sciences and Engineering	23.2%	25.9%	26.1%	29.0%	30.4%
Physics	38.4	45.4	50.2	52.2	51.4
Chemistry	39.7	52.8	48.8	51.8	47.2
Biosciences	46.6	48.7	53.3	59.0	62.7

SOURCE: National Research Council, Survey of Earned Doctorates

Table 2.2

TOTAL NUMBER[1] OF POSTDOCTORALS IN U.S. UNIVERSITIES,
1974-79

	1974	1975	1976	1977	...	1979
All Departments	11975	12665	13705	14069		13856
Departmental Field						
Mathematical Sciences	139	164	180	146		199
Physics	1492	1419	1447	1552		1443
Chemistry	2350	2483	2581	2628		2616
Earth Sciences	282	275	375	376		329
Engineering	1019	1153	1169	1213		1069
Agricultural Sciences	371	342	441	376		245
Biosciences - Graduate Schools	2607	3023	3228	3329		3374
Biosciences - Medical Schools	3046	3225	3596	3770		3738
Psychology	293	341	358	354		446
Social Sciences	376	240	330	325		397

[1]Includes both U.S. and foreign citizens who hold a Ph.D., M.D., or other doctoral degree.

SOURCE: National Science Foundation, Survey of Graduate Science Student Support and Postdoctorals.

"employment position" was not available. Among physicists and life scientists the fraction was lower, an estimated 19 percent, but among chemists it was as high as 37 percent. The fraction was higher the more years since the degree. Among postdoctorals who had held the degree 2 years, the figure was approximately 37 percent; among those who had been out 3 years, it was 46 percent.[55] It seems that many postdoctorals, like planes waiting to land, were stacked in a holding pattern. Postdoctoral appointments were playing a new role in the lives of young investigators.

The Congress was sufficiently concerned by the relation of predoctoral and postdoctoral training to national needs that in 1974 it required the Secretary of Health, Education, and Welfare to consult with the National Academy of Sciences before determining the number of fellowships and traineeships National Institutes of Health and the Alcohol, Drug Abuse, and Mental Health Administrations should award in the biomedical and behavioral sciences. The academy was asked to "establish the Nation's overall need" for "research personnel" in these sciences, identifying particular subject areas and the number of people needed in each, and to "identify the kinds of research positions available to and held by individuals" after completion of their training. The academy, if it agreed to assume this responsibility, was required to report to the secretary each year.[56] The academy accepted the responsibility and, starting in 1975, has submitted five reports under the act.

In 1977 the American Physical Society undertook a study of the changing character of the postdoctoral role and the subsequent employment of those who have completed postdoctoral appointments. The study findings, based on survey responses from more than 850 physicists who had held postdoctoral appointments in 1973, are somewhat distressing. Many of these physicists felt that they had not received adequate career counseling and did not consider their postdoctoral experience valuable in helping them achieve their career objectives.

> If they had to do it over again, most would still go into physics; 30%, however, would have chosen other areas, medicine and engineering predominating. Looking ahead, less than half would recommend physics as a career to others. To a large extent this was based on the very tight job market they saw in the future and the high degree of insecurity they had experienced.
>
> These relatively negative attitudes among many of our brightest young physicists should be a matter of continuing concern to the physics community.[57]

---

[55]National Science Foundation (1975), pp. 296, 299.
[56]U.S. Congress (1974).
[57]Porter (1979), p. 23.

Another change since 1969 is a growing concern with the opportunities in science for women and members of minority groups. With
our current-day consciousness of equal rights, the many quotations in
this chapter which refer to "men" as if they are the only people in
science strike one as strangely obtuse. Women and members of minority
groups have in fact played their part in the developments described
here. In 1920, for example, the National Research Council awarded a
special fellowship to support the work at Howard University of the
black zoologist Ernest Everett Just, recognizing that "because of his
color [he] was unable to enter the larger universities in the
country." He held the fellowship for 11 years. The council's records
note that he published 27 papers during this time, "fully justifying"
the award of the fellowship.[58] A Ph.D. recipient from the University of Chicago, Just, who stayed at Howard until his death in 1941,
continued to publish significant work.

We do not know how many young black scientists received regular
National Research Fellowships. The records do include the names of
some women recipients, however. Some held their awards in circumstances that reflect sadly on the status accorded them in the profes-
sion. One was Jane Mary Dewey, the youngest daughter of the
philosopher John Dewey, who obtained her doctorate in physical
chemistry at MIT in 1925. After 2 years with Niels Bohr in Copen-
hagen, she won a National Research Fellowship to study at Princeton.
As a woman she was not welcomed by the physics faculty, but the dean
of the graduate school, William F. Magie, a physicist, insisted they
take her. In 1929 her mentor, Karl T. Compton, wrote all over the
country to help her find a faculty position. The only sympathetic
response came from a member of the physics department at Berkeley, who
reported, however, that his colleagues simply refused to have a woman
on the staff. After 2 more years as a research fellow at Princeton
(in other words, after a total of 6 postdoctoral years), she joined
the faculty at Bryn Mawr.[59]

Four decades later, the study for The Invisible University found
that women on postdoctoral appointments were much more likely than men
to hold them for a third year or longer. While less than 10 percent
of male postdoctorals were "long-term" in this way, nearly 20 percent
of women were long-term. The study commmittee made the observation:

> The fact that U.S. males have a greater chance of obtain-
> ing faculty appointments . . . may partially explain the
> distribution of long-term postdoctorals. Many of the
> women are either faculty or student wives who are not
> able to receive faculty positions because of institu-
> tional rules on nepotism. There are, of course, some

[58]National Research Council (1932), pp. 237-8.
[59]Kevles (1979), p. 207.

women who find the postdoctoral status to their liking,
allowing them to do research part-time while remaining
a wife and mother. Nevertheless, it is clear that the
majority are simply taking the best position that is
open to women who want to do research and to live with
their husbands and children.[60]

The issue was not discussed further in The Invisible University.
Today, we are acutely concerned with the obstacles which stand in the
way of women's careers.

These questions about career opportunity, however, are not
questions about the intrinsic worth of postdoctoral study. The
intellectual opportunity it offers the individual scholar and the
stimulus it gives to the nation's research are no longer significant
issues. The postdoctoral appointment is an accepted feature of the
research university. Gilman would be pleased to see how effective his
merging of the English fellow and the German privat-docent has been in
advancing American science. The problems of the postdoctoral appointment today are important just because of its established role in
American science.

References

American Council on Learned Societies. Bulletin No. 12. New
    York: American Council on Learned Societies, December 1929.
Appleton, C. E. The Endowment of Research as a Form of Produc-
    tive Expenditure. In C. E. Appleton (ed.) Essays
    in the Endowment of Research. London: King & Co., 1876.
Association of American Universities. Journal of Proceedings
    and Addresses, First and Second Annual Conferences, 1900
    and 1901. Washington, D.C.: Association of American
    Universities, 1902.
_____. Journal of Proceedings and Addresses, 36th Annual
    Conference, 1934. Washington, D.C.: Association of
    American Universities, 1935.
_____. Journal of Proceedings and Addresses, 39th Annual
    Conference, 1937. Washington, D.C.: Association of
    American Universities, 1938.
Berelson, B. Graduate Education in the United States. New York:
    McGraw-Hill, 1960.
Bush, V. Science, The Endless Frontier, A Report to the
    President on a Program for Postwar Scientific Research.
    Washington, D.C.: U.S. Government Printing Office, 1945
    (reprinted July 1960 by the National Science Foundation).

---

[60]National Research Council (1969), p. 104.

Childs, H. An American Genius: The Life of Ernest Orlando Lawrence. New York: E. P. Dutton, 1968.

Coben, S. The Scientific Establishment and the Transmission of Quantum Mechanics to the United States, 1919-32. American Historical Review 76(2):450, April 1971.

Conant, J. B. My Several Lives. New York: Harper & Row, 1970.

Fosdick, R. B. The Story of the Rockefeller Foundation. New York: Harper, 1952.

French, J. C. A History of the University Founded by Johns Hopkins. Baltimore: Johns Hopkins Press, 1946.

Gilman, D. C. University Problems in the United States. New York: The Century Co., 1898.

_____. The Launching of a University. New York: Dodd, Mead & Company, 1906.

Hawkins, H. Pioneer: A History of the Johns Hopkins University, 1874-1889. Ithaca: Cornell University Press, 1960.

John Simon Guggenheim Memorial Foundation. Outline of Purposes of the John Simon Guggenheim Memorial Foundation. New York: John Simon Guggenheim Memorial Foundation, 1925.

_____. Reports of the Secretary and Treasurer (1935 and 1936). New York: John Simon Guggenheim Memorial Foundation, 1936.

Kevles, D. J. The Physicists. New York: Vintage Books, 1979.

McMillan, J. H. Our Universities' Research-Associate Positions in Physics. Physics Today, August 1958.

Millikan, R. A. The Autobiography of Robert A. Millikan. New York: Prentice-Hall, 1950.

Mitchell, W. C. Annual Report of the Chairman, 1926, Social Science Research Council. Political Science Quarterly 41(4):16-8, December 1926.

Monod, J. From Enzymatic Adaptation to Allosteric Transitions. Science 101:475, 1966.

National Academy of Sciences. Proceedings of the National Academy of Sciences. Washington, D.C.: National Academy of Sciences, 1919.

National Research Council. Consolidated Report Upon the Activities of the National Research Council, 1919 to 1932. Washington, D.C.: National Academy of Sciences, 1932.

_____. National Research Fellowships, 1919-1938. Washington, D.C.: National Academy of Sciences, 1938.

_____. Chemistry: Opportunities and Needs. Washington, D.C.: National Academy of Sciences, 1965.

_____. Physics: Survey and Outlook. Washington, D.C.: National Academy of Sciences, 1966.

_____. The Invisible University. Washington. D.C.: National Academy of Sciences, 1969.

_____. Research Excellence Through the Year 2000. Washington, D.C. National Academy of Sciences, 1979.

National Science Foundation. Characteristics of Doctoral Scientists and Engineers in the United States, 1973, Detailed Statistical Tables, Appendix B. Washington, D.C.: U.S. Government Printing Office, 1975.

42

Pickering, E. C. An Address on the Endowment of Research. Presented
    to the American Association for the Advancement of Science.
    Salem, 1877.

Porter, B. F. Summary of Transition-A Follow-Up Study of 1973 Post-
    doctorals. In The Transition in Physics Doctoral
    Employment, 1960-1990, Executive Summary. New York: Ameri-
    can Physical Society, 1979.

Rand, M. J. The National Research Fellowships. The Scientific
    Monthly 73(2):79, August 1951.

Science, 41(1046):86-7, January 15, 1915.

Science, 41(1052):316, February 26, 1915.

Social Science Research Council. Fellows of the Social Science Re-
    search Council, 1925-1939. New York: Social Science
    Research Council, 1939.

Spencer, R. R. National Cancer Institute Program of Postgraduate
    Training for Physicians. Public Health Reports 64(24):
    750-6, June 17, 1949.

U.S. Congress, Public Law 75-244, National Cancer Institute Act.
    Washington, D.C. 1937.

_____. Public Law 78-410, Public Health Service Act, Washing-
    ton, D.C. 1944.

_____. Public Law 93-348, National Research Service Award Act.
    Washington, D.C. 1974.

U.S. Department of Health, Education, and Welfare. Research Fellows
    of the National Cancer Institute, January 1, 1938-April 1,
    1958. Wshington, D.C.: U.S. Government Printing Office, 1959.
    (PHS Publication No. 658).

U.S. Department of the Interior. Research-A National Resource;
    Part I, Relation of the Federal Government to Research. Report
    of the Science Committee to the National Resources Commmittee.
    Washington, D.C.: U.S. Government Printing Office, November
    1938.

Visher, S. S. Scientists Starred, 1903-1943, in American Men of
    Science. Baltimore: The Johns Hopkins Press, 1947.

3. CHANGING EMPLOYMENT PATTERNS

Fundamental to this study of the postdoctoral role in the sciences and engineering is an understanding of the system by which students completing their graduate education enter careers in these fields. The system is a dynamic one in which both supply and demand respond to a variety of economic, demographic, and other factors. On the supply side, for example, the career choices of undergraduate and graduate students are influenced by their perceptions of employment prospects, relative earnings, and educational costs, as well as by their own academic interests. On the demand side, the availability of positions, nearly 60 percent of which lie in the academic sector, is primarily determined by the level of the national investment in research, total enrollments in colleges and universities, and rates of labor force attrition. In the past few years several concerted efforts[1] have been made to model the Ph.D. labor market and to analyze the supply-demand outlook for the next decade or two. Of particular relevance are the forecasts recently completed by Radner and Kuh[2] and by the National Science Foundation,[3] both of which examine in some detail the flow of graduate students into the Ph.D. labor force. Later in this chapter we summarize the findings from these forecasts and examine the major factors contributing to the findings. First, however, we present a schematic description of the Ph.D. labor force which, unlike the supply-demand models used in most employment market forecasts, incorporates the postdoctoral role in early career patterns.

---

[1]A detailed critique by Donald J. Hernandez of five recent forecasts of Ph.D. supply and demand is published in National Research Council (1979), Appendix B.
[2]Radner and Kuh (1978).
[3]National Science Foundation (1979).

Career Paths

Figure 3.1 shows alternative career pathways Ph.D. recipients follow in entering the science labor force after graduate school. The estimate associated with each pathway represents the average number of individuals per year who followed that particular route during the period from March 1973 through February 1979. For purposes here, the science fields have been aggregated. In Chapter 4 this same supply diagram is presented with separate estimates for engineering and each major field of science.

During the 6-year span an average of approximately 14,500 individuals each year earned science doctorates and entered the U.S. labor force[4] through paths A, B, and C. The majority (66 percent) have taken nonpostdoctoral employment in the science workforce (path B). Another 30 percent chose postdoctoral appointments in these fields (path C), while the remaining 4 percent found positions in engineering, the humanities, education, or professional fields (path A). It must be emphasized that the fraction of graduates following paths B or C has varied considerably among the major fields of science. In the biosciences and physics, for example, the postdoctoral route has been followed more frequently than the direct path to employment in these fields. In the social sciences, on the other hand, less than 5 percent of the recent graduates have taken postdoctoral appointments.

An average of approximately 1,050 doctorate recipients each year entered the science labor force from other fields of graduate study. The majority of these field-switchers were either humanities and education graduates who found positions in related social science and psychology fields or engineers moving into areas within the physical sciences. Most of these individuals took employment in the workforce (path E) rather than entering through the postdoctoral route (path D).

The total science labor force (including postdoctorals as well as all other doctorate recipients employed in these fields) expanded from an estimated 180,500 individuals in 1973 to 251,000 individuals[5] by 1979. This represents an average expansion of 6 percent, or 11,750 persons per year. The two major factors contributing to this growth are readily apparent in the supply diagram presented. An average of 14,975 doctorate recipients have entered the science labor force each year, either directly into the workforce (via paths B and E) or through the postdoctoral routes (paths C and D). This 7 percent accretion has been partially offset by an estimated annual attrition

---

[4]Excluded from the data reported in this chapter are (a) scientists who, after receiving doctorates from U.S. universities, expected to be employed outside the United States; and (b) scientists who took positions in the United States after receiving doctorates from foreign universities.

[5]See Table 3.6 in the supplement to this chapter.

ALL FIELDS OF SCIENCE

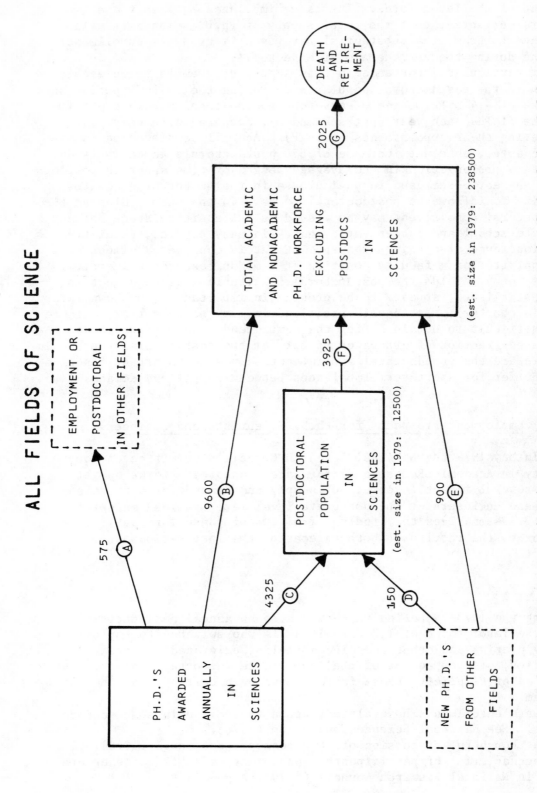

FIGURE 3.1 Components contributing to the average annual growth of the doctoral labor force during the period from March 1973 through February 1979. Estimates represent the average annual number of individuals following particular pathways during this 6-year period. No estimates have been made for field-switching, immigration, emigration, or re-entry into the labor force.

due to death and retirement[6] of only 2,025 scientists--less than 1 percent of the labor force. The large imbalance between these two factors guarantees that the total supply of Ph.D. scientists will continue to grow at a substantial rate even if graduate enrollments decline during the next decade as expected.[7]

Of particular importance in this supply diagram is the sizeable growth in the postdoctoral population. During the 1973-79 period an average of 4,475 Ph.D. recipients took postdoctoral appointments in science fields each year (paths C and D), compared with only 3,925 completing their appointments (path F). As will be discussed in the next chapter, this net increase of 550 postdoctorals annually is due both to a prolongation in the average length of time spent in postdoctoral apprenticeship and to an increase in the number of graduates choosing to follow the postdoctoral route. In the supply diagram the postdoctoral appointment may be viewed as a transition stage between graduate school and career employment. In many physics, chemistry, and bioscience disciplines the appointment is considered almost a prerequisite for a faculty position at a major research university. In most other fields the postdoctoral institution, although not as well established, appears to be growing in importance (as shown later in this chapter). As faculty positions in many science fields become more difficult to obtain during the next decade, we may expect an increased fraction of graduates to opt for the postdoctoral route. In this regard the postdoctoral appointment serves an important function as a buffer for short-term imbalances between supply and demand.[8]

Employment Prospects for Ph.D. Scientists and Engineers

In May 1979 the National Research Council's Committee on Continuity in Academic Research Performance sponsored a workshop[9] at which several recent forecasts of supply and demand for both scientists and engineers at the doctorate level were examined in detail. Table 3.1 summarizes the findings from two of these forecasts. According to the results of both forecasts, the most serious supply-

---

[6]During the 1973-79 period there was also an annual net attrition from the labor force of 1,200 individuals who switched to employment in engineering and other nonscience fields, emigrated to foreign countries, or dropped out of the labor force for other reasons. For purposes of simplicity these factors have been omitted from the supply diagram.

[7]Graduate enrollments have already begun to decline in some science fields. See National Science Foundation (1978).

[8]For a thoughtful discussion of this concept, see Shull (1978).

[9]The agenda, list of participants, and summary of this workshop are given in National Research Council (1979), Appendix B.

Table 3.1

ALTERNATIVE FORECASTS OF UTILIZATION OF PH.D. SCIENTISTS
AND ENGINEERS, BY MAJOR FIELD OF SCIENCE

	Bureau of Labor Statistics Projection			National Science Foundation Projection		
	Labor Force (thousands)	Requirements [1] (thousands)	%Excess of Labor Force over Requirements	Labor Force (thousands)	Requirements [2] (thousands)	%Excess of Labor Force over Requirements
Physical Sciences	90.0	81.1	10%	95	87	8%
Engineering	60.5	65.7	none	72	59	18%
Life Sciences	109.4	87.5	20%	103	91	12%
Mathematical Sciences	24.8	17.4	30%	28	22	21%
Social Sciences	128.0	94.0	27%	113	84	26%
All Science and Engineering	412.7	346.0	16%	412	342	17%

[1] Projected Ph.D. scientists and engineers in "traditional employments."

[2] Projected "science and engineering utilization of science and engineering Ph.D.'s."

NOTE: Bureau of Labor Statistics projection is for 1985; National Science Foundation projection is for 1987.

SOURCE: Braddock (1978)
        National Science Foundation (1979)

demand imbalances during the next 5-7 years are expected in mathematics and the social sciences. Considerably smaller imbalances are anticipated for engineers and physical scientists--in fact, recent data suggest that there is now a significant undersupply of doctoral personnel in engineering. Although the magnitude of the projected oversupply in each field varies according to the methodologies and assumptions used in each forecast, the basic message is quite apparent.

> Barring any unforeseen major increase in demand for Ph.D.'s, or a large drop in Ph.D. output, holders of doctorates in most fields will continue to experience keen competition in obtaining the types of jobs Ph.D.'s have traditionally held. Consequently, many Ph.D.'s will continue to experience delays in obtaining permanent employment in traditional jobs--and may experience job dissatisfaction.[10]

Some caution must be exercised in interpreting projected supply-demand imbalance in a particular field. First, in response to changing employment prospects and relative salaries, some students may alter their career plans. Even the more sophisticated forecasting models which incorporate "feedback mechanisms"[11] do not accurately predict the magnitude of such an adjustment or the associated time lags. Nor do they provide any information about changes in the caliber of students choosing to pursue careers in particular fields. Furthermore, the implementation of new federal programs could have an important impact on the availability of academic employment opportunities in particular fields.[12] Also, although some of the forecasts give consideration to demand in the nonacademic sectors, the forces controlling demand in these sectors are not well understood. In the face of waning prospects for faculty positions, one might expect a significant increase in the numbers of doctoral graduates hired outside academia. Recent trends in this direction have already been

---

[10]Braddock (October 1978), p. 50.

[11]Two of the more promising approaches which utilize feedback mechanisms are those employed by Freeman (1976) and National Science Foundation (1979).

[12]For example, the National Research Council Committee on Continuity in Academic Research Performance recommended the establishment of 5-year, nonrenewable awards for tenured and nontenured faculty members nominated by their departments. The Committee urged that 30 such awards per year be offered immediately in both mathematics and physics. A complete description of the program is presented in National Research Council (1979), Chapter V. After reviewing this recommendation the National Science Foundation has decided not to fund such a program.

observed in the mathematical sciences, psychology, and the social sciences.[13] Finally, it must be emphasized that even a large oversupply of doctoral personnel in a particular field is unlikely to be manifest in high rates of unemployment (relative to the general level of unemployment in the economy). Such highly qualified personnel will almost certainly find employment in nontraditional areas, although some may not consider themselves to be fully utilizing their research skills.

Two factors principally account for the projected decline in employment prospects in most science fields. The first is the expected absence of significant growth in the total number of university and college faculty positions.

> Viewed in the aggregate, then, the 1970's are a period in which the higher education system has begun to make a rather abrupt transition from conditions of rapid growth to conditions of steady, or perhaps modestly declining, demands for its services. This trend is almost certain to produce a significant reduction in the number of academic positions opening up for new Ph.D.'s.[14]

For the next 15 years there will be a substantial drop in the college-age population. This will mean a modest decline or, at best, a stabilization in total undergraduate and graduate enrollments.[15] Moreover, while federal R and D levels cannot be predicted with any degree of confidence, during the next decade large increases are highly unlikely in view of recent trends.[16] Since faculty hiring is closely tied to both enrollments and research funding, we can expect little or no expansion in university science faculties.

A second and equally important factor contributing to the projected oversupply is the anticipated low rate of labor force attrition. As illustrated in Figure 3.1, during the 1973-79 period an average of 2,025 scientists, less than 1 percent of the total pool, retired or died each year. This rate is considerably below what might be considered a steady-state condition,[17] with an annual attrition rate of approximately 3 percent. The reason for this low attrition is

---

[13]Between 1973 and 1979 there has been an annual growth in the nonacademic sectors in each of these three fields of more than 10 percent. See Table 3.6 in the supplement to this chapter.

[14]National Research Council (1979), pp. 14-5.

[15]For a comprehensive analysis of enrollment projections see Cartter (1976), Freeman (1976), Dresch (1975b), or Carnegie Foundation (1975).

[16]Since 1968 total federal expenditures for research and development have declined (in constant dollars). See National Science Foundation (1979a).

[17]The attrition rate for a steady-state conditon is based on an expected 35-year career for a scientist.

a significant imbalance in the age distribution. As shown in Figure 3.2, less than 30 percent of the doctoral personnel who were employed in science and engineering fields in 1979 were over 50 years old, and less than 10 percent were over 60 years old. If one assumes that all doctoral scientists and engineers 50 years or older in 1979 will vacate their positions by the year 1994, then an estimated 72,700 openings will become available during this 15-year span, or an average of 4,850 openings a year. The annual incoming supply of science and engineering Ph.D. recipients is at the present time nearly four times this size.

Faculty Aging

During the transition period of the 1970's several changes have been observed in the employment situations of doctoral scientists and engineers. Perhaps the change receiving the most attention[18] has been what is sometimes referred to as "the faculty aging problem." As the number of new faculty hires in many fields began to decline, the overall proportion of faculty appointments held by recent graduates also fell. Figure 3.3(a) describes the decline in young faculty at major research universities.[19] Between 1973 and 1979 the percentage of science and engineering faculty in these institutions who had received their doctorates in the preceding 7 fiscal years dropped from 38 to 30 percent. The decline in young faculty in engineering and the mathematical and physical science fields was noticeably more abrupt than that experienced in the life sciences or social sciences.

The implications of these trends for universities and the national research enterprise are not fully understood. More definitive information is needed about the roles young faculty members play in academic science and about the relationship between age and research productivity. There is, nevertheless, a consensus within the academic community that a continuing flow of young investigators into university faculty positions is essential to maintain the vitality of the research effort. Another National Research Council committee examined this issue in detail.

> In our view, a steady flow of "new blood" and in part "young blood" into academic departments is important in large part because of its impact on the overall research environment of the department and on the maintenance of a generational mix conducive to good communication and

---

[18]Atelsek and Gomberg (1976 and 1979).
[19]Included are 59 institutions that together accounted for approximately two-thirds of the total research expenditures by universities in 1977.

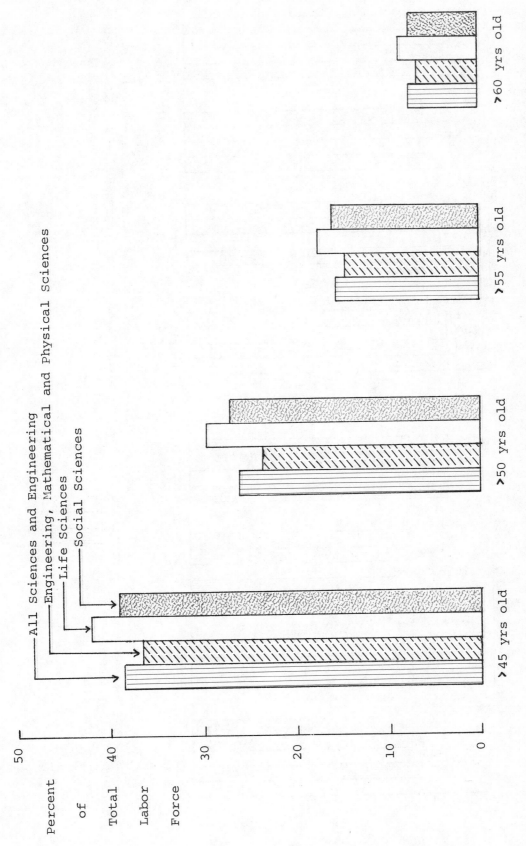

FIGURE 3.2 Age distribution of total doctoral labor force in science and engineering fields in 1979. From National Research Council, Survey of Doctorate Recipients, 1979.

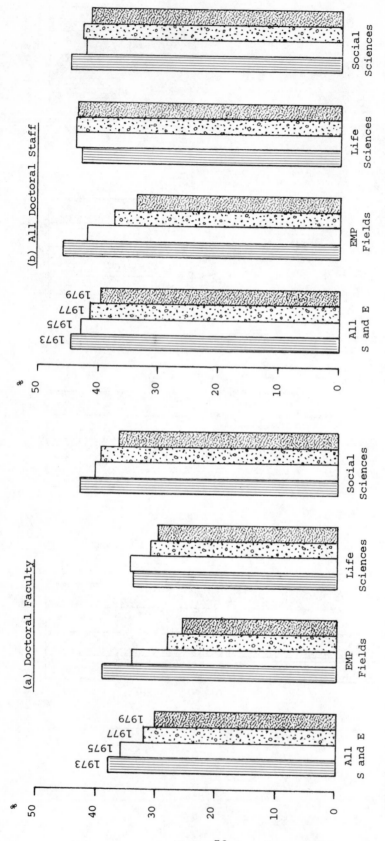

FIGURE 3.3 Percent of (a) doctoral faculty and (b) all doctoral staff in major research universities who had earned their doctorates in the preceding seven fiscal years, 1973-79. EMP fields include engineering and the mathematical and physical sciences. From National Research Council, Survey of Doctorate Recipients.

the most effective motivation of successive cohorts of
independent investigators. Some of the effects we have
pointed to are subtle and indirect. They have not for
the most part been quantified in the existing literature
on sociology of science--and perhaps some of them cannot
be in the present state of the art. . . . But in the
absence of definitive research, we have based our analysis on our experience and understanding of the function-
ing of the academic research system and on the testimony
of other experienced observers. That experience leads
us to believe that the vitality of academic science
would be seriously impaired by sharp restrictions on
the hiring of new faculty.[20]

It is important to recognize that this aging problem is not
nearly as serious for the total doctoral labor force in academia
(including postdoctorals and other nonfaculty doctoral staff) as for
faculty alone. As shown in Figure 3.3(b), the percent of all
scientists and engineers at major research universities who had
received doctorates in the preceding 7 fiscal years only decreased
from 45 percent in 1973 to 40 percent 6 years later. In the life
sciences, the proportion of young staff in academia has remained
almost constant during this period. Whether an increase in
postdoctorals and other nonfaculty doctoral research staff can, in
part, compensate for a decline in junior faculty is an important
issue--and one that will be addressed in Chapter 6.

Postdoctoral Increases

In the face of decreasing numbers of appointments to faculty
positions in many fields of science, there has been a marked increase
in postdoctoral appointments during the past decade. Figure 3.4
describes recent trends in the numbers of doctorate recipients from
U.S. universities who held postdoctoral appointments in this country
during the period between February 1972 and February 1979. By far the
largest increase (in absolute numbers) has occurred in the biosciences. The postdoctoral population in this field has steadily grown
from an estimated 3,650 individuals in 1972 to 7,325 in 1979--an
average annual rate of growth of more than 10 percent in this field.
What is most astonishing about this growth is that it took place
during a period when the number of Ph.D. awards in the biosciences
remained constant at approximately 3,650 each year.[21] Consequently,
by 1979 the number of individuals holding bioscience postdoctoral
appointments was almost twice the number receiving doctorates in the
field that year.

---

[20]National Research Council (1979), pp. 65-6.

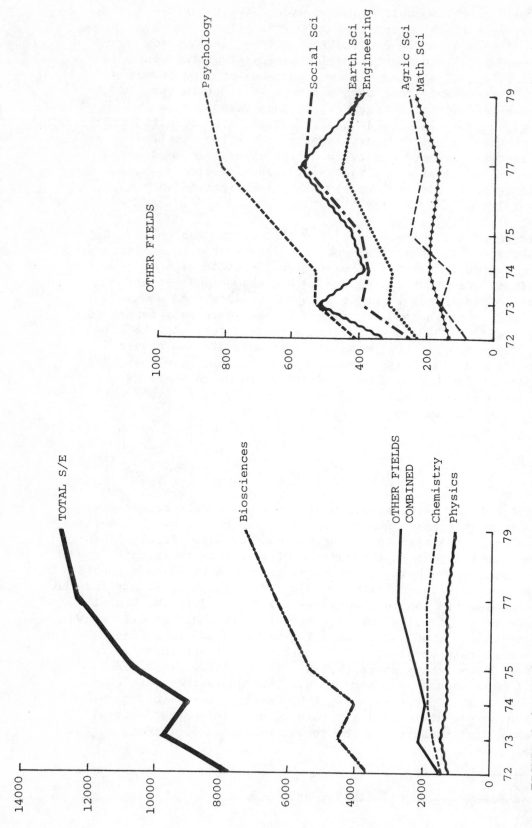

FIGURE 3.4 Estimated number of individuals holding postdoctoral appointments in science and engineering fields, 1972-79. These estimates exclude those who had received their doctorates from foreign institutions. From National Research Council, Survey of Doctorate Recipients and Survey of Earned Doctorates.

The postdoctoral populations in chemistry and physics have also been large, but a substantial drop in doctoral awards during the 1970's has limited the postdoctoral expansion in these fields. The number of postdoctorals in chemistry increased from an estimated 1,400 in 1972 to 1,675 7 years later--an annual growth of less than 3 percent. In physics the postdoctoral population shrunk by approximately 100 individuals during this same period.

The sizes of the postdoctoral populations in most other fields of science are still comparatively small, but rapidly growing. In fact, in three fields--agricultural sciences, psychology, and social sciences--postdoctoral growth has exceeded 10 percent annually. In engineering, however, we have seen a significant decrease during the past 2 years in the postdoctoral numbers (excluding persons with doctorates from foreign institutions).

It is uncertain to what extent these increases in postdoctorals in science fields reflect shortages of alternative employment opportunities for recent graduates, a genuine need for more advanced training in a particular area of research, a recognition that for some careers the postdoctoral is considered a necessary credential, or other factors. The issue is an important one and will be considered in the following chapter.

Other Changes in Employment Patterns

During the past decade we have also witnessed a significant growth in other nonfaculty positions in universities as well as in employment outside the academic sector. Table 3.2 illustrates the growth of other "nonfaculty staff" in universities. Included in this group are doctoral scientists and engineers employed in the academic sector who were considered neither faculty members nor postdoctoral appointees. Between 1973 and 1979 the nonfaculty Ph.D. staff in sciences and engineering expanded at a rate of approximately 8 percent per year--a rate of growth even greater than that for the postdoctoral population.

Although members of this group represented only about 8 percent of the total doctoral scientists and engineers employed by colleges and universities in 1979, there is testimonial evidence[22] to suggest that they have made important contributions to both teaching and research. The chairman of a behavioral science department with a large research program told our committee:

---

[21] See Table 3.7 in the supplement to this chapter for trend data on the number of science and engineering doctorates awarded by U.S. universities.

[22] See Teich (1978) and National Research Council (1978), Chapter 4, for a fuller discussion of the research contributions made by nonfaculty doctoral staff members.

Table 3.2

NUMBER OF DOCTORAL SCIENTISTS AND ENGINEERS WHO HELD ACADEMIC
STAFF POSITIONS OTHER THAN FACULTY OR POSTDOCTORAL APPOINTMENTS, 1973-79

	1973 (N)	1975 (N)	1977 (N)	1979 (N)	Annual Rate of Growth(%)
All Sciences and Engineering	7,752	8,861	10,169	12,195	7.8
Mathematical Sciences	370	516	637	594	(8.2)
Physics	701	944	1,045	1,097	(7.7)
Chemistry	627	716	906	762	(3.3)
Earth Sciences	512	454	537	735	(6.2)
Engineering	735	874	881	882	(3.1)
Agricultural Sciences	419	440	510	701	(9.0)
Biosciences	2,239	2,217	2,988	3,709	8.8
Psychology	1,173	1,279	1,286	2,047	9.7
Social Sciences	976	1,421	1,379	1,668	9.3

NOTE: Estimates reported in the first four columns of this table are derived
from a sample survey and are subject to sampling errors of less than
10 percent of the reported estimates, unless otherwise indicated. Growth
percentages (last column) which are based on survey estimates with
sampling errors of 10 percent or more are reported in parentheses. See
Appendix G for a description of the formula used to calculate approximate
sampling errors.

SOURCE: National Research Council, Survey of Doctorate Recipients and Survey
of Earned Doctorates.

The research program of the [department] could not be carried on without the use of doctoral research staff. Meeting the needs of a long-term longitudinal research program
requires not only staff continuity but a substantial number of well-trained (i.e., doctoral) behavioral scientists
who can spend at least half of their time at research. It
is simply not feasible to secure the kind of staff needed
through academic appointments to regular departments,
though a number of senior and junior faculty are involved
part-time in this enterprise. Few of the postdocs at [this
department] contribute as much to the research program as
do those who are employed on the doctoral research staff
and in some respects, at least, postdoctoral fellowships
have simply become a source of support for persons who
have shown a little promise rate researchers. . . .
Also since their research skills are often far more
sophisticated than those of the postdoctorals they
(doctoral research staff) can bring to bear a level of
expertise not only beyond that of the postdoctorals but
often beyond that of most available faculty members.[23]

In an earlier report our committee examined in detail the characteristics and employment situations of members of the nonfaculty doctoral
research staff. Approximately half of the nonfaculty staff devoted
the majority of their time to teaching, administation, and other
nonresearch activities.[24] For example, in the mathematical and
social sciences many had part-time or temporary teaching assignments that were not considered regular faculty appointments. In
psychology, many were involved in consulting and clinicial services.
In the physical and life sciences and in engineering, on the other
hand, a majority of the nonfaculty staff in universities were
primarily engaged in basic and applied research.

Employment in science and engineering fields outside the academic
sector has also swelled in recent years. As shown in Table 3.3, the
total number of doctoral scientists and engineers employed in government, industry, and other nonacademic sectors grew by roughly 7
percent annually between 1973 and 1979. The largest proportional
growth occurred in those fields in which most members of the labor
force have traditionally worked in colleges and universities. For
instance, the number of mathematical scientists (including computer
scientists) holding jobs outside academia more than doubled during
this 6-year period, as a result of an increase of an estimated 2,800

[23]From a department chairman's response to our committee's request for information on postdoctoral and nonfaculty doctoral research staff.
[24]National Research Council (1978), Table 4, p. 16.

Table 3.3

NUMBER OF DOCTORAL SCIENTISTS AND ENGINEERS WHO HELD POSITIONS
OUTSIDE THE ACADEMIC SECTOR, 1973-79

	1973 (N)	1975 (N)	1977 (N)	1979 (N)	Annual Rate of Growth(%)
All Sciences and Engineering	91,345	106,242	119,684	137,162	7.0
Mathematical Sciences	3,278	3,811	6,077	6,947	13.3
Physics	7,637	8,171	8,598	9,063	2.9
Chemistry	17,165	19,565	20,307	22,439	4.6
Earth Sciences	5,116	6,267	6,829	8,707	9.3
Engineering	23,068	27,956	29,702	32,858	6.1
Agricultural Sciences	4,091	5,093	5,965	6,487	8.0
Biosciences	15,054	15,900	17,797	20,677	5.4
Psychology	11,028	13,396	16,416	19,531	10.0
Social Sciences	4,908	6,083	7,993	10,453	13.4

NOTE: Estimates reported in the first four columns of this table are derived
from a sample survey and are subject to sampling errors of less than
5 percent of the reported estimates. See Appendix G for a description
of the formula used to calculate approximate sampling errors.

SOURCE: National Research Council, Survey of Doctotate Recipients and Survey
of Earned Doctorates.

Ph.D. recipients in business and industrial employment.[25]   In the
social sciences the large expansion in the nonacademic sectors was
primarily attributable to an increase of 3,500 Ph.D. recipients in
government employment.   As already noted, the forces contributing to
expanded demand in the nonacademic sectors are not as well understood
as those contributing to academic demand.

Field-Switching

During the transitional period of the 1970's we have also
witnessed considerable mobility among the major fields of science and
engineering.   The frequency of field-switching by recent graduates is
illustrated in Table 3.4.   The third column in this table reports the
percentage of FY1972-78 Ph.D. recipients in each major field who in
1979 held employment positions outside their field of graduate training.   More than 35 percent of the physics graduates have switched
fields.   Most of these physicists found positions in engineering,
computer sciences, and the earth sciences.[26]
     The sixth column in this table reports the percentage of
FY1972-78 graduates employed in each major field who had earned their
doctorates in other fields.   As many as 40 percent of those employed
in the earth sciences had received their doctoral education in other
disciplines--primarily in engineering, physics, and the biosciences.
As shown in the last two columns of the table, the result has been a
net increase to the earth sciences labor force of an estimated 1,600
persons (41 percent of all recent Ph.D. recipients in the field).   In
contrast, the physics labor force experienced a net loss through
field-switching of roughly 1,950 recent graduates (24 percent of the
doctorate total).   These field changes may correct, to a significant
extent, for short-term imbalances in the supply and demand for doctoral personnel in particular fields[27].   In Chapter 4 we discuss the
important role postdoctoral education has played in facilitating
field-switching.

Difficulties in Finding Employment

It should be restated that, even with a rapidly declining job
market in certain fields of science, high levels of unemployment for
doctoral personnel are not expected.   There is, nevertheless, some

---

[25]See Table 3.6 in the supplement to this chapter for detailed data
on growth patterns within industry, government, and other nonacademic
sectors.
[26]A detailed analysis of the mobility patterns among science and
engineering fields is presented in National Research Council (1975).
[27]Grodzins (1979).

Table 3.4

FIELD-SWITCHING BY FY1972-78 PH.D. RECIPIENTS IN 1979
SCIENCE AND ENGINEERING LABOR FORCE

Field of Science	Doctoral Field			Employment Field			Net Change[1]	
	Total (N)	Employed in Other Field (N)	(%)	Total (N)	Doctorate in Other Field (N)	(%)	(N)	(%)
Mathematical Sci	7,088	1,131	16	8,541	2,584	30	1,453	20
Physics	8,187	2,900	35	6,236	949	15	-1,951	-24
Chemistry	11,340	2,018	18	10,584	1,262	12	-756	-7
Earth Sciences	3,849	587	15	5,427	2,165	40	1,578	41
Engineering	17,264	3,329	19	16,466	2,531	15	-798	-5
Agricultural Sciences	4,805	1,102	23	4,683	980	21	-122	-2
Biosciences	24,383	2,853	12	25,146	3,616	14	763	3
Psychology	17,641	1,807	10	16,224	390	2	-1,417	-8
Social Sciences	21,952	4,909	22	19,578	2,535	13	-2,374	-11

[1]Percent based on the total doctorates awarded in the field (column 1).

NOTE: Percentage estimates reported in this table are derived from a sample survey and are subject
        to an absolute sampling error of less than 3 percentage points. See Appendix G for a description
        of the formula used to calculate approximate sampling errors.

SOURCE: National Research Council, Survey of Doctorate Recipients, 1979.

60

evidence to indicate that recent graduates in many fields have
encountered more difficulty in finding jobs than graduates of the
mid-1960's. As shown in Figure 3.5, the percentage of science and
engineering graduates who were still seeking employment positions
at the time they were awarded their doctorates[28] has climbed
significantly since the expansion era in the 1960's. By the late
1970's almost 20 percent of the Ph.D. recipients in psychology and the
other social science fields had not found positions at the time of
graduation. These graduates have apparently found it increasingly
difficult in recent years to find jobs after receiving their
degrees—at least those jobs they wanted. The situation for doctorate
recipients in engineering and the mathematical and physical sciences,
on the other hand, may have improved slightly in the last several
years. In fact, other evidence leads us to believe that there are now
significant shortages of doctoral personnel in engineering and the
computer sciences.

As might be suspected, recent doctoral graduates have encountered
considerably more difficulty in obtaining faculty appointments than
other types of positions.   As shown in Figure 3.6, FY1978 Ph.D.
recipients in every field had less success in their quests for faculty
appointments than they had for either postdoctoral appointments or
positions outside the academic sector. Apparently the fields in which
it has been most difficult to obtain faculty offers were physics,
mathematical sciences, psychology, and chemistry. Graduates in these
fields received, on the average, one job offer for every 10 or more
inquiries made. By far the most promising prospects for faculty
positions were in engineering. Doctorate recipients in this field
received an average of between three and four offers for every ten
faculty positions they sought.

Compared with faculty positions, postdoctoral appointments have
been much more readily available to young scientists and engineers.
In every field except the mathematical sciences,[29] in fact, FY1978
graduates were successful, on the average, in better than 40 percent
of the postdoctoral inquiries they made. Prospects for employment in
business and industry, government, and other nonacademic sectors have
also been more promising than faculty opportunities. On the average,
science and engineering graduates received one job offer for every
three positions they sought outside the academic sector. As shown in
Tables 14C and 14D in Appendix E, the employment prospects for
engineers in industry and for psychologists in government have been
particularly favorable. On the basis of the information presented in
Figure 3.6, it is not at all surprising that we have found rapid
expansion in the numbers of scientists and engineers employed in
industry or government or holding postdoctoral appointments. It must
be recognized, however, that these data reflect the experiences of
those earning doctorates 2 years ago and that employment patterns in a
field can change significantly in a short period of time.

---

[28]The validity of the "SEEK" variable (described in Figure 3.5) has
been explored in an unpublished report by Freeman (1977).

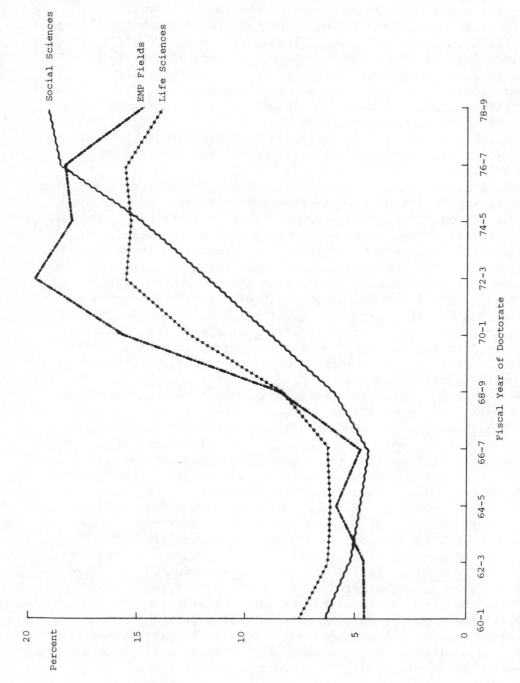

FIGURE 3.5 Percent of doctorate recipients in science and engineering fields who were seeking employment positions at the time they received their degrees, 1960-79. EMP fields include engineering and the mathematical and physical sciences. From National Research Council, Survey of Earned Doctorates.

62

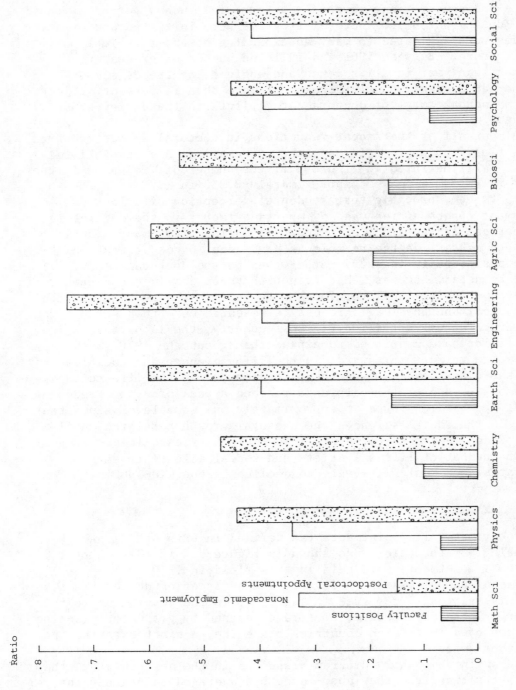

FIGURE 3.6 Ratio of the median number of job offers for faculty, postdoctoral, and nonacademic positions to the median number of inquiries made by FY1978 Ph.D. recipients. From National Research Council, Survey of Scientists and Engineers, 1979.

Adjustments in the Labor Market

During the past decade some significant reductions have occurred in the numbers of students earning doctorates in certain fields of science and engineering. These reductions followed a period of rapid growth during which new doctoral programs were initiated and existing programs were augmented to meet an expanding demand for highly skilled investigators. Between 1961 and 1971 the number of graduates[30] produced each year in all science and engineering fields almost tripled--an average annual increase of more than 11 percent. Since then the annual total of doctorate recipients in these fields has declined.

Almost all of the recent reductions in doctoral awards occurred in the fields of engineering and the mathematical and physical sciences. As illustrated in Figure 3.7, the number of graduates in these fields fell from a peak of approximately 8,350 in 1970 to 6,200 in 1979. It seems probable that students' perception of a lack of employment opportunities was an important factor in the decline in the mathematical and physical sciences. In engineering, many baccalaureate and masters degree recipients have been induced to take high-paying positions in industry rather than pursue doctoral study. It should be noted, however, that even with these declines the number of graduates entering the labor force each year in engineering and the mathematical and physical sciences represented more than seven times the average annual attrition.[31] Consequently, the labor forces in these fields have continued to expand throughout the 1970's.

Growth in doctoral awards in the life sciences and social sciences has also slowed during the past decade. In the life sciences the number of doctorate recipients reached a peak of 4,450 graduates in 1971 and has continued at approximately the same level since that time. In the social sciences the doctoral growth persisted until 1977. Recent decreases[32] in first-year graduate enrollments suggest that the number of life scientists and social scientists earning doctorates each year will begin to decline by the mid-1980's.

---

[29]Few postdoctoral appointments (as defined in this study) have been available in mathematics. As shown in Figure 3.4 in this chapter, only 200 appointments were held in this field in 1979.
[30]The total annual awards of science and engineering doctorates from U.S. universities is reported in Table 3.7 in the supplement to this chapter. These data exclude doctorates earned by graduates planning to be employed in foreign countries since they are not entering the U.S. labor force.
[31]As shown in the supply diagram presented in the next chapter, the annual attrition from the labor force has averaged only 1 percent per year in each of these fields.
[32]Data on first-year graduate enrollments are available from the National Science Foundation (1978).

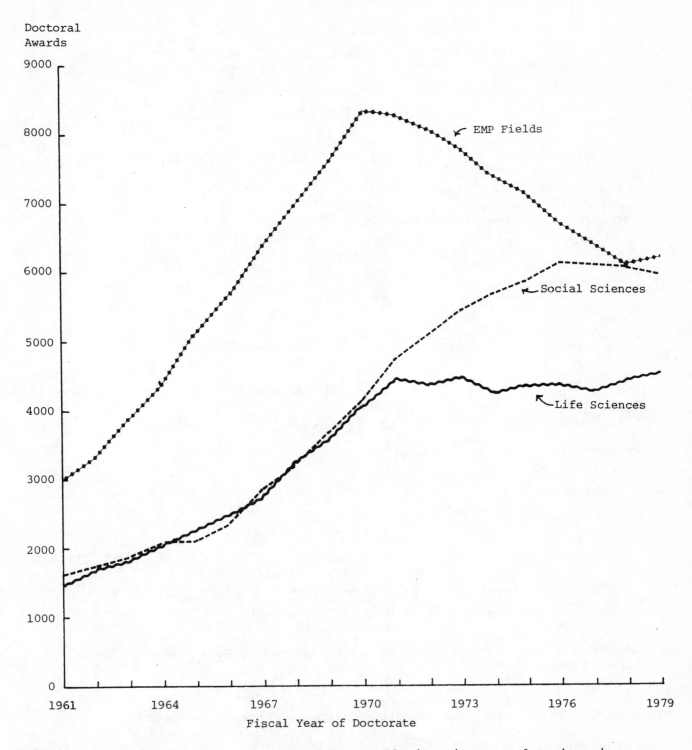

FIGURE 3.7 Number of doctorates awarded annually in sciences and engineering, 1961-79. Data exclude doctorates earned by graduates planning to be employed in foreign countries. EMP fields include engineering and the mathematical and physical sciences. From National Research Council, Survey of Earned Doctorates.

Table 3.5

MEDIAN SALARIES OF RECENT DOCTORAL GRADUATES EMPLOYED FULL-TIME IN
SCIENCES AND ENGINEERING IN THE ACADEMIC AND NONACADEMIC SECTORS, 1973 AND 1979

Employed in Universities and Colleges[1]

	1973 Salaries[2]	1979 Salaries[3]	Annual Increment
All Sciences and Engineering	$15,000	$19,500	4.5%
Engineering and the Mathematical and Physical Sciences	15,000	19,500	4.5%
Life Sciences	14,700	19,800	5.1%
Social Sciences	15,300	19,200	3.9%

Employed Outside the Academic Sector[1]

	1973 Salaries[2]	1979 Salaries[3]	Annual Increment
All Sciences and Engineering	$17,800	$24,300	5.3%
Engineering and the Mathematical and Physical Sciences	18,100	25,400	5.8%
Life Sciences	16,600	22,300	5.0%
Social Sciences	17,900	22,200	3.7%

[1] Excludes those holding postdoctoral appointments.

[2] Median estimates based on 1973 salaries reported by FY1971-72 doctorate recipients.

[3] Median estimates based on 1979 salaries reported by FY1977-78 doctorate recipients.

SOURCE: National Research Council, Survey of Doctorate Recipients.

Nonetheless during the next 5 years the total doctoral supply in these fields will almost certainly expand at an annual rate of more than 4 percent.[33]

We have also witnessed some other important changes in the labor market recently. Starting salaries for doctoral scientists and engineers have not kept up with inflation during the 1970's. As reported in Table 3.5, the median salaries of recent graduates holding full-time (nonpostdoctoral) positions in universities and colleges increased by an average of 4-5 percent a year in each field during the 1973-79 period. Salaries in the nonacademic sectors grew at only a slightly higher rate. During the 1973-77 period prices, as measured by the Gross National Product price deflator,[34] climbed at an annual average rate of 7.5 percent. Some[35] view the decline in real salaries as an important factor contributing to the recent decreases in first-year graduate enrollments. Whether this interpretation is correct or not, it is quite apparent that significant changes have already occurred in both the supply and demand for doctoral scientists and engineers during the past decade

References

Atelsek, F. J. and I. L. Gomberg. Young Doctorate Faculty in Selected Science and Engineering Departments, 1975 to 1980. Higher Education Panel Report No. 30. Washington, D.C.: American Council on Education, 1976

_____. Young Doctorate Faculty in Science and Engineering: Trends in Composition and Research Activity. Higher Education Panel Report No. 43. Washington, D.C.: American Council on Education, 1979.

Braddock, D. The Oversupply of Ph.D.'s to Continue through 1985. Monthly Labor Review: 48-50, October 1978.

Carnegie Foundation for the Advancement of Teaching. More Than Survival: Prospects for Higher Education in a Period of Uncertainty. New York: Jossey Bass, 1975.

Cartter, A. M. Ph.D.'s and the Academic Labor Market. New York: McGraw Hill, 1976.

Dresch, S. P. Demography, Technology, and Higher Education: Toward a Formal Model of Educational Adaptation. Journal of Political Economy, 83:535-69, June 1975a.

---

[33]Annual attrition from the labor force in the life sciences and social sciences will remain at less than 2 percent during the next 5 years, as discussed in the next chapter.

[34]U.S. Bureau of the Census (1978), p. 441.

[35]Freeman (1976) and Dresch (1975a).

_____. Educational Saturation: A Demographic-Economic Model. AAUP Bulletin: 239-47, Autumn 1975b.

Freeman, R. B. The Overeducated American. New York: Academic Press, 1976.

_____. Employment Opportunities in the Doctorate Manpower Market: Biosciences and Psychology, unpublished, January 1977.

Grodzins, L. Supply and Demand V: Studies of the Mobility of Scientists and Engineers, unpublished, December 1979.

National Research Council. Field Mobility of Doctoral Scientists and Engineers. Washington, D.C.: National Academy of Sciences, 1975.

_____. Nonfaculty Doctoral Research Staff in Science and Engineering in United States Universities. Washington, D.C.: National Academy of Sciences, 1978.

_____. Research Excellence Through the Year 2000. Washington, D.C.: National Academy of Sciences, 1979.

National Science Foundation. Graduate Science Education: Student Support and Postdoctorals. Technical Notes and Detailed Statistical Tables. Washington, D.C.: U.S. Government Printing Office, 1978 (NSF78-315).

_____. Projections of Science and Engineering Doctorate Supply and Utilization 1982 and 1987. Washington, D.C.: U.S. Government Printing Office, 1979 (NSF79-303).

Radner, R. and C. V. Kuh. Preserving a Lost Generation: Policies to Assure a Steady Flow of Young Scholars Until the Year 2000. A Report to the Carnegie Council on Policy Studies in Higher Education, October 1978.

Shull, Harrison. The Ph.D. Employment Cycle--Damping the Swings. In The National Research Council in 1978. Washington, D.C.: National Academy of Sciences, 1978.

Teich, A. H. Trends in the Organization of Academic Research: The Role of ORU's and Full-Time Researchers. Report submitted to the National Science Foundation, June 1978.

U.S. Bureau of the Census. Statistical Abstract of the United States: 1978. Washington, D.C.: U.S. Government Printing Office, 1978.

Supplementary Tables for Chapter 3 Follow.

Table 3.6

ESTIMATED NUMBER OF DOCTORAL SCIENTISTS AND ENGINEERS BY
TYPE OF POSITIONS, 1973-79

| | Total All Fields | | | | Annual Rate of Growth(%) |
	1973	1975	1977	1979	
Total Labor Force	216,142	245,871	272,750	298,929	5.6
Academic Sectors	122,226	137,127	149,629	158,656	4.4
Faculty Positions	107,003	120,008	129,565	136,019	4.1
Professor	42,390	47,884	51,006	58,054	5.4
Associate Professor	31,260	35,961	39,418	39,905	4.2
Assistant Professor/Instructor	33,353	36,163	39,141	38,060	2.2
Nonfaculty Positions	15,223	17,119	20,064	22,637	6.8
Postdocs	7,471	8,258	9,895	10,442	5.7
Other Staff	7,752	8,861	10,169	12,195	7.8
Nonacademic Sectors	91,345	106,242	119,684	137,162	7.0
Postdocs	2,288	2,416	2,520	2,422	1.0
Other Positions	89,057	103,826	117,164	134,740	7.1
In FFRDC Labs	9,036	11,374	11,906	12,488	5.5
In Government	16,055	19,047	22,485	26,697	8.8
In Business/Industry	48,333	58,925	65,015	75,027	7.6
In Other Sectors	15,633	14,480	17,758	20,528	4.6
Unemployed--Seeking Position	2,571	2,502	3,437	3,111	3.2

NOTE: Estimates reported in the first four columns of this table are derived from a sample survey and are subject to sampling errors of less than 10 percent of the reported estimates. See Appendix G for a description of the formula used to calculate approximate sampling errors.

SOURCE: National Research Council, Survey of Doctorate Recipients and Survey of Earned Doctorates.

Table 3.6

ESTIMATED NUMBER OF DOCTORAL SCIENTISTS AND ENGINEERS BY
TYPE OF POSITIONS, 1973-79

	Mathematical Sciences				Annual Rate of Growth (%)
	1973	1975	1977	1979	
Total Labor Force	14,836	16,548	19,711	21,139	6.1
Academic Sectors	11,387	12,653	13,462	14,123	3.7
Faculty Positions	10,910	12,015	12,719	13,329	3.4
Professor	3,573	4,029	4,344	5,066	6.0
Associate Professor	3,234	3,820	4,354	4,350	5.1
Assistant Professor/Instructor	4,103	4,166	4,021	3,913	-0.8
Nonfaculty Positions	477	638	743	794	(8.9)
Postdocs	107	122	106	200	(11.0)
Other Staff	370	516	637	594	(8.2)
Nonacademic Sectors	3,278	3,811	6,077	6,947	13.3
Postdocs	52	66	54	39	(-4.7)
Other Positions	3,226	3,745	6,023	6,908	13.5
In FFRDC Labs	509	615	669	882	(9.6)
In Government	516	667	905	1,052	(12.6)
In Business/Industry	1,787	2,273	4,053	4,613	17.1
In Other Sectors	414	190	396	361	(-2.3)
Unemployed--Seeking Position	171	84	172	69	(-14.0)

NOTE: Estimates reported in the first four columns of this table are derived from a sample survey and are subject to sampling errors of less than 10 percent of the reported estimates, unless otherwise indicated. Growth percentages (last column) which are based on survey estimates with sampling errors of 10 percent or more are reported in parentheses. See Appendix G for a description of the formula used to calculate approximate sampling errors.

SOURCE: National Research Council, Survey of Doctorate Recipients and Survey of Earned Doctorates.

Table 3.6

ESTIMATED NUMBER OF DOCTORAL SCIENTISTS AND ENGINEERS BY
TYPE OF POSITIONS, 1973-79

Physics

	1973	1975	1977	1979	Annual Rate of Growth(%)
Total Labor Force	16,634	17,383	18,295	18,843	2.1
Academic Sectors	8,693	8,830	9,417	9,529	1.5
Faculty Positions	6,965	7,092	7,500	7,579	1.4
Professor	2,861	3,094	3,323	3,709	4.4
Associate Professor	2,015	2,409	2,432	2,464	3.4
Assistant Professor/Instructor	2,089	1,589	1,745	1,406	-6.4
Nonfaculty Positions	1,728	1,738	1,917	1,950	2.0
Postdocs	1,027	794	872	853	(-3.0)
Other Staff	701	944	1,045	1,097	(7.7)
Nonacademic Sectors	7,637	8,171	8,598	9,063	2.9
Postdocs	459	474	430	293	(-7.2)
Other Positions	7,178	7,697	8,168	8,770	3.4
In FFRDC Labs	2,521	3,008	3,002	3,219	4.2
In Government	957	1,040	1,183	1,465	7.4
In Business/Industry	3,213	3,282	3,535	3,558	1.7
In Other Sectors	487	367	448	528	(1.4)
Unemployed--Seeking Position	304	382	280	251	(-3.1)

NOTE: Estimates reported in the first four columns of this table are derived from a sample survey and are
subject to sampling errors of less than 10 percent of the reported estimates, unless otherwise
indicated. Growth percentages (last column) which are based on survey estimates with sampling
errors of 10 percent or more are reported in parentheses. See Appendix G for a description of the
formula used to calculate approximate sampling errors.

SOURCE: National Research Council, Survey of Doctorate Recipients and Survey of Earned Doctorates.

Table 3.6

ESTIMATED NUMBER OF DOCTORAL SCIENTISTS AND ENGINEERS BY
TYPE OF POSITIONS, 1973-79

	Chemistry				Annual Rate of Growth(%)
	1973	1975	1977	1979	
Total Labor Force	28,484	32,396	33,833	36,566	4.3
Academic Sectors	10,718	12,433	13,060	13,687	4.2
Faculty Positions	8,655	10,235	10,604	11,471	4.8
Professor	3,649	4,566	4,792	5,709	7.7
Associate Professor	2,556	3,083	2,968	3,239	4.0
Assistant Professor/Instructor	2,450	2,586	2,844	2,523	0.5
Nonfaculty Positions	2,063	2,198	2,456	2,216	1.2
Postdocs	1,436	1,482	1,550	1,454	0.2
Other Staff	627	716	906	762	(3.3)
Nonacademic Sectors	17,165	19,565	20,307	22,439	4.6
Postdocs	287	356	364	232	(-3.5)
Other Positions	16,878	19,209	19,943	22,207	4.7
In FFRDC Labs	980	1,157	1,230	1,390	6.0
In Government	1,107	1,342	1,463	1,623	6.6
In Business/Industry	13,559	15,669	16,050	18,010	4.8
In Other Sectors	1,232	1,041	1,200	1,184	(-0.7)
Unemployed--Seeking Position	601	398	466	440	(-5.1)

NOTE: Estimates reported in the first four columns of this table are derived from a sample survey and are subject to sampling errors of less than 10 percent of the reported estimates, unless otherwise indicated. Growth percentages (last column) which are based on survey estimates with sampling errors of 10 percent or more are reported in parentheses. See Appendix G for a description of the formula used to calculate approximate sampling errors.

SOURCE: National Research Council, Survey of Doctorate Recipients and Survey of Earned Doctorates.

72

Table 3.6

ESTIMATED NUMBER OF DOCTORAL SCIENTISTS AND ENGINEERS BY
TYPE OF POSITIONS, 1973-79

Earth Sciences

	1973	1975	1977	1979	Annual Rate of Growth(%)
Total Labor Force	10,069	11,666	12,663	14,224	5.9
Academic Sectors	4,889	5,307	5,747	5,468	1.9
Faculty Positions	4,155	4,585	4,826	4,409	1.0
Professor	1,761	1,868	2,100	2,096	2.9
Associate Professor	1,227	1,524	1,453	1,273	0.6
Assistant Professor/Instructor	1,167	1,193	1,273	1,040	(-1.9)
Nonfaculty Positions	734	722	921	1,059	(6.3)
Postdocs	222	268	384	324	(6.5)
Other Staff	512	454	537	735	(6.2)
Nonacademic Sectors	5,116	6,267	6,829	8,707	9.3
Postdocs	101	92	80	90	(-1.9)
Other Positions	5,015	6,175	6,749	8,617	9.4
In FFRDC Labs	566	861	676	948	(9.0)
In Government	1,964	2,162	2,622	3,137	8.1
In Business/Industry	2,022	2,797	3,011	4,038	12.2
In Other Sectors	463	355	440	494	(1.1)
Unemployed--Seeking Position	64	92	87	49	(-4.4)

NOTE: Estimates reported in the first four columns of this table are derived from a sample survey and are subject to sampling errors of less than 10 percent of the reported estimates, unless otherwise indicated. Growth percentages (last column) which are based on survey estimates with sampling errors of 10 percent or more are reported in parentheses. See Appendix G for a description of the formula used to calculate approximate sampling errors.

SOURCE: National Research Council, Survey of Doctorate Recipients and Survey of Earned Doctorates.

Table 3.6

Estimated Number of Doctoral Scientists and Engineers by
Type of Positions, 1973-79

Engineering

	1973	1975	1977	1979	Annual Rate of Growth(%)
Total Labor Force	35,618	41,281	43,829	47,951	5.1
Academic Sectors	12,273	13,049	13,860	14,780	3.1
Faculty Positions	11,125	11,886	12,470	13,511	3.3
Professor	4,755	5,505	5,924	7,173	7.1
Associate Professor	3,665	3,856	3,951	3,988	1.4
Assistant Professor/Instructor	2,705	2,525	2,595	2,350	-2.3
Nonfaculty Positions	1,148	1,163	1,390	1,269	1.7
Postdocs	413	289	509	387	(-1.1)
Other Staff	735	874	881	882	(3.1)
Nonacademic Sectors	23,068	27,956	29,702	32,858	6.1
Postdocs	105	124	74	16	(-26.9)
Other Positions	22,963	27,832	29,628	32,842	6.1
In FFRDC Labs	2,378	3,260	3,471	3,518	6.7
In Government	2,375	2,884	3,518	3,788	8.1
In Business/Industry	16,756	21,138	21,841	24,766	6.7
In Other Sectors	1,454	550	798	770	(-10.1)
Unemployed--Seeking Position	277	276	267	313	(2.1)

NOTE: Estimates reported in the first four columns of this table are derived from a sample survey and are subject to sampling errors of less than 10 percent of the reported estimates, unless otherwise indicated. Growth percentages (last column) which are based on survey estimates with sampling errors of 10 percent or more are reported in parentheses. See Appendix G for a description of the formula used to calculate approximate sampling errors.

SOURCE: National Research Council, Survey of Doctorate Recipients and Survey of Earned Doctorates.

Table 3.6

Estimated Number of Doctoral Scientists and Engineers by
Type of Positions, 1973-79

Agricultural Sciences

	1973	1975	1977	1979	Annual Rate of Growth(%)
Total Labor Force	10,763	12,979	14,322	15,022	5.7
Academic Sectors	6,618	7,835	8,289	8,413	4.1
Faculty Positions	6,033	7,146	7,565	7,527	3.8
Professor	2,979	3,523	3,658	4,070	5.3
Associate Professor	1,761	1,963	2,116	2,213	3.9
Assistant Professor/Instructor	1,293	1,660	1,791	1,244	-0.6
Nonfaculty Positions	585	689	724	886	(7.2)
Postdocs	166	249	214	185	(1.8)
Other Staff	419	440	510	701	(9.0)
Nonacademic Sectors	4,091	5,093	5,965	6,487	8.0
Postdocs	0	0	0	58	--
Other Positions	4,091	5,093	5,965	6,429	7.8
In FFRDC Labs	701	793	1,062	440	(-7.5)
In Government	1,289	1,542	1,808	2,348	10.5
In Business/Industry	1,813	2,514	2,826	3,228	10.1
In Other Sectors	288	244	269	413	(6.2)
Unemployed--Seeking Position	54	51	68	122	(14.5)

NOTE: Estimates reported in the first four columns of this table are derived from a sample survey and are subject to sampling errors of less than 10 percent of the reported estimates, unless otherwise indicated. Growth percentages (last column) which are based on survey estimates with sampling errors of 10 percent or more are reported in parentheses. See Appendix G for a description of the formula used to calculate approximate sampling errors.

SOURCE: National Research Council, Survey of Doctorate Recipients and Survey of Earned Doctorates.

75

Table 3.6

Estimated Number of Doctoral Scientists and Engineers by
Type of Positions, 1973-79

	Biosciences				Annual Rate of Growth(%)
	1973	1975	1977	1979	
Total Labor Force	47,343	51,373	57,025	64,243	5.2
Academic Sectors	31,773	34,860	38,257	42,771	5.1
Faculty Positions	25,985	28,371	30,008	33,018	4.1
Professor	10,117	10,931	11,080	12,383	3.4
Associate Professor	7,468	7,984	8,960	9,796	4.6
Assistant Professor/Instructor	8,400	9,456	9,968	10,839	4.3
Nonfaculty Positions	5,788	6,489	8,249	9,753	9.1
Postdocs	3,549	4,272	5,261	6,044	9.3
Other Staff	2,239	2,217	2,988	3,709	8.8
Nonacademic Sectors	15,054	15,900	17,797	20,677	5.4
Postdocs	921	1,072	1,129	1,277	5.6
Other Positions	14,133	14,828	16,668	19,400	5.4
In FFRDC Labs	1,120	1,350	1,461	1,372	3.4
In Government	4,144	4,557	4,682	5,591	5.1
In Business/Industry	5,072	5,691	6,438	7,363	6.4
In Other Sectors	3,797	3,230	4,087	5,074	5.0
Unemployed--Seeking Position	516	613	971	795	(7.5)

NOTE: Estimates reported in the first four columns of this table are derived from a sample survey and are subject to sampling errors of less than 10 percent of the reported estimates, unless otherwise indicated. Growth percentages (last column) which are based on survey estimates with sampling errors of 10 percent or more are reported in parentheses. See Appendix G for a description of the formula used to calculate approximate sampling errors.

SOURCE: National Research Council, Survey of Doctorate Recipients and Survey of Earned Doctorates.

Table 3.6

Estimated Number of Doctoral Scientists and Engineers by
Type of Positions, 1973-79

	Psychology				Annual Rate of Growth(%)
	1973	1975	1977	1979	
Total Labor Force	25,622	30,316	34,039	37,978	6.8
Academic Sectors	14,304	16,683	17,147	17,937	3.8
Faculty Positions	12,818	14,866	15,301	15,325	3.0
Professor	4,596	5,443	5,418	6,156	5.0
Associate Professor	3,645	4,412	4,438	4,312	2.8
Assistant Professor/Instructor	4,577	5,011	5,445	4,857	1.0
Nonfaculty Positions	1,486	1,817	1,846	2,612	9.9
Postdocs	313	538	560	565	(10.3)
Other Staff	1,173	1,279	1,286	2,047	9.7
Nonacademic Sectors	11,028	13,396	16,416	19,531	10.0
Postdocs	208	86	262	300	(6.3)
Other Positions	10,820	13,310	16,154	19,231	10.1
In FFRDC Labs	139	153	128	110	(-3.8)
In Government	1,939	2,250	2,615	2,905	7.0
In Business/Industry	2,997	4,037	5,393	6,940	15.0
In Other Sectors	5,745	6,870	8,018	9,276	8.3
Unemployed--Seeking Position	290	237	476	510	(9.9)

NOTE: Estimates reported in the first four columns of this table are derived from a sample survey and are subject to sampling errors of less than 10 percent of the reported estimates, unless otherwise indicated. Growth percentages (last column) which are based on survey estimates with sampling errors of 10 percent or more are reported in parentheses. See Appendix G for a description of the formula used to calculate approximate sampling errors.

SOURCE: National Research Council, Survey of Doctorate Recipients and Survey of Earned Doctorates.

Table 3.6

Estimated Number of Doctoral Scientists and Engineers by
Type of Positions, 1973-79

Social Sciences

	1973	1975	1977	1979	Annual Rate of Growth(%)
Total Labor Force	26,773	31,929	39,033	42,963	8.2
Academic Sectors	21,571	25,477	30,390	31,948	6.8
Faculty Positions	20,357	23,812	28,572	29,850	6.6
Professor	8,099	8,925	10,367	11,692	6.3
Associate Professor	5,689	6,910	8,746	8,270	6.4
Assistant Professor/Instructor	6,569	7,977	9,459	9,888	7.1
Nonfaculty Positions	1,214	1,665	1,818	2,098	9.5
Postdocs	238	244	439	430	(10.4)
Other Staff	976	1,421	1,379	1,668	9.3
Nonacademic Sectors	4,908	6,083	7,993	10,453	13.4
Postdocs	155	146	127	117	(-4.6)
Other Positions	4,753	5,937	7,866	10,336	13.8
In FFRDC Labs	122	177	207	609	(30.7)
In Government	1,764	2,603	3,689	4,788	18.1
In Business/Industry	1,114	1,524	1,868	2,511	14.5
In Other Sectors	1,753	1,633	2,102	2,428	5.6
Unemployed--Seeking Position	294	369	650	562	(11.4)

NOTE: Estimates reported in the first four columns of this table are derived from a sample survey and are subject to sampling errors of less than 10 percent of the reported estimates, unless otherwise indicated. Growth percentages (last column) which are based on survey estimates with sampling errors of 10 percent or more are reported in parentheses. See Appendix G for a description of the formula used to calculate approximate sampling errors.

SOURCE: National Research Council, Survey of Doctorate Recipients and Survey of Earned Doctorates.

78

Table 3.7

NUMBER OF DOCTORATES[1] AWARDED IN SCIENCE AND ENGINEERING FIELDS, 1960-79

Fiscal Year of Doctorate

Field of Doctorate	1960	1961	1962	1963	1964	1965	1966	1967	1968	1969
All Sciences & Engin	5725	6126	6771	7582	8466	9529	10442	11994	13466	14887
Mathematical Sci	259	305	353	451	538	639	697	783	910	994
Physics	492	538	639	749	802	954	966	1209	1336	1319
Chemistry	997	1073	1053	1203	1241	1335	1489	1644	1701	1836
Earth Sciences	217	212	216	277	269	327	356	370	399	435
Engineering	740	883	1098	1238	1529	1891	2119	2419	2675	3040
Agricultural Sci	338	354	369	387	413	445	435	454	525	645
Biosciences	1151	1148	1307	1427	1626	1814	2020	2281	2710	2979
Psychology	744	794	818	861	970	922	1084	1236	1408	1682
Social Sciences	787	819	918	989	1078	1202	1276	1598	1802	1957

Fiscal Year of Doctorate

Field of Doctorate	1970	1971	1972	1973	1974	1975	1976	1977	1978	1979
All Sciences & Engin	16551	17521	17537	17762	17354	17331	17088	16739	16526	16685
Mathematical Sci	1132	1150	1155	1100	1097	1033	901	880	891	903
Physics	1512	1523	1439	1435	1196	1176	1119	1043	994	1011
Chemistry	2085	2001	1816	1728	1670	1652	1505	1481	1452	1482
Earth Sciences	447	489	541	580	556	577	574	610	576	594
Engineering	3180	3149	3148	3028	2853	2713	2539	2391	2172	2218
Agricultural Sci	723	829	770	794	739	820	721	695	770	763
Biosciences	3304	3637	3561	3642	3522	3519	3653	3561	3616	3755
Psychology	1797	2026	2181	2391	2523	2637	2786	2911	2996	3016
Social Sciences	2371	2717	2926	3064	3198	3204	3290	3167	3059	2943

[1]Numbers exclude doctorate recipients planning employment outside the United States after graduation.

SOURCE: National Research Council, Survey of Earned Doctorates

4. POSTDOCTORAL PATH TO CAREERS IN RESEARCH

The postdoctoral expansion during the past decade may be viewed as a continuation of a trend that began 20 or more years ago. Since the early 1960's we have witnessed major increases in the numbers of students completing doctoral programs in the sciences and engineering. During this same period there have been even larger increases in the fraction of graduates continuing their education at the postdoctoral level. This trend is quite apparent in Figure 4.1. In FY1960-61 approximately 10 percent of all doctorate recipients in sciences and engineering planned to take postdoctoral appointments after graduate school. By 1978-79 more than 30 percent of the graduates planned postdoctoral study. The most striking increases have occurred in the biosciences. As many as 63 percent of the most recent graduates in this field expected to take postdoctoral appointments. In the fields of physics and chemistry approximately half of the most recent doctorate recipients intended to hold such appointments. In other fields there has been a more modest, but continuous, increase over the past two decades in the fraction of graduates planning postdoctoral study.

Several factors are often cited to explain these trends. In many areas of science and engineering, especially the interdisciplinary and transdisciplinary ones, the nature of research has become increasingly complex and has required young investigators to develop highly specialized skills. Frequently these skills can be acquired more effectively through an intensive postdoctoral apprenticeship than through a graduate research assistantship.

It is more likely postdoctoral education has arisen in some fields because those fields are so rich in subtleties of technique and sophisticated ideas that the single research project required for the doctoral thesis does not provide the student with a sufficient grasp of his field to permit him to become an independent faculty member. On the other hand, not everyone who earns a Ph.D. in those fields intends to continue in research on the frontier. To require that everyone spend another two years to acquire the mastery that is essential for further research contributions is both inefficient and

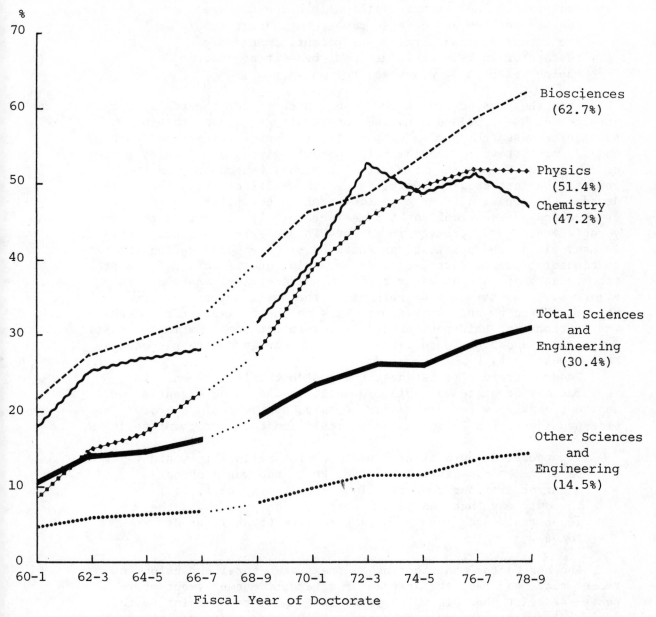

FIGURE 4.1 Percent of doctorate recipients in sciences and engineering planning postdoctoral study after graduate school, 1960-79. Because of a change in definition, FY1969-79 data are not strictly comparable with data from earlier years. From National Research Council, Survey of Earned Doctorates.

redundant. The present system allows the college teacher and the nonacademic researcher to get about their business and permits the potential academic researcher to have the additional benefit of experiencing research in a new environment.[1]

From the perspective of the young investigator the postdoctoral appointment has provided a unique opportunity to concentrate on a particular research problem without the burden of either the teaching and administrative responsibilities usually given to a faculty member or the formal degree requirements of a graduate student. As the competition for research positions has intensified during the past decade, the opportunity as a postdoctoral to establish a strong record of research publications has become increasingly attractive to many young scientists interested in careers in academic research. In fact, in many fields the publications authored or coauthored during the postdoctoral period have become an essential qualification for most faculty appointments at major research universities. As shown in Figure 4.2, an estimated 88 percent of the assistant professors recently hired by chemistry departments in the 59 largest research institutions had held postdoctoral appointments sometime in the past. For physics and bioscience departments the corresponding percentages were almost as high.

Under certain circumstances the postdoctoral experience in research may be quite valuable, as well, to the young scientist or engineer seeking a research career outside the academic sector. The vice-president of a large pharmaceutical firm told our committee:

> In general I would think a postdoctoral fellowship would be a tremendous asset to a young Ph.D. who would choose a career with our company. In fact, in many ways, it is the only way that the person will get accepted . . . the industrial market can be more selective (than it used to be).[2]

Another factor contributing to the postdoctoral expansion in recent years has been the absence of alternative employment prospects--at least those in which young investigators were interested. Table 4.1 reports the primary reasons FY1978 doctorate recipients gave for taking their first postdoctoral appointments. As many as 16 percent of the science and engineering graduates who had taken postdoctoral appointments indicated that they had done so principally because they could not find other employment they wanted. The major-

---

[1]National Research Council (1969), p. 243.
[2]This comment was written in response to our committee's request for opinions concerning the value of postdoctoral experience for careers in research outside the academic sector.

83

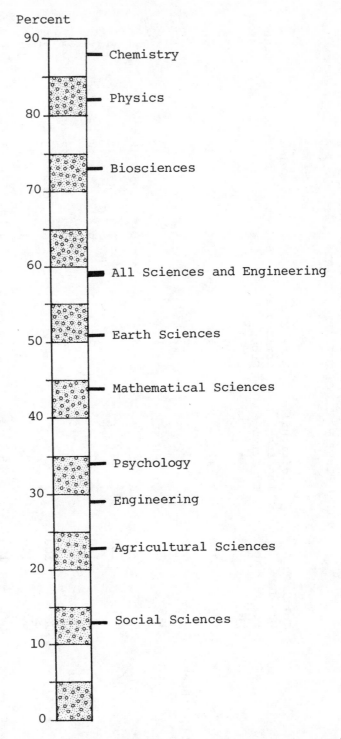

Percent

90 — Chemistry
— Physics
80 —
— Biosciences
70 —
— All Sciences and Engineering
60 —
— Earth Sciences
50 —
— Mathematical Sciences
40 —
— Psychology
30 — Engineering
— Agricultural Sciences
20 —
— Social Sciences
10 —

0 —

FIGURE 4.2 Percent of the last five assistant professors hired by departments in major research universities who had held postdoctoral appointments sometime in the past. Major research universities include 59 institutions which together accounted for approximately two-thirds of the total research expenditures by universities in 1977. From National Research Council, Survey of Science and Engineering Department Chairmen, 1979.

Table 4.1

PRIMARY REASON FY1978 PH.D. RECIPIENTS GAVE FOR TAKING
THEIR FIRST POSTDOCTORAL APPOINTMENT

	Total Ph.D.'s Who Took Postdoc Appts N	%	Additional Research Experience %	Work With Particular Group %	Switch Fields %	Other Employment Unavailable %	Other Reason %
All 1978 Ph.D.'s	4,106	100	47	17	14	16	6
Mathematical Sciences	106	100	(39)	(35)	1	19	7
Physics	389	100	56	18	9	14	3
Chemistry	576	100	36	20	20	19	5
Earth Sciences	174	100	54	16	10	15	5
Engineering	175	100	43	22	9	26	1
Agricultural Sciences	99	100	42	10	2	24	21
Biosciences	1,880	100	52	17	16	13	2
Psychology	471	100	41	11	13	16	20
Social Sciences	236	100	35	14	18	22	12

NOTE: Percentage estimates reported in this table are derived from a sample survey and are subject to an absolute sampling error of less than 5 percentage points, unless otherwise indicated. Estimates with sampling errors of 5 or more percentage points are reported in parentheses. See Appendix G for a description of the formula used to calculate approximate sampling errors.

SOURCE: National Research Council, Survey of Scientists and Engineers, 1979.

ity state that they have taken appointments in order to acquire additional experience in research or to work with a particular research group or mentor.

In the preceding discussion of the general factors contributing to the postdoctoral trends in sciences and engineering, we have ignored several important questions:

(1) What alternative paths have been available to recent graduates interested in careers in research?

(2) To what extent have those taking postdoctoral appointments prolonged their appointments because alternative opportunities they sought were unavailable?

(3) How successful have graduates with experience as postdoctorals been in pursuing careers in research, compared with other graduates?

The answer to each of these questions is, as one might expect, highly dependent upon the established postdoctoral patterns in a particular field or subfield. In the analyses that follow we examine these questions for five separate groups of fields: (1) biosciences; (2) physics and chemistry; (3) psychology and social sciences; (4) earth sciences and agricultural sciences; and (5) engineering and mathematical sciences. The analyses presented in this chapter are limited to an examination of changes in the employment patterns of recent doctorate recipients in each of these fields. We ignore, for example, the question of whether the early career patterns of the most promising young investigators have differed significantly from the career patterns of other graduates. This and other issues relevant to career decisions of young scientists are addressed in Chapter 5.

Biosciences

In 1979 an estimated 7,325 scientists (excluding foreign immigrants) held postdoctoral appointments in bioscience fields. The total postdoctoral population in all other science and engineering fields combined numbered only 5,550 persons. The rapid expansion of the postdoctoral population in the biosciences began in the late 1950's with large increases in the federal investment in health-related research.

During the subsequent years [following 1960] research in all areas of biomedical science flourished to a degree that few could have foreseen. The rapid growth in research on life processes in normal and diseased tissues led to an immediate need for large numbers of highly skilled and creative investigators. To meet this need, federal programs for the support of graduate and postgraduate research training were quickly expanded.[3]

Although the growth in federal expenditures for biomedical research began to slow in the late 1960's, the postdoctoral expansion has continued to the present. As noted in the previous chapter, the number of postdoctoral appointees in the biosciences more than doubled between 1972 and 1979. What is most remarkable about this expansion is that during this same period the number of bioscientists completing doctoral programs each year did not significantly increase.

Figure 4.3 describes the alternative pathways followed by recent Ph.D. recipients pursuing careers in the biosciences during the 6-year span between 1973 and 1979. The numerical estimates in this supply diagram represent the average number of individuals each year who have followed alternative pathways into the workforce. Depicted on the left is the incoming supply of 4,125 bioscience Ph.D. recipients each year. To the right is the active labor force--an estimated 7,300 postdoctorals and 56,900 doctoral bioscientists employed in the academic and nonacademic sectors in 1979. The attrition from the labor force due to death and retirement has averaged only 600 bioscientists (1 percent of the total Ph.D. workforce[4]) each year. During this same period an estimated 200 bioscience Ph.D. recipients a year have found positions in other fields (path A), while 550 graduates from chemistry and other disciplines have taken postdoctoral appointments (path D) or other employment (path E) in the biosciences. Consequently, there has been an annual net growth in the bioscience labor force (including postdoctorals) of approximately 3,325 scientists, or more than 5 percent per annum.

The postdoctoral expansion in the biosciences is described by the rates of flow through paths C, D, and F. During the 1973-79 period an average of 1,975 bioscience Ph.D. recipients (55 percent) each year have taken postdoctoral appointments in this field, along with 275 graduates from other fields. At the same time an average of 1,775 individuals have completed postdoctoral appointments in the biosciences and moved into the regular workforce. As a result, the postdoctoral population in this field has grown at an astonishing rate of 475 individuals per year, or 9 percent annually.

Two factors explain this growth. First, there has been a significant increase in the number of bioscience Ph.D. recipients who have taken postdoctoral appointments. From the committee's surveys we estimate that 1,900 bioscience graduates in FY1978 held postdoctoral appointments within a year after receiving their doctorates, compared with 1,650 graduates in FY1972.[5] This increase is a reflection of the continuous rise (described in Figure 4.1) in the fraction of graduates taking postdoctoral appointments. A second, equally

---

[3]Coggeshall et al. (1978), p. 487.
[4]The low rate of attrition is explained by the skewed age distribution of the labor force. More than three-fourths of the bioscientists in the active labor force in 1979 were under the age of 50.

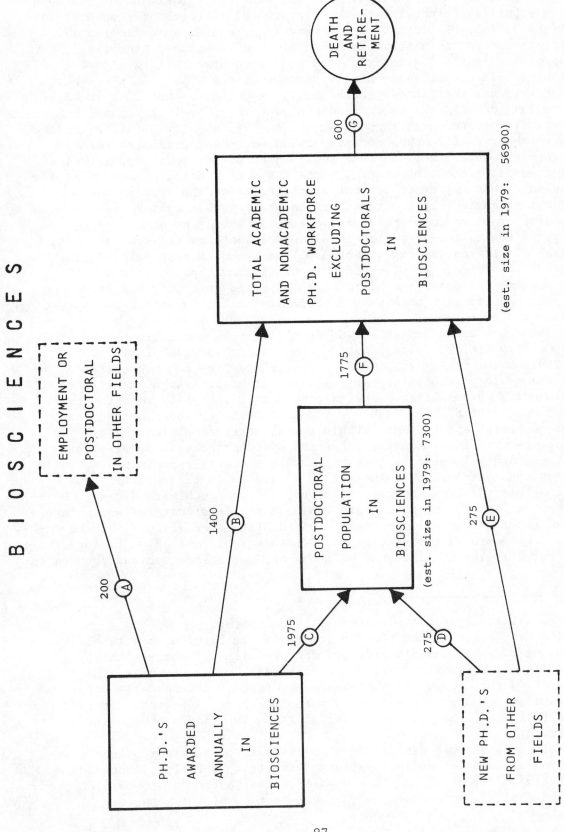

FIGURE 4.3 Components contributing to the average annual growth of the doctoral labor force during the period from March 1973 through February 1979. Estimates represent the average annual number of individuals following particular pathways during this six-year period. No estimates have been made for field-switching, immigration, emigration, or re-entry into the labor force.

87

88

important, factor contributing to the postdoctoral expansion has been
the significant increase in the average total length of time bioscientists held appointments. As shown in Figure 4.4, an estimated 57
percent of the 1976 cohort who had planned[6] to take postdoctoral
appointments after graduation had held appointments longer than 24
months. In comparison, only 34 percent of the 1969 cohort had held
appointments that long. Furthermore, we estimate that 35 percent of
the 1975 cohort were on postdoctoral appointments longer than 36
months, compared with 12 percent of the 1968 cohort. Similar trends
were observed for other cohorts--the more recent graduates were
generally more likely to have remained on postdoctoral appointments
for longer periods of time. On the basis of a detailed analysis of
these trends, we conclude that almost half[7] of the 1972-79 postdoctoral expansion can be attributed to prolongation in the average
length of time spent on appointments. As one might expect, these
trends toward longer postdoctoral apprenticeships reflect, in part, a
lack of alternative employment opportunities. Nearly half[8] of the
FY1972 bioscience Ph.D. recipients who had held postdoctoral
appointments longer than 24 months indicated that they had prolonged
their appointments because of difficulty in finding other employment
they wanted.

The preceding analysis ignores differences among bioscience
specialty fields. Data from the committee's surveys of FY1972 and
FY1978 Ph.D. recipients indicate that there has been considerable
variance in postdoctoral participation of graduates in the various
biomedical disciplines. The last column in Table 4.2 reports the
percentage of FY1978 graduates in each specialty who had taken
postdoctoral appointments within a year after receiving their
doctorates. More than three-fourths of the biochemists, biophysi-
cists, and molecular biologists took postdoctoral appointments, while
less than one-fourth of the FY1978 graduates in biostatistics,
biomathematics, environmental health, and public health did so. More
than half of the bioscientists who have held postdoctoral appointments
had received their doctorates in one of five specialties: biochemistry, microbiology, physiology, pharmacology, or molecular biology.
Apparently the postdoctoral build-up has not been a serious concern in

---

[5]See Table 4.2 presented later in this chapter.
[6]It must be noted that these percentages are based on the total
number of graduates planning postdoctoral study. Some of these
graduates, however, never took appointments. Consequently, the
reported percentages underestimate the percent who actually held
postdoctoral appointments for a specified length of time. It is
unlikely that this discrepancy significantly affects the reported
trends.
[7]This estimate was derived from an analysis of the year of doctorate
of those holding postdoctoral appointments in the biosciences during
the 1972-77 period. See Table 4.11 in the supplement to this chapter.
[8]See Table 4.5 presented in the next section of this chapter.

89

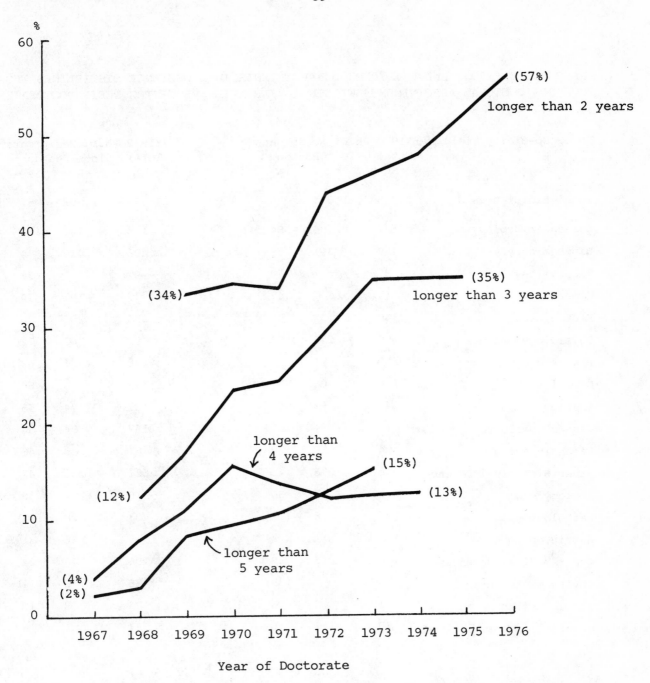

FIGURE 4.4 Percent of bioscientists planning postdoctoral study who had held
appointments longer than 2 - 5 years, by year of doctorate. Reported percentages probably underestimate the percent actually holding appointments for a
specified period of time since some of those planning postdoctoral study may
have in fact never taken appointments. From National Research Council, Survey
of Doctorate Recipients, 1973-79.

Table 4.2

PERCENT OF FY1972 AND FY1978 PH.D. RECIPIENTS IN BIOSCIENCE DISCIPLINES WHO
TOOK POSTDOCTORAL APPOINTMENTS WITHIN A YEAR AFTER RECEIVING THEIR DOCTORATES

Ph.D. Specialty Field	FY1972 Ph.D. Recipients			FY1978 Ph.D. Recipients		
	Total N	Took Postdoc[1] N	%	Total N	Took Postdoc[1] N	%
Total Biosciences	3,298	1,635	50	3,347	1,908	57
Molecular Biology	127	106	84	139	120	86
Biochemistry	479	361	75	496	419	84
Biophysics	91	71	78	92	71	77
Immunology	15	7	(47)	77	57	74
Microbiology	340	192	56	293	205	70
Physiology, Animal	290	152	52	282	203	72
Pharmacology	159	91	57	190	131	69
Genetics	116	66	57	103	66	64
Anatomy	148	59	40	131	74	56
General Biology	113	51	45	157	84	54
Bioengineering	64	18	28	61	28	46
Other Biological Sciences	696	278	40	621	259	42
Zoology	325	97	30	216	82	38
Pathology	70	26	(37)	83	28	(34)
Nutrition	N/A	N/A	N/A	65	20	31
Other Medical Sciences	174	48	28	196	46	24
Environmental Health	20	7	(35)	28	6	(21)
Public Health	51	3	6	83	8	10
Biometrics, Biostatistics	20	2	10	34	1	3

[1]Excludes graduates who took their first postdoctoral appointments more than
a year after they had received their doctorates.

NOTE: Percentage estimates reported in this table are derived from a sample
survey and are subject to an absolute sampling error of less than 5
percentage points, unless otherwise indicated. Estimates with sampling
errors of 5 or more percentage points are reported in parentheses. See
Appendix G for a description of the formula used to calculate approximate
sampling errors.

SOURCE: National Research Council, Survey of Scientists and Engineers, 1979.

many of the smaller, more applied disciplines that did not typically
utilize large research teams. Nevertheless, a comparison of the third
and sixth columns in this table indicates that in almost every
specialty the fraction of graduates taking postdoctoral appointments
increased between 1972 and 1978.

What are the implications of these findings? From the perspective of the national investment in research, the postdoctoral build-
up, in the short run, may be beneficial. The availability of a highly
skilled group of investigators at a very reasonable cost should improve both the quantity and quality of the research product. In the
long run, on the other hand, there is the risk that declining
prospects for career employment will discourage some of the most
promising young investigators from pursuing careers in biomedical
research.[9]

From the perspective of the young bioscientist, the key question
is: what will become of those caught in the postdoctoral "holding
pattern"? It is probably still too early to reach a definitive answer
to this question since many of those graduates taking postdoctoral
appointments in the early 1970's have not yet come up for tenure
review. Nonetheless, on the basis of results from the committee's
survey of FY1972 doctorate recipients, we have a preliminary
indication of how successful bioscience graduates have been in
pursuing careers in research. Table 4.3 compares the recent (April
1979) employment situations of 1972 graduates who took postdoctoral
appointments within a year after completing their doctorates with the
situations of other bioscience graduates who have never held such
appointments.[10] From the table we find:

- A total of about 60 percent of each group were employed
  in universities, colleges, and medical schools.
- As might be expected, the former postdoctorals were more
  likely to be located in major research universities than
  were the other graduates.
- However, 150 of the estimated 1,000 former postdoctorals
  employed in academia held staff appointments which were
  considered to be outside the faculty ladder.
- Furthermore, only one-fifth of the former postdoctorals
  in academia had received tenure, compared with more than
  three-fifths of the other graduates.
- The unemployment rate for the former postdoctorals, while
  not alarmingly high, was three times the rate for graduates who had never held postdoctoral appointments.

---

[9]The possible decline in the caliber of graduate students who elect
to take postdoctoral appointments is discussed in the next chapter.
[10]This table excludes graduates who had taken their first postdoctoral appointment more than a year after they had received their
doctorates.

Table 4.3

COMPARISON OF 1979 EMPLOYMENT SITUATIONS OF FY1972 BIOSCIENCE PH.D.
RECIPIENTS WHO TOOK POSTDOCTORAL APPOINTMENTS WITHIN A YEAR AFTER
RECEIPT OF THEIR DOCTORATES WITH THE SITUATIONS OF OTHER FY1972
GRADUATES WHO HAVE NEVER HELD APPOINTMENTS

Employment Position in 1979	Took Postdoc Within Year After Graduation		Never Held Postdoc	
	N	%	N	%
Total 1972 Bioscience Ph.D.'s[1]	1,571	100	1,472	100
Major Research Universities[2]	446	28	230	16
Tenured Faculty	77	5	130	9
Nontenured Faculty	281	18	69	5
Nonfaculty Staff	88	6	31	2
Other Universities and Colleges	548	35	649	44
Tenured Faculty	116	7	410	28
Nontenured Faculty	369	24	195	13
Nonfaculty Staff	63	4	44	3
Nonacademic Sectors	537	34	580	39
FFRDC Laboratories	30	2	12	1
Government	171	11	243	16
Business/Industry	183	12	214	14
Other Sectors	153	10	111	8
Unemployed and Seeking Job	40	2	13	1

[1] Excludes graduates not active in the labor force in 1979.

[2] Included are 59 universities whose total R and D expenditures in 1977 represented two-thirds of the total expenditures of all universities and colleges.

NOTE: Percentage estimates reported in this table are derived from a sample survey and are subject to an absolute sampling error of less than 5 percentage points. See Appendix G for a description of the formula used to calculate approximate sampling errors.

SOURCE: National Research Council, Survey of Scientists and Engineers, 1979.

Table 4.4 presents additional data comparing former postdoctorals and other 1972 Ph.D. recipients with respect to their median salaries, time spent on research activities in 1979, and their publication records. It is not surprising to find that the former postdoctorals were more likely to devote an average of almost 30 percent more of their time to basic and applied research activities than were other bioscience graduates who had never held postdoctoral appointments. These differences were observed for those employed in the nonacademic sectors as well as those in universities and colleges. It is also not surprising to find that the former postdoctorals had published more articles (including those authored during their postdoctoral apprenticeship) than had other graduates during their careers. However, the 1979 median salaries of those with postdoctoral experience were substantially lower than the salaries of the other group. In the nonacademic sectors the difference in salaries was as much as $4,000.

The differences we have found in salaries and tenure success can be partly explained by the fact that those FY1972 graduates not taking postdoctoral appointments entered the regular workforce 1 to 3 years before those who had pursued postdoctoral study. Nonetheless, on the basis of the magnitude of these differences, one must question whether the postdoctoral experience has been advantageous to those pursuing careers in research. It appears that many of the bioscience graduates who have taken postdoctoral appointments will not be successful in meeting their career goals. The frustrations of those caught in a "postdoctoral holding pattern" were expressed by many young bioscientists responding to our committee's survey. For example, one biochemist commented:

> Frankly, many of us are concerned about our future prospects in these times, after many years of training. We are becoming increasingly discouraged by the decline of tenure-track positions, and the increasing difficulty in obtaining grant support. An opinion that is often expressed is that we postdocs provide a cheap labor source for "established" investigators. Especially in recent years many of us have been completely bypassed by the economic trends, so that we have been unable to purchase homes, have families, etc., while pursuing advanced training necessary to secure "a respectable position." For many of us it is becoming reasonable to ask: "Is it worth it?"[11]

The preceding analysis of the postdoctoral holding pattern in the biosciences neglects the important question of whether it has been primarily the less talented young investigators who have been unable

---

[11]The comment was provided by a FY1978 bioscience Ph.D. recipient, in response to item #15 in the committee's survey.

Table 4.4

COMPARISON OF 1979 SALARIES, RESEARCH INVOLVEMENT, AND PUBLICATION RECORDS OF FY1972 BIOSCIENCE PH.D. RECIPIENTS WHO TOOK POSTDOCTORAL APPOINTMENTS WITHIN A YEAR AFTER RECEIPT OF THEIR DOCTORATES WITH THOSE OF OTHER FY1972 GRADUATES WHO HAVE NEVER HELD APPOINTMENTS

Employment in 1979	Median Salaries in 1979		Involved in Some Research[2]		Median Number of Articles[3]	
	Took Postdoc[1]	No Postdoc	Took Postdoc[1]	No Postdoc	Took Postdoc[1]	No Postdoc
Total 1972 Bioscience Ph.D.'s	$24,200	$26,500	78%	49%	6	4
Universities and Colleges	22,700	24,200	84	52	7	4
Faculty	23,500	24,300	84	51	7	4
Nonfaculty Staff	17,000	--	87	60	5	3
Nonacademic Sectors	26,500	30,400	66	44	5	4
Government[4]	27,300	29,200	76	58	7	7
Business/Industry	29,200	33,100	58	36	4	3
Other Sectors	24,000	31,100	64	28	4	3

[1]Excludes graduates who had taken their first postdoctoral appointment more than a year after they had received their doctorates.

[2]Percent of FY1972 Ph.D. recipients who spent at least one-fourth of their time in basic or applied research activities.

[3]Included are all articles of which the respondent had been principal author and which had been published in refereed journals.

[4]Includes positions in FFRDC laboratories as well as other government employment.

NOTE: Median and percentage estimates reported in this table are derived from a sample survey and are subject to sampling errors of varying sizes. See Appendix G for a description of the formula used to calculate approximate sampling errors.

SOURCE: National Research Council, Survey of Scientists and Engineers, 1979.

to find employment they wanted after completing postdoctoral appointments. This question is addressed in the next chapter.

Physics and Chemistry

The postdoctoral tradition in physics and chemistry in this
country had its origin in the establishment of the National Research
Fellowship Program in 1919.

> The stated purpose of the fellowship was three-fold: to
> open a scientific career to a larger number of investiga-
> tors and to give investigators a more thorough training
> in research, to increase knowledge relating to the funda-
> mental principles of physics and chemistry "upon which the
> progress of all the sciences and the development of in-
> dustry depend," and to create more favorable conditions
> for research in the educational institutions of the
> country.[12]

Although the importance of its contributions to the development of
talented young investigators is unquestioned,[13] the program was
quite small by today's standards. It was not until the late 1950's,
when the federal investment in research was substantially augmented,
that significantly increasing numbers of young physicists and chemists
began taking postdoctoral appointments. For the next 15 years the
postdoctoral expansion in these fields was quite remarkable. Figure
4.5 describes the numbers of physics and chemistry Ph.D. recipients
planning postdoctoral study after completion of their graduate
programs. In chemistry the group expecting to take postdoctoral
appointments steadily climbed from approximately 75 graduates in 1958
to 965 in 1972. In physics the increase was just as remarkable--from
only 25 graduates planning postdoctoral study in 1958 to a peak of 670
in 1973.

The postdoctoral growth during this period can be attributed to
both an increase in doctoral graduates and an increase in the fraction
of graduates taking postdoctoral appointments. As reported in Table
3.7 in the supplement to Chapter 3, the number of doctorates awarded
annually in physics tripled between 1958 and 1973, and the number of
doctoral awards in chemistry nearly doubled. At the same time the
fraction of graduate planning to take postdoctoral appointments also
rose sharply, as illustrated in Figure 4.1. Approximately half of all
physics and chemistry Ph.D. recipients in 1973 expected to hold postdoctoral appointments after graduation.

The postdoctoral expansion in physics and chemistry did not continue during the decade of the 1970's, as it did in the biosciences.

---

[12]National Research Council (1960), p. 16.
[13]Results from an evaluation of this program were presented in M.
Rand (1951).

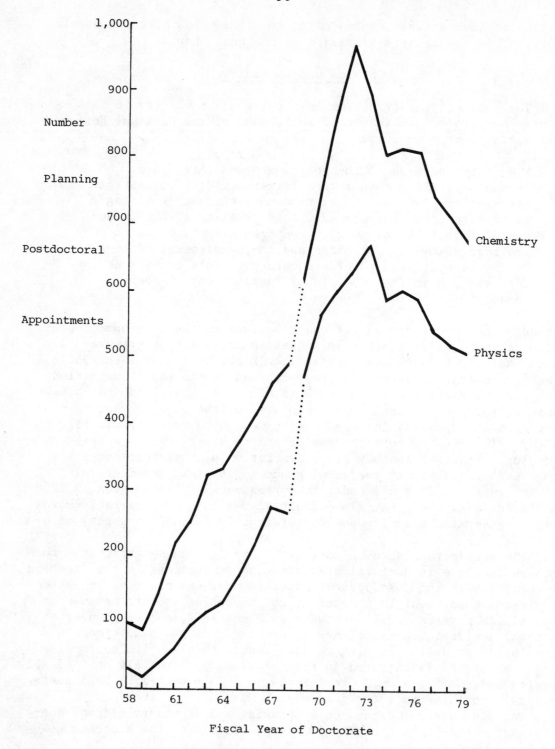

FIGURE 4.5 Number of Ph.D. recipients in physics and chemistry planning to take postdoctoral appointments after graduation, 1958-79.
Because of a change in definition, FY1969-79 data are not strictly
comparable with data from earlier years. From National Research
Council, Survey of Doctorate Recipients.

By the early 1970's, stabilizing (or declining) enrollments and tighter research budgets had had an impact on both graduate and postdoctoral education in the fields of physics and chemistry. A recent study of postdoctorals in physics in 1973 observes:

> By the 1970's the job market had changed. Academic tenure track openings became scarce, extremely so at many top research universities, and employment at FFR&DC's had declined. Projections pointed to an increasingly tight academic market through the 1980's and little growth in the FFR&DC's. Thus, the employment spheres where postdocs usually found later regular employment were very tight and apparently would continue to remain so in the near future.[14]

The employment situation in chemistry during the past decade has been quite similar, although it may have improved in recent years.[15] In both fields annual doctoral awards began to decline in the early 1970's (see Figure 3.7 in the preceding chapter). Accompanying this decline was a more than 30 percent decrease in the number of doctoral graduates taking postdoctoral appointments. From the committee's survey we found that only an estimated 390 of the FY1978 Ph.D. recipients in physics had taken postdoctoral appointments within a year after receiving their doctorates, compared with 565 individuals in the FY1972 cohort.[16] Similarly, only 575 of the FY1978 graduates in chemistry had taken postdoctoral appointments, compared with 960 of the graduates 6 years earlier.

Despite these declines the total sizes of the postdoctoral populations in physics and chemistry did not shrink appreciably. The reason for this can be seen from Figures 4.6 and 4.7 which describe the annual flow through the components of the doctoral labor forces in physics and chemistry, respectively, during the 1973-79 period. An average of 525 (46 percent) of the 1,150 physics Ph.D. recipients each year took postdoctoral appointments in physics (path C), along with another 25 graduates from other fields (path D). During this same period an estimated 600 individuals completed their postdoctoral education in physics each year and moved into the regular workforce (path F). As a net result, the postdoctoral population in this field only declined by approximately 50 scientists annually. In chemistry there was a net decrease of 25 postdoctorals a year between 1973 and 1979. Of the 1,550 doctorate recipients, an average of 625 (40

---

[14]Porter (1979), p. 17.
[15]For a description of the changing employment market in chemistry, see "Employers Intensify Their Search for Chemical Professionals" in Chemical and Engineering News (October 23, 1978).
[16]See the analysis of question 10 in Appendix D and the analysis of question 10 in Appendix E.

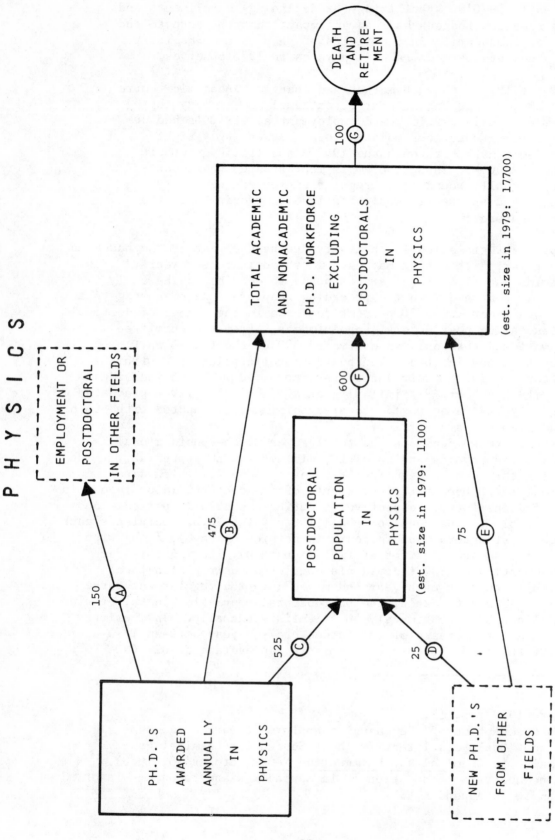

P H Y S I C S

FIGURE 4.6 Components contributing to the average annual growth of the doctoral labor force during the period from March 1973 through February 1979. Estimates represent the average annual number of individuals following particular pathways during this six-year period. No estimates have been made for field-switching, immigration, emigration, or re-entry into the labor force.

98

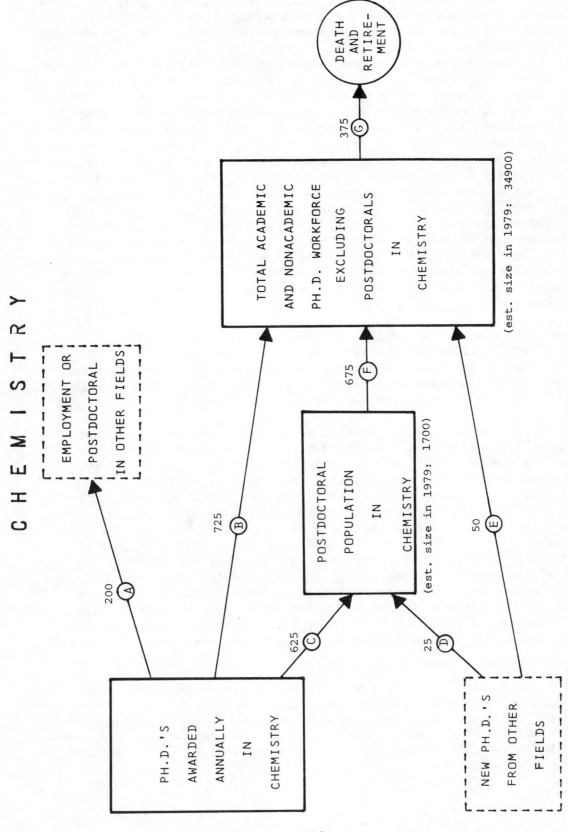

99

FIGURE 4.7 Components contributing to the average annual growth of the doctoral labor force during the period from March 1973 through February 1979. Estimates represent the average annual number of individuals following particular pathways during this six-year period. No estimates have been made for field-switching, immigration, emigration, or re-entry into the labor force.

percent) took postdoctoral appointments in chemistry (path C), along with 25 graduates from other fields (path D). Approximately 675 of those holding postdoctoral appointments in chemistry completed their apprenticeships each year (path F).

Although the postdoctoral populations in these fields have not expanded significantly during the past decade, there may be reason for concern. From responses to the committee's survey of FY1972 Ph.D. recipients, we found convincing evidence that many young physicists and chemists had prolonged their postdoctoral apprenticeships because they could not find other employment that they wanted. As reported in Table 4.5, approximately 36 percent of the FY1972 physics graduates who had taken postdoctoral appointments had extended their appointments for this reason. As many as 38 percent of the chemists had done the same. Of those chemistry graduates who had held postdoctoral appointments more than 2 years, over two-thirds indicated that they had prolonged their appointments because other employment opportunities were unavailable. The frustrations of those graduates caught in a "postdoctoral holding pattern" are apparent from several of the comments made by respondents to our survey. For example, one young chemist noted:

> I got my degree in 1971 (FY1972). There are colleagues of mine still doing post-docs from that time because university/research jobs are not around. Disappointment and disgust abound. Expectations have not been fulfilled, and the era of the perpetual postdoc is upon us.[17]

Although the survey results suggest that chemistry postdoctorals[18] have prolonged their appointments more frequently than either the physicists or bioscientists, the situation for chemists may not be as serious. As the data in the first column of Table 4.5 indicate, the chemists were not as likely to hold postdoctoral appointments for long periods of time. Thirty-seven percent of the chemistry postdoctorals had remained on appointments longer than 2 years, compared with approximately half of the physicists and bioscientists. Furthermore, only 13 percent of the chemists reported that they had held postdoctoral appointments for more than 3 years, while more than one-fourth of the postdoctorals in the other two fields had extended their appointments that long. One might infer from these differences that although many chemistry postdoctorals indicated they had prolonged their appointments because of difficulty

---

[17]The comment was provided by a FY1972 chemistry Ph.D. recipient, in response to item #17 in the committee's survey.
[18]For the analysis presented here, the "chemistry postdoctorals" include all Ph.D. recipients in chemistry who had taken postdoctoral appointments after graduation, regardless of what field they held their appointments in.

TABLE 4.5

PERCENT OF FY1972 DOCTORATE RECIPIENTS IN PHYSICS, CHEMISTRY, AND BIOSCIENCES
WHO HAD PROLONGED THEIR POSTDOCTORAL APPOINTMENTS BECAUSE OF DIFFICULTY
IN FINDING OTHER EMPLOYMENT THEY WANTED

	Held Postdoc N	Prolonged Postdoc %
Physics Ph.D. Recipients		
Total Who Took Postdoctoral Appts	563	36
Held Appts. Longer Than:		
12 Months	442	45
24 Months	272	56
36 Months	168	64
48 Months	87	74
Chemistry Ph.D. Recipients		
Total Who Took Postdoctoral Appts.	952	38
Held Appts. Longer Than:		
12 Months	749	48
24 Months	356	68
36 Months	126	(73)
48 Months	46	(72)
Bioscience Ph.D. Recipients		
Total Who Took Postdoctoral Appts.	1,617	28
Held Appts. Longer Than:		
12 Months	1,323	33
24 Months	816	47
36 Months	423	58
48 Months	217	62

NOTE: Percentage estimates reported in this table are derived from a sample survey and are subject to an absolute sampling error of less than 5 percentage points, unless otherwise indicated. Estimates with sampling errors of 5 or more percentage points are reported in parentheses. See Appendix G for a description of the formula used to calculate approximate sampling errors.

SOURCE: National Research Council, Survey of Scientists and Engineers, 1979.

in finding other employment, they had been more successful in securing alternative positions than their counterparts in physics and the biosciences.

What types of employment have young physicists and chemists found? An analysis of the subsequent employment situations of FY1972 Ph.D. recipients reveals that less than half of those who had taken postdoctoral appointments shortly after graduation have obtained faculty positions. Of the estimated 550 former postdoctorals in physics, fewer than 35 percent held faculty appointments and only 14 percent had received tenure by 1979 (Table 4.6). Even a smaller fraction of the former postdoctorals in chemistry were employed as faculty--only 22 percent of these graduates held tenure track positions in colleges and universities in 1979 (Table 4.7). In contrast, almost 29 percent of the chemists who had never taken postdoctoral appointments were employed on academic faculties at this time. For the majority of these young physicists and chemists the postdoctoral path has led to careers outside the academic sector. Most of the chemists who had followed this path eventually found industrial positions. Many of the physicists eventually found employment in government and federally funded research and development center (FFRDC) laboratories as well as in industry. Further consideration of the applicability of postdoctoral experience for careers in the nonacademic sectors is presented in the next chapter.

Of paramount importance to this analysis is the question of how many of the FY1972 graduates with experience on postdoctoral appointments were successful in obtaining positions which allowed them to function as independent investigators. As reported in Table 4.8, approximately three-fourths of the physicists with this experience were involved to a significant degree[19] in basic or applied research activities, regardless of the sector in which they worked. In fact, those employed in nonacademic sectors were more active in research and had published almost as many articles as their colleagues in universities. Similarly, as many as three-fourths of the chemistry graduates who had held postdoctoral appointments devoted a significant fraction of their time to research activities (Table 4.9), although those employed outside the academic sector had published, on the average, only two articles during their careers. On the basis of this information, it appears that the majority of former postdoctorals in both fields were utilizing their research training--regardless of the sector in which they were employed.

For the young physicist or chemist interested in a position in a major research university, 1 or 2 years experience as a postdoctoral may be considered almost essential. Of the small group employed in the largest research institutions, an estimated 71 percent of the physicists and 89 percent of the chemists had been postdoctorals

---

[19]For purposes of this analysis this group includes those who devoted at least one-fourth of their time to research activities.

Table 4.6

COMPARISON OF 1979 EMPLOYMENT SITUATIONS OF FY1972 PHYSICS PH.D.
RECIPIENTS WHO TOOK POSTDOCTORAL APPOINTMENTS WITHIN A YEAR AFTER
RECEIPT OF THEIR DOCTORATES WITH THE SITUATIONS OF OTHER FY1972
GRADUATES WHO HAVE NEVER HELD APPOINTMENTS

Employment Position in 1979	Took Postdoc Within Year After Graduation		Never Held Postdoc	
	N	%	N	%
Total 1972 Physics Ph.D.'s[1]	557	100	632	100
Major Research Universities[2]	115	21	46	7
Tenured Faculty	28	5	19	3
Nontenured Faculty	53	10	19	3
Nonfaculty Staff	34	6	8	1
Other Universities and Colleges	132	24	166	26
Tenured Faculty	49	9	113	18
Nontenured Faculty	63	11	41	6
Nonfaculty Staff	20	4	12	2
Nonacademic Sectors	308	55	418	66
FFRDC Laboratories	91	16	82	13
Government	71	13	107	17
Business/Industry	126	23	186	29
Other Sectors	20	4	43	7
Unemployed and Seeking Job	2	0	2	0

[1] Excludes graduates not active in the labor force in 1979.

[2] Included are 59 universities whose total R and D expenditures in 1977
represented two-thirds of the total expenditures of all universities and
colleges.

NOTE: Percentage estimates reported in this table are derived from a sample
survey and are subject to an absolute sampling error of less than 5
percentage points. See Appendix G for a description of the formula
used to calculate approximate sampling errors.

SOURCE: National Research Council, Survey of Scientists and Engineers, 1979.

Table 4.7

COMPARISON OF 1979 EMPLOYMENT SITUATIONS OF FY1972 CHEMISTRY PH.D.
RECIPIENTS WHO TOOK POSTDOCTORAL APPOINTMENTS WITHIN A YEAR AFTER
RECEIPT OF THEIR DOCTORATES WITH THE SITUATIONS OF OTHER FY1972
GRADUATES WHO HAVE NEVER HELD APPOINTMENTS

Employment Position in 1979	Took Postdoc Within Year After Graduation		Never Held Postdoc	
	N	%	N	%
Total 1972 Chemistry Ph.D.'s [1]	941	100	615	100
Major Research Universities [2]	142	15	18	3
Tenured Faculty	42	4	18	3
Nontenured Faculty	64	7	0	0
Nonfaculty Staff	36	4	0	0
Other Universities and Colleges	119	13	166	27
Tenured Faculty	25	3	117	19
Nontenured Faculty	79	8	41	7
Nonfaculty Staff	15	2	8	1
Nonacademic Sectors	680	72	416	68
FFRDC Laboratories	38	4	0	0
Government	78	8	86	14
Business/Industry	501	53	287	47
Other Sectors	63	7	43	7
Unemployed and Seeking Job	0	0	15	2

[1] Excludes graduates not active in the labor force in 1979.

[2] Included are 59 universities whose total R and D expenditures in 1977 represented two-thirds of the total expenditures of all universities and colleges.

NOTE: Percentage estimates reported in this table are derived from a sample survey and are subject to an absolute sampling error of less than 5 percentage points. See Appendix G for a description of the formula used to calculate approximate sampling errors.

SOURCE: National Research Council, Survey of Scientists and Engineers, 1979.

Table 4.8

COMPARISON OF 1979 SALARIES, RESEARCH INVOLVEMENT, AND PUBLICATION RECORDS OF FY1972 PHYSICS PH.D. RECIPIENTS WHO TOOK POSTDOCTORAL APPOINTMENTS WITHIN A YEAR AFTER RECEIPT OF THEIR DOCTORATES WITH THOSE OF OTHER FY1972 GRADUATES WHO HAVE NEVER HELD APPOINTMENTS

Employment in 1979	Median Salaries in 1979		Involved in Some Research[2]		Median Number of Articles[3]	
	Took Postdoc[1]	No Postdoc	Took Postdoc[1]	No Postdoc	Took Postdoc[1]	No Postdoc
Total 1972 Physics Ph.D.'s	$26,200	$28,100	76%	52%	5	2
Universities and Colleges	21,600	22,700	73	38	5	2
Faculty	22,000	22,400	70	34	6	2
Nonfaculty Staff	19,800	--	82	--	5	--
Nonacademic Sectors	29,600	30,900	78	59	4	2
Government[4]	28,800	30,800	85	70	6	3
Business/Industry	30,300	32,200	74	55	4	2
Other Sectors	--	--	--	--	--	--

[1]Excludes graduates who had taken their first postdoctoral appointment more than a year after they had received their doctorates.

[2]Percent of FY1972 Ph.D. recipients who spent at least one-fourth of their time in basic or applied research activities.

[3]Included are all articles of which the respondent had been principal author and which had been published in refereed journals.

[4]Includes positions in FFRDC laboratories as well as other government employment.

NOTE: Median and percentage estimates reported in this table are derived from a sample survey and are subject to sampling errors of varying sizes. See Appendix G for a description of the formula used to calculate approximate sampling errors.

SOURCE: National Research Council, Survey of Scientists and Engineers, 1979.

Table 4.9

COMPARISON OF 1979 SALARIES, RESEARCH INVOLVEMENT, AND PUBLICATION RECORDS OF FY1972 CHEMISTRY PH.D. RECIPIENTS WHO TOOK POSTDOCTORAL APPOINTMENTS WITHIN A YEAR AFTER RECEIPT OF THEIR DOCTORATES WITH THOSE OF OTHER FY1972 GRADUATES WHO HAVE NEVER HELD APPOINTMENTS

Employment in 1979	Median Salaries in 1979		Involved in Some Research[2]		Median Number of Articles[3]	
	Took Postdoc[1]	No Postdoc	Took Postdoc[1]	No Postdoc	Took Postdoc[1]	No Postdoc
Total 1972 Chemistry Ph.D.'s	$27,300	$28,000	77%	39%	3	2
Universities and Colleges	22,300	22,400	79	20	7	1
Faculty	22,800	23,000	80	22	11	1
Nonfaculty Staff	--	--	--	--	--	--
Nonacademic Sectors	29,200	30,200	77	46	2	2
Government[4]	--	--	--	--	1	--
Business/Industry	29,600	30,400	82	53	2	2
Other Sectors	--	--	--	--	--	--

[1]Excludes graduates who had taken their first postdoctoral appointment more than a year after they had received their doctorates.

[2]Percent of FY1972 Ph.D. recipients who spent at least one-fourth of their time in basic or applied research activities.

[3]Included are all articles of which the respondent had been principal author and which had been published in refereed journals.

[4]Includes positions in FFRDC laboratories as well as other government employment.

NOTE: Median and percentage estimates reported in this table are derived from a sample survey and are subject to sampling errors of varying sizes. See Appendix G for a description of the formula used to calculate approximate sampling errors.

SOURCE: National Research Council, Survey of Scientists and Engineers, 1979.

(Tables 4.6 and 4.7). On the other hand, several respondents to the committee's survey questioned whether the experience as a postdoctoral was an asset to a physics or chemistry Ph.D. recipient interested in pursuing a research career outside the academic sector. From a financial perspective, it may well have been a liability. Besides receiving low pay as postdoctorals,[20] those taking postdoctoral appointments also forfeited 1 to 3 years of experience that might be counted toward promotion. Often the years spent as a postdoctoral are not fully counted in determining the starting salary of a young investigator. As reported in Tables 4.8 and 4.9, the median salaries of former postdoctorals were as much as $1,000 to $2,000 below those of other physicists and chemists in the nonacademic sectors.

From a career perspective, the value of a postdoctoral apprenticeship depends on the type of nonacademic position being sought and the nature of the postdoctoral experience. For physics and chemistry graduates interested in research positions in either FFRDC's or large government laboratories, one or two years of post-Ph.D. research experience may be viewed as desirable as it is for faculty appointments in major research universities. For candidates seeking careers in industry, this experience is less important unless it has direct relevance to the research problem which is to be worked on. The vice-president in charge of an industrial laboratory which had hired 19 physicists and chemists within the past 2 years told our committee:

> Our observations of postdoctorals vis-a-vis fresh Ph.D.'s make us extremely wary of generalizing. It does mean, however, that the experience is not very beneficial unless the research training for the Ph.D. was deficient. In such cases it is most important that the appointment be at another institution. The other exception is when the fresh Ph.D. has a burning desire to pursue a line of enquiry that can best be done as a postdoctoral. In most cases it appears that postdoctorals are in holding patterns awaiting an academic appointment that will not materialize . . . The best generalization we can make is that the experience represents additional value to us only when the postdoctoral activity was congruent with the specific topics of concern to these laboratories. In most situations this is unlikely, and the time must be considered to have been spent in a not very efficient manner.[21]

---

[20]Differences between postdoctoral stipends and the starting salaries paid to other graduates are considered in Chapter 5.
[21]From a response to our committee's request for information from managers of industrial laboratories.

Psychology and Social Sciences

In comparison with trends in physics and chemistry the post-doctoral expansion in psychology and the social sciences has been a more recent phenomenon. In the late 1950's fewer than 5 percent of the doctorate recipients in psychology and 2 percent of those in the social sciences intended to take postdoctoral appointments after they had received their degrees.[22] Since then there have been continuous increases in both the annual total of doctoral graduates in these fields and the fraction who planned continued study. As shown in Figure 4.8, the number of psychology graduates expecting to hold postdoctoral appointments climbed steadily from approximately 30 individuals in FY1958 to more than 500 in FY1979. During this same 21-year period the number of social scientists planning postdoctoral study rose from 15 to over 200 graduates annually. Furthermore, in recent years the overall growth in the postdoctoral populations in these fields has shown no signs of slowing, as it has in physics and chemistry. Between 1972 and 1979 the total number of individuals holding postdoctoral appointments in psychology and the social sciences has more than doubled--a rate of increase 12 percent or more in each field.[23] By 1979 there were an estimated 850 postdoctorals in psychology and 550 in the social sciences.

Despite these remarkable postdoctoral growth trends, the fractions of doctoral graduates taking postdoctoral appointments in these two fields are still quite small in comparison with the fractions in physics, chemistry, and the biosciences. Figure 4.9 describes the early career patterns of both psychologists and social scientists during the period between 1973 and 1979. The numerical estimates represent the average number of individuals each year who have followed alternative pathways into the workforce. For purposes of comparison the estimates for psychologists (P) and social scientists (SS) are reported in the same figure. An average of only 375 (14 percent) of the graduates in psychology took postdoctoral appointments in this field each year (path C), along with another 50 graduates from other fields (path D). Among the doctorate recipients in the social sciences, an average of only 150 (5 percent) followed the postdoctoral pathway in this field. During the 1973-79 period, then, there has been an annual net growth in the postdoctoral populations of approximately 50 psychologists and 25 social scientists.[24]

---

[22]See Table 4.12 in the supplement to this chapter.
[23]The postdoctoral growth patterns in these two fields are presented in Figure 3.4 of the preceding chapter.
[24]The net growth in the postdoctoral population can be determined from the difference between the estimated number taking postdoctoral apointments (paths C and D) and the number completing their appointments (path F).

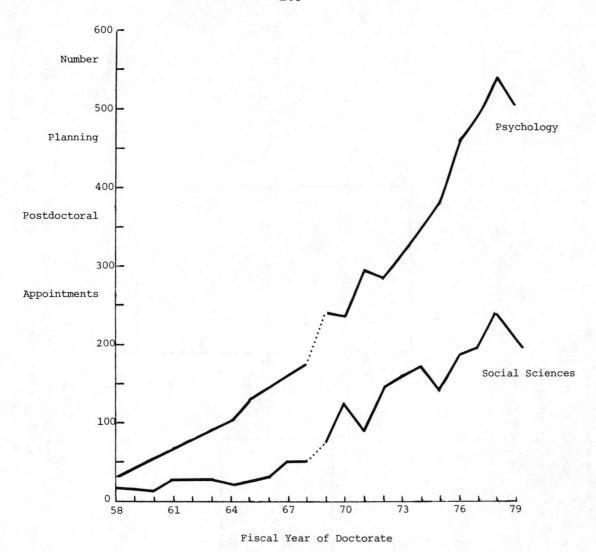

FIGURE 4.8 Number of Ph.D. recipients in psychology and the social sciences planning to take postdoctoral appointments after graduation, 1958-79. Because of a change in definition, FY1969-79 data are not strictly comparable with data from earlier years. From National Research Council, Survey of Earned Doctorates.

PSYCHOLOGY (P) AND SOCIAL SCIENCES (SS)

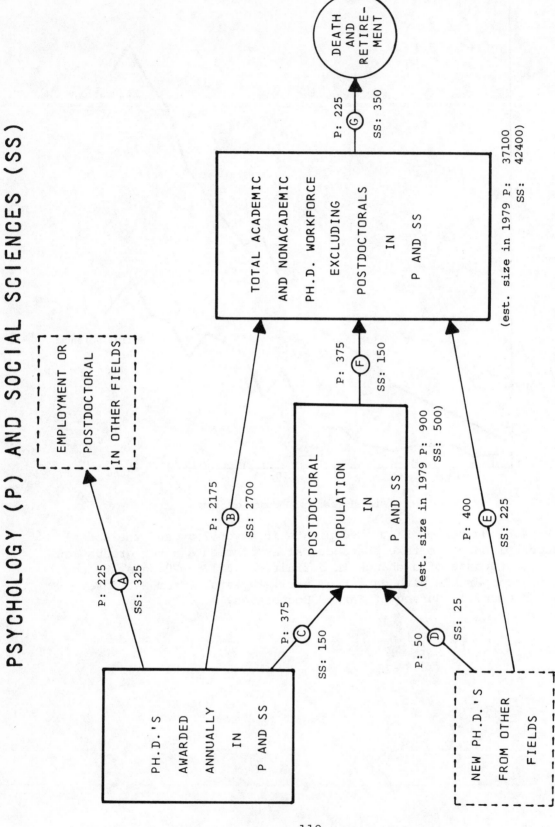

FIGURE 4.9 Components contributing to the average annual growth of the doctoral labor force during the period from March 1973 through February 1979. Estimates represent the average annual number of individuals following particular pathways during this six-year period. No estimates have been made for field-switching, immigration, emigration, or re-entry into the labor force.

110

At the same time the regular doctoral workforce (excluding postdoctorals) in each field has been expanding by 2,725 scientists per year.[25]

Although the postdoctoral appointment may still be regarded as a departure from the usual career pattern for the majority of young psychologists and social scientists, in recent years the appointment has been frequently utilized by graduates in certain disciplines--in particular, those directly related to health and behavioral research.

Postdoctoral research training has been acknowledged as an important means to strengthen or develop skills in such areas as population research, including demographic and fertility studies, in evaluation research and computer simulation methods, and in the role of behavior in disease development. Such training is also viewed as a means to extend the cooperative study of brain functions by neuro- and behavioral scientists with respect to such processes as learning, sensation and perception, sleep, aging, and emotion. Finally in the area of behavior development, postdoctoral research training may provide the skills necessary to elaborate more precise methods for diagnosing hyperkinesis, autism, and various forms of mental retardation and to provide techniques to better understand the interaction of individual, family, and society in adolescent development.[26]

Figure 4.10 presents the percentage of FY1978-79 doctorate recipients in selected disciplines who expected to take postdoctoral appointments after graduation. More than two-thirds of the physiological psychologists were planning postdoctoral study. Many of these graduates, of course, will eventually seek faculty and other research staff positions in medical schools. Of those receiving doctorates in experimental and developmental psychology, approximately one-fourth expected to take postdoctoral appointments. Graduates in the three aforementioned disciplines, along with those in clinical psychology, accounted for two thirds[27] of all psychology Ph.D. recipients planning postdoctoral appointments after graduation. Among the social scientists, the sociologists and anthropologists constituted more than half[28] of the FY1978-79 graduates planning postdoctorals. Postdoctoral appointments were taken most frequently by anthropologists--approximately one-fifth of these graduates expected to take such appointments.

---

[25]The net growth in the regular doctoral workforce can be determined from the difference between the estimated number entering the workforce (paths B, E, and F) and the annual attrition (path G).
[26]National Research Council (1977), p. 102.
[27]Of the 1,044 psychology graduates planning postdoctoral appointments, a total of 704 were in these four disciplines.
[28]Of the 452 Ph.D. recipients in the social sciences who planned postdoctoral appointments, 234 were in these two disciplines.

Percent Planning Postdoctoral Appointments

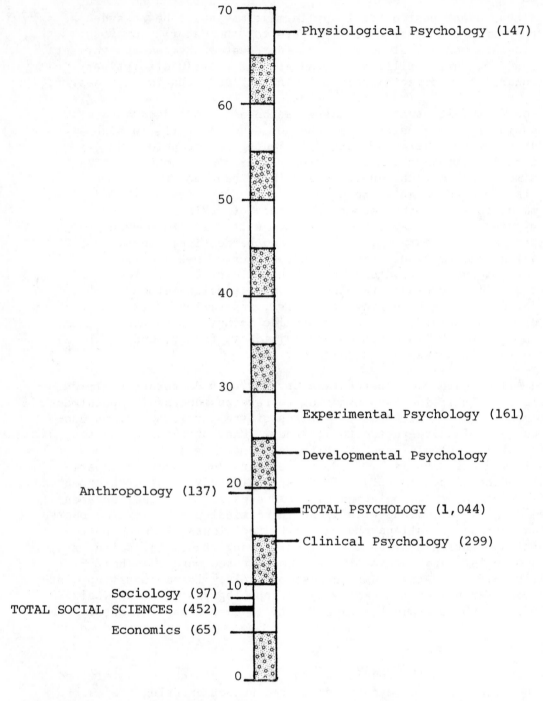

FIGURE 4.10 Percent of FY1978-79 Ph.D. recipients in selected disciplines within psychology and the social sciences who planned to take postdoctoral appointments after graduation. Numbers given in parentheses represent the actual number of graduates planning postdoctoral appointments. From National Research Council, Survey of Earned Doctorates.

The numbers of psychologists and social scientists who have had experience as postdoctorals are not sufficiently large to permit a detailed analysis of the postdoctoral "holding pattern" in these fields, as was presented in the preceding sections of this chapter. Nonetheless, there is evidence to suggest that a lack of employment opportunities in some areas of psychology and the social sciences has influenced the early career decisions of a significant fraction of recent graduates. Of the estimated 240 social science Ph.D. recipients in FY1978 who took postdoctoral appointments, more than one-fifth[29] indicated that they had done so primarily because other employment they wanted was not available. On the other hand, less than 10 percent of the FY1972 graduates in this field who had taken postdoctoral appointments reported that they had prolonged their appointments because of difficulty in finding other employment (Table 4.10). Several of the comments provided by respondents to the committee's survey suggest that FY1978 graduates in the social sciences may have encountered more difficulty in finding employment than their FY1972 colleagues. For example, one young sociologist still on a postdoctoral appointment commented:

> I received my current "postdoctoral" position in 1977 FY1978). At the time the job market in my field was terrible, but I did have several faculty job options. I took this research position (a postdoctoral at a major research university) because it was a unique opportunity to work with special people. But now, two years later, the job market in my field has collapsed. Though I have been very productive in terms of publications, etc., I have no idea what the future will bring at this point. I've talked to many other young, productive sociologists about these issues lately, and the level of stress and anger is alarming.[30]

From the evidence available it appears that the situation for young psychologists may also be of some concern. Approximately 16 percent of the FY1978 graduates taking postdoctoral appointments had done so primarily because they could not find other employment; 14 percent of the FY1972 graduates who had held appointments had prolonged their period of postdoctoral education as a result of not being able to obtain other employment they preferred. Nonetheless, only 14 percent of the FY1972 psychology graduates with experience as postdoctorals and 16 percent of their colleagues in the social sciences had remained on appointments longer than 2 years (Table 4.10).

---

[29]See Table 4.1 presented earlier in this chapter.
[30]The commmment was provided by a FY1978 social science Ph.D. recipient in response to item #15 in the committee's survey.

Table 4.10

PERCENT OF FY1972 DOCTORATE RECIPIENTS IN PSYCHOLOGY AND THE SOCIAL SCIENCES
WHO HAD PROLONGED THEIR POSTDOCTORAL APPOINTMENTS BECAUSE OF DIFFICULTY IN
FINDING OTHER EMPLOYMENT THEY WANTED

	Held Postdoc N	Prolonged Postdoc %
Psychology Ph.D. Recipients		
Total Who Took Postdoctoral Appts.	303	14
Held Appts. Longer Than:		
12 Months	145	28
24 Months	41	(44)
Social Science Ph.D. Recipients		
Total Who Took Postdoctoral Appts.	228	9
Held Appts. Longer Than:		
12 Months	54	(39)
24 Months	36	(53)

NOTE: Percentage estimates reported in this table are derived from a sample
survey and are subject to an absolute sampling error of less than 5
percentage points, unless otherwise indicated. Estimates with sampling
errors of 5 or more percentage points are reported in parentheses.
See Appendix G for a description of the formula used to calculate
approximate sampling errors.

SOURCE: National Research Council, Survey of Scientists and Engineers, 1979.

The postdoctoral growth that has occurred in certain psychology
and social science disciplines is too recent a phenomenon to evaluate
how successful those who have taken postdoctoral appointments in these
disciplines have been in pursuing careers in research. Nevertheless,
some general comments can be made about employment prospects for
graduates in these fields. First, it should be emphasized that at the
present time the total numbers of psychologists and social scientists
who have been forced to prolong their postdoctoral apprenticeships are
still quite small. Of the total 4,700 individuals who had earned
doctorates in these two fields in FY1972, less than 2 percent[31]
had held postdoctoral appointments longer than 2 years. Secondly,
increasing numbers of psychologists and social scientists have found
employment outside the academic sector in recent years. Between 1973
and 1979 the total number of psychologists employed in government,
business/industry, and other nonacademic sectors grew at a rate of
approximately 10 percent per year.[32] The rate of growth for nonacademic employment in the social sciences was even greater. The availability of employment opportunities outside academia is further
substantiated by the high ratio of job offers to inquiries made by
FY1978 Ph.D. recipients who sought nonacademic positions. In both
fields the ratio for graduates seeking nonacademic employment was
approximately four times that for graduates seeking faculty positions
(see Figure 3.6 in the preceding chapter). By comparison the prospects for academic employment have not been as promising. A very
recent study of the employment outlook for behavioral scientists
(including psychologists, anthropologists, and sociologists)
concluded:

> The Committee has been, and continues to be, concerned
> that academic demand for behavioral scientists will de-
> cline in the mid-1980's due to a levelling off of growth
> in college and university enrollments and to the relative-
> ly young age of tenured faculty.[33]

For many young psychologists and social scientists, then, the efficacy
of postdoctoral experience will depend on the extent to which it
prepares them for research careers outside the university and college
setting.

Earth Sciences and Agricultural Sciences

Early development of the postdoctoral appointment in both the
earth and the agricultural sciences followed a course quite similar

---

[31]Based on data reported in Table 4.10.
[32]See Table 3.6 in Chapter 3.
[33]National Research Council (1980), p. 56.

to that in psychology and social sciences, although the postdoctoral
populations in the former set of fields were somewhat smaller. Between 1958 and 1973 there were substantial increases in the numbers of
earth and agricultural scientists earning doctorates each year, as
well as in the fractions of these graduates taking postdoctoral
appointments. By 1973 more than 140 graduates in each field planned
to hold postdoctoral appointments after completing their doctoral
programs (Figure 4.11). Since that time, the number of agricultural
scientists planning postdoctoral study has declined slightly, while
the number in the earth sciences continued to grow. In each of the
past 2 years more than 175 (30 percent) of the earth science graduates
expected to take postdoctoral appointments. These increases led to a
modest expansion in the aggregate postdoctoral population[34] in this
field, as illustrated in Figure 3.4 in the previous chapter. The
total number of individuals holding such appointments in the earth
sciences grew from an estimated 325 in 1973 to 425 in 1979. The
postdoctoral population in the agricultural sciences also grew during
this same period (from approximately 75 to 250 individuals), despite
the recent decline in the number of graduates in this field planning
postdoctoral study.

These growth patterns are depicted in Figure 4.12, which presents
the estimated number of scientists each year who followed alternative
career tracks. As shown in this figure, the majority of graduates in
both fields entered the workforce directly (path B), and did not opt
for appointments as postdoctorals (path C). Of the average 600 earth
science graduates each year (during the 1973-79 period), approximately
25 percent took postdoctoral appointments in this field. Of the 750
graduates in the agricultural sciences, only 13 percent took postdoctoral appointments in the field. During this 6-year period the postdoctoral population in each field expanded by only slightly more than
25 persons.[35]

The majority of earth scientists pursuing postdoctoral education
had earned their doctorates in one of three disciplines: geophysics
(including atmospheric sciences), oceanography, and geochemistry.
More than one-third of the FY1978-79 graduates in each of these
disciplines expected to hold postdoctoral appointments after
completion of their doctoral programs (Figure 4.13). Nearly half of
those in geophysics, in fact, planned postdoctoral study. In all
other earth science disciplines such appointments were scarce. One
important reason for this was the lack of postdoctoral support.

---

[34]Included in this population are all persons holding postdoctoral
appointments in the earth sciences, irrespective of their doctoral
field or year of graduation.
[35]There were increases of approximately 100 postdoctorals in each
field between 1973 and 1979.

117

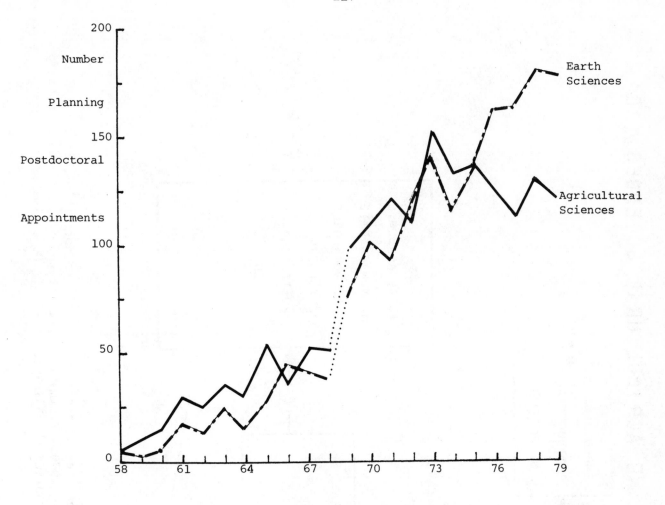

Fiscal Year of Doctorate

FIGURE 4.11 Number of Ph.D. recipients in earth and agricultural sciences planning to take postdoctoral appointments after graduation, 1958-79. Because of a
change in definition, FY1969-79 data are not strictly comparable with data from
earlier years. From National Research Council, Survey of Earned Doctorates.

EARTH SCIENCES (EA) AND AGRICULTURAL SCIENCES (AG)

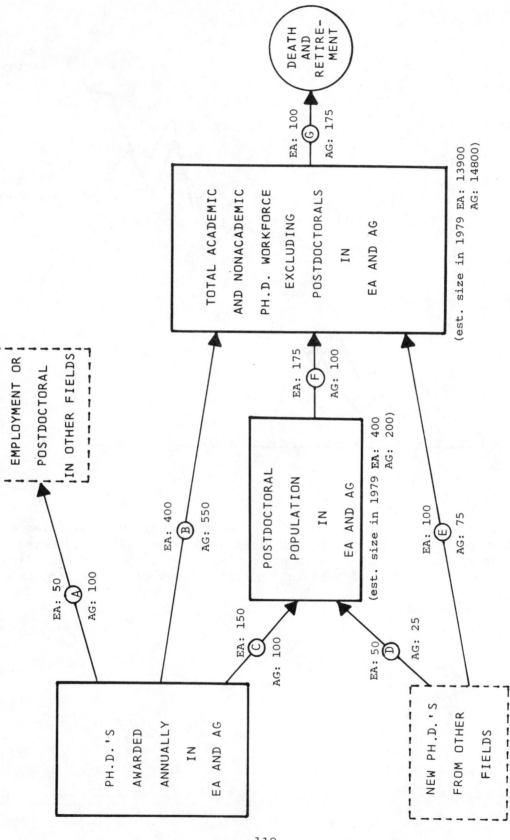

FIGURE 4.12 Components contributing to the average annual growth of the doctoral labor force during the period from March 1973 through February 1979. Estimates represent the average annual number of individuals following particular pathways during this six-year period. No estimates have been made for field-switching, immigration, emigration, or re-entry into the labor force.

118

Percent Planning Postdoctoral Appointments

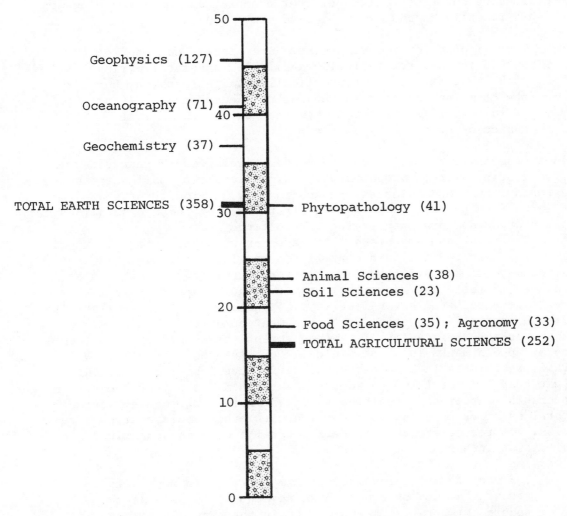

FIGURE 4.13 Percent of FY1978-79 Ph.D. recipients in selected disciplines within earth and agricultural sciences who planned to take postdoctoral appointments after graduation. Numbers given in parentheses represent the actual number of graduates planning postdoctoral appointments. From National Research Council, Survey of Earned Doctorates.

Several of the recent graduates we surveyed indicated that they would have preferred to have taken postdoctoral appointments, but could not find funding for such positions. For example, one marine ecologist who had recently earned his doctorate commented:

> They [postdoctoral appointments] are needed and beneficial, but so few are realistically available in coastal marine work, that they are not practically available to any but the creme de la creme in the field. Those of us that are of less intellectual bent than the genius stand little chance of ever seeing such a position.[36]

In the agricultural sciences the postdoctorals were concentrated in five disciplines: phytopathology, animal sciences, soil sciences, agronomy, and food sciences. Approximately one-fourth of the FY1978-79 Ph.D. recipients in the first three of these disciplines had planned postdoctoral study after graduation.

The total numbers of recent graduates with postdoctoral experience in these two fields are still too small to permit a quantitative assessment of the utility of postdoctoral training for subsequent careers in research. Nevertheless, it is quite apparent from the comments received from several survey respondents that the availability of substantially higher paying employment opportunities[37] has been an important disincentive for young scientists considering postdoctoral appointments in these fields. More than half of all FY1978 Ph.D. recipients in both earth and agricultural sciences indicated that they had not taken postdoctoral appointments either because "more promising career opportunities were available" or because "postdoctoral salaries were too low compared with other employment opportunities." A recent graduate in agricultural economics summarized the situation in his own discipline:

> For many in my field, including myself, employment with a research agency of the federal government is seen as a secure, high paying means to obtain the same advantages of a postdoctoral appointment. It provides research experience and an opportunity to learn new techniques in preparation for an academic or other position without the restrictions of a postdoc.[38]

As for those who have taken postdoctoral appointments, very few have encountered difficulty in finding subsequent employment. The earth

---

[36]The comment was provided by a FY1978 earth science Ph.D. recipient in response to item #15 in the committee's survey.
[37]A discussion of employment opportunities in these and other science fields is presented in Chapter 3.
[38]The comment was provided by a FY1978 agricultural science Ph.D. recipient in response to item #15 in the committee's survey.

scientists have been particularly successful in this regard. Of the
estimated 110 FY1972 graduates in this field who took postdoctoral
appointments after graduation, only 6 percent indicated that they had
prolonged their appointments because they were unable to find other
employment they preferred.[39] Furthermore, less than one-third of
this group held appointments for longer than 2 years.[40]

Engineering and Mathematical Sciences

Postdoctoral trends in engineering and the mathematical sciences
(including computer sciences and applied mathematics) differ markedly
from patterns in the other science fields considered in the preceding
sections of this chapter. Figure 4.14 illustrates the 1958-79 postdoctoral trends in these two fields for those that had earned doctorates at U.S. universities. The number of engineers who expected to
take postdoctoral appointments after completion of their doctoral
programs (at U.S. universities) has dropped significantly during the
past 7 or 8 years. This decline followed a 5-year period of growth in
which the number of engineering postdoctorals had increased at a rate
nearly comparable to that in physics. In contrast, there has been
minimal growth over the past two decades in the number of mathematical
science graduates planning postdoctoral study. By 1972 the total
number of mathematicians expecting to hold postdoctorals reached a
peak of only 100 graduates--the fewest in any science field--and has
remained at that level since then.

The overwhelming majority of recent doctorate recipients in
both fields have entered the regular workforce directly rather than
follow the postdoctoral route. Between 1973 and 1979 an average of
only 13 percent of the graduates in engineering and 8 percent of those
in mathematical sciences took postdoctoral appointments (Figure 4.15).
The aggregate postdoctoral population[41] in each field constituted as
little as 1 percent of the total Ph.D. labor force in 1979. Furthermore, this population has not grown much in either field since 1973,
as shown in Figure 3.4 in the preceding chapter.[42] The absence of
postdoctoral expansion in engineering may be largely explained by the
availability of substantially higher paying career opportunities for

---

[39]See the analysis of question 11C in Appendix D.
[40]See the analysis of question 12B in Appendix D.
[41]For the purpose of this analysis the postdoctoral population
excludes individuals who held appointments in the United States but
had earned their doctorates from foreign universities. In engineering
this group was quite large. However, we have no means of estimating
the growth pattern for this foreign group.
[42]In engineering, in fact, the postdoctoral group shrank during the
1973-79 period.

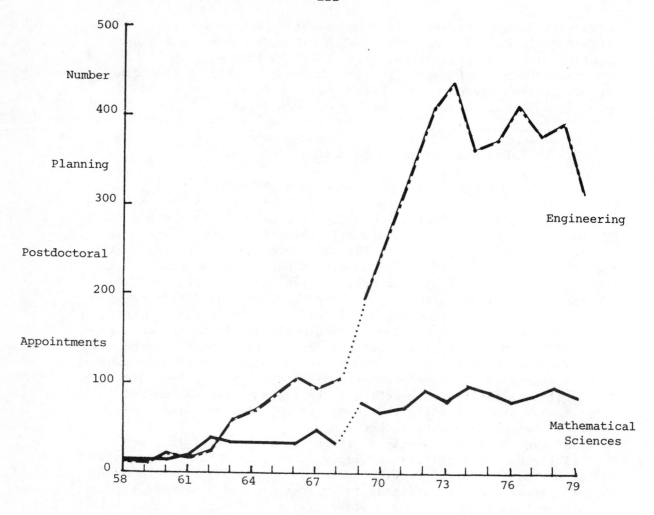

Fiscal Year of Doctorate

FIGURE 4.14 Number of Ph.D. recipients in engineering and mathematical sciences planning to take postdoctoral appointments after graduation, 1958-79. Because of a change in definition, FY1969-79 data are not strictly comparable with data from earlier years. From National Research Council, Survey of Earned Doctorates.

ENGINEERING (E) AND MATHEMATICAL SCIENCES (M)

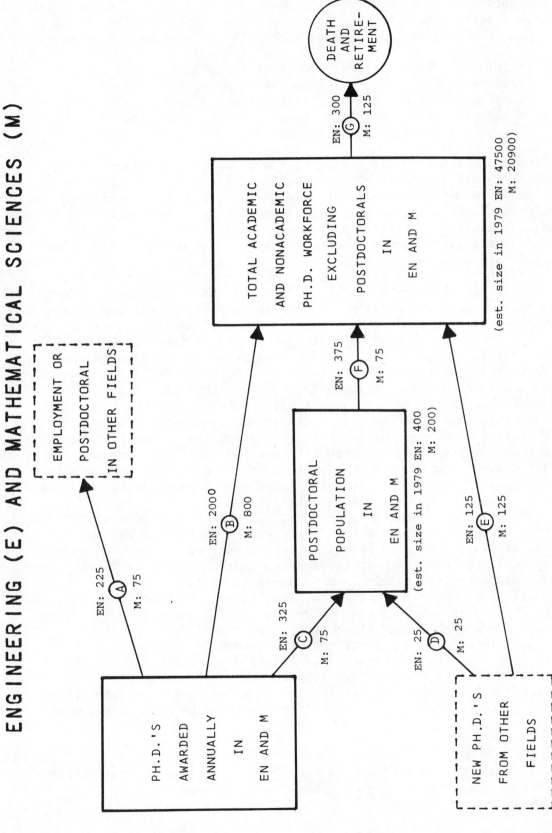

FIGURE 4.15 Components contributing to the average annual growth of the doctoral labor force during the period from March 1973 through February 1979. Estimates represent the average annual number of individuals following particular pathways during this six-year period. No estimates have been made for field-switching, immigration, emigration, or re-entry into the labor force.

123

young engineers. The majority of these opportunities lay outside the academic sector, as mentioned in the previous chapter. The recent experience of a young bioengineer highlights the job market situation:

> I left my post-doc after 4 months because I could not afford to live on $12,500. I am now earning $35,000 in industry, but have academic affiliations. Nonetheless I would have rather stayed in a hospital setting doing research and working with patients.[43]

An important factor contributing to the absence of postdoctoral expansion in mathematical sciences has been a lack of available funding for such appointments. Furthermore, as reported in Table 3.3 in the previous chapter, much of the recent hiring in mathematics has been for positions outside the academic sector--positions for which postdoctoral experience was most likely not considered an important qualification.

Figure 4.16 presents the number and percent of FY1978-79 Ph.D. recipients in selected areas of engineering and mathematical sciences who had expected to hold postdoctoral appointments after completion of their doctoral programs. Only those areas with at least 25 graduates (within the 2-year period) planning postdoctoral study are included. It is not at all surprising to find that postdoctoral appointments were most frequently taken by biomedical engineers--44 percent of them expected to hold such appointments. It is likely that many of these graduates sought medical school faculty positions for which postdoctoral experience was regarded as almost a prerequisite. As shown in the figure, more than one-fourth of the graduates in materials science and metallurgy also expected to hold postdoctoral appointments. In other areas of engineering the postdoctoral percentages were smaller, although the areas of electrical and mechanical engineering produced the largest numbers of graduates planning postdoctoral study.

Within the mathematical sciences there are three sets of disciplines with quite different patterns of employment and postdoctoral activity: core mathematics (including pure mathematics and classical applied mathematics), statistics and operations research, and computer sciences. In core mathematics there are a small number of what might be called "classical postdoctoral fellowships," including those established by the National Science Foundation a few years ago. In addition, there are numerous "quasi-postdoctoral appointments." These are temporary, nontenure-track instructorships or assistant professorships--primarily in major research departments --that provide talented young mathematicians an opportunity to do research while having relatively light teaching loads and few other faculty responsibilities. The Peirce appointments at Harvard, Moore

---

[43]The comment was provided by a FY1978 engineering Ph.D. recipient in response to item #15 in the committee's survey.

Percent Planning Postdoctoral Appointments

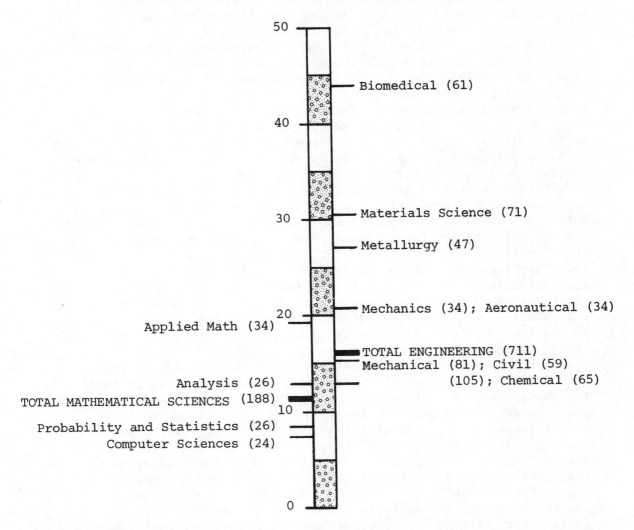

FIGURE 4.16 Percent of FY1978-79 Ph.D. recipients in selected disciplines within mathematical sciences and engineering who planned to take postdoctoral appointments after graduation. Numbers given in parentheses represent the actual number of graduates planning postdoctoral appointments. From National Research Council, Survey of Earned Doctorates.

at MIT, and Gibbs at Yale are examples of such positions (but many do not carry named titles). Individuals are usually not permitted to hold appointments of this type longer than 2 or 3 years, although they may subsequently accept similar positions at other institutions. In contrast to the situation in the 1960's when tenure-track positions in major research departments were generally available to the most promising young investigators, these "quasi-postdoctoral appointments" have been the primary academic research positions open to many talented young mathematicians in the 1970's. In almost all postdoctoral and "quasi-postdoctoral" positions in core mathematics, the responsibility for the choice of direction of research is that of the young investigator who may choose to work in areas of senior faculty interest or in his or her own area of interest.

Within statistics and operations research, the postdoctoral opportunities lie primarily in the areas of application and research methods. Anecdotal information suggests that many of these positions are supported by federal research grant and contract funds. Within the computer sciences, very few Ph.D. recipients have taken postdoctoral appointments. Of the individuals earning doctorates in FY1978-79, fewer than 8 percent planned postdoctoral study. The availability of lucrative career opportunities for computer scientists in business and industry has undoubtedly been a key factor underlying the lack of postdoctoral activity in this field--just as it has been in many engineering disciplines.

Further analysis of the postdoctoral trends in engineering reveals that an increasingly large fraction of the recent postdoctorals were foreign citizens who held temporary visas (and consequently were not expected to remain in the U.S. workforce after completion of their postdoctoral apprenticeships). By FY1978-79 foreign citizens on temporary visas constituted a majority of the engineering Ph.D. recipients from U.S. universities[44] who planned to hold postdoctoral appointments in the United States (Figure 4.17). Eight years earlier the foreign engineers made up only about one-fourth of those planning postdoctoral study in this country. The availability of high-paying career opportunities in industry for U.S. citizens has been an important factor underlying the increase in recent years in the postdoctoral fraction of foreign engineers. As the chairman of an engineering department which has hosted both U.S. and foreign postdocs noted,

> [Many universities] are offering temporary postdoctoral
> appointments at salary levels well below those in industry.
> The job is temporary and often not very educational, and is

---

[44]In FY1978-79 approximately 25 percent of the engineers who received doctorates from U.S. universities were foreign citizens here on temporary visas. More than one-third of this group expected to remain in the United States on postdoctoral appointments.

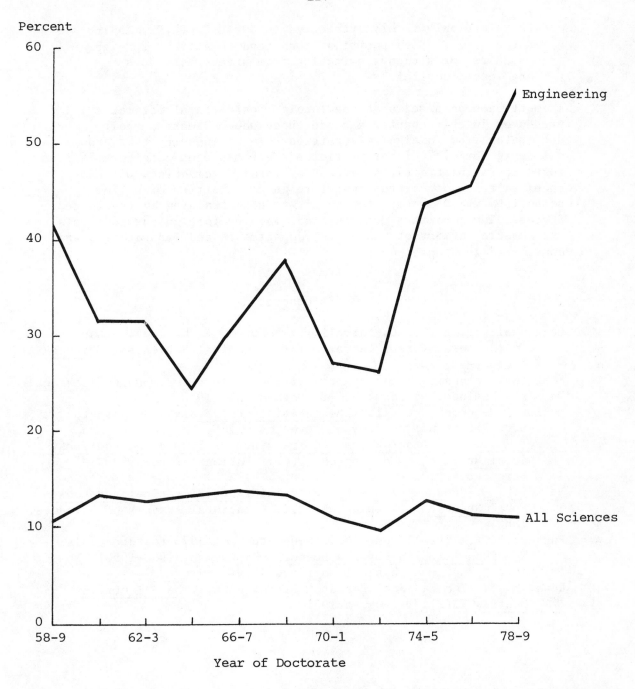

FIGURE 4.17 Percent of graduates planning to take postdoctoral appointments who were foreign citizens on temporary visas. Percentages exclude those planning to hold appointments outside the United States. From National Research Council, Survey of Doctorate Recipients.

128

therefore only rarely attractive to our U.S. Ph.D. candidates. . . . Such positions then tend to attract foreign
students, or students switching from areas where jobs
are less plentiful.[45]

It must be emphasized that the foreign postdoctoral estimates
presented in this chapter exclude those who had earned their
doctorates from foreign universities. In engineering this group
was quite large.[46] In other fields there has been considerably less
postdoctoral participation either by foreign scientists who had
received their doctorates from foreign universities or by foreign
scientists who had completed their graduate training in the United
States. The important contributions made by foreign postdoctorals to
the research effort of their host departments and laboratories are
considered in Chapter 6.

References

Coggeshall, P. E., J. C. Norvell, L. Bogorad, R. M. Bock. Changing
    Postdoctoral Career Patterns for Biomedical Students. Science
    202:487-93, 1978.
Employers Intensify Their Search for Chemical Professionals. Chemical
    and Engineering News: 26-8, October 23, 1978.
National Research Council. The Invisible University. Washington,
    D.C.: National Academy of Sciences, 1969.
_____. Personnel Needs and Training for Biomedical and Behav-
    ioral Research. Washington, D.C.: National Academy of
    Sciences, 1977.
_____. Personnel Needs and Training for Biomedical and Behav-
    ioral Research. Washington, D.C.: National Academy of Sciences,
    1980.
Porter, B. F. Transition-A Follow-Up Study of 1973 Postdoctorals.
    The Transition in Physics Doctoral Employment 1960-1990. New
    York: American Physical Society, 1979.
Rand, M. J. The National Research Fellowships. The Scientific
    Monthly 73(2):79, August 1951.

---

[45]From a response to our committee's request for information from
chairmen of science and engineering departments which hosted postdoctorals.
[46]An estimate of the total numbers of foreign citizens holding
postdoctoral appointments at U.S. universities in 1979 is given in
Chapter 6.

SUPPLEMENTARY TABLES FOR CHAPTER 4

Table 4.11

AN ESTIMATION OF THE PORTION OF THE 1972-77 INCREASE IN BIOSCIENCE POSTDOCTORALS
THAT IS ATTRIBUTABLE TO PROLONGATION IN THE AVERAGE TIME SPENT ON APPOINTMENTS

Year of Doctorate	Planned Postdoc (A)	Hold 1972 Postdoc[1] (B)	Ratio B:A (C)
1971	1,600	1,400	.88
1970	1,500	1,000	.67
1969	1,400	600	.43
1968	1,300	300	.23
1967	800	100	.13
Total	6,600	3,400	

Year of Doctorate	Planned Postdoc (D)	Hold 1977 Postdoc[2]	Projected 1977 Postdocs[3] (C) X (D)
1976	2,300	2,100	2,000
1975	2,000	1,600	1,300
1974	1,800	1,000	800
1973	1,500	600	300
1972	1,700	300	200
Total	9,300	5,600	4,600

[1]Excludes 300 postdoctorals who received their doctorates prior to 1967.

[2]Excludes 700 postdoctorals who received their doctorates prior to 1972.

[3]On the basis of postdoctoral plans we would expect 4,600 graduates in the
1972-76 cohorts to have held appointments in 1977; an actual total of
5,600 did hold appointments. The difference of 1,000 individuals
represents the portion of postdoctoral increase between 1972 and 1977
that can be attributed to a prolongation of the average time spent on
postdoctoral appointments. Therefore, almost half of the net increase
of 2,200 postdoctorals is explained by the prolongation factor.

SOURCE: National Research Council, Survey of Doctorate Recipients,
         1973 and 1977, and Survey of Earned Doctorates, 1967-76.

130

Table 4.12

PERCENT OF SCIENCE AND ENGINEERING PH.D. RECIPIENTS FROM U.S.
UNIVERSITIES PLANNING POSTDOCTORAL STUDY AFTER RECEIVING THEIR
DOCTORATES, 1960-79

Fiscal Year of Doctorate

Field of Doctorate		1960	1961	1962	1963	1964	1965	1966	1967	1968	1969
All Sciences & Engineering	%	9.1	11.9	13.5	14.7	14.3	15.3	15.9	16.3	16.3	21.2
Mathematical Sciences	%	6.7	6.3	11.3	8.3	6.9	5.1	5.3	6.4	3.8	8.6
Physics	%	7.9	10.6	14.9	15.4	16.4	17.5	22.3	22.7	19.9	35.7
Chemistry	%	14.4	20.6	23.9	26.7	26.3	27.7	27.4	28.1	28.6	34.1
Earth Sciences	%	2.8	9.1	6.3	9.3	5.7	8.6	12.9	11.4	9.5	18.0
Engineering	%	2.6	1.8	2.3	4.9	4.5	4.8	4.8	3.9	4.0	6.4
Agricultural Sciences	%	4.5	8.5	6.8	9.3	7.3	12.0	8.0	11.4	9.7	15.0
Biosciences	%	18.4	24.2	27.1	27.6	29.2	30.5	31.2	33.5	36.4	43.1
Psychology	%	7.6	8.2	9.8	10.6	10.5	14.2	13.6	13.0	12.3	14.3
Social Sciences	%	1.5	2.9	2.7	2.7	1.9	2.2	2.4	3.2	2.8	3.9

Fiscal Year of Doctorate

Field of Doctorate		1970	1971	1972	1973	1974	1975	1976	1977	1978	1979
All Sciences & Engineering	%	22.6	23.6	25.7	26.0	25.3	27.0	28.9	29.1	31.0	29.8
Mathematical Sciences	%	6.5	6.8	9.0	8.3	9.5	9.4	9.7	10.9	12.0	10.3
Physics	%	37.2	39.6	43.9	46.8	49.0	51.3	52.5	51.8	52.4	50.4
Chemistry	%	36.2	43.3	53.2	52.4	48.2	49.4	53.7	49.9	49.1	45.4
Earth Sciences	%	22.9	19.0	22.2	24.6	20.8	23.1	28.4	26.9	31.2	30.0
Engineering	%	7.8	10.3	13.7	14.5	12.8	13.8	16.3	16.0	18.2	14.3
Agricultural Sciences	%	15.1	14.6	14.3	19.2	18.0	16.7	17.5	16.2	17.1	15.8
Biosciences	%	46.6	46.6	48.7	48.7	49.9	56.6	57.7	60.3	62.9	62.6
Psychology	%	13.1	14.6	13.0	13.0	13.8	14.5	16.3	16.9	18.0	16.8
Social Sciences	%	5.3	3.4	5.0	5.2	5.3	4.3	5.7	6.1	7.9	7.2

SOURCE: National Research Council, Survey of Earned Doctorates.

5. AN EXAMINATION OF ISSUES FROM
THE PERSPECTIVE OF POSTDOCTORALS

In the interim report on postdoctorals our committee identified a number of policy issues[1] that needed to be addressed in this study. The most important of these dealt with (a) the desirability, from the perspective of the young scientist or engineer, of taking a postdoctoral appointment; and (b) the contributions of postdoctoral appointees to the research effort of their host departments and laboratories. The former topic (a) has been considered at some length in the preceding chapter. The latter topic (b) is the subject of Chapter 6. In pages immediately following we address, on the basis of what we have learned in the study, a variety of other topics that were raised in the interim report:

- a possible decine in postdoctoral interest on the part of the most promising young investigators;
- the adequacy of postdoctoral financing;
- the level of postdoctoral participation by minority scientists and engineers;
- the status of women postdoctorals in science and engineering;
- the efficacy of postdoctoral experience for those interested in careers outside outside the academic sector.

Although the topics listed cover quite a broad range of issues, they share a common link. Each is concerned with whether or not the postdoctoral institution is adequately meeting the needs of young scientists and engineers who are interested in careers in research. A number of questions might be raised in this regard. For example, have declining prospects for career employment discouraged some of the most promising young investigators from pursuing careers in academic research (via the postdoctoral route)? Have the most promising young

---

[1]A total of 12 specific policy issues are identified and considered in some detail in the interim report of our committee. For a listing of these issues, see National Research Council (1978), p. 74.

scientists and engineers who took postdoctoral appointments encountered difficulty in finding employment positions after completing
their appointments? Has the postdoctoral stipend been too low to
attract many of the most talented young investigators? Is the fraction of minority scientists and engineers taking postdoctoral appointments different from that for other doctorate recipients, and if so,
what factors contribute to the difference? Were women scientists and
engineers more likely than men to have been caught in what might be
called a "postdoctoral holding pattern"? Has experience as a
postdoctoral been an asset or a liability for the young scientist or
engineer who was interested in a research career in government or
industry? These and many other related questions are addressed in the
following sections of this chapter. The answers to such questions
largely depend, of course, on the established career patterns and
employment situations in the various fields of science and engineering. For this reason the analyses that follow pay particular attention to field differences. A major section in this chapter is devoted
to the opinions of recent graduates with regard to the advantages and
disadvantages of postdoctoral experience from their individual
perspectives.

Qualitative Trends

As shown in the preceding chapter, there have been large increases during the past 20 years in the numbers of Ph.D. recipients
who elected to take postdoctoral appointments. In certain fields
(i.e., the biosciences, psychology, the social sciences, and the earth
sciences) these increases have continued to the present time. In
other fields the numbers of graduates planning postdoctoral study have
stabilized or even declined somewhat in recent years. These trends
seem to reflect, in part, the changing state of the employment market
in the various science and engineering fields. For example, the large
build-up in the postdoctoral population in the biosciences may be at
least partly attributed[2] to the increasing difficulty recent
graduates in this field have encountered in finding employment positions they desired. The decrease in physics postdoctorals may also be
attributed to a worsening employment outlook that, since the late
1960's, appears to have discouraged many students from pursuing graduate studies in this field. In the analysis presented in the preceding chapter, we examined the quantitative impact that changing
employment market conditions appear to have had on the postdoctoral
populations in the biosciences, physics, and other fields. Was there
a qualitative impact in certain fields as well? One might speculate,
for instance, that in the face of rapidly diminishing opportunities in

---

[2]For a discussion of the factors contributing to the postdoctoral
build-up, see the section on "Biosciences" in Chapter 4.

academic research an increasing fraction of the most promising young
investigators have sought other types of positions for which experience as a postdoctoral was not considered a prerequisite.

To test this hypothesis, we have examined the postdoctoral plans
of two groups of highly promising graduates and compared our findings
with the plans of all graduates. The two groups include: (a) those
who had earned their doctorates from the twenty largest research universities;[3] and (b) those who completed doctoral programs at major
research universities within less than 5 years after receiving their
baccalaureate degrees.[4] The findings are presented in Figure 5.1
for selected fields. Although members of both of these groups were
more likely to have planned postdoctoral study than other graduates,
the differences were not as large as might be expected in any of the
fields examined. Furthermore, the recent trends fail to support the
hypothesis that in recent years an increasing fraction of the most
promising graduates [i.e., those in groups (a) and (b)] were choosing
not to follow the postdoctoral path to careers in research.

Another related issue is whether or not the most talented young
investigators have encountered as much difficulty as other Ph.D.
recipients in finding alternative employment after completion of their
postdoctoral appointments. One might speculate that it has been
primarily the "weaker" graduates who have been caught in what we have
called a "postdoctoral holding pattern." The data reported in Table
5.1, however, do not support such a hypothesis. Of the estimated
1,540 scientists and engineers who had earned doctorates from the 20
largest research universities in FY1972 and had subsequently taken
postdoctoral appointments, 26 percent indicated that they had prolonged their appointments because of difficulty in finding other
employment. This percentage is somewhat lower than that for doctorate
recipients from "other major research universities,"[5] but not significantly different from the percentage for graduates of other institutions with smaller research budgets. Furthermore, in each of the
fields we examined, graduates of the "other major research universities" were more likely than either of the other groups to have prolonged their postdoctoral apprenticeships. Unfortunately we do not
have available valid measures that would enable us to identify a small
number (perhaps 5 percent) of the most promising young investigators
in each field. Nevertheless, on the basis of the anecdotal evidence

---

[3] It is assumed that graduates of those universities which (in
FY1977) had the largest total expenditures for R and D were among the
most talented young investigators.
[4] For purposes of this analysis it is assumed that graduates who had
earned doctorates in less than 5 years after receiving their
baccalaureate degrees were also among the most talented investigators.
Some graduates, of course, may be included in both groups (a) and (b).
[5] For a description of this set of institutions, see footnote 3 in
Table 5.1.

134

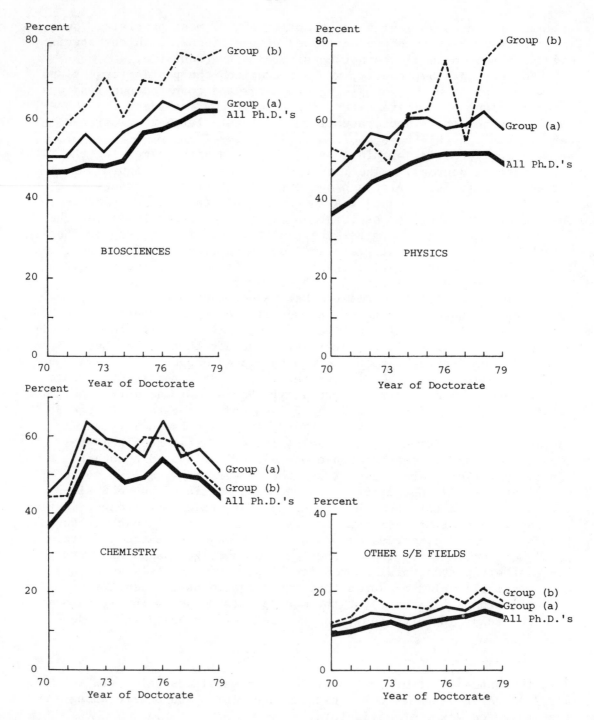

FIGURE 5.1 Percent of Ph.D. recipients in selected fields of science and engineering who planned to take postdoctoral appointments after graduation. Group (a) includes graduates who had earned their doctorates from the twenty largest research universities; group (b) includes graduates who had completed doctoral programs at major research universities within less than five years after receiving their baccalaureate degrees. From National Research Council. Survey of Earned Doctorates.

Table 5.1

PERCENT OF FY1972 PH.D. RECIPIENTS TAKING POSTDOCTORAL APPOINTMENTS
WHO HAD PROLONGED THEIR APPOINTMENTS BECAUSE
OF DIFFICULTY IN FINDING OTHER EMPLOYMENT THEY WANTED

Field and Institution of Ph.D.	Total Who Took Postdoc. Appt.[1] N	Prolonged Appt. Because Couldn't Find Job %
All Sciences and Engineering		
Twenty largest research universities[2]	1,540	26
Other major research universities[3]	1,380	33
Ph.D. recipients from other institutions	1,331	27
Biosciences		
Twenty largest research universities	519	27
Other major research universities	575	30
Ph.D. recipients from other institutions	523	27
Physics		
Twenty largest research universities	233	36
Other major research universities	182	41
Ph.D. recipients from other institutions	148	31
Chemistry		
Twenty largest research universities	261	(34)
Other major research universities	347	(42)
Ph.D. recipients from other institutions	344	(38)
Other Sciences and Engineering		
Twenty largest research universities	527	18
Other major research universities	276	(22)
Ph.D. recipients from other institutions	316	12

[1]Total FY1972 Ph.D. recipients who had taken postdoctoral appointments within a year after receiving their doctorates.

[2]Included are Ph.D. recipients from the twenty universities with the largest total R and D expenditures in 1977.

[3]Included are Ph.D. recipients from the next 39 largest universities, in terms of total R and D expenditures in 1977. These, combined with the twenty largest institutions, accounted for approximately two-thirds of the total R and D expenditures by universities in 1977.

NOTE: Percentage estimates reported in this table are derived from a sample survey and are subject to an absolute sampling error of less than 5 percentage points, unless otherwise indicated. Estimates with sampling errors of 5 or more percentage points are reported in parentheses. See Appendix G for a description of the formula used to calculate approximate sampling errors.

SOURCE: National Research Council, Survey of Scientists and Engineers, 1979.

compiled in this study, the committee is convinced that challenging
and rewarding career opportunities in academic research are still
accessible to the most talented investigators in every field.

Postdoctoral Financing

In the preceding chapter the postdoctoral expansion (or decline)
has been explained primarily in terms of changes in the number of
indivdiuals completing doctoral programs and their interest in taking
postdoctoral appointments. Another important factor, of course, is
the availability of federal and nonfederal support for these appointments. An earlier National Research Council study of postdoctoral
education in the United States found that the federal government
funded more than two-thirds of the postdoctoral appointments in
1969.[6] This funding has been an continues to be furnished through
three separate mechanisms. In the physical sciences and engineering,
for example, federal research grant and contract funds have provided
the majority of postdoctoral support, with principal investigators
selecting their postdoctoral research associates in accordance with
the particular requirements of the research project. The federal
postdoctoral fellowship has been used most frequently to support young
psychologists and biological scientists. It has the advantage of
providing direct support to talented young investigators who have been
chosen through national competition and allows them some flexi-
bility in selecting the mentor with whom they will work. A third
mechanism of federal support for postdoctorals, the training grant,
has been extensively utilized in the biomedical fields. These awards
are made to one or more graduate school or medical school programs,
with the trainees appointed by the training grant director. The award
generally provides full tuition and stipend support as well as partial
assistance for faculty salaries, equipment, supplies, and other training expenses. Much of the stipend support for postdoctorals in mathematical sciences, agricultural sciences, and the social sciences has
come from nonfederal sources--in particular, university and state
funding. Although the research grant, fellowship, and training grant
programs differ in the mechanisms by which they furnish postdoctoral
support, they are not all that different with respect to the benefits
they afford to the individual and to the sponsors of research.

> Many of the postdoctorals are supported on [federal] re-
> search grants and make positive contributions to scien-
> tific and scholarly knowledge. It is, in fact, this
> creation of knowledge that the sponsors of these postdoc-
> torals are purchasing; under research grants postdoctoral
> training is a by-product. Conversely, those postdoctorals

---

[6]National Research Council (1969), pp. 233-5.

supported by fellowships or traineeships, presumably established to create or to promote new talent,
are also performing research. The roles of prime
purpose and by-product are reversed but the conse-
quence is similar. To abstract the costs attributable to the postdoctoral and to identify these costs
as the costs of postdoctoral education is to ignore
the side benefits. The sponsors are simultaneously
purchasing research and training postdoctorals.[7]

During the past decade there have been significant changes in the
numbers of science and engineering postdoctorals receiving federal
support. Table 5.2 reports the numbers and percentages of FY1972 and
FY1978 Ph.D. recipients in each field who within a year after graduation had taken postdoctoral appointments that were primarily supported by federal training and research funds. A comparison of the
FY1972 and FY1978 data reveals several important findings. Although
there was an estimated 3 percent drop in total science and engineering
graduates taking postdoctoral appointments, the number who has received federal support increased approximately 4 percent (from an
estimated, 2,830 postdoctorals to 2,950). Almost 72 percent[8] of the
FY1978 Ph.D. recipients taking these appointments had been federally
funded, compared with 67 percent of the FY1972 cohort. Nearly all of
the growth in federal funding has been in research grants and contracts. In chemistry and physics there have been substantial decreases in support for research training--a result of the severe
cutbacks in the NSF-sponsored postdoctoral fellowship program. In the
biosciences, on the other hand, the number of federally supported
fellows and trainees, most of whom were sponsored by the NIH,[9] increased somewhat between FY1972 and FY1978. In the mathematical
sciences, psychology, and the social sciences there has been a small,
but nonetheless significant, expansion in research support for postdoctorals. In contrast, the number of engineering graduates with
postdoctoral funding from federal research grants and contracts
declined sharply. Although these findings clearly indicate that the
postdoctoral support patterns in each field have been quite different
and are rapidly changing, it is evident that the federal government
still plays a leading role in providing postdoctoral support in
science and engineering fields. By FY1978 more than half of the
graduates in every field who had taken postdoctoral appointments were

---

[7]National Research Council (1969), pp. 224-5.
[8]It should be noted that some postdoctorals who received stipends
from their host departments may not know the actual source of these
funds.
[9]A detailed account of the numbers of postdoctoral trainees and
fellows sponsored by NIH is available from National Institutes of
Health (1979), Table 29.

138

Table 5.2

PRIMARY SOURCE OF FEDERAL SUPPORT FOR FY1972 and FY1978 PH.D. RECIPIENTS IN
SCIENCES AND ENGINEERING WHO TOOK POSTDOCTORAL APPOINTMENTS

		Total Taking Postdocs N	Total N	%	Source of Federal Support Training Grant/ Fellowship N	%	Research Grant/ Contract N	%
All Fields,	1972	4,251	2,834	67	1,187	28	1,647	39
	1978	4,106	2,954	72	1,189	29	1,765	43
Math. Sci.,	1972	144	40	(28)	12	8	28	(19)
	1978	106	55	(52)	12	11	43	(41)
Physics,	1972	563	417	74	90	16	327	58
	1978	389	333	86	45	12	288	74
Chemistry,	1972	952	632	66	219	23	413	43
	1978	576	466	81	78	14	388	67
Earth Sci.,	1972	109	86	79	14	13	72	(66)
	1978	174	131	75	21	12	110	63
Engineering,	1972	256	127	(50)	29	11	98	(38)
	1978	175	91	52	30	17	61	35
Agric. Sci.,	1972	79	55	(70)	3	4	52	(66)
	1978	99	52	52	4	4	48	48
Biosciences,	1972	1,617	1,181	73	631	39	550	34
	1978	1,880	1,407	75	757	40	650	35
Psychology,	1972	303	229	76	176	58	53	18
	1978	471	291	62	176	37	115	24
Social Sci.,	1972	228	67	29	13	6	54	24
	1978	236	128	54	66	28	62	26

NOTE: Percentage estimates reported in this table are derived from a sample survey and are subject to an absolute sampling error of less than 5 percentage points, unless otherwise indicated. Estimates with sampling errors of 5 or more percentage points are reported in parentheses. See Appendix G for a description of the formula used to calculate approximate sampling errors.

SOURCE: National Research Council, Survey of Scientists and Engineers, 1979.

primarily supported by federal funds. Only in psychology has there
been a significant increase in the fraction of postdoctoral assistance
from nonfederal sources.

From the comments received from the recent Ph.D. recipients the
committee surveyed, we found (not surprisingly) that the meager postdoctoral stipend was an important deterrent for those considering
taking an appointment. For example, a young physicist who had by-
passed a postdoctoral opportunity in favor of an industrial position
told our committee:

> [The] postdoc position seemed to be little more than a glori-
> fied grad. student--the pay was barely subsistence and you
> were still expected to work 12 hrs./day in the lab. Who
> needs more of that?! I graduated in order to leave that at-
> mosphere (i.e., slavery). [Don't get me wrong. I still
> spend 10 hrs./day in the lab.--but I get paid better for
> it.][10]

Several recent graduates who had been awarded NIH postdoctoral fellowships or traineeships were particularly distressed about the "payback
provision" they had been asked to sign. Since the National Research
Service Award Act[11] was instituted in 1974, all recipients of NIH
and ADAMHA[12] fellowship and traineeship awards (both postdoctoral
and predoctoral) have been required, after completion of their
training, to pursue careers in health-related research and teaching
for a period of time equivalent to the total months they had received
support. Failure to do so may result in the individual's being
required to pay back the support he or she had received (unless a
special waiver can be obtained from the Secretary HEW). A young
molecular biologist who had signed the payback agreement complained:

> I don't feel that postdoctoral appointees are treated as
> professionals. Salaries are lower than laboratory tech-
> nicians, many secretaries, janitors, etc. Furthermore,
> NIH postdocs are required to sign a demeaning statement
> which is reminiscent of indentured servitude and implies
> that the postdoc has taken the appointment with the intent,
> in some cases, to cheat the government by taking some non-
> research position in the future. It's ridiculous and
> insulting.[13]

---

[10]The comment was provided by a FY1978 physics Ph.D. recipient, in
response to item #15 in the committee's survey.

[11]A copy of the NRSA legislation may be found in National Research
Council (1978b), Appendix A.

[12]Alcohol, Drug Abuse, and Mental Health Administration.

[13]The comment was provided by a FY1978 bioscience Ph.D. recipient,
in response to item #15 in the committee's survey.

140

The meagerness of the postdoctoral stipend is apparent from the figures reported in Table 5.3. This table compares the median postdoctoral stipend paid to FY1978 Ph.D. recipients (as of April 1979) with the median salary of other members of this cohort who were employed full-time in other types of positions. Medians are presented by field and sector so that valid comparisons can be made. For the science and engineering group as a whole, salaries exceeded postdoctoral stipends by as much as $9,300 (i.e., $21,300 vs. $12,000). As expected, the median salary level for faculty and other academic staff was substantially below that for those employed in business and government. Similar differences were found for postdoctoral stipends. Postdoctorals holding appointments in government laboratories received an average annual stipend of nearly $18,000, compared with the $11,500 paid to university postdoctorals. A field-by-field analysis reveals that in every field except the mathematical sciences the wages paid to postdoctorals were well below those paid to other graduates employed in the same sector. In the mathematical sciences the average postdoctoral stipend was only $800 less than the median salary of other university employees. There are two apparent reasons for this. First, some mathematicians not on postdoctorals held instructorships or nontenure-track university positions (described in Chapter 4). Often these positions paid lower salaries than regular faculty appointments. Secondly, the average postdoctoral stipend in the mathataical sciences was significantly higher than in any other field--perhaps in recognition of the greater teaching responsibilities given to postdoctorals in this field. Postdoctorals in the biosciences, chemistry, and psychology received the lowest stipends--with an average of $11,000 or less paid to those holding appointments in universities. Many of these postdoctorals held NIH or ADAMHA fellowships and traineeships that carried a starting stipend of $10,000. When the starting stipend for these awards is increased to $13,400 in FY1981, as planned, we expect the averages in these fields to rise significantly.

Undoubtedly the large differential between postdoctoral stipends and alternative starting salaries has discouraged many young scientists and engineers from pursuing the postdoctoral route to careers in academic research. The fact that postdoctorals cannot expect, after completion of their appointments, to earn salaries comparable to those received by other graduates who had not taken these temporary appointments (as was demonstrated in the previous chapter[14]) serves as an additional deterrent. On the other hand, the career opportunities that are accessible only to those with postdoctoral experience may override the substantial differences between postdoctoral stipends and salaries.

[14]Subsequent salary differences between those who had held postdoctoral appointments and those who had not are considered in the previous chapter in the "Biosciences" and "Physics and Chemistry" sections.

Table 5.3

COMPARISON OF MEDIAN POSTDOCTORAL STIPENDS AND FULL-TIME EMPLOYED SALARIES
OF FY1978 SCIENCE AND ENGINEERING PH.D. RECIPIENTS, 1979

| | | Academic Sector | | | Other Sectors | | |
	Total	Total	Major Research Univ.	Other Univ.	Indus./ Busn.	Govt.	Other
All Fields							
Median F-T Salary	$21,300	$19,400	$20,100	$19,400	$25,500	$23,000	$21,000
Median Postdoc Stipend	12,000	11,500	11,500	11,500	--	18,000	12,600
Mathematical Sciences							
Median F-T Salary	18,900	17,800	18,400	16,600	24,000	--	--
Median Postdoc Stipend	17,000	17,000	--	--	--	--	--
Physics							
Median F-T Salary	24,000	17,600	18,000	16,000	25,000	24,000	--
Median Postdoc Stipend	15,000	14,000	14,000	13,400	--	18,000	--
Chemistry							
Median F-T Salary	24,000	16,500	--	14,300	25,000	--	--
Median Postdoc Stipend	12,000	11,000	10,800	11,000	--	--	--
Earth Sciences							
Median F-T Salary	21,600	18,900	--	18,900	25,200	23,000	--
Median Postdoc Stipend	14,900	14,900	14,900	--	--	--	--
Engineering							
Median F-T Salary	26,000	23,000	23,200	23,000	27,800	28,000	--
Median Postdoc Stipend	15,000	15,200	14,600	--	--	--	--
Agricultural Sciences							
Median F-T Salary	21,000	20,000	20,000	20,000	22,000	24,000	--
Median Postdoc Stipend	12,000	12,000	11,400	--	--	--	--
Biosciences							
Median F-T Salary	20,000	19,400	20,000	19,000	24,600	22,000	18,200
Median Postdoc Stipend	11,500	11,000	11,000	11,500	--	16,000	12,400
Psychology							
Median F-T Salary	20,000	18,800	18,800	18,900	26,500	20,200	20,200
Median Postdoc Stipend	10,500	10,400	10,400	10,400	--	--	--
Social Sciences							
Median F-T Salary	20,900	20,400	20,400	20,100	26,000	23,100	25,000
Median Postdoc Stipend	11,000	11,000	11,000	--	--	--	--

NOTE: Median estimates reported in this table are derived from a sample survey and are
subject to sampling errors. Estimates have been rounded to the nearest hundred
dollars.

SOURCE: National Research Council, Survey of Scientists and Engineers, 1979.

As far as benefits are concerned, from the point of view
of the postdoctoral himself the difference between his
postdoctoral stipend is defrayed in whole or in part by
his opportunity to obtain further research training under
a certain mentor as well as his expectation of being able
to secure a subsequent position in an institution which
he respects and of being able to make significant contributions in his field.[15]

The decision of whether or not to take a postdoctoral appointment
largely rests on the graduate's perception of future career prospects
in his or her field and on the current availability of alternative
employment. For doctoral engineers, the availability of industrial
positions with starting salaries of $25,000 or more makes the postdoc-
toral route seem most unattractive. More and more physical scientists
may also prefer nonacademic careers to the postdoctoral appointment.
Furthermore, as the prospects for faculty positions in major research
universities diminish along with reduced enrollments, we may expect to
find fewer of the most promising young investigators following the
postdoctoral path to careers in research.

Postdoctoral Participation By Minority Scientists and Engineers

There can be no doubt of the need to increase participation in
science and engineering of members of racial/ethnic minority groups--
blacks, Hispanics, Asians, and American Indians. At the present time
these groups constitute less than 9 percent[16] of the total doctoral
labor force in science and engineering. Nor can there be any doubt
that the issues involved in increasing minority participation are
complex ones that will require intervention at all levels of the educational ladder. Here we limit our concerns to only those issues
pertinent to postdoctoral training, recognizing full well that, in
terms of attracting minority students to careers in science and
engineering, the greatest impact is to be made at the graduate and
undergraduate levels or even at the pre-college levels of education.

Over the past 5 years there have been small, but significant,
increases in the numbers of minority graduates earning doctorates in
science and engineering fields. Of the approximately 14,550 U.S.

---

[15]National Research Council (1969), p. 224.
[16]Based on 1979 Survey of Doctorate Recipients data that include
foreign scientists and engineers who were employed in the United
States and held either permanent or temporary visas as well as U.S.
citizens. The inclusion of the foreign groups undoubtedly inflates
the reported percentage of minority group members.

citizens[17] who received science and engineering doctorates from U.S. universities in FY1979, 930 identified themselves as belonging to one of the racial/ethnic groups mentioned above (Table 5.4). This represents an increase of approximately 38 percent over the number of minority graduates in FY1975. Despite this increase, there has been a decline in the number of minority scientists and engineers taking postdoctoral appointments. As shown in Table 5.5, between FY1972 and FY1978 there was an estimated 21 percent gain in the total number of minority scientists and engineers receiving doctorates, but a 19 percent drop in the number who took postdoctoral appointments. In every set of fields except the social sciences the percentage of minority graduates taking postdoctoral appointments also fell between FY1972 and FY1978, while the corresponding percentage for whites increased significantly. By far the largest decine occurred in physical and mathematical sciences. Only about one-fourth of the FY1978 minority graduates in these fields had held postdoctoral appointments, compared with almost half of the graduates 6 years earlier. Furthermore, FY1978 minority Ph.D. recipients in all fields except the social sciences were significantly less likely to take these appointments than were their white colleagues.

The principal factors contributing to the observed decline in postdoctoral participation by minority graduates are not fully understood. The primary reasons given by these graduates for deciding not to take postdoctoral appointments[18] do not differ much from the reasons given by other Ph.D. recipients—more promising career opportunities were available; the appointment was perceived as being of little or not benefit in terms of the graduate's career aspirations; and the postdoctoral stipend was considered too low compared with alternative salaries being offered. One might speculate that the increasing uncertainty about careers in academic research may have had greater influence on the career decisions of minority scientists than othe graduates. Earlier studies[19] have shown that minority graduates tend to be older and have more dependents at the time they receive their doctorates than their white colleagues. For these reasons many minority Ph.D. recipients may be unwilling to spend additional years in postdoctoral training, receiving stipends well below salaries offered by alternative employment. A second and equally important reason for the decline in minority participation at the postdoctoral level is the availability of alternative employment

---

[17]Excluded are approximately 1,000 foreign citizens on permanent visas in the United States and 2,700 on temporary visas. Neither of these groups is considered to belong to one of the five "protected" racial/ethnic minority groups, as defined by the U.S. Office of Civil Rights.
[18]See analysis of question 10, Appendix E.
[19]Gilford and Snyder (1977), Chapter 1, and National Research Council (1977), Chapter 8.

Table 5.4

RACIAL/ETHNIC IDENTIFICATION OF U.S. CITIZENS EARNING DOCTORATES, FY1975 AND FY1979

	All S/E		Physical/Math Sciences		Engineering		Life Sciences		Social Sciences	
	1975	1979	1975	1979	1975	1979	1975	1979	1975	1979
Total Ph.D.'s[1]	14,977	14,553	3,758	3,369	1,769	1,356	3,916	4,191	5,534	5,637
White	13,319	12,217	3,350	2,855	1,551	1,084	3,539	3,597	4,879	4,681
Total Minority	674	933	135	191	93	115	163	223	283	404
Asian	211	343	53	86	62	78	56	113	40	66
Black	268	327	41	49	11	17	55	52	161	209
Hispanic	138	189	27	37	15	16	37	43	59	93
American Indian	57	74	14	19	5	4	15	15	23	36
Unknown	984	1,403	273	323	125	157	214	371	372	552

[1]Data exclude all non-U.S. citizens on either temporary or permanent visas.

SOURCE: National Research Council, Survey of Earned Doctorates, 1975 and 1979.

144

145

Table 5.5

NUMBER AND PERCENT OF THE MINORITY GRADUATES WHO TOOK POSTDOCTORAL APPOINTMENTS
WITHIN A YEAR AFTER RECEIVING THEIR DOCTORATES, FY1972 AND FY1978 PH.D. RECIPIENTS

| | FY1972 Ph.D. Recipients | | | FY1978 Ph.D. Recipients | | |
| | Total | Took Postdoc | | Total | Took Postdoc | |
	N	N	%	N	N	%
All S/E[1]						
Minority graduates	716	234	33	865	190	22
Other graduates	14,559	4,017	28	13,197	3,916	30
Physical/Math Sci						
Minority graduates	209	100	(48)	192	49	26
Other graduates	4,166	1,668	40	3,018	1,196	40
Engineering						
Minority graduates	117	6	(5)	110	5	4
Other graduates	2,240	250	11	1,200	170	14
Life Sciences						
Minority graduates	213	111	52	186	79	42
Other graduates	3,651	1,585	43	3,725	1,900	51
Social Sciences						
Minority graduates	177	17	(10)	377	57	15
Other graduates	4,502	514	11	5,254	650	12

[1]Data exclude all non-U.S. citizens on either temporary or permanent visas.

NOTE: Percentage estimates reported in this table are derived from a sample survey and are subject to an absolute sampling error of less than 5 percentage points, unless otherwise indicated. Estimates with sampling errors of 5 or more percentage points are reported in parentheses. See Appendix G for a description of the formula used to calculate approximate sampling errors.

SOURCE: National Research Council, Survey of Scientists and Engineers, 1979.

opportunities. Affirmative action programs and a general recognition by employers of the importance of hiring minority scientists and engineers have greatly increased the demand for this group. This attitude is reflected in the data reported in Figure 5.2, which compares the median number of faculty job offers (per inquiry) received by minority graduates and other FY1978 Ph.D. recipients. As shown in the figure, minority graduates in all fields except engineering[20] have been more successful than other graduates in receiving offers for faculty positions. The strong interest in hiring minority Ph.D. recipients was confirmed by anecdotal information our committee received from university deans and department chairmen. As the dean of a large graduate school commented, ". . . Ph.D. minority persons are in such demand that they can't be bothered by taking added training as a postdoc." Many of the minority scientists and engineers took faculty positions immediately after completion of their doctoral programs.[21] Consequently there is concern that the lack of postdoctoral experience may limit the ultimate career achievement of minority scientists, especially in fields like the biosciences, physics, and chemistry in which such experience is generally regarded as valuable to careers in academic research. The committee believes that it is as important for the scientific community as it is for young minority scientists that they be given greater encourgement to pursue postdoctoral education.

Utilization of Women Scientists and Engineers

The issues most important to the participation of women in science and engineering activities are quite different from those discussed in the preceding section. During the past decade there have been large increases in the number of women earning Ph.D. degrees from U.S. universities. In fact, by FY1979 women constituted approximately one-third of the doctorate recipients in the social science fields (including psychology) and one-fourth of those in the life sciences.[22] In the physical sciences and engineering the fractions of women graduates were considerably smaller—only 12 percent and 3 percent, respectively—but still growing. There have been corresponding increases in all science and engineering fields in the numbers of women taking postdoctoral appointments after receiving their doctorates. As shown in Table 5.6, it is estimated that the total number of women graduates taking postdoctoral appointments rose nearly 80 percent between 1972 and 1978 while the number of men dropped 15 percent.

---

[20]In engineering, many of the minority Ph.D. recipients are foreign citizens who, because of their citizenship and language difficulties, may have encountered more problems in finding positions in the United States than other minority graduates.
[21]See analysis of question 4 in Appendix E.
[22]See National Research Council (1980).

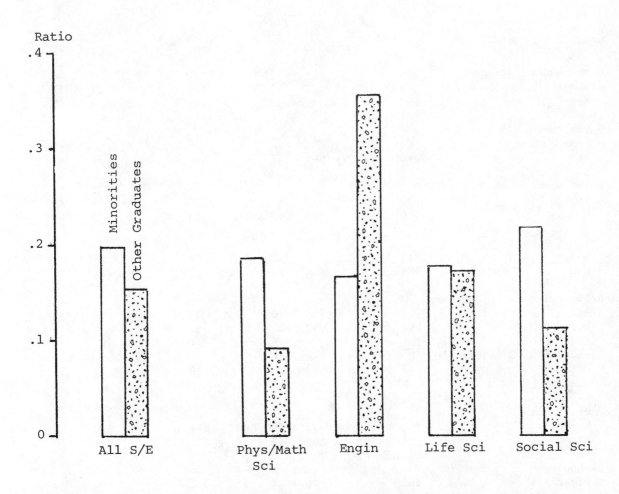

FIGURE 5.2 Ratio of the median number of faculty job offers to the
median number of inquiries made by minority graduates and other FY1978
Ph.D. recipients. From National Research Council, Survey of Scientists
and Engineers, 1979.

Table 5.6

NUMBER AND PERCENT OF WOMEN AND MEN PH.D. RECIPIENTS IN SCIENCES AND ENGINEERING
WHO TOOK POSTDOCTORAL APPOINTMENTS WITHIN A YEAR AFTER RECEIVING THEIR DOCTORATES,
FY1972 AND FY1978 PH.D. RECIPIENTS

| | FY1972 Ph.D. Recipients | | | FY1978 Ph.D. Recipients | | |
| | Total | Took Postdoc | | Total | Took Postdoc | |
	N	N	%	N	N	%
All S/E						
Women	1,796	501	28	3,031	899	30
Men	13,479	3,750	28	11,031	3,207	29
Mathematical Sciences						
Women	78	13	17	101	13	13
Men	943	131	14	609	93	15
Physics						
Women	24	1	4	30	18	(60)
Men	1,240	562	45	758	371	49
Chemistry						
Women	140	63	45	146	59	40
Men	1,470	889	60	1,043	517	50
Earth Sciences						
Women	16	6	(38)	56	15	27
Men	464	103	22	467	159	34
Engineering						
Women	13	0	0	31	6	(19)
Men	2,344	256	11	1,279	169	13
Agricultural Sciences						
Women	12	3	(25)	38	11	(29)
Men	618	76	12	587	88	15
Biosciences						
Women	580	325	56	841	460	55
Men	2,654	1,292	49	2,445	1,420	58
Psychology						
Women	560	78	14	1,071	189	18
Men	1,557	225	14	1,817	282	16
Social Sciences						
Women	373	12	3	717	128	18
Men	2,189	216	10	2,026	108	5

NOTE: Percentage estimates reported in this table are derived from a sample
survey and are subject to an absolute sampling error of less than 5
percentage points, unless otherwise indicated. Estimates with sampling
errors of 5 or more percentage points are reported in parentheses.
See Appendix G for a description of the formula used to calculate
approximate sampling errors.

SOURCE: National Research Council, Survey of Scientists and Engineers, 1979.

149

The largest increases in women postdoctorals were in those fields with the largest growth in women Ph.D. recipients: the biosciences, psychology, and other social sciences. In the social sciences women graduates in FY1978 were more than three times as likely to hold postdoctoral appointments as men. This difference can be partly attributed to the fact that the women earning doctorates in the social sciences were concentrated in anthropology and sociology--two fields that together included the majority[23] of the postdoctoral population in the social sciences.

The data in Table 5.6 indicate that, in general, women were as likely to take postdoctoral appointments as men. What these data do not reveal, however, is that the postdoctoral decision was significantly affected by the marital status and sex of the graduate. The evidence for this finding is presented in Figure 5.3. In every field men who were married at the time they received their doctorates were less likely to opt for postdoctoral appointments than were single men. In the life sciences, for example, 64 percent of the single men earning Ph.D. degrees in FY1978 took postdoctoral appointments compared with 44 percent of the married men in that cohort. On the basis of these findings it would seem that some men, faced with the responsibilities of supporting families, were unable or unwilling to make the financial sacrifice required in taking postdoctoral appointments. Married women also were less likely than single women to hold these appointments, although the percentage differences were not nearly as large as those observed for men.

As for the motivation in taking or not taking an appointment, we found essentially no differences in the primary reasons men and women gave for their decisions.[24] However, we did find that women graduates in all fields of science and engineering were much more likely to be influenced by geographic considerations. Of the 900 women graduates in FY1978 who took postdoctoral appointments, more than half indicated that limitations in their geographic mobility had an important influence on their decision to accept an appointment (Table 5.7). As might be expected, geographic restrictions were considerably more imporant to married women than single. As many as 70 percent of the former considered this an important factor in their decision to take an appointment. On the other hand, only about one-fourth of the men--either married or single--indicated that limitations in geographic mobility significantly influenced their postdoctoral plans.

Survey data reported in Table 5.8 reveal that women in the FY1972 cohort who had taken postdoctoral appointments held them longer than men and were more likely to have prolonged them because of difficulty in finding alternative employment positions. The largest differences in the postdoctoral tenure of women and men were found in the physical sciences and the life sciences--the fields in which the postdoctoral

[23]See Figure 4.9 in Chapter 4.
[24]See analyses of question 10 in Appendixes D and E.

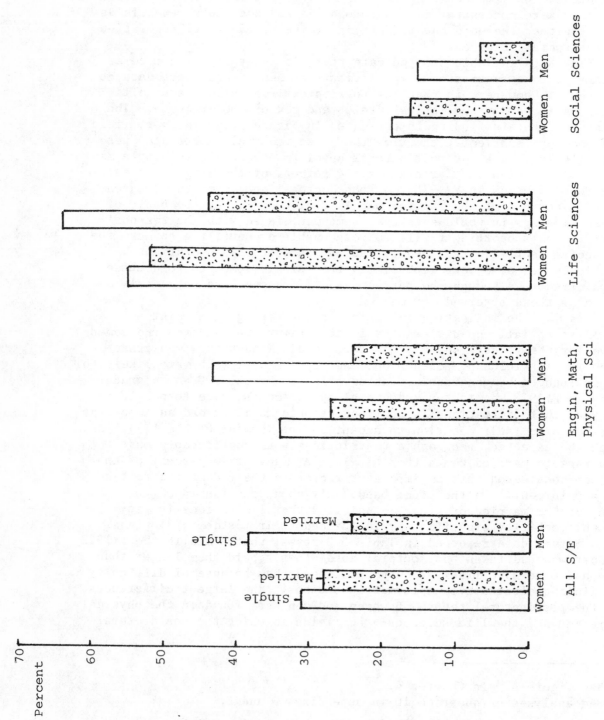

FIGURE 5.3 Percent of FY1978 Ph.D. recipients in sciences and engineering who took postdoctoral appointments, by sex and marital status at the time they received their doctorates. From National Research Council, Survey of Scientists and Engineers, 1979.

150

Table 5.7

EXTENT TO WHICH LIMITATIONS IN GEOGRAPHIC MOBILITY INFLUENCED DECISION
TO TAKE A POSTDOCTORAL APPOINTMENT, FY1978 WOMEN AND MEN PH.D. RECIPIENTS

	Total Taking Postdoc N	Geographic Limitations		
		Important Factor %	Incidental Factor %	Not a Factor %
All S/E				
Women, single	463	33	23	44
married	436	70	8	22
Men, single	1,465	22	25	52
married	1,742	26	25	50
Engin, Math, Physical Sci				
Women, single	59	24	17	59
married	52	(60)	4	(36)
Men, single	704	22	29	49
married	605	26	23	51
Life Sciences				
Women, single	234	26	22	52
married	237	71	8	21
Men, single	554	16	25	58
married	954	25	25	50
Social Sciences				
Women, single	170	(44)	26	29
married	147	(73)	10	18
Men, single	207	(40)	13	(47)
married	183	28	27	44

NOTE: Percentage estimates reported in this table are derived from a sample survey and are subject to an absolute sampling error of less than 5 percentage points, unless otherwise indicated. Estimates with sampling errors of 5 or more percentage points are reported in parentheses. See Appendix G for a description of the formula used to calculate approximate sampling errors.

SOURCE: National Research Council, Survey of Scientists and Engineers, 1979.

152

Table 5.8

PERCENT OF FY1972 WOMEN AND MEN PH.D. RECIPIENTS WHO PROLONGED THEIR
POSTDOCTORAL APPOINTMENTS BECAUSE OF DIFFICULTY IN FINDING OTHER
EMPLOYMENT THEY WANTED AND PERCENT WHO HELD APPOINTMENTS LONGER THAN 36 MONTHS

		Total Taking Postdoc N	Prolonged Postdoc %	Held Appt. >36 Months %
All S/E				
Women,	Total	501	30	23
	Single	230	25	21
	Married	271	34	24
Men,	Total	3,750	28	18
	Single	1,033	35	24
	Married	2,717	26	15
Engin, Math, Physical Sci				
Women,	Total	83	(43)	20
	Single	35	(43)	(20)
	Married	48	(44)	(21)
Men,	Total	1,941	32	16
	Single	594	36	20
	Married	1,347	31	13
Life Sciences				
Women,	Total	328	31	29
	Single	152	25	25
	Married	176	36	32
Men,	Total	1,368	28	24
	Single	354	37	33
	Married	1,014	25	21
Social Sciences				
Women,	Total	90	14	3
	Single	43	(14)	7
	Married	47	(15)	0
Men,	Total	441	11	6
	Single	85	21	7
	Married	356	9	6

NOTE: Percentage estimates reported in this table are derived from a
sample survey and are subject to an absolute sampling error of
less than 5 percentage points, unless otherwise indicated.
Estimates with sampling errors of 5 or more percentage points
are reported in parentheses. See Appendix G for a description
of the formula used to calculate approximate sampling errors.

SOURCE: National Research Council, Survey of Scientists and Engineers, 1979.

"holding pattern" was most apparent. Further analysis of these data reveal major differences between graduates who were married at the time they earned their doctorate and those who were not. Approximately 34 percent of the married women who had been postdoctorals indicated that they had prolonged their appointments because they could not secure other positions they preferred, compared with 25 percent of the single women. From this result it appears that limitations in geographic mobility may have restricted the career options of married women after they had taken postdoctoral appointments (as well as before). On the other hand, married men were significantly less likely to prolong postdoctoral apprenticeships than were single men. In the life sciences, for example, 37 percent of the single men who had taken postdoctoral appointments indicated that they had extended their appointments because of difficulty in obtaining employment they desired, compared with 25 percent of the married men. This difference may be explained by the same factors cited earlier to account for the smaller fraction of married men who took postdoctoral appointments--i.e., married men were less willing to bear the financial sacrifice required in prolonging their postdoctoral apprenticeships.

Results from the survey of 1972 Ph.D. recipients also reveal that the subsequent employment of former postdoctorals varies signficantly according to sex and field. Women with doctorates in engineering and the mathematical and physical sciences were more likely to be employed in academia than were men (Table 5.9). Of the estimated 80 women in these fields with postdoctoral experience, almost two-thirds held university or college positions in 1979. Only 36 percent of the men surveyed in these fields worked in the academic sector. On the other hand, men in engineering and the mathematical and physical sciences who had held postdoctoral appointments were approximately three times as likely to be employed by industry or business as were women. Among the life science graduates the differences were smaller, but nonetheless significant. Only about 4 percent of the women with postdoctoral experience worked in the industrial or business sector, compared with 15 percent of the men. The situation for social scientists was quite different. Women in these fields were more likely than men to have held positions in government or business/industry.

Although as many as two-thirds of the women graduates in FY1972 who had taken postdoctoral appointments were employed in the academic sector in 1979, only a small number had received faculty tenure. Of the estimated 340 women scientists and engineers in academia, only one in seven had been given tenure. In contrast, approximately one-third of men holding academic positions had tenured faculty appointments. More than one-fifth of the women employed in this sector held positions that were considered to lie outside the faculty track. Some of them still held postdoctoral appointments, while others had doctoral research staff positions (supported by research grants or contract funds) or temporary teaching assignments. On the basis of the foregoing results, it is quite apparent that men have been more successful than women in pursuing faculty careers. From the data

Table 5.9

1979 EMPLOYMENT SITUATIONS OF WOMEN AND MEN WHO HAD TAKEN POSTDOCTORAL
APPOINTMENTS AFTER RECEIVING DOCTORATES IN FY1972

	Total Taking Postdoc N	Universities and Colleges				Nonacademic Sector			
		Total Acad %	Tenured Faculty %	Other Faculty %	Nonfaculty Staff %	Total %	Govt %	Business Industry/Other %	Other %
All S/E									
Women	501	68	10	43	15	32	16	7	9
Men	3,750	51	17	27	7	49	15	27	7
Engin, Math, Physical Sci									
Women	83	(62)	12	(34)	16	(38)	19	14	5
Men	1,941	36	14	16	6	64	18	41	5
Life Sciences									
Women	328	70	8	45	17	30	16	4	10
Men	1,368	62	14	40	9	38	13	15	10
Social Sciences									
Women	90	(65)	13	(46)	6	(35)	14	10	11
Men	441	77	41	30	6	23	9	6	8

NOTE: Percentage estimates reported in this table are derived from a sample survey and are subject to
an absolute sampling error of less than 5 percentage points, unless otherwise indicated. Estimates
with sampling errors of 5 or more percentage points are reported in parentheses. See Appendix G
for a description of the formula used to calculate approximate sampling errors.

SOURCE: National Research Council, Survey of Scientists and Engineers, 1979.

154

155

available it is not clear what factors have contributed to these
findings. Some of the difference in the tenure rates for men and
women might be attributed to the fact that some women, after completing doctorates, have left the labor force for a few years to start
families. Other survey data, however, indicate that married women in
the FY1972 cohort have been somewhat more successful in acquiring
tenure than single women.[25]

Survey information on the 1979 median salaries of former postdoctorals shows that men were also earning significantly higher
salaries than women--in both the academic and nonacademic sectors
(Figure 5.4). Similar differences were found in each set of fields
examined. Men with FY1972 doctorates in engineering and the mathematical and physical sciences earned an average of $2,800 more than
women in academia, and $2,900 more in other sectors. In the life sci-
ences men's median salary exceeded women's by $1,600 in the academia
sector and $950 outside this sector. In social sciences the salary
difference for men and women employed in universities and colleges was
approximately $1,600.[26] These findings clearly suggest that women
with postdoctoral experience[27] have not been as successful as men in
pursuing careers in sciences and engineering. Some further analysis,
beyond the scope of this study, is required to determine the major
factors contributing to this situation.

The women responding to the committee's survey expressed varying
opinions regarding the value of postdoctoral experience for careers in
science. The majority of their comments were not dissimilar from those
expressed by their male counterparts. However, certain unique advantages and disadvantages of the postdoctoral appointment were mentioned
by women with families. One woman with a Ph.D. in biochemistry cited
some positive aspects:

> Postdoctoral appointments have made it possible for me to
> remain professionally active at a time when geographical
> and personal constraints and a lack of other employment
> opportunities worked in the opposite direction.[28]

Some women who had taken time from their careers to start families
commented that the postdoctoral appointment afforded them an oppor-

---

[25]Approximately 12 percent of the married women in the FY1972 cohort
who had postdoctoral exprience held tenured faculty appointments in
FY1979, compared with 7 percent of the single women.
[26]There were not enough survey responses to report the median
salaries of women social scientists who were employed outside the
academic sector.
[27]Other survey data not reported here reveal that women without any
postdoctoral experience received lower salaries than men.
[28]The comment was provided by a FY1972 bioscience Ph.D. recipient,
in response to item #17 in the committee's survey.

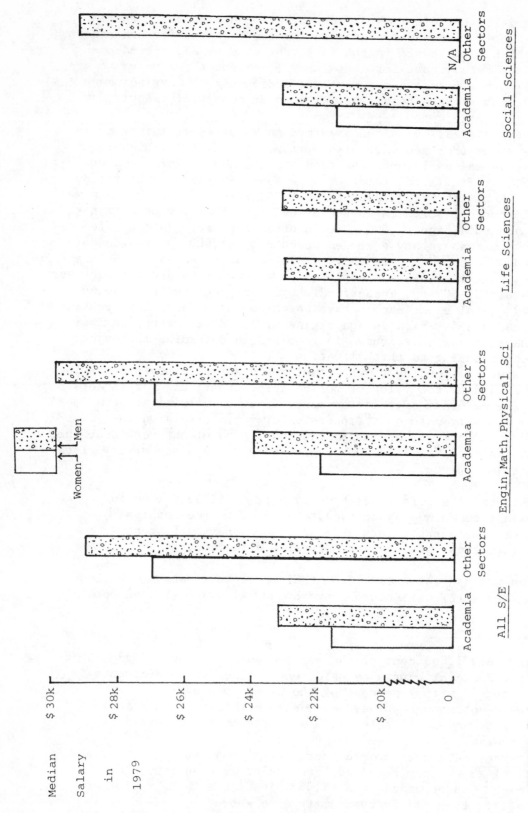

FIGURE 5.4 Median salaries in 1979 of women and men who had received doctorates in FY1972 and had held postdoctoral appointments. Salaries are reported for only those who were employed full-time in the academic or other sectors. From National Research Council, Survey of Scientists and Engineers, 1979.

tunity to get back into research. On the other hand, some found the appointment undesirable. A FY1972 graduate in immunology mentioned a number of negative aspects:

> As a married woman, I find the stringent work requirements and pay-back conditions of current postdoctoral fellowships (of the NIH) prohibitive. Limited job opportunities would almost certainly force a change in location upon the family. The beginning salary of post-postdoctorals cannot compensate for the loss of employment position and income of the husband who usually commands the larger salary. . . .Thus, despite the potential advantages to my own career, these conditions were untenable. Clearly, these postdoctorals are an opportunity offered to the young, male scientists.[29]

Comments from Young Scientists and Engineers

A large number of the FY1972 and FY1978 Ph.D. recipients responding to our survey questions offered their own opinions concerning the advantges and disadvantages of postdoctoral appointments in their own particular fields. Although the comments are anecdotal and do not lend themselves to statistical analyses, many of the comments are thoughtful and provide an insight into certain issues which cannot be adequately addressed from the responses to specific survey questions. The comments were particularly important in helping us understand the early career decisions of scientists and engineers who have recently completed their postdoctoral or graduate study. The comments also provide a general picture of the employment situation in particular fields, from the recent graduates' perspective. In all approximately 1,500 of the FY1978 Ph.D. recipients and 1,000 of the FY1972 Ph.D. recipients offered their views on postdoctoral experience (Table 5.10). The majority of the comments were provided by graduates who either presently held or had formerly held postdoctoral appointments. Nevertheless, we also received statements from more than 1,000 of the FY1978 and FT1972 Ph.D. recipients who had never taken postdoctoral appointments.

In the pages that follow we have made an attempt to summarize the comments provided by graduates in each field, with emphasis on the factors that have influenced their decisions to take or not take postdoctoral appointments. To the extent possible we have used direct quotations of the graduates, both here and in other sections of the report. Many of the respondents have acclaimed the advantages of postdoctoral experience, while others have been highly critical. Although it is obviously not possible to mention all the views

---

[29]The comment was provided by a FY1972 bioscience Ph.D. recipient, in response to item #17 in the committee's survey.

Table 5.10

NUMBER OF SURVEY RESPONDENTS PROVIDING COMMENTS ON THE ADVANTAGES AND DISADVANTAGES OF POSTDOCTORAL APPOINTMENTS, FY1972 AND FY1978 PH.D. RECIPIENTS

FY1972 Ph.D. Recipients

Field of Doctorate	Total Survey Respondents	Total Comments	Comments From Former Postdocs	Comments From Other Ph.D.'s
All Sciences and Engin	3,680	992	549	443
Mathematical Sciences	176	33	12	21
Physics	639	159	99	60
Chemistry	326	98	62	36
Earth Sciences	127	33	12	21
Engineering	227	52	19	33
Agricultural Sciences	118	24	11	13
Biosciences	1,405	426	276	150
Psychology	395	107	41	66
Social Sciences	267	60	17	43

FY1978 Ph.D. Recipients

Field of Doctorate	Total Survey Respondents	Total Comments	Comments From Former Postdocs	Comments From Other Ph.D.'s
All Sciences and Engin	4,231	1,543	926	617
Mathematical Sciences	180	36	14	22
Physics	543	194	117	77
Chemistry	255	74	47	27
Earth Sciences	194	67	33	34
Engineering	267	81	38	43
Agricultural Sciences	157	46	24	22
Biosciences	1,821	771	529	242
Psychology	527	177	85	92
Social Sciences	287	97	39	58

SOURCE: National Research Council, Survey of Scientists and Engineers, 1979.

expressed, we have tried to present a balanced summary of how the graduates in each field viewed the postdoctoral situation in their own field. We have also attempted to estimate the approximate fraction of the graduates who considered the advantages of postdoctoral experience in their field to outweigh the disadvantages. In many instances it was difficult to categorize a respondent's comments as either supportive or critical of the postdoctoral experience since both positive and negative aspects were mentioned. Thus, the estimates reported in the summaries for each set of fields represent rough aprroximations based on subjective evaluations, and are provided only to give the reader a general impression of how the respondents regarded the situation in their field.

Several general comments regarding the advantages and disadvantages of postdoctoral experience were repeated by many FY1978 and FY1972 Ph.D. recipients in different fields. On the positive side, the appointment afforded the young scientist an opportunity to devote his or her full attention to a research problem without the encumbrance of course work, teaching, or administrative duties. As a research fellow in operations research commented,

> [The postdoctoral appointment] enables a recent graduate to develop a great research momentum with no distractions or conflicts. If I had accepted a faculty position initially, I would not have obtained the present quantity and quality of research and would not be as marketable as I currently am.[30]

Other graduates pointed out that their experience as postdoctorals allowed them to broaden their horizons beyond the narrow focus of their dissertation work. At the same time several respondents felt that the appointment had helped them bridge the gap between graduate school, where their research had been largely directed by their mentor, and independent research. For example, a physical chemist who has since moved to industrial research wrote:

> The intellectual maturity I gained while I was a postdoctoral researcher was invaluable. It gave me a much-needed new perspective of research.[31]

In terms of career prospects, many survey respondents emphasized the publication record they had established as postdoctorals as well as the important contacts made. Both of these factors were considered most advantageous for those who would be seeking faculty appointments at major research universities.

---

[30]The comment was provided by a FY1978 Ph.D. recipient in mathematics, in response to item #15 in the committee's survey.
[31]Comment from a FY1972 Ph.D. recipient in chemistry.

On the negative side, the most frequent complaint about the post-doctoral institution pertained to the low stipend and lack of benefits generally offered by such appointments. A recent graduate in elementary particle physics summarized the situation:

> The low pay scale is extremely demoralizing: low salary, no health insurance, no retirement fund; moving to private industry would double my earnings. . . . I expect that within two years I will be forced to leave my field (after six years of graduate training) and become a full-time computer hack in order to allow my wife and me to be able to afford to have children.[32]

A second disadvantage mentioned frequently by survey respondents was the postdoctorals' lack of status within the university structure. In some places postdoctorals have been treated as "second class citizens," with the rights and privileges of neither faculty members nor students. Consequently, some postdoctorals felt they had been "exploited" by their mentor, the department, or the university itself. An environmental toxicologist who had decided against taking a postdoctoral appointment observed:

> They [postdocs] are rapidly becoming a source of labor to which senior people owe no responsibility; postdocs are cheap, non-tenured, have no seniority rights, and don't dare complain, since they exist at the supervisor's discretion. . . .[33]

This respondent went on to note that, from his observation, the situation was much worse in those fields in which employment opportunities outside the academic sector were scarce.

The temporary nature of the appointment and the lack of employment prospects after completing postdoctoral apprenticeships were other concerns of several respondents to the survey. Some respondents questioned the prudence of providing federal and institutional support for postdoctorals who, after completing their appointments, may not be able to find more permanent positions that will allow them to utilize their training. A recent graduate in solid state physics who had left his field of research for an industrial job in engineering summarized the plight of many of his colleagues:

> Postdocs seem to be a "holding pattern" in most Ph.D.'s careers, judging from my associates' experiences, where-in one trades peak earning years (already substantially deferred) for a low salary, ill-defined working condi-

---

[32]Comment from a FY1978 Ph.D. recipient in physics.
[33]Comment from a FY1972 Ph.D. recipient in the biosciences.

tions, and no accrued benefits after a one or two year
stint. These reasons are the basis for my not choosing
that course of employment. I believe there should be
fewer postdocs funded, and at salaries commensurate with
faculty (or industry) positions, to make them more competitive and more of a credit to a recipient.[34]

In general, the FY1978 Ph.D. recipients seemed to be more pessimistic
about the employment prospects for postdoctorals than were the FY1972
graduates. One explanation for this difference, of course, is that
the scientists and engineers in the older group were further along in
their careers and had a better perspective of where they were headed.
Another explanation is that the academic employment prospects for
graduates in most fields have declined considerably in recent years.
We suspect that both factors had an important influence on the
opinions expressed by survey respondents.

Graduates commenting on the postdoctoral situation in the mathematical sciences were fairly evenly split between those who urged that
there be more support available for postdoctoral appointments and
those who saw no need for such appointments. The majority of those in
the latter group were involved in computer science, an area in which
there have been abundant employment opportunities in recent years.
Several of those favoring additional postdoctoral support pointed out
that there are numerous temporary (nontenured-track) teaching positions offered, but that these do not provide an adequate opportunity
for research.

There are relatively few postdoctoral appointments in
mathematics. There are a number of "visiting" positions,
the purpose of which is usually to fill in for a faculty
member on leave of absence. I think that it would be beneficial to basic research in mathematics if there were more
postdoctoral appointments (i.e., temporary appointments
made on the basis of research, instead of mainly teaching).[35]

In terms of the overall employment situation in the mathematical
sciences, the comments we received confirm the results presented in
earlier chapters. Recent graduates in this field have encountered considerable difficulty in obtaining tenure-track faculty appointments,
with the result that increasing numbers have taken positions outside
the academic sector. Often, however, these nonacademic positions do
not involve research.

More than two-thirds of the engineers commenting on postdoctoral
appointments held the opinion that the appointment was not an attractive employment option. The stipend offered was significantly below

---

[34]Comment from a FY1978 Ph.D. recipient in physics.
[35]Comment from a FY1978 Ph.D. recipient in number theory.

162

the starting salary for an assistant professor and far below salaries being paid to doctoral graduates going to industry. In fact as one respondent pointed out, the postdoctoral stipend was even lower than the average starting salary for baccalaureate graduates in industry. As a result, engineering schools have encountered considerable difficulty in attracting postdoctorals (as well a junior faculty) and have had to recruit large numbers of foreign graduates. An associate professor at a large engineering school wrote:

> At present (November, 1979) the pay for postdocs is so low that it is very difficult to find American citizen engineering candidates. Most (if not all) the candidates who applied for my two postdoctoral positions were of foreign origin and citizenship (from India, Taiwan, Africa--i.e., third world countries). At least in engineering I think we have the makings of a future crisis.[36]

Some respondents felt that, for engineers interested in academic careers, 1 or 2 years experience in industry might be more valuable than a postdoctoral appointment. Others pointed out that the postdoctoral opportunity to do research, although worthwhile, would probably not improve one's credentials signficantly. Biomedical engineers were an exception. Many of these graduates observed that experience as a postdoctoral was considered important, if not essential, for candidates interested in faculty appointments in medical school. Furthermore, in this field there has been an apparent shortage of faculty openings for recent graduates. In other fields of engineering many schools have not been able to fill all of their faculty positions.[37]

The comments received from psychologists and other social scientists we surveyed were, in general, quite supportive of postdoctoral training in these fields. The FY1972 Ph.D. recipients in psychology, in particular, thought that the advantages of this training--i.e., an opportunity to do independent research, to work with a distinquished mentor, to establish a publication record--clearly compensated for what one respondent termed "the abysmal salaries" paid to postdoctorals. For graduates in physiological psychology a 2-year postdoctoral term was regarded as essential for those aspiring to academic careers in major research universities. For those in the areas of experimental, developmental, and clinical psychology and the neurosciences, experience as a postdoctoral was also considered quite valuable (although not essential). In certain clinical areas of psychology some licensing agencies and employers have required post-

---

[36]Comment from a FY1972 Ph.D. recipient in sanitary and environmental engineering.
[37]Acute shortages of engineering faculty are described in a March 28, 1980, memorandum from the American Society for Engineering Education and the American Association of Engineering Societies.

doctoral internships that might involve both clinical and research training. In other fields of psychology postdoctoral opportunities were quite limited in number. Several survey respondents were concerned that there were no mid-career training opportunities available. This training would be very helpful, in particular, to women who were trying to re-enter the workforce, to psychologists who wanted to switch fields, and to some senior faculty who needed to rejuvenate their research skills. A recent graduate in social psychology who held a teaching position at a small 4-year college wrote:

> I would like to mention that many universities and four-year colleges do not have an effective sabbatical program for further educational opportunities and enrichment of their long-term faculty (either tenured or non-tenured). The result that I think I am observing is that many faculty go stale after about 10-15 years in the field and become, scientifically speaking, non-productive. How about a postdoctoral program to address the needs of these more long-term faculty? I think that these older faculty members could benefit, if anything, slightly more than recent graduates as they know from long experience where their strengths and weaknesses lie and what type of further study would enhance their research.[38]

Survey respondents from a variety of psychology disciplines complained that a better system for advertising and publicizing the availability of postdoctoral opportunities (other than federal fellowships) was much needed. Respondents also complained about the inadequacy of the stipends offered--in some cases graduates had to rely on personal resources to supplement stipends of as little as $5,000 to $8,000 a year. In general, the FY1978 graduates were more critical of the stipend level and the career prospects for post-doctorals than were FY1972 graduates. An experimental psychologist explained his recent decision to accept an administrative position in the Federal government rather than a postdoctoral appointment:

> Because of the employment picture for research psychologists (i.e., GRIM) one is generally well advised to take a job when available, since the situation is more likely to get worse than better over the one-to-two years of a postdoc.[39]

Comments from graduates in the social science fields (other than psychology) suggest that the postdoctoral situation was quite similar to that in psychology. In most areas of the social sciences there

---

[38]Comments from a FY1972 Ph.D. recipient in social psychology.
[39]Comment from a FY1978 Ph.D. recipient in experimental psychology.

were few postdoctoral training opportunities available, and many
respondents wanted to see more postdoctoral support in their field.
Those who had held postdoctoral appointments generally felt that the
experience had been valuable to their careers. In the fields of sociology and anthropology this experience has become increasingly
important for those seeking faculty positions in many of the larger
university departments. However, rapidly declining employment prospects in these and many other social science fields have led to some
skepticism on the part of recent graduates. A FY1978 Ph.D. recipient
in sociology who had taken a postdoctoral appointment in a leading
program commented on her situation:

> I received my current postdoctoral position in 1977. At
> the time the job market in my field was terrible, but I did
> have several faculty options. I took this research position
> because it was a unique opportunity to work with special
> people. But now, two years later, the job market in my
> field has collapsed. Though I have been very productive
> in terms of publications, etc., I have no idea what the
> future will bring at this point. I've talked to many other
> young, productive sociologists about these issues lately,
> and the level of stress and anger is alarming. More post-
> docs is one partial answer, but their main drawback is that
> they are temporary.[40]

In economics, on the other hand, there were apparently still employment opportunities available outside the academic sector. This
situation has resulted in many young economists deciding to bypass
academic opportunities for considerably more lucrative positions in
business and government.

In most physical science fields postdoctoral appointments were
held by large fractions of graduates, and many of them had strong
opinions about the utility of such appointments. In physics FY1972
graduates were fairly evenly divided between those who thought postdoctoral experience had been valuable to their careers and those who
thought otherwise. For graduates during this period the postdoctoral apprenticeship represented a gamble at a time when employment
demand was falling. Those who were eventually able to secure faculty
positions in major research universities or staff positions in
federally funded research and development centers considered their
experience as postdoctorals essential to their career development.
Those who were unsuccessful in getting the type of position they
wanted often regretted the postdoctoral experience. Many of the
latter group were forced to seek employment in other fields.

---

[40]Comment from a FY1978 Ph.D. recipient in sociology.

I have switched from my original field (theoretical
physics) to chemical engineering. In this new field
postdoctoral positions are rare, and I think this is
better for the field. Postdoctoral positions serve
only as a source of dedicated cheap labor and do not
help the appointee at all. I feel that except in
rare instances such as the Oppenheimer Fellowship,
postdoctoral appointments should be abolished. They
only delay facing the inevitable problem of either
finding a suitable position in your field of training
or switching fields. After two years of postdoctoral
positions in physics-related fields, I switched to
engineering and got a permanent position.[41]

Several other physics Ph.D. recipients, however, mentioned that their
postdoctoral training had been quite helpful in enabling them to
transfer into new areas of research with more promising employment
prospects.

A large majority (more than two-thirds) of the FY1978 Ph.D.
recipients in physics who provided comments were highly critical of
the postdoctoral situation. Numerous respondents complained about the
lack of employment prospects in academic research for those who have
recently taken postdoctoral appointments. From these responses it
appears that the situation has already had a significant effect on the
attitudes of young graduates and may well have a long-term impact on
basic research. A young theoretical physicist who had taken a postdoctoral appointment in a leading research laboratory because he could
not find other employment wrote:

Since there are no secure jobs for intelligent young scientists, some of the best people are forced to go into
other fields. This will have a definite negative effect
on the quality of science this country will produce in the
future![42]

From the comments of both FY1978 and FY1972 graduates it is quite
apparent that the postdoctoral appointment has come to be held in considerably less esteem than it once was. One recent Ph.D. recipient
viewed it as a "consolation prize" for those who were not offered
permanent positions. An astronomer who had resigned from a postdoctoral position in the early 1970's in order to find more permanent
employment summarized the postdoctoral situation in his field:

At the time it was, and remains, my opinion that the
postdoctoral concept, at least in astronomy, has in

---

[41]Comment from a FY1972 Ph.D. recipient in elementary particles.
[42]Comment from a FY1978 Ph.D. recipient in general physics.

many instances been transformed from a temporary
educational/maturing experience into a semi-permanent
holding pattern permitting a denial of employment
realities and a kind of "futures" speculation against
an improbable massive increase in demand for academic
faculty. For all too many people whom I know person-
ally, the speculation failed and the chain of postdoctorals ended with financial exhaustion, and under- or
unemployment.

Hopefully, the decline in production of doctorates from recent unsupportable levels, as well as
the continuing liquidation of past excess is reliev-
ing some of the demand for postdoctorals as the
employment of last resort, yet in any event I urge
your committee to consider replacing the serial
postdoctoral with increased candor on employment options, and to urge Federal and institutional policies which will restore the postdoctoral to its
place as a valuable and unique developmental experience for new scientists.[43]

In general the chemists--both FY1972 and FY1978 graduates-- were
more enthusiastic about the advantages of postdoctoral experience than
were the physicists. This difference may be largely explained by the
fact that chemists have apparently encountered less difficulty in
finding employment in their field. As academic opportunities have
diminished in recent years, chemists have been able to obtain industrial research positions, with minimal disruption (in most cases) to
their careers. Most of those who eventually took positions outside
the academic sector felt that postdoctoral experience was of little
value in helping them to secure a nonacademic position and was rarely
relevant to their work. A FY1972 Ph.D. recipient in organic chemistry
who had had 3 years of postdoctoral training commented:

[Postdoctoral training was] not particularly valuable
in my experience in obtaining industrial employment,
but essential for academic. My particular postdoc . . .
was of great personal value, but limited professional
value. This may be fairly typical of postdocs for
people going into industry.[44]

Among those who were able to secure faculty positions, on the other
hand, the postdoctoral apprenticeship was generally considered quite
valuable--in terms of both enhancing their credentials and providing
them with productive research experience. In fact, for a faculty

[43]Comment from a FY1972 Ph.D. recipient in astronomy.
[44]Comment from a FY1978 Ph.D. recipient in organic chemistry.

position in a chemistry department with a large research budget, post-doctoral experience was regarded as nearly essential. Thus, in this field postdoctoral training was viewed almost exclusively as a means to acquire an academic research position. A recent graduate who had decided not to take a postdoctoral appointment observed:

> The lack of postdoc experience did inhibit me from obtain-
> ing a faculty position. I did apply for five or six post-
> doc positions and received two offers, but subsequently
> refused both after deciding on an industrial career. A
> postdoc would <u>not</u> have helped me in my current position
> as laboratory manager.[45]

As discussed in the preceding chapter, the postdoctoral appointment has been considerably less common in the earth sciences than in the other physical sciences or life sciences. Some earth scientists expressed concern about an apparent shortage of postdoctoral funding in this field, while others indicated that they had turned down post-doctoral opportunities in favor of more lucrative and stable employ-ment. Of those who had held postdoctoral appointments, less than one-third felt that they had wasted their time. Although experience as a postdoctoral was generally considered to be advantageous, it was not regarded, in most instances, as essential for candidates seeking faculty positions. Employment opportunities in recent years have not been as scarce in the earth sciences as in the other physical sciences and mathematical sciences—a situation which has attracted large numbers of field-switchers into the earth sciences. For many the postdoctoral experience has provided a unique opportunity to make career changes. For example, a FY1972 Ph.D. recipient currently in-volved in atmospheric research at a large, nonprofit research insti-tute commented:

> My postdoc [in atmospheric research] was designed to help
> young scientists change fields. I feel that such postdocs
> are an enormous aid in allowing talented people in over-
> populated fields (mine was nuclear physics) to find reward-
> ing applications of their skills.[46]

In the biosciences postdoctoral experience has been regarded as a requirement not only for most faculty positions in major research uni-versities, but also for many other types of positions involving re-search in the academic and nonacademic sectors. For example, a few of the large pharmaceutical laboratories have been primarily recruiting candidates with this experience. In certain medical science speciali-ties 1 year or more of postdoctoral training has been required for

---

[45]Comment from a FY1978 Ph.D. recipient in biochemistry.
[46]Comment from a FY1972 Ph.D. recipient in nuclear physics.

board certification. It is not surprising then that a large majority of the FY1972 Ph.D. recipients in the biosciences considered the postdoctoral apprenticeship an important, and often necessary, step in their career development. As many noted, experience as a postdoctoral was essential for those wishing to continue in research. Even for those pursuing faculty careers in the smaller and less research-oriented universities, this experience was generally regarded as important. Those graduates who had not held postdoctoral appointments found their career options quite restricted. A human anatomist who had accepted a nontenure-track teaching appointment in a medical school immediately after earning her doctorate in FY1972 observed:

> I feel that a postdoctoral experience would have been immensely helpful to me, but as I indicated earlier [on the survey questionnaire] none was available in my field and geographic area. For that reason I took a faculty appointmentwhere there was no senior investigator in my field with whom I could work and from whom I could continue to learn. This has been a serious disadvantage to me in developing my career.[47]

A large majority (as many as three-fourths) of FY1972 biosciences graduates also felt their postdoctoral apprenticeships had been highly rewarding experiences in terms of: (1) the breadth of training received; (2) the opportunity to do independent research without other distractions and responsibilities; (3) the enhancement of one's publication record; (4) the refinement of technical skills; or (5) the chance to move into emerging areas of research. Some respondents, on the other hand, pointed out that the postdoctoral experience had generated false hopes for many graduates who have been subsequently unable to secure the research positions they sought. Approximately one-fifth of the FY1972 bioscience Ph.D. recipients were highly critical of their experiences as postdoctorals for this reason.

A much larger fraction of the FY1978 graduates in this field (an estimated three-fourths) were dissatisfied with their postdoctoral experience. Although the more recent graduates also recognized the necessity of this experience in order to obtain a research position, the majority thought that the disadvantages outweighed the advantages. A biochemist who had received his graduate training at a large state university and now held a posdoctoral appointment at a medical school commented:

> There is increasing dissatisfaction among peers at the low salary, no cost of living increases, lack of positions higher than postdoc, bleak future. Therefore many of us find this intolerable and are dropping out or already have.

---

[47]Comment from a FY1972 Ph.D. recipient in human anatomy.

> Not one graduate or postdoc from my former department has
> yet found a permanent position in the last seven years.[48]

There can be no doubt that the difference in the attitudes of FY1978
and FY1972 graduates commenting on the postdoctoral situation largely
reflects the rapidly diminishing career opportunities in recent years.
Other factors have also contributed, however. Several respondents
expressed outrage over the "payback provision" of the National
Research Service Award Act[49] which penalizes NIH traineeship/fel-
ship recipients who decide to leave research or teaching. Many others
complained about the low stipends paid to postdoctoral--starting at
$10,000 per year[50]--and about the lack of benefits and privileges
accorded other university staff. Another frequent criticism was the
failure of university faculty to counsel graduate students and
postdoctorals regarding the alternative employment opportunities
available.

> As a graduate student in the biomedical sciences, I was
> "groomed" for only one career option--the traditional aca-
> demic sequence of postdoc, junior faculty member, and
> tenured research/teaching faculty. This experience has al-
> so been true for my peers. In reality, however, this op-
> tion is becoming an increasingly unrealistic goal. . . .
> Tenure-track positions simply are not to be had, relative
> to the number of qualified individuals seeking them. . . .
> The point is that academia has no place for many of us,
> and our alternative is in private industry. Unfortunately,
> graduate programs seem to be exceedingly reluctant to pro-
> vide the counseling and advice necessary to prepare their
> graduates to compete for these jobs. While I was encour-
> aged to take extra physiology and anatomy courses to in-
> crease my chances for a teaching appointment in a medical
> school, I wish now that I had been advised to take a
> course in business administration or the like.[51]

As shown in Table 4.2 in the preceding chapter, there has been
considerably less postdoctoral participation by graduates in many of
the newer and smaller biosciences disciplines (e.g., biometrics/bio-
statistics, public health). This has also been true for many of the
agricultural science disciplines. It is not surprising then that the

---

[48]Comment from a FY1978 Ph.D. recipient in biochemistry.
[49]The act, which was passed in late 1974, requires the awardee to
"payback" each year of support with a year spent in research or
teaching. See National Research Council (1980), Appendix A.
[50]In FY1981 the starting stipend for NIH postdoctoral fellowships/
traineeships will be increased by approximately 35 percent.
[51]Comment from a FY1978 Ph.D. recipient in neurosciences.

majority of both the FY1972 and FY1978 doctorate recipients in these fields who provided comments saw little or not advantage in postdoctoral experience. Several respondents pointed out that the stipend offered was substantially less than the alternative salaries paid to young agricultural scienctists in the industrial, government, and academic sectors. Other respondents noted that postdoctoral experience in basic research was not likely to be as valuable to future careers as would be more practical experience in applied research, management, or teaching. For this reason many graduates preferred staff positions in university-affiliated agricultural experiment stations or government laboratories. A recent Ph.D. recipient in agricultural economics explained his reasons for not taking a postdoctoral appointment after earning his doctorate:

> For many in my field, including myself, employment with a research agency of the Federal government is seen as a secure, high paying means to obtain the same advantages of a postdoctoral appointment. It provides research experience and an opportunity to learn new techniques in preparation for an academic or other position without the restriction of a postdoc.[52]

Research Careers Outside the Academic Sector

In the comments provided by survey respondents mention was made of the advantages and disadvantages of postdoctoral training for careers outside the academic sector. As discussed in the preceding section, some respondents considered their postdoctoral experience quite helpful--both in terms of acquiring a nonacademic position and in terms of their professional advancement in jobs outside academia. Other respondents regarded the experience to be of little or not benefit for those seeking careers in industry, government, and other types of nonacademic employment. The issue is of particular importance in the fields of engineering, chemistry, and physics, in all of which a majority of recent graduates had pursued careers outside the academic sector. If recent trends continue[53] and increasing numbers of graduates in the mathematical sciences, the social sciences, and the life sciences find employment outside the university, we can except the issue to become increasingly important in these fields as well.

Table 5.11 summarizes the attitudes of FY1972 Ph.D. recipients with respect to the importance of postdoctoral experience in helping them attain their current (as of April 1979) employment positions. For purposes of comparision, data are presented for those employed in

---

[52]Comment from a FY1978 Ph.D. recipient in agricultural economics.
[53]See Table 3.3 in Chapter 3.

Table 5.11

IMPORTANCE OF THE POSTDOCTORAL APPOINTMENT IN ATTAINING PRESENT
EMPLOYMENT POSITION (IN 1979), FY1972 PH.D. RECIPIENTS

	Total Taking Postdoc N	Essential %	Helpful %	No Difference %	Can't Determine %
All Sciences & Engineering					
Academic Sector	2,153	48	31	15	6
Nonacademic Sectors	1,952	30	42	25	4
Mathematical Sciences					
Academic Sector	94	(44)	(38)	11	7
Nonacademic Sectors	48	0	(58)	(38)	(4)
Physics					
Academic Sector	247	52	29	14	5
Nonacademic Sectors	308	30	34	34	3
Chemistry					
Academic Sector	261	(62)	(25)	6	6
Nonacademic Sectors	680	26	49	21	4
Earth Sciences					
Academic Sector	69	(30)	(58)	0	(12)
Nonacademic Sectors	40	(25)	(60)	15	0
Engineering					
Academic Sector	66	(18)	(29)	(47)	6
Nonacademic Sectors	162	7	(55)	(38)	0
Agricultural Sciences					
Academic Sector	33	9	(36)	(24)	(30)
Nonacademic Sectors	46	(17)	(46)	(28)	(9)
Biosciences					
Academic Sector	994	57	28	10	4
Nonacademic Sectors	537	42	33	20	5
Psychology					
Academic Sector	203	32	42	21	5
Nonacademic Sectors	91	(44)	(40)	14	2
Social Sciences					
Academic Sector	186	8	(34)	(50)	(9)
Nonacademic Sectors	40	(29)	(16)	(55)	0

NOTE: Percentage estimates reported in this table are derived from a sample
survey and are subject to an absolute sampling error of less than 5
percentage points, unless otherwise indicated. Estimates with sampling
errors of 5 or more percentage points are reported in parentheses. See
Appendix G for a description of the forumla used to calculate sampling
errors.

SOURCE: National Research Council, Survey of Scientists and Engineers, 1979.

universities and colleges, as well as for those working outside academia. As expected, the former group were much more likely to consider postdoctoral experience essential to attaining their current position than were the latter group. The differences in the responses of these two groups were particularly significant in the fields of physics and chemistry. A majority of the graduates in these fields who currently held university or college positions regarded their experience as postdoctorals as essential, while only approximately one-fourth of the graduates who held positions in other sectors felt the same way. In psychology and the social sciences, on the other hand, a larger fraction of the nonacademic employees considered postdoctoral experience essential than did academic employees (albeit the number of graduates employed outside universities and colleges was quite small). In engineering, as well as in the social sciences, more than one-third of those employed in either the academic or nonacademic sectors felt that their training appointments had made no difference at all in enabling them to attain their current positions.

Table 5.12 reports similar findings regarding the importance of postdoctoral training for professional advancement. A majority of the scientists and engineers employed in universities and colleges considered this training "extremely valuable." In comparison, only about one-third of the FY1972 cohort employed outside academia felt the same way. Nonetheless, only about 17 percent of the nonacademic group reported that their postdoctoral experience had not been at all useful to their professional advancement. Approximately 30 percent of the physicists working in industry and government viewed this experience as not useful; in all other fields the percentage was considerably smaller.

One must be careful, however, not to generalize from the findings in Tables 5.11 and 5.12. From the comments provided by survey respondents we inferred that the value of postdoctoral experience depends on the training background of the young scientist or engineer and, in particular, on the employment situation in which the individual will be involved. In order to explore this issue in detail, the committee contacted more than 50 managers in government and industrial laboratories.[54]

We found that, in general, administrators at large government laboratories and federally funded research and development centers (FFRDC's) viewed postdoctoral experience as an asset for candidates seeking permanent employment in their laboratory. An administrative officer at an FFRDC that is noted as a center for physics research told our committee:

---

[54]In the preliminary phase of the study letters were sent to more than 50 managers in government and industrial laboratories. Later committee members and staff interviewed several managers and postdoctorals in each of six different laboratories.

Table 5.12

VALUE OF THE POSTDOCTORAL EXPERIENCE TO PROFESSIONAL ADVANCEMENT,
FY1972 PH.D. RECIPIENTS

	Total Taking Postdoc N	Extremely Valuable %	Useful %	Not Useful %	Can't Determine %
All Sciences & Engineering					
Academic Sector	2,153	57	31	7	6
Nonacademic Sector	1,952	35	41	17	8
Mathematical Sciences					
Academic Sector	94	(67)	(19)	11	3
Nonacademic Sector	48	(27)	(58)	(10)	(4)
Physics					
Academic Sector	247	62	23	12	3
Nonacademic Sectors	308	27	37	30	7
Chemistry					
Academic Sector	261	(62)	(30)	4	4
Nonacademic Sectors	680	33	42	15	11
Earth Sciences					
Academic Sector	69	(49)	(41)	3	7
Nonacademic Sectors	40	(32)	(58)	10	0
Engineering					
Academic Sector	66	(33)	(58)	3	6
Nonacademic Sectors	162	7	(62)	13	18
Agricultural Sciences					
Academic Sector	33	(36)	(46)	12	6
Nonacademic Sectors	46	(54)	(24)	(17)	4
Biosciences					
Academic Sector	994	62	27	7	5
Nonacademic Sectors	537	44	35	16	4
Psychology					
Academic Sector	203	47	47	4	2
Nonacademic Sectors	91	(59)	(29)	10	2
Social Sciences					
Academic Sector	186	(34)	(36)	7	(23)
Nonacademic Sectors	40	(45)	(45)	(10)	0

NOTE: Percentage estimates reported in this table are derived from a sample survey and are subject to an absolute sampling error of less than 5 percentage points, unless otherwise indicated. Estimates with sampling errors of 5 or more percentage points are reported in parentheses. See Appendix G for a description of the formula used to calculate sampling errors.

SOURCE: National Research Council, Survey of Scientists and Engineers, 1979.

Most of our Divisions weigh experience in a postdoctoral
position heavily in the consideration of applicants for
regular staff research positions. . . . It was the
opinion of all the Directors that postdoctoral work is
a definite asset (almost a necessity) for a scientist
going into a government laboratory.[55]

The associate director at another FFRDC summarized the advantages of
postdoctoral experience.

Postdoctoral study is an unquestioned asset for young scientists about to go into industrial or government research.
New Ph.D.'s just out of academia are usually highly paro-
chial and narrowly trained; often sub-disciplines in
industry or other non-academic institutions may not even
exist in academia; all experience broadening the young
scientist's abilities and horizons are of great value.[56]

Managers in the industrial laboratories we contacted were
generally less enthusiastic about the efficacy of postdoctoral training than were government administrators. Most of these industrial
managers, in reviewing candidates for a position in their laboratory,
attached more weight to relevant experience in industrial research
than to postdoctoral experience. The vice-president for research at a
major company that had hired 89 Ph.D. scientists and engineers in a
recent 2-year period noted that only 19 of those hired had held postdoctoral appointments. Of the remaining 70 employees, 58 had just
completed graduate school, and 12 others had previously worked in
industry or had held other types of positions. Commenting on this
distribution the vice-president observed:

The value of postdoctoral experience varies widely and
needs to be addressed on an individual basis. The best
generalization we can make is that the experience represents additional value to us only when the postdoctoral
activity was congruent with the specific topics of concern to these laboratories. In most situations this is
unlikely, and the time must be considered to have been
spent in a not very efficient manner. Starting salaries
for postdoctorals are generally the same as for fresh
Ph.D.'s unless the postdoctoral research area was
congruent with our specific interests. In this situation we generally reward the experience.[57]

_____

[55]From a response to the committee's preliminary request for
information from industrial and government administrators.
[56]Comment from an administrator in an FFRDC laboratory.
[57]Comment from a vice-president in an industrial laboratory.

The associate director for university relations at a leading chemical company was similarly skeptical:

> The value of a postdoctoral presents a moot question.
> Assuming a postdoctoral in a research field different
> than the doctoral thesis where the learning curve is
> steep, it should be of some value. Postdoctorals
> longer than 1-2 years tend to be a liability since
> questions arise regarding motivation and real career
> goals. There are no situations where preference
> would be given to a postdoctoral per se.[58]

Senior staff scientists at a prestigious industrial laboratory visited by members of our committee pointed out that the laboratory had a tradition of looking for the younger doctoral scientist or engineer who has "jumped all the academic hurdles in short order." Since they were usually not looking for candidates with extensive experience, the time spent as a postdoctoral could work against a candidate. As one staff scientist put it, laboratory administrators were not inclined to favor the candidate who was willing to "fool around as a postdoc." They preferred the young scientist who had completed work for the doctorate without any wasted time and was likely to continue "beating the system" at the laboratory.

Employers hiring life scientists seemed to have a higher regard for postdoctoral experience than did those hiring physical scientists and engineers. A group vice-president at a chemical company that employs both life scientists and chemists discussed differences in his company's hiring practices:

> Our research managers exercise considerable independent
> judgement of what credentials best qualify new employees
> for positions in the different areas of research. Some of
> our research managers prefer new Ph.D.'s without postdoc-
> toral training, on the ground that they get scientists
> this way who are more flexible and adaptable to program
> needs in the areas of their first assignments. Others of
> our research managers, and particularly those in the life
> sciences, prefer and even require that candidates have
> postdoctoral training, on the ground that such people
> are better trained for highly complex and demanding
> research.[59]

The senior vice-president for science and technology at a leading pharmaceutical company that we visited was emphatic about the desira- bility of postdoctoral experience:

---

[58]Comment from a manager in a chemical company.
[59]Comment from a manager in a chemical company.

In general, I would think a postdoctoral fellowhip would
be a tremendous asset to a young Ph.D. who would choose
a career with our company. In fact, in many ways, it
is the only way that the person would get accepted.[60]

Others at this same company confirmed this statement. A manager who
had recently come from a senior university post indicated that he
would hire a new Ph.D. recipient only under the rarest circumstances.
These comments are supported by the opinions of former postdoctorals
themselves. As reported earlier in Table 5.12, almost half of the
life scientists employed outside the academic sector considered their
postdoctoral experience extremely valuable to their professional advancement. A much smaller fraction of the physical scientists and
engineers in nonacademic employment regarded their postdoctoral
experience as highly.

References

American Society for Engineering Education and American Association of
Engineering Societies. Memorandum on Engineering Education, un-
published, March 1980.
Gilford, D. G., and J. Snyder. Women and Minority Ph.D.'s in the
1970's: A Data Book. Washington, D.C.: National Academy of
Sciences, 1977.
National Institutes of Health, Basic Data Relating to the National
Institutes of Health. Washington, D.C.: U.S. Government
Printing Office, 1979.
National Research Council. The Invisible University. Washington,
D.C.: National Academy of Sciences, 1969.
_____. Personnel Needs and Training for Biomedical and Behavioral
Research. Washington, D.C.: National Academy of Sciences, 1977.
_____. Interim Report and Proposal for Continuation of Study of
Postdoctorals in Science and Engineering in the United States.
Washington, D.C.: National Academy of Sciences, 1978a.
_____. Personnel Needs and Training for Biomedical and Behavioral
Research. Washington, D.C.: National Academy of Sciences,
1978b.
_____. Summary Report 1979--Doctorate Recipients from United
States Universities. Washington, D.C.: National Academy of
Sciences, 1980.

---

[60]Comment from a manager in a pharmaceutical firm.

6. POSTDOCTORAL CONTRIBUTION TO RESEARCH

The preceding two chapters have focused on a variety of issues relevant to the value of postdoctoral experience for young scientists and engineers interested in careers in research. This chapter deals with another issue of major significance to federal policy--the contributions of postdoctoral appointees to the ongoing research effort in sciences and engineering. In the face of declining graduate enrollments and reduced faculty hiring in many fields, university departments are likely to be under increasing pressure to appoint young investigators to temporary (nontenure-track) positions in order to maintain the present level of the research effort within the department. Likewise, senior investigators are likely, in the absence of graduate research assistants, to hire more postdoctorals (if available) to work on their research grants and contracts. In this final chapter we examine in detail changes during the past decade in the numbers of postdoctorals and other academic research personnel. We also consider some quality-related aspects of the postdoctoral contribution, based on the opinions of department chairmen and the postdoctorals themselves. Finally, we examine the unique role played by foreign scientists and engineers who hold postdoctoral appointments in U.S. universities.

The specific role that a postdoctoral plays in the research effort may depend on a variety of different factors such as the field of investigation, the policies of the host institution and department, the overall size of the research team, the modus operandi of the senior investigator, the nature of the research problem, and the experience and talents of the young scientist. Not all of these factors can be quantified and analyzed. In the analyses that follow particular attention is paid to both the fields of investigation and the type of institution in which the research is being performed. Many of the figures and tables cited in these analyses are included in a supplement at the end of this chapter.

Postdoctoral Presence

As a group, postdoctorals made up only about 4 percent of the
total Ph.D. labor force in all sciences and engineering in 1979
(Figure 6.1). Yet there can be little doubt that they have in the
past and will continue in the future to play a vital role in academic
research. Commenting on the importance of postdoctorals to the
overall research effort in his department, a chemistry chairman
summarized the collective opinion of his colleagues:

> Effect is out of proportion to their numbers. They are
> often the only people who are dedicated to research, as
> they often have no other competing duties, and as they
> also are in that magic period of having the necessary
> background to make them mature enough, but are not yet
> stultified or overburdened. It is thus often hard to
> measure the intangible factors, how their presence keeps
> both the senior staff and the graduate students inter-
> ested and/or dedicated to research. We firmly believe
> that the biggest single factor making the very leading
> departments what they are is not their superior staff,
> students, or equipment, but the quality of the postdoc-
> toral transients.[1]

The overall impact that postdoctorals have on the research
enterprise is closely tied, of course, to their total numbers. Thus
significant changes in the size of the postdoctoral population in a
given field can have an appreciable effect on the national research
effort in that field. As shown in Figure 6.1, since 1973 the postdoctoral fraction of the Ph.D. labor force in the biosciences has grown
rapidly. By 1979 postdoctorals constituted more than 10 percent of
the labor force in this field. In physics and chemistry the postdoctoral fraction has declined during these 6 years, but still made up
more than 4 percent of the doctoral labor force in each field in 1979.
In all other sciences and engineering, postdoctorals accounted for
less than 2 percent of the total Ph.D. labor force. These figures,
however, underrepresent the actual contribution postdoctorals made to
research. Among research personnel within the major universities the
postdoctoral group represented a much larger fraction (as will be
discussed in the next section). Furthermore, postdoctorals spend
substantially more time in the laboratories than do either faculty or
graduate students. The chairman of a molecular biology department
wrote:

---

[1]From a response to the committee's preliminary request for information from university deans and department chairmen.

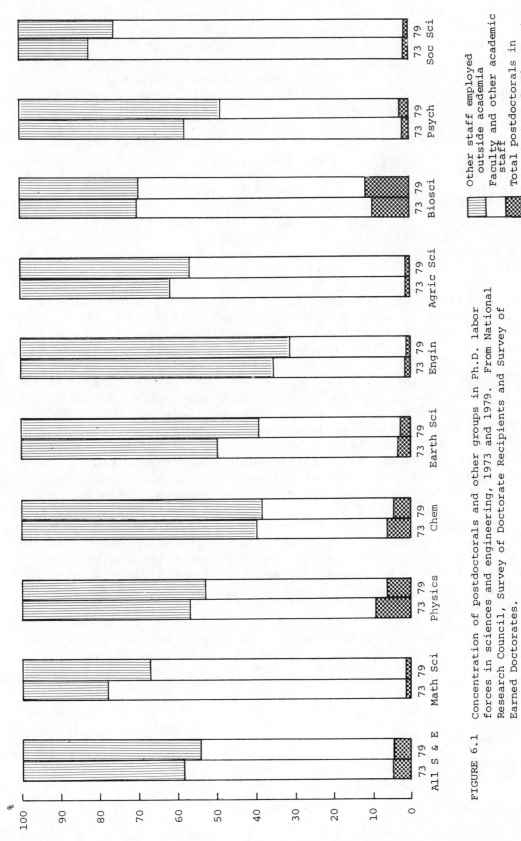

FIGURE 6.1 Concentration of postdoctorals and other groups in Ph.D. labor
forces in sciences and engineering, 1973 and 1979. From National
Research Council, Survey of Doctorate Recipients and Survey of
Earned Doctorates.

FIGURE 6.1 Concentration of postdoctorals and other groups in Ph.D. labor forces in sciences and engineering, 1973 and 1979. From National Research Council, Survey of Doctorate Recipients and Survey of Earned Doctorates.

179

The contribution of postdoctoral personnel to the
research is vast. There would be a major effect in the
productivity of our research activities should there be a
decrease in their numbers or quality. The reason for this
is simple. Professional staff have multiple obligations
including teaching, editorial work, journal refereeing,
public lecturing, administrative chores within the department, grant application writing, and laboratory administrative work. Postdoctoral people have one principal
responsibility: RESEARCH. While they may be less experienced than the people who are their supervisors, they
generally do the bulk of arduous, time-consuming, hands-on
work which gives rise to publications from laboratories.
There are important and notable exceptions to this, but I
think it is a valid generalization that much of the creative research which is done in biomedical research today
is actually accomplished by people at the postdoctoral
level.[2]

The importance of the postdoctoral contribution varies markedly
by research specialty as well as by broad field. Table 6.1 lists the
specialties within each major field that had the largest postdoctoral
participation. Of the FY1979 Ph.D. recipients planning employment in
molecular biology, for example, 93 percent had decided to take postdoctoral appointments. In many other areas of bioscience (especially
all of those not listed in the table), the percentage is considerably
smaller. From this table we conclude that (a) there has been greater
postdoctoral participation, in general, in the more established
disciplines which utilize large research teams, and (b) the variations
among specialty areas are quite large within every major field.

Although in the analyses that follow we focus almost exclusively
on the postdoctoral contribution to academic research, one must
recognize that not an insignificant fraction of postdoctoral activity
takes place outside the university environs. Almost one-fifth of the
1979 postdoctoral population in sciences and engineering were located
in federally funded research and development centers (FFRDC's), other
government and industrial laboratories, hospitals and clinics, and
other nonprofit institutions (Table 6.2). The nonacademic share of
postdoctorals was greatest in the fields of psychology and physics and
smallest in engineering. In the biosciences, psychology, and the
social sciences the majority of postdoctorals outside academia were in
hospitals and clinics. In the mathematical and physical science
fields the majority were in FFRDC's. The modest increase between 1973
and 1979 in the total number of postdoctorals outside the academic

---

[2]From a response to the committee's preliminary request for information from university deans and department chairmen.

Table 6.1

PERCENT OF FY1979 PH.D. RECIPIENTS PLANNING EMPLOYMENT IN SELECTED SPECIALTY
AREAS WHO EXPECTED TO TAKE POSTDOCTORAL APPOINTMENTS

Biosciences
molecular biology 93%
embryology 92%
immunology 83%
genetics 82%
biochemistry 80%
animal physiology 78%
biophysics 75%
pharmacology 74%
plant physiology 68%
cytology 65%

Physics
elementary particles 81%
nuclear structure 77%
astrophysics 74%
atomic and molecular 59%
astronomy 53%
plasma physics 53%

Chemistry
theoretical chemistry 89%
organic 50%
physical 49%
inorganic 47%

Earth Sciences
atmospheric sciences 48%
geochemistry 43%
oceanography 40%
geophysics 39%

Psychology
physiological 72%
comparative 38%
personality 26%
developmental 24%
experimental 23%
clinical 15%

Agricultural Sciences
phytopathology 26%
animal husbandry 21%
agronomy 20%
soil sciences 16%
animal sciences 15%

Engineering
biomedical 37%
metallurgy 26%
engin physics 20%
agricultural 20%
ceramic 18%
mechanics 18%
aeronautical 15%
chemical 13%

Mathematical Sciences
number theory 31%
geometry 30%
applied math 15%
analysis 14%
logic 13%
statistics 10%

Social Sciences
econometrics 19%
anthropology 13%
social statistics 10%
urban planning 8%
international relations 8%
sociology 7%

SOURCE: National Research Council, Survey of Earned Doctorates.

Table 6.2

PERCENT OF SCIENCE AND ENGINEERING POSTDOCTORALS HOLDING APPOINTMENTS
OUTSIDE THE ACADEMIC SECTOR, 1973 AND 1979

	Total Postdoctorals[1] N	Nonacademic Sectors					
		Total %	FFRDC %	Govt %	Industry %	Hosp/ Clinic %	Other %
All S/E							
1973	9,759	23	4	6	2	4	7
1979	12,864	19	3	5	1	6	4
Mathematical Sci							
1973	159	(33)	5	(13)	0	0	(14)
1979	239	(16)	(9)	0	1	0	(7)
Physics							
1973	1,486	31	16	7	4	0	4
1979	1,146	26	16	2	4	2	2
Chemistry							
1973	1,723	17	5	5	2	3	2
1979	1,686	14	7	3	0	2	1
Earth Sciences							
1973	323	(31)	7	(16)	5	0	4
1979	414	(22)	12	6	0	0	3
Engineering							
1973	518	(20)	3	6	5	6	0
1979	403	4	1	0	0	3	0
Agricultural Sci							
1973	166	0	0	0	0	0	0
1979	243	(24)	0	(12)	(12)	0	0
Biosciences							
1973	4,470	21	1	6	1	5	7
1979	7,321	17	1	6	0	7	4
Psychology							
1973	521	(40)	2	4	0	17	17
1979	865	(35)	0	8	0	(23)	4
Social Sciences							
1973	393	(40)	0	9	4	0	(27)
1979	547	(21)	0	1	0	0	(21)

[1] Total includes postdoctorals in the academic and nonacademic sectors.

NOTE: Percentage estimates reported in this table are derived from a sample
survey and are subject to an absolute sampling error of less than 5
percentage points, unless otherwise indicated. Estimates with sampling
errors of 5 or more percentage points are reported in parentheses. See
Appendix G for a description of the formula used to calculate approximate
sampling errors.

SOURCE: National Research Council, Survey of Doctorate Recipients.

sector may be attributed entirely to increases in the life sciences and psychology.

From the written comments we received and the interviews we conducted, it appears that most FFRDC's and other government laboratories that host postdoctorals consider this group as much more than trainees. The postdoctorals have made a significant contribution to their laboratory's research effort and, as at universities, have provided an influx of fresh ideas and new techniques. Furthermore, many of these laboratories have found the postdoctoral appointments to be a valuable mechanism for attracting candidates who have not yet decided between academic and nonacademic careers; for hiring candidates who cannot accept permanent positions (e.g., foreign scientists or engineers on temporary visas); and for maintaining a flow of young talent when openings in permanent positions are unavailable. The National Research Council administers the Postdoctoral Resident Research Associateship program, which supports more than 400 postdoctoral associates in federally funded laboratories. A senior administrator at one of these places listed the advantages to his laboratory:

(a) Their research supplements the ongoing inhouse research. Postdoctorals often make very significant contributions to the over all research effort [in this laboratory].

(b) In some cases, postdoctorals provide specialized skills not existing among permanent staff.

(c) Postdoctorals serve as an incentive for the younger permanent staff to continue their education in pursuit of an advanced degree.

(d) Postdoctorals and colleagues . . . establish fruitful peer relationships which continue for years.

(e) Postdoctorals bring fresh ideas into the [laboratory's] ongoing research activities.

(f) Senior postdoctorals often serve as informal consultants to employees on problems in the disciplinary specialty of the postdoctorals.

(g) Postdoctorals help bring permanent staff up to date on new advances in academia.

(h) Postdoctorals often publicize the research activities at the [laboratory] after their departure.[3]

From the perspective of the postdoctoral, these appointments have the important advantage of offering substantially higher stipends than most university appointments. In 1979 science and engineering postdoctorals at FFRDC's and government laboratories were paid an average of almost $6,500 more a year than university postdoctorals.[4]

---

[3]From a response to the committee's preliminary request for information from industrial and government administators.
[4]See Table 5.3 in Chapter 5.

Postdoctoral Involvement in Academic Research

By far the largest overall impact of postdoctorals on the national research effort has been in the universities. In this section we quantify this impact in terms of the numbers of postdoctorals compared with the numbers of other categories of university research personnel and in terms of the full-time equivalent (FTE) contribution of each group. In the section that follows we examine the importance of the postdoctoral contribution to the productivity and quality of the research effort, as perceived by department chairmen, postdoctorals, and other young scientists and engineers. Although in the next two sections we make some generalizations about the importance of the postdoctoral contribution in different fields, it should be emphasized that the effectiveness of an individual depends very much on the type of postdoctoral appointment he or she holds. For this reason there is undoubtedly considerable variation in the postdoctoral roles in research within each field.

In the tables and figures that follow, many data are presented for two different sets of institutions: all Ph.D.-granting schools and the major research universities, neither of which is a subset of the other. The latter set is comprised of 59 universities whose total R and D expenditures in 1977 represented two-thirds of the total research expenditures of all colleges and universities. Included are medical and other professional schools that are attached to these 59 universities. Professional schools, however, are not included in the set of Ph.D.-granting schools. The exclusion of professional schools in this set significantly reduces the postdoctoral estimates for the biosciences and for certain specialty areas within other fields (e.g., biomedical engineering, physiological psychology, and pharmaceutical chemistry).

The size of the postdoctoral cadre in relation to the total numbers of university research personnel varies widely among the different fields of science and engineering. This variation is seen from Figure 6.2, which describes the percent distribution of FTE research personnel employed in academia in 1979. The personnel categories include faculty, postdoctorals, other Ph.D. staff, and graduate research assistants. The FTE estimates are based on the average fraction of time each group devoted to research activities. For purposes of estimation it is assumed that graduate research assistants have devoted an average of 40 percent of their time to these activities.

The postdoctoral fraction of FTE research personnel in Ph.D.-granting schools is estimated to have ranged from as little as 2 percent in engineering to as much as 22 percent in chemistry, with an overall average of approximately 10 percent for all sciences and engineering in 1979. In the major research universities the postdoctoral involvement was significantly greater. In these 59 institutions science and engineering postdoctorals made up 16 percent of all FTE research personnel, with a spread from 3 percent in the agricultural sciences to 27 percent in the biosciences.

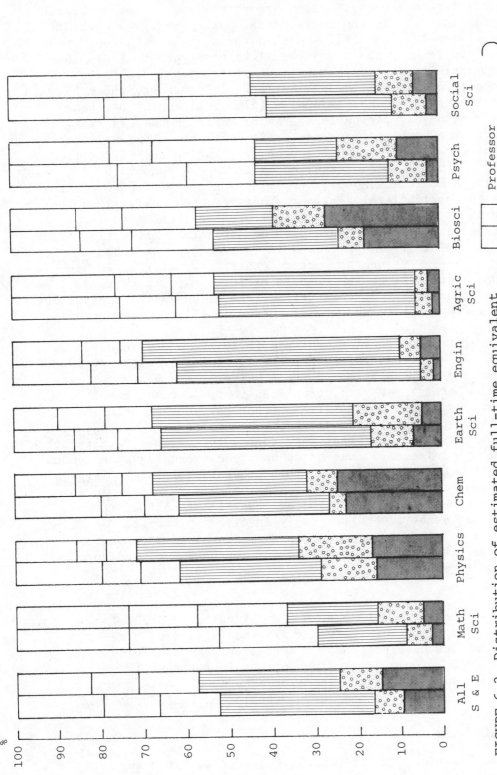

FIGURE 6.2 Distribution of estimated full-time equivalent research personnel employed in academia in sciences and engineering, 1979. FTE estimates are based on the average fraction of time each group devoted to research activities. Estimates for major research universities include those employed in medical schools and other branches of the university which may not grant Ph.D. degrees. From National Research Council, Survey of Doctorate Recipients and Survey of Earned Doctorates and National Science Foundation, Survey of Graduate Science Student Support and Postdoctorals.

Changes over the 1973-79 period in the composition of the pool of personnel in sciences and engineering are shown in Table 6.3. Within the Ph.D.-granting schools the postdoctoral population grew by 1,300 scientists between 1975 and 1977 and then shrank by 800 in the 2 years following. As a result, there has been little net growth (less than 1 percent per year) in the total numbers of postdoctorals in Ph.D.-granting schools during the 1973-79 period. In contrast, there has been significant postdoctoral expansion (almost 8 percent per year) during this same 6-year period in the major research universities. By 1979, in fact, the number of postdoctorals in these 59 universities exceeded that in all Ph.D.-granting schools. During the period from 1973 to 1979 there have been large increases in the numbers of postdoctorals in medical schools; these increases, which have more than offset the postdoctoral decline in physics and chemistry in the major research universities, are not reflected in the counts for Ph.D.-granting schools. It should also be noted that all estimates of academic personnel that are presented in this chapter exclude scientists and engineers who had earned their doctorates at foreign institutions. Estimates of the numbers of foreign postdoctorals holding appointments at U.S. universities are given in the analysis of question 16 in Appendix C, and are discussed in a later section of this chapter.

The annual rate of postdoctoral growth in the major research universities was more than twice the rate for faculty. Between 1973 and 1979 the faculty population in these universities grew at a rate of less than 4 percent per year, with less than 3 percent growth in the numbers of assistant professors/instructors. On the other hand, there have been substantial increases in the numbers of Ph.D. staff holding university positions that were considered neither faculty nor postdoctoral appointments. This group has been expanding at an annual rate of nearly 12 percent. In 1979 this group was almost as large as the postdoctoral population in major research universities. In an earlier report[5] our committee estimated that almost half of these nonfaculty staff members were primarily involved in research activities. The remaining members held temporary teaching assignments or administrative positions, which may or may not have included some participation in research.

CHEMISTRY. As shown in Table 6.4, the total numbers of chemistry postdoctorals at both Ph.D.-granting schools and major research universities have not changed appreciably in recent years. There have also been only minor fluctuations in the numbers of assistant professors. In Ph.D.-granting schools the only groups to expand significantly during the 1973-79 period have been the full

---

[5]See National Research Council (1978), Chapter II, for a detailed description of the positions held by nonfaculty staff members.

Table 6.3

ESTIMATED NUMBER OF FACULTY, POSTDOCTORALS, AND GRADUATE STUDENTS IN PH.D.-GRANTING AND MAJOR RESEARCH UNIVERSITIES, 1973-79

All Scientists and Engineers at Ph.D.-Granting Schools					6-year annual growth(%)
	1973	1975	1977	1979	
Total Ph.D. Staff[1]	81,167	86,221	93,160	95,014	2.7
Faculty Positions	70,410	74,789	79,897	81,414	2.5
Professor	29,386	31,876	34,124	36,813	3.8
Associate Professor	20,588	22,408	23,769	22,338	1.4
Asst. Prof./Instructor	20,436	20,505	22,004	22,263	1.4
Nonfaculty Positions	10,757	11,432	13,263	13,600	4.0
Postdoctorals	5,947	5,711	7,036	6,194	0.7
Other Staff	4,810	5,721	6,227	7,406	7.5
Graduate Research Assistants[2]	35,629	39,946	43,599	48,907	5.4

All Scientists and Engineers at Major Research Universities (Including Professional Schools)[3]					6-year annual growth(%)
	1973	1975	1977	1979	
Total Ph.D. Staff[1]	42,602	47,497	52,018	56,271	4.7
Faculty Positions	34,583	37,760	40,260	42,407	3.5
Professor	15,354	16,751	17,871	19,365	3.9
Associate Professor	9,169	10,191	10,896	11,165	3.3
Asst. Prof./Instructor	10,060	10,818	11,493	11,877	2.8
Nonfaculty Positions	8,019	9,737	11,758	13,864	9.6
Postdoctorals	4,646	5,266	6,701	7,227	7.6
Other Staff	3,373	4,471	5,057	6,637	11.9
Graduate Research Assistants[2]	22,900	25,007	27,095	30,083	4.7

[1]Excludes those who had earned their doctorates from foreign universities.

[2]Estimates of the number of graduate research assistants in 1973 in the biosciences and social sciences are based on an incomplete response to the Survey of Graduate Science Student Support and Postdoctorals that year and may be underestimated.

[3]Includes medical schools and other branches of the university which may not grant Ph.D. degrees and hence are not included above under Ph.D.-granting schools.

NOTE: Estimates reported in the first four columns of this table are derived from a sample survey and are subject to sampling errors of less than 10 percent of the reported estimates. See Appendix G for a description of the forumla used to calculate approximate sampling errors.

SOURCE: National Research Council, Survey of Doctorate Recipients and Survey of Earned Doctorates and National Science Foundation, Survey of Graduate Science Student Support and Postdoctorals.

Table 6.4

ESTIMATED NUMBER OF FACULTY, POSTDOCTORALS, AND GRADUATE STUDENTS
IN PH.D.-GRANTING AND MAJOR RESEARCH UNIVERSITIES, 1973-79

Chemists at Ph.D.-Granting Schools

	1973	1975	1977	1979	6-year annual growth(%)
Total Ph.D. Staff[1]	6,153	6,840	7,271	6,940	2.0
Faculty Positions	4,426	5,132	5,384	5,292	3.0
Professor	1,981	2,459	2,505	2,844	6.2
Associate Professor	1,319	1,519	1,585	1,356	0.5
Asst. Prof./Instructor	1,126	1,154	1,294	1,092	(-0.5)
Nonfaculty Positions	1,727	1,708	1,887	1,648	-0.8
Postdoctorals	1,289	1,291	1,330	1,222	-0.9
Other Staff	438	417	557	426	(-0.5)
Graduate Research Assistants	2,884	3,174	3,534	4,129	6.2

Chemists at Major Research Universities
(Including Professional Schools)[2]

	1973	1975	1977	1979	6-year annual growth(%)
Total Ph.D. Staff[1]	2,809	3,384	3,405	3,440	3.4
Faculty Positions	1,754	2,179	2,132	2,306	4.7
Professor	803	947	1,098	1,126	(5.8)
Associate Professor	459	603	525	724	(7.9)
Asst. Prof./Instructor	492	629	509	456	(-2.4)
Nonfaculty Positions	1,055	1,205	1,273	1,134	(1.2)
Postdoctorals	823	891	892	809	(-0.3)
Other Staff	232	314	381	325	(5.8)
Graduate Research Assistants	1,863	2,020	2,251	2,443	4.6

[1]Excludes those who had earned their doctorates from foreign universities.

[2]Includes medical schools and other branches of the university which may not grant Ph.D. degrees and hence are not included above under Ph.D.-granting schools.

NOTE: Estimates reported in the first four columns of this table are derived from a sample survey and are subject to sampling errors of less than 10 percent of the reported estimates, unless otherwise indicated. Growth percentages (last column) which are based on survey estimates with sampling errors of 10 percent or more are reported in parentheses. See Appendix G for a description of the formula used to calculate approximate sampling errors.

SOURCE: National Research Council, Survey of Doctorate Recipients and Survey of Earned Doctorates and National Science Foundation, Survey of Graduate Science Student Support and Postdoctorals.

professors and graduate research assistants. At the major research universities there has also been growth in the numbers of associate professors and nonfaculty staff.

Figure 6.3 describes the distribution of effort contributed to research by the various categories of academic staff in 1979. The estimates are reported in terms of full-time equivalent (FTE) research personnel. The postdoctoral contribution in chemistry is seen to have been quite substantial--far outweighing the estimated contribution of assistant professors. Postdoctorals accounted for an estimated one-fourth of the FTE research personnel in chemistry in the major research universities. Faculty and graduate research assistants each represented another one-third of the estimated total FTE researchers.

PHYSICS. Data in Table 6.5 reveal a significant drop between 1973 and 1979 in the numbers of physics postdoctorals. Within the Ph.D.-granting schools the postdoctoral group decreased approximately 4 percent per year during these 6 years; within the major research universities the rate of decline was even greater. There has also been an appreciable drop in the numbers of assistant professors. On the other hand, there have been significant increases in the numbers of nonfaculty staff (other than postdoctorals), most of whom were heavily involved in research activities.[6] It is quite apparent from these trends that this nonfaculty group is being called upon to play an increasingly important role in physics research as faculty hiring and graduate enrollments diminish.

In terms of FTE research personnel (Figure 6.4), the post-doctorals and other nonfaculty staff together represented a major portion of the total research effort in 1979. Within the Ph.D.-granting schools the two groups accounted for almost 30 percent of the estimated total FTE research personnel in 1979. In the 59 major research universities the contribution of these two groups even exceeded that of either the faculty or the graduate research assistants. The postdoctorals alone made up between 16 and 17 percent of all FTE research personnel in physics in both sets of institutions.

BIOSCIENCES. In the biosciences the differences between the data for the two sets of institutions reported in Table 6.6 are particularly pronounced because many postdoctorals and other nonfaculty staff were employed in medical schools and consequently are not counted in the data for Ph.D.-granting schools. The populations of both Ph.D.

---

[6]Of the nonfaculty staff employed in physics in 1977, 90 percent devoted some time to research and nearly 70 percent considered research to be their primary work activity. See National Research Council (1978), Tables 3 and 4.

190

Chemists at Ph.D.-Granting Schools

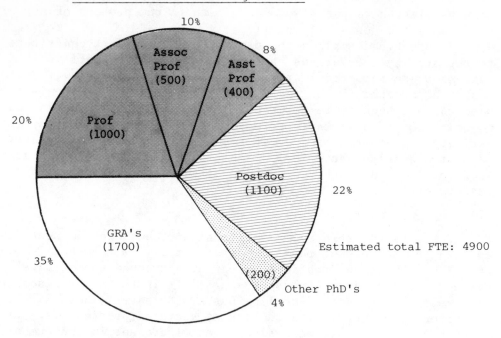

Chemists at Major Research Universities (Including Professional Schools)

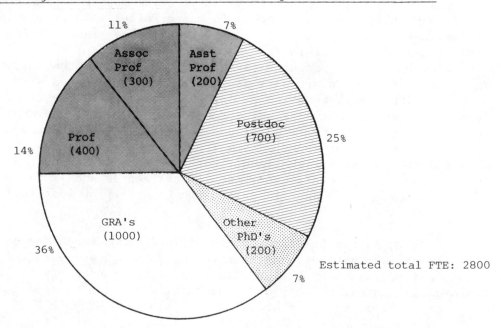

FIGURE 6.3 Distribution of estimated full-time equivalent research personnel employed in academia in chemistry, 1979. FTE estimates are based on the average fraction of time each group devoted to research activities. Estimates for major research universities include those employed in medical schools and other branches of the university which may not grant Ph.D. degrees. From National Research Council, Survey of Doctorate Recipients and Survey of Earned Doctorates and National Science Foundation, Survey of Graduate Science Student Support and Postdoctorals.

Table 6.5

ESTIMATED NUMBER OF FACULTY, POSTDOCTORALS, AND GRADUATE STUDENTS
IN PH.D.-GRANTING AND MAJOR RESEARCH UNIVERSITIES, 1973-79

Physicists at Ph.D.-Granting Schools

	1973	1975	1977	1979	6-year annual growth(%)
Total Ph.D. Staff[1]	6,219	6,214	6,577	6,378	0.4
Faculty Positions	4,651	4,663	4,848	4,724	0.3
Professor	2,173	**2,276**	2,514	2,606	3.1
Associate Professor	1,259	**1,463**	1,302	1,246	-0.2
Asst. Prof./Instructor	1,219	924	1,032	872	(-5.4)
Nonfaculty Positions	1,568	**1,551**	1,729	1,654	0.9
Postdoctorals	1,004	777	837	787	(-4.0)
Other Staff	564	774	892	867	(7.4)
Graduate Research Assistants	3,372	3,238	3,229	3,694	1.5

Physicists at Major Research Universities (Including Professional Schools)[2]

	1973	1975	1977	1979	6-year annual growth(%)
Total Ph.D. Staff[1]	3,470	3,384	3,736	3,534	0.3
Faculty Positions	2,330	2,212	2,508	2,242	-0.6
Professor	1,187	1,127	1,342	1,126	(-0.9)
Associate Professor	491	576	561	701	(6.1)
Asst. Prof./Instructor	652	509	605	415	(-7.3)
Nonfaculty Positions	1,140	1,172	1,228	1,292	2.1
Postdoctorals	740	569	555	523	(-5.6)
Other Staff	400	603	673	769	(11.5)
Graduate Research Assistants	2,411	2,325	2,318	2,651	1.6

[1] Excludes those who had earned their doctorates from foreign universities.

[2] Includes medical schools and other branches of the university which may not grant Ph.D. degrees and hence are not included above under Ph.D.-granting schools.

NOTE: Estimates reported in the first four columns of this table are derived from a sample survey and are subject to sampling errors of less than 10 percent of the reported estimates, unless otherwise indicated. Growth percentages (last column) which are based on survey estimates with sampling errors of 10 percent or more are reported in parentheses. See Appendix G for a description of the formula used to calculate approximate sampling errors.

SOURCE: National Research Council, Survey of Doctorate Recipients and Survey of Earned Doctorates and National Science Foundation, Survey of Graduate Science Student Support and Postdoctorals.

Physicists at Ph.D.-Granting Schools

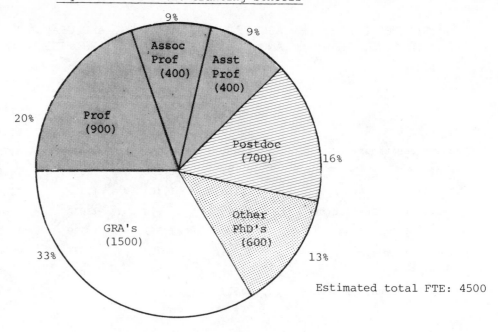

Estimated total FTE: 4500

Physicists at Major Research Universities (Including Professional Schools)

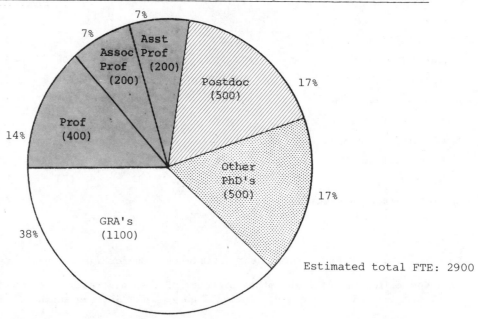

Estimated total FTE: 2900

FIGURE 6.4 Distribution of estimated full-time equivalent research personnel employed in academia in physics, 1979. FTE estimates are based on the average fraction of time each group devoted to research activities. Estimates for major research universities include those employed in medical schools and other branches of the university which may not grant Ph.D. degrees. From National Research Council, Survey of Doctorate Recipients and Survey of Earned Doctorates and National Science Foundation, Survey of Graduate Science Student Support and Postdoctorals.

Table 6.6

ESTIMATED NUMBER OF FACULTY, POSTDOCTORALS, AND GRADUATE STUDENTS
IN PH.D.-GRANTING AND MAJOR RESEARCH UNIVERSITIES, 1973-79

	Bioscientists at Ph.D.-Granting Schools				6-year annual growth(%)
	1973	1975	1977	1979	
Total Ph.D. Staff[1]	20,260	18,419	20,725	20,864	0.5
Faculty Positions	16,473	14,903	16,217	16,471	0.0
Professor	6,659	6,100	6,330	6,162	-1.3
Associate Professor	4,759	4,368	4,840	4,599	-0.6
Asst. Prof./Instructor	5,055	4,435	5,047	5,710	2.1
Nonfaculty Positions	3,787	3,516	4,508	4,393	2.5
Postdoctorals	2,477	2,285	3,007	2,780	1.9
Other Staff	1,310	1,231	1,501	1,613	3.5
Graduate Research Assistants[2]	6,103	7,095	8,414	10,069	8.7

	Bioscientists at Major Research Universities (Including Professional Schools)[3]				6-year annual growth(%)
	1973	1975	1977	1979	
Total Ph.D. Staff[1]	12,964	14,483	16,627	19,248	6.8
Faculty Positions	9,572	10,378	11,086	12,352	4.3
Professor	3,903	4,218	4,363	4,723	3.2
Associate Professor	2,565	2,698	3,185	3,339	4.5
Asst. Prof./Instructor	3,104	3,462	3,538	4,290	5.5
Nonfaculty Positions	3,392	4,105	5,541	6,896	12.6
Postdoctorals	2,268	2,749	3,810	4,470	12.0
Other Staff	1,124	1,356	1,731	2,426	13.7
Graduate Research Assistants[2]	3,817	4,373	5,177	6,079	8.1

[1]Excludes those who had earned their doctorates from foreign universities.

[2]Estimates of the number of graduate research assistants in 1973 in the biosciences and social sciences are based on an incomplete response to the Survey of Graduate Science Student Support and Postdoctorals that year and may be underestimated.

[3]Includes medical schools and other branches of the university which may not grant Ph.D. degrees and hence are not included above under Ph.D.-granting schools.

NOTE: Estimates reported in the first four columns of this table are derived from a sample survey and are subject to sampling errors of less than 10 percent of the reported estimates. See Appendix G for a description of the formula used to calculate approximate sampling errors.

SOURCE: National Research Council, Survey of Doctorate Recipients and Survey of Earned Doctorates and National Science Foundation, Survey of Graduate Science Student Support and Postdoctorals.

194

postdoctorals and other nonfaculty Ph.D. staff in major research
universities have approximately doubled during the 1973-79 period.
This growth has, in part, been offset by a decline in the number of
postdoctorals with M.D. or other professional doctorates.[7] In the
Ph.D.-granting schools the postdoctoral and doctoral research staff
populations have shown only modest growth. Similar, but smaller,
differences were noted in the faculty growth rates. The total number
of faculty members in Ph.D.-granting schools in 1979 was almost
identical to the number 6 years earlier; in major research universities, on the other hand, there has been a 4 percent annual growth in
Ph.D. faculty. This increase in faculty hiring presumably reflects
the recent increases in federal support for biomedical research--
between 1973 and 1978 the national expenditures for life sciences R
and D at colleges and universities have been growing at an annual rate
of 3 percent in constant dollars.[8] The graduate research assistant
population in both sets of institutions has expanded at an average
annual rate of more than 8 percent--higher than in engineering or any
other science field.

The magnitude of the postdoctoral involvement in bioscience
research is evident from the information presented in Figure 6.5. In
1979 postdoctorals constituted an estimated 18 percent of the FTE
research personnel in Ph.D.-granting schools and 27 percent in the
major research universities. Postdoctorals and other nonfaculty Ph.D.
staff together accounted for almost two-fifths of the FTE research
personnel in the latter set of institutions.

OTHER FIELDS OF SCIENCE AND ENGINEERING. The numbers of postdoctorals and other groups of academic research personnel in engineering
and the five science fields not discussed above are given in Tables
6.12-6.17 in the supplement to this chapter. The postdoctoral population in each of these six fields was much smaller than that found in
chemistry, physics, or the biosciences--as a matter of fact, in each
there were fewer than 400 postdoctorals at Ph.D.-granting schools in
1979. Since the data presented are based on an 8-16 percent sample of
small populations, minor fluctuations in postdoctoral estimates may
not represent significant trends. Nevertheless, an interesting
observation can be made. In every one of these fields--mathematical
sciences, earth sciences, engineering, agricultural sciences,
psychology, and the social sciences--the estimated number of postdoctorals at major research universities in 1979 exceeded the number in
1973. During this same period the annual rates of growth for faculty
at these institutions ranged between 1 percent in psychology and the
earth sciences and nearly 6 percent in the social sciences. In every
one of these fields there were appreciable increases in the numbers
of graduate research assistants as well.

---

[7]National Research Council (1980), Chapter 2.
[8]National Science Foundation (1974-79).

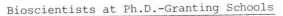

Bioscientists at Ph.D.-Granting Schools

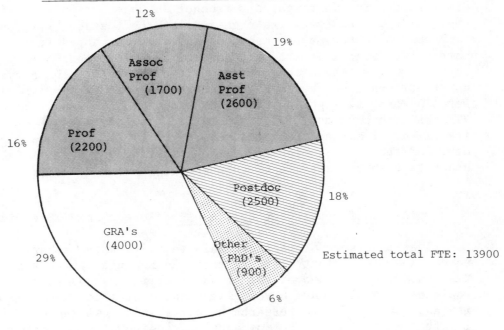

Bioscientists at Major Research Universities (Including Professional Schools)

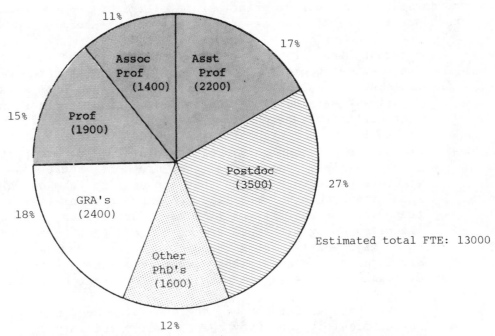

FIGURE 6.5 Distribution of estimated full-time equivalent research personnel employed in academia in biosciences, 1979. FTE estimates are based on the average fraction of time each group devoted to research activities. Estimates for major research universities include those employed in medical schools and other branches of the university which may not grant Ph.D. degrees. From National Research Council, Survey of Doctorate Recipients and Survey of Earned Doctorates and National Science Foundation, Survey of Graduate Science Student Support and Postdoctorals.

Figures 6.7-6.12 at the end of this chapter illustrate the 1979 distribution in FTE research personnel in these same five sciences and engineering. The estimated magnitude of the postdoctoral contribution to research in the major research universities ranged from approximately 3-5 percent in the mathematical sciences, engineering, and the agricultural sciences to 10 percent in psychology. The corresponding contributions in each field to the research effort in Ph.D.-granting schools were, as might be expected, significantly less. In terms of FTE research personnel, the faculty constituted the largest group in the fields of mathematical sciences, agricultural sciences, psychology, and the social sciences. In engineering and earth sciences the graduate research assistants outnumbered the FTE faculty.

Opinions of Department Chairmen and Recent Ph.D. Recipients

The importance of postdoctorals to university research goes well beyond what is reflected by quantitative measures such as the size of the postdoctoral group or the amount of time devoted to research. Postdoctorals also make a very important contribution to the creativity and quality of the research effort. This quality-related aspect is often mentioned in the comments we received from department chairmen and young scientists and engineers as well as in other anecdotal evidence we compiled. A principal investigator who employed four postdoctorals in his own research group volunteered:

> A cursory inspection of the 1977 edition of the ACS [American Chemical Society] Directory of Graduate Research reveals that roughly one-half of the papers published from this department were based on postdoctoral research--thus the impact of their research effort is quite significant. In terms of quality of research it should be pointed out that many of the more significant advances in chemistry involve postdoctoral associates because (a) they are more mature than graduate students, and (b) they are able to take on "high risk" research problems; i.e., research problems which have a reasonable probability of failure. Furthermore, postdoctorals often bring with them expertise in a particular technique which is essential for a research problem. Obviously, a significant increase in the number or quality of these individuals would have a marked effect on the research effort.[9]

From the onset of the study the committee recognized that it would be difficult to quantify the character and importance of the

---

[9]From a response to the committee's preliminary request for information from university deans and department chairmen.

postdoctorals' contribution. We concluded that the best measure was, in fact, the subjective judgment of those involved in the research effort. Consequently, in our surveys of department chairmen and FY1972 and FY1978 Ph.D. recipients, we included identical questions[10] calling for an evaluation of the contributions of postdoctorals and other research personnel. Those surveyed were asked to rate:

(1) the contributions of faculty, postdoctoral appointees, other doctoral staff, graduate research assistants, and nondoctoral staff (e.g., technicians) to the overall productivity of the research effort; and

(2) the contributions of postdoctorals, in particular, to (a) determining the basic directions of the research project, (b) intellectual vigor of the research effort, (c) infusion of new research techniques, (d) publication of research findings, and (e) training of graduate students.

A summary of the findings from each survey is presented in Tables 6.7 and 6.8.

The survey data confirm an impression already shared by many members of our committee--namely, that in many fields the contribution of postdoctorals to the overall productivity of the research effort in major university laboratories is very important, if not essential. As shown in Table 6.7, FY1972 Ph.D. recipients as well as chairmen of departments that had one or more postdoctorals rated the contributions of these postdoctorals as valuable as any other group except faculty, even though in many cases the numbers of postdoctorals involved in the research effort may be quite small. The FY1978 Ph.D. recipients, many of whom held postdoctoral appointments at the time of the survey, rated the postdoctoral contribution as important as that of faculty. Interestingly, the differences in the ratings provided by survey respondents in each of the major fields were quite small.[11]

In terms of the importance of postdoctorals to various aspects of the research project (Table 6.8), the opinions of FY1978 Ph.D. recipients were similar to those expressed by department chairmen and FY1972 graduates. All groups concurred that the most valuable contribution of postdoctorals has been to the intellectual vigor of the research effort. The chairman of a leading department of biology wrote:

---

[10]Copies of the survey questionnaires are included in the front of Appendixes C, D, and E.
[11]For a comparison of the survey data by field, see the analyses of question 12A in Appendix C, question 15A in Appendix D, and question 12 in Appendix E.

Table 6.7

IMPORTANCE OF POSTDOCTORALS AND OTHER GROUPS TO THE OVERALL PRODUCTIVITY
OF THE RESEARCH EFFORT, BASED ON THE OPINIONS OF SCIENTISTS AND
ENGINEERS INVOLVED IN ACADEMIC RESEARCH

Research Personnel	Opinion of Dept. Chairmen (avg. rating[1])	Opinion of FY1972 Ph.D.'s (avg. rating[1])	Opinion of FY1978 Ph.D.'s (avg. rating[1])
Faculty	2.0	1.8	1.7
Postdoctoral Appointees	1.3	1.4	1.7
Other Doctoral Staff	1.3	1.5	1.4
Graduate Research Assistants	1.3	1.3	1.2
Nondoctoral Staff (e.g., Technicians)	1.3	1.4	1.2

[1]Rating scale: 2 = essential   1 = important   0 = unimportant
(Those with no opinion are not included in the calculation
of the average rating.)

SOURCES: National Research Council, Survey of Science and Engineering
Department Chairmen, 1979, and Survey of Scientists and Engineers,
1979.

Table 6.8

IMPORTANCE OF POSTDOCTORALS TO VARIOUS ASPECTS OF THE RESEARCH PROJECT,
BASED ON THE OPINIONS OF SCIENTISTS AND ENGINEERS INVOLVED
IN ACADEMIC RESEARCH

	Opinion of Dept. Chairmen (avg. rating[1])	Opinion of FY1972 Ph.D.'s (avg. rating[1])	Opinion of FY1978 Ph.D.'s (avg. rating[1])
Determining the basic directions of the research project	0.8	0.8	1.3
Intellectual vigor of the research effort	1.3	1.3	1.6
Infusion of new research techniques	1.2	1.2	1.4
Publication of research findings	1.2	1.1	1.4
Training of graduate students	0.7	0.6	0.7

[1]Rating scale: 2 = essential   1 = important   0 = unimportant
(Those with no opinion are not included in the calculation
of the average rating.)

SOURCES: National Research Council, Survey of Science and Engineering
Department Chairmen, 1979, and Survey of Scientists and Engineers,
1979

> They [postdoctorals] bring new ideas and new techniques to
> the graduate students and staff. They pass along their own
> research experience to the graduate students. They general-
> ly are indispensible to the maintenance of a professional
> environment and help maintain productivity when the instruc-
> tor is busily occupied teaching or in commmittee work.
> Seminars and journal clubs are made much more exciting and
> stimulating by their presence, and they act as critical
> advisors in all aspects of the research activities of a
> thriving laboratory.[12]

The importance of the contribution is likely to grow if, as expected,
faculty hiring in many science departments declines and fewer graduate
research assistants are available.

Also considered highly valuable was the postdoctorals' involvement in the publication of research findings and the infusion of new
research techniques. As one graduate dean observed, "their [the
postdoctorals'] contribution is almost inevitably recognized by
inclusion as co-authors or sometimes sole authors of research publications." Findings from our survey of FY1972 Ph.D. recipients demon-
strate that those with postdoctoral experience have authored many more
publications than their colleagues.[13] Furthermore, since most postdoctorals take appointments in departments other than the one from
which they received their doctorate,[14] their experience with
alternative approaches to the research problem was considered to be a
valuable asset. A biologist noted:

> Because they [postdoctorals] come from other institutions,
> they most frequently bring invigorating new perspectives to
> bear upon research programs. Moreover, they are vehicles
> to transplant technology between laboratories and even some
> disciplines in fields of biology.[15]

It is not at all surprising that the postdoctorals' importance to
the training of graduate students or to determining the basic directions of the research project was not as highly regarded by survey
respondents. We estimate that as few as 27 percent of the university
departments permitted their postdoctorals to assume primary responsibility for teaching courses.[16] Significantly fewer, in fact, had

---

[12]From a response to the committee's preliminary request for
information from university deans and department chairmen.
[13]See the analysis of question 14 in Appendix D.
[14]Less than 10 percent of the postdoctorals in university departments had earned their doctorate in the same department. See the
analysis of question 2 in Appendix C.
[15]Written comment from the chairman of a department of biology.
[16]See the analysis of question 6 in Appendix C.

postdoctorals who were actually teaching during the spring semester in 1979.

It appears that far too often postdoctorals are expected only to carry out the research of their mentor and are not given the independence to follow their own investigative paths. Their dissatisfaction with their lack of independence in the laboratory was expressed by many of the postdoctorals responding to our survey (as described in Chapter 5). Although the university administrators and faculty we contacted were not explicitly asked to comment on this issue, several volunteered commments expressing similar concerns. The provost at a leading research institution told our committee:

> I have the impression that our universities do not give
> sufficient attention to the contributions and needs of
> postdoctorals. In the extreme there are cases of
> exploitation--simply employing the postdoc as a highly
> skilled technician with little regard to his/her profes-
> sional development.[17]

In the committee's view, freedom both in the choice of the research problem and in the manner in which it is pursued is important to the postdoctoral's development as an independent investigator.

Foreign Postdoctorals in U.S. Universities

Not to be overlooked is the research contribution of foreign engineers and scientists who hold postdoctoral appointments at U.S. universities. For many years now this group has played a valuable role in research in this country. As one chemistry department chairman wrote, "Foreign postdoctoral fellows have probably [made] the most underestimated contribution to U.S. research efforts in the golden age."[18] Twelve years ago, when the last comprehensive study of postdoctoral education was done, foreign engineers and scientists constituted as many as 45 percent of all postdoctorals in U.S. universities (Figure 6.6). We now estimate the foreign component to be approximately 38 percent.

Engineering had by far the largest fraction of foreign post-doctorals. In 1979 nearly 70 percent of all postdoctorals in engineering departments were foreign citizens. Almost half of the university postdoctoral populations in mathematical sciences and chemistry were foreign. In other fields of science foreign citizens made up a smaller, but by no means insignificant, fraction of the postdoctoral groups.

---

[17]Written comment from a university provost.
[18]From a response to the committee's preliminary request for information from university deans and department chairmen.

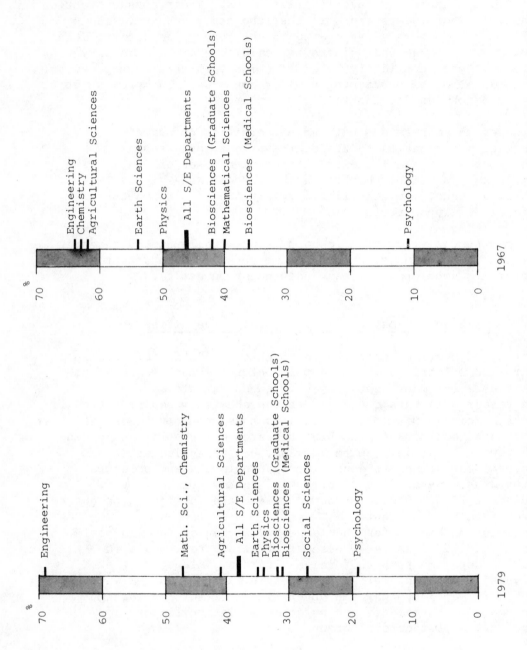

FIGURE 6.6 Percent of postdoctorals in science and engineering departments who were foreign citizens, 1967 and 1979. From National Research Council, Survey of Science and Engineering Department Chairmen, 1979, and The Invisible University, 1969.

In all fields except engineering, mathematical sciences, and psychology, the fraction of foreign postdoctorals is estimated to have fallen during the period between 1967 and 1979.[19] This decline is probably due to a number of different factors. In many European and other countries young scientists have encountered increasing difficulty in finding teaching and research positions. Under these circumstances it is likely that many young scientists have been hesitant to give up positions in their own homelands in order to accept temporary appointments in the United States. Furthermore, in the last decade it has become more difficult for foreign scientists to obtain permanent positions in this country--both the job market and visa regulations have stood in the way. Undoubtedly the fall in the value of the U.S. dollar also has reduced the attractiveness of the postdoctoral stipends for candidates from countries with currencies that have appreciated relative to the dollar. Finally, it is believed by some that the decline in foreign postdoctorals is due, in part, to the growing strength of science in other countries of the world. For young scientists in some foreign countries postdoctoral experience in a U.S. laboratory may not be considered as important to their career development as it once was.

There has been little change in the list of countries from which the postdoctorals have come. According to both the 1967 and the 1979 surveys, more than 40 percent of all foreign postdoctorals were from three countries--India, Japan, and the United Kingdom. The first eight countries listed in Table 6.9 accounted for nearly two-thirds of the foreign postdoctorals in both years. In this 12-year span there appears to have been a significant increase in the postdoctoral share from India, Japan, Hong Kong, and the Netherlands, and a decrease in the share from the United Kingdom and West Germany. In 1979, as well as in 1967, only about 21 percent of the foreign postdoctorals in this country had earned their doctorates from U.S. universities.[20]

From the statements of university deans and department chairmen it is quite clear that the academic community holds the foreign postdoctoral in high regard. Only 8 percent of the department chairmen we surveyed considered the foreign postdoctorals less productive than their American colleagues.[21] From the chairman of an astronomy department came this comment:

> We have always tried to have foreign as well as domestic
> postdoctoral fellows in roughly equal mix. Astronomy is
> an extraordinarily international subject, and we feel
> that our program and future as well as that of this field

---

[19]Unfortunately there are no reliable longitudinal data available on the actual numbers of foreign scientists and engineers holding postdoctoral appointments in U.S. universities during the 1967-79 period.
[20]See the analyses of questions 2 and 16 in Appendix C.
[21]See the analysis of question 18.1 in Appendix C.

Table 6.9

PERCENT OF FOREIGN POSTDOCTORALS IN U.S. UNIVERSITIES WHO CAME
FROM DIFFERENT COUNTRIES, 1967 AND 1979

Country of Citizenship	1979	1967
India	18%	13%
Japan	15%	13%
United Kingdom	11%	15%
Taiwan	6%	4%
Canada	4%	5%
Israel	4%	3%
West Germany	3%	7%
Australia	3%	3%
Hong Kong	3%	*
Poland	2%	1%
France	2%	2%
Korea	2%	2%
Netherlands	2%	1%

*Less than 0.5 percent.

SOURCES: National Research Council, Survey of Foreign Scientists
and Engineers, 1979 and the Invisible University, 1969.

are enriched in this way. Also we can, in a sense, do
better for many foreign scholars . . . in view of the
very high quality of American astronomical equipment and
facilities compared with those abroad.[22]

Department chairmen saw a number of advantages in hiring foreign
postdoctorals. Approximately one-third of the chairmen we surveyed
indicated that the primary reason their department appointed foreign
postdoctorals was to utilize the special research skills or training
of these foreign scientists and engineers (Table 6.10). Another 23
percent of the chairmen indicated that the foreign group had been
appointed because they were better qualified than the available U.S.
candidates. Often the foreign postdoctoral is older, more mature, and
has had several years of research experience, while the U.S. candidate
may have only recently completed his or her graduate program. In many
cases--in the fields of engineering and chemistry, in particular--
there were no U.S. candidates available for the postdoctoral positions. As many as 61 percent of the engineering chairmen and 41
percent of the chemistry chairmen identified this situation as the
primary reason for appointing foreign citizens.

In these two fields many departments would find it difficult, if
not impossible, to maintain their research productivity without the
participation of foreign postdoctorals. As shown in Table 6.11, as
many as 93 percent of all engineering and chemistry departments with
one or more postdoctorals had at least some participation by foreign
citizens. Moreover, in an estimated 66 percent of the engineering
departments and 45 percent of the chemistry departments, the foreign
group outnumbered the U.S. appointees. More than one-third of the
engineering departments had only foreign postdoctorals. Many of the
chairmen we contacted in this field pointed out that the strong demand
in industry has drawn students away from doctoral and postdoctoral
study. The chairman of a department of metallurgy commented:

. . . a relatively large proportion of our graduates end
up with advanced degrees doing research and development
work. However, the great majority of our students go to
work in industry, at the B.S., M.S., and Ph.D. levels.
Since our students enjoy an excellent job market, many
don't go on to graduate school. Of those who do, many
who could get a Ph.D. stop with an M.S. Similarly at
the Ph.D. level the student asks why he or she should
take a job at $1000/month as a postdoc when they can
get twice as much at an industrial research and development lab.[23]

---

[22]From a response to the committee's preliminary request for
information from university deans and department chairmen.
[23]Comment from the chairman of a department of metallurgy in a
school of engineering.

Table 6.10

PRIMARY REASON FOR APPOINTING FOREIGN POSTDOCTORALS

Departmental Field	Total Depts with foreign Postdoctorals N	Foreign better qualified than U.S. Candidates %	Foreign had special skills or training %	No U.S. candidates available %	Other reasons %
Departmental Field	1,136	23	33	32	12
Mathematical Sciences	20	(30)	15	20	(35)
Physics	112	48	26	21	5
Chemistry	149	30	25	41	4
Earth Sciences	40	22	45	25	8
Engineering	191	11	25	61	4
Agricultural Sciences	38	(37)	(37)	(14)	11
Biosci-Grad Schl	264	16	(44)	33	7
Biosci-Med Schl	276	23	(36)	21	20
Psychology	16	(25)	(25)	0	(50)
Social Sciences	30	7	(30)	0	(63)

NOTE: Percentage estimates reported in this table are derived from a sample survey and are subject to an absolute sampling error of less than 5 percentage points, unless otherwise indicated. Estimates with sampling errors of 5 or more percentage points are reported in parentheses. See Appendix G for a description of the formula used to calculate approximate sampling errors.

SOURCE: National Research Council, Survey of Science and Engineering Department Chairmen, 1979.

206

Table 6.11

FRACTION OF ALL POSTDOCTORALS IN A DEPARTMENT
WHO ARE FOREIGN CITIZENS

	Total Depts	Foreign fraction of postdoctorals			
		All	> 1/2	> 1/4	Some
	N	%	%	%	%
Departmental Field	1,601	13	30	59	72
Mathematical Sciences	28	21	39	64	71
Physics	152	8	23	60	75
Chemistry	162	4	45	87	95
Earth Sciences	67	17	27	52	61
Engineering	205	38	66	89	93
Agricultural Sciences	65	20	31	(49)	(58)
Biosciences-Grad Schl	372	10	25	54	72
Biosciences-Med Schl	430	6	15	50	67
Psychology	62	0	10	16	26
Social Sciences	58	21	(32)	(41)	(54)

NOTE: Percentage estimates reported in this table are derived from a sample survey and are subject to an absolute sampling error of less than 5 percentage points, unless otherwise indicated. Estimates with sampling errors of 5 or more percentage points are reported in parentheses. See Appendix G for a description of the forumla used to calculate approximate sampling errors.

SOURCE: National Research Coucnil, Survey of Science and Engineering Department Chairmen, 1979.

Not surprisingly most (more than 70 percent)[24] of the foreign
scientists and engineers holding postdoctoral appointments in this
country were employed on U.S federal research grants and contracts.
Only about 12 percent[25] were supported by funds from their own
governments. A majority[26] of the foreign group were expected to
return to their homelands after completion of their appointments.
Thus foreign postdoctorals have been called upon to make a valuable
contribution to the research efforts of university investigators,
without significantly increasing the future supply of doctoral
personnel in the United States. Their role has been especially
important in fields like engineering and chemistry in which there has
been a sharp decline in the numbers of young investigators. Also,
there is little doubt that the availability of foreign postdoctorals
has reduced the cost of doing research. On the other hand, a few of
the department chairmen we contacted expressed concern about the
long-term impact on academic research. The chairman of a materials
science department commented:

> One of the problems . . . is the fact that many
> places . . . are offering temporary postdoctoral appoint-
> ments at salary levels well below those in industry. The
> job is temporary, and often not very educational, and is
> therefore only rarely attractive to our U.S. Ph.D. candi-
> dates, who would prefer to go overseas, or start their
> careers. Such positions then tend to attract foreign
> students, or students switching from areas where jobs are
> less plentiful. This kind of "budget-stretching" is
> deplorable on ethical grounds. Furthermore it prevents
> these laboratories from reaching our best U.S. people; in
> the long run the laboratories will suffer.[27]

It must be emphasized, however, that the committee has found no
evidence to suggest that there has been a decline in the quality of
research. Almost all the department chairmen we surveyed shared the
opinion that foreign postdoctorals make as valuable a contribution to
the intellectual vigor of the research effort as their U.S. colleagues.[28]

---

[24]See the sixth column of the analysis of question 16 in Appendix C.
[25]See the fourth column of the analysis of question 16 in Appendix
C.
[26]Science and engineering department chairmen estimated that
approximately 60 percent of the foreign postdoctorals would return
home immediately after completing their appointments. See last column
of the analysis of question 16 in Appendix C.
[27]Comment from the chairman of a department of materials science in
a school of engineering.
[28]See the analysis of question 18.3 in Appendix C.

209

In addition, foreign postdoctorals make an important, although less recognized, contribution to the international exchange of science. One chairman we contacted described this contribution as follows:

> Foreign postdoctorals serve several valuable functions. In my opinion, one of the most important things they do is create the basis for good communication in the work among different countries. This is most important for the graduate students with whom the postdoctoral fellow will interact. I believe it critically important that workers in common fields interact with each other on a personal basis. The journals and published papers simply do not convey the sufficient detail and spirit of the work. Foreign postdoctoral appointments play an extremely important role in enhancing this communication.[29]

The importance of foreign postdoctorals in transmitting new research techniques and approaches between U.S. and foreign laboratories as well as in promoting international understanding and good will should not be underestimated.

Possible Trends

The findings presented in this chapter delineate many significant differences in the role of postdoctorals in research in each major field of science and engineering. In three fields--physics, chemistry, and the biosciences--postdoctorals continue to play a leading role in the research effort in universities. In other fields that role is considerably smaller, but may very well expand during the next two decades. The future roles of postdoctorals will depend on how universities and the scientific community as a whole adapt to anticipated changes in enrollments, faculty hiring patterns, and other factors affecting the supply and demand for research personnel. One of the most pressing problems facing the scientific community is the mismatch in many fields between the importance of postdoctorals in support of the nation's research enterprise, on the one hand, and the availability of subsequent career opportunities for postdoctorals, on the other. The resolution of this problem may be quite different in different fields. In the remaining pages of this chapter we consider some possible developments that are based on recent changes we have observed in the career patterns and utilization of young doctorate recipients in each science and engineering field.

In some fields we may witness a significant expansion of the postdoctoral population in order to meet a growing demand for academic

---

[29]Comment from the chairman of a department of psychology.

research personnel and to provide temporary employment for young
investigators unable to find faculty positions. This phenomenon has
already occurred in the biosciences. During a period when there were
many more bioscience graduates seeking university faculty positions
than were available, a large number of graduates have prolonged their
period of education in hopes of eventually meeting their career goals.
Those taking postdoctorals have undoubtedly made a very valuable
contribution to the research effort in this field. As we have seen,
however, this situation can lead to frustration and disappointment for
many talented young investigators.

If, as anticipated, faculty hiring in most fields of science
falls well below its current level, we can also expect increases in
the numbers of doctorate recipients pursuing other careers--either
within the academic sector or in government and industrial
laboratories. Trends in this direction have already begun in many
fields. In physics, for example, there has been sizable expansion
during the past 6 years in the nonfaculty doctoral staff groups in
universities. By 1979 members of this group outnumbered the
postdoctorals in major research universities[30] and have made
significant contributions to academic research in this field. In the
mathematical sciences, psychology, and the social sciences rapidly
growing fractions of the doctoral labor force have taken positions
outside the academic sector.[31] There have been substantial
increases in industrial and government hiring in engineering,
chemistry, and the earth sciences, as well. It is still too early to
determine what the long-term impact of these trends will be on the
quality and productivity of university research. Nonetheless, there
is already serious concern[32] about the decline in the numbers of
young investigators entering faculty careers in physics, mathematics,
engineering, and chemistry.

On the supply side, we can expect significant changes during the
next 15 years in the numbers of doctoral graduates in many science and
engineering fields. These changes may be due in part to demographic
factors, in part to student career choices, and in part to the availability of student support. During the past decade the numbers of
annual doctoral awards in mathematical sciences, physics, chemistry,
and engineering have fallen by more than 25 percent. We believe that
these decreases are largely attributable to changes in students'
perceptions of the career prospects in these fields and in the level
of federal support for graduate education. In the last few years
employment opportunities--mostly outside the academic sector--seem to

---

[30]See Figure 6.4 in this chapter.
[31]Nonacademic employment in these three fields has nearly doubled
during the past 6 years. See Table 3.3 in Chapter 3.
[32]Another National Research Council committee has examined this
issue in detail. A summary of that committee's findings is presented
in Chapter 3.

have opened up in all four fields (especially in engineering), and some adjustments in the doctoral supply have already occurred.[33] Such adjustments, however, may lag several years behind demand. Despite a strong demand for Ph.D. engineers for the last few years, market forces have done little as yet to reverse the decline in young investigators pursuing careers in academic research.

Significant changes can also be expected in the supply of postdoctoral candidates in science and engineering fields. The postdoctoral supply in a particular field is determined by a variety of different factors including the number of recent doctoral graduates in that field, the availability and attraction of alternative employment opportunities, the adequacy of postdoctoral stipends (compared with salaries offered in alternative employment), and students' perceptions of the long-term career prospects for those completing postdoctoral appointments in that field. We have seen from this study that the numbers of postdoctorals in a field can change quite rapidly.[34] Within the past six years the postdoctoral population in the biosciences has more than doubled.[35] In physics and chemistry the postdoctoral populations have recently declined. In the next two decades we can expect even greater changes in some fields as universities, the primary loci for basic research, adjust to an environment which is likely to be considerably different from that in the past two decades.

References

National Research Council. Nonfaculty Doctoral Research Staff in Science and Engineering in United States Universities. Washington, D.C.: National Academy of Sciences, 1978.

National Science Foundation. Federal Funds for Research and Development, and Other Scientific Activities. Washington, D.C.: U.S. Government Printing Office, 1974-79.

---

[33]In all four fields there was a modest increase in doctoral awards between FY1978 and FY1979. See Table 3.7 in the supplement to Chapter 3.

[34]To a certain extent the availability of foreign postdoctorals can temper these fluctuations.

[35]See Figure 3.4 in Chapter 3.

SUPPLEMENTARY TABLES AND FIGURES FOR CHAPTER 6

Table 6.12

ESTIMATED NUMBER OF FACULTY, POSTDOCTORALS, AND GRADUATE STUDENTS
IN PH.D.-GRANTING AND MAJOR RESEARCH UNIVERSITIES, 1973-79

Mathematical Scientists at Ph.D.-Granting Schools

	1973	1975	1977	1979	6-year annual growth(%)
Total Ph.D. Staff[1]	7,295	7,956	8,111	8,863	3.3
Faculty Positions	7,000	7,486	7,619	8,285	2.8
Professor	2,355	2,718	2,884	3,402	6.3
Associate Professor	2,091	2,354	2,494	2,450	2.7
Asst. Prof./Instructor	2,554	2,414	2,241	2,433	-0.8
Nonfaculty Positions	295	470	492	578	(11.9)
Postdoctorals	71	120	104	162	(14.7)
Other Staff	224	350	388	416	(10.9)
Graduate Research Assistants	1,226	1,325	1,438	1,652	5.1

Mathematical Scientists at Major Research Universities (Including Professional Schools)[2]

	1973	1975	1977	1979	6-year annual growth(%)
Total Ph.D. Staff[1]	3,148	3,574	3,538	4,137	4.7
Faculty Positions	2,974	3,246	3,219	3,702	3.7
Professor	1,136	1,263	1,354	1,651	6.4
Associate Professor	717	838	855	873	(3.3)
Asst. Prof./Instructor	1,121	1,145	1,010	1,178	(0.8)
Nonfaculty Positions	174	328	319	435	(16.5)
Postdoctorals	17	112	75	155	(44.5)
Other Staff	157	216	244	280	(10.1)
Graduate Research Assistants	919	852	916	1,078	2.7

[1]Excludes those who had earned their doctorates from foreign universities.

[2]Includes medical schools and other branches of the university which may not grant
Ph.D. degrees and hence are not included above under Ph.D.-granting schools.

NOTE: Estimates reported in the first four columns of this table are derived from a
sample survey and are subject to sampling errors of less than 10 percent of
the reported estimates, unless otherwise indicated. Growth percentages (last
column) which are based on survey estimates with sampling errors of 10 percent
or more are reported in parentheses. See Appendix G for a description of the
formula used to calculate approximate sampling errors.

SOURCE: National Research Council, Survey of Doctorate Recipients and Survey of
Earned Doctorates and National Science Foundation, Survey of Graduate
Science Student Support and Postdoctorals.

Mathematical Scientists at Ph.D.-Granting Schools

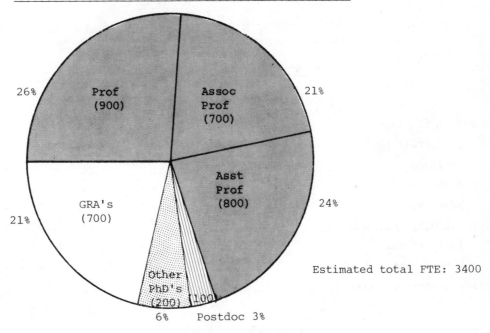

Mathematical Scientists at Major Research Universities
(Including Professional Schools)

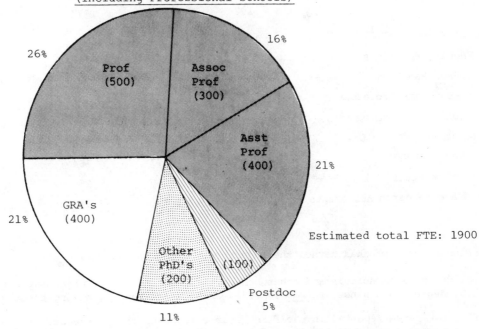

FIGURE 6.7 Distribution of estimated full-time equivalent research
personnel employed in academia in mathematical sciences, 1979. FTE
estimates are based on the average fraction of time each group devoted
to research activities. Estimates for major research universities
include those employed in medical schools and other branches of the
university which may not grant Ph.D. degrees. From National Research
Council, Survey of Doctorate Recipients and Survey of Earned Doctorates
and National Science Foundation, Survey of Graduate Science Student
Support and Postdoctorals.

Table 6.13

ESTIMATED NUMBER OF FACULTY, POSTDOCTORALS, AND GRADUATE STUDENTS IN PH.D.-GRANTING AND MAJOR RESEARCH UNIVERSITIES, 1973-79

Earth Scientists at Ph.D.-Granting Schools

	1973	1975	1977	1979	6-year annual growth(%)
Total Ph.D. Staff[1]	3,418	3,922	4,011	3,763	1.6
Faculty Positions	2,822	3,269	3,264	2,881	0.3
Professor	1,355	1,432	1,550	1,384	0.4
Associate Professor	795	1,058	848	777	(-0.4)
Asst. Prof./Instructor	672	779	866	720	(1.2)
Nonfaculty Positions	596	653	747	882	(6.8)
Postdoctorals	222	268	363	304	(5.4)
Other Staff	374	385	384	578	(7.5)
Graduate Research Assistants	2,501	2,757	3,146	3,489	5.7

Earth Scientists at Major Research Universities (Including Professional Schools)[2]

	1973	1975	1977	1979	6-year annual growth(%)
Total Ph.D. Staff[1]	1,885	2,028	2,175	2,211	2.7
Faculty Positions	1,461	1,611	1,661	1,582	1.3
Professor	697	673	727	671	(-0.6)
Associate Professor	409	498	443	442	(1.3)
Asst. Prof./Instructor	355	440	491	469	(4.8)
Nonfaculty Positions	424	417	514	629	(6.8)
Postdoctorals	140	177	264	192	(5.4)
Other Staff	284	240	250	437	(7.4)
Graduate Research Assistants	1,628	1,799	2,043	2,218	5.3

[1] Excludes those who had earned their doctorates from foreign universities.

[2] Includes medical schools and other branches of the university which may not grant Ph.D. degrees and hence are not included above under Ph.D.-granting schools.

NOTE: Estimates reported in the first four columns of this table are derived from a sample survey and are subject to sampling errors of less than 10 percent of the reported estimates, unless otherwise indicated. Growth percentages (last column) which are based on survey estimates with sampling errors of 10 percent or more are reported in parentheses. See Appendix G for a description of the formula used to calculate approximate sampling errors.

SOURCE: National Research Council, Survey of Doctorate Recipients and Survey of Earned Doctorates and National Science Foundation, Survey of Graduate Science Student Support and Postdoctorals.

Earth Scientists at Ph.D.-Granting Schools

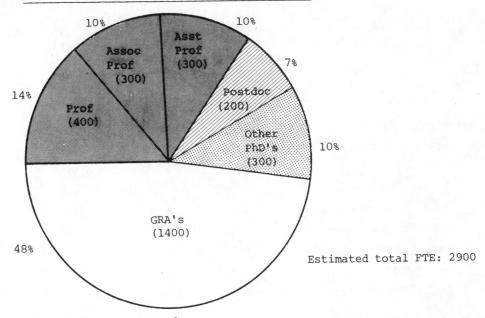

Earth Scientists at Major Research Universities (Including Professional Schools)

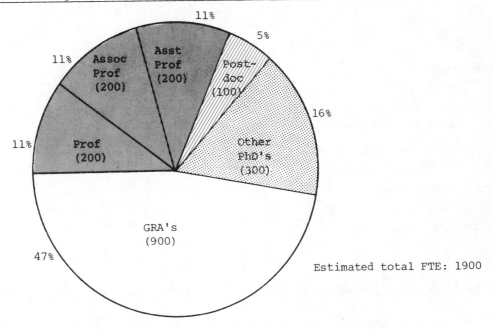

FIGURE 6.8 Distribution of estimated full-time equivalent research personnel employed in academia in earth sciences, 1979. FTE estimates are based on the average fraction of time each group devoted to research activities. Estimates for major research universities include those employed in medical schools and other branches of the university which may not grant Ph.D. degrees. From National Research Council, Survey of Doctorate Recipients and Survey of Earned Doctorates and National Science Foundation, Survey of Graduate Science Student Support and Postdoctorals.

Table 6.14

ESTIMATED NUMBER OF FACULTY, POSTDOCTORALS, AND GRADUATE STUDENTS
IN PH.D.-GRANTING AND MAJOR RESEARCH UNIVERSITIES, 1973-79

Engineers at Ph.D.-Granting Schools

	1973	1975	1977	1979	6-year annual growth(%)
Total Ph.D. Staff[1]	10,571	11,108	11,672	12,491	2.8
Faculty Positions	9,714	10,088	10,530	11,612	3.0
Professor	4,143	4,805	5,210	6,428	7.6
Associate Professor	3,231	3,334	3,423	3,228	0.0
Asst. Prof./Instructor	2,340	1,949	1,897	1,956	-2.9
Nonfaculty Positions	857	1,020	1,142	879	(0.4)
Postdoctorals	277	235	482	303	(1.5)
Other Staff	580	785	660	576	(-0.1)
Graduate Research Assistants	10,193	10,993	11,902	12,737	3.8

Engineers at Major Research Universities
(Including Professional Schools)[2]

	1973	1975	1977	1979	6-year annual growth(%)
Total Ph.D. Staff[1]	5,053	5,422	5,784	6,185	3.4
Faculty Positions	4,499	4,796	4,977	5,340	2.9
Professor	2,122	2,390	2,530	3,169	6.9
Associate Professor	1,307	1,321	1,464	1,501	2.3
Asst. Prof./Instructor	1,070	1,085	983	670	(-7.5)
Nonfaculty Positions	554	626	807	845	(7.3)
Postdoctorals	232	139	264	365	(7.8)
Other Staff	322	487	543	480	(6.9)
Graduate Research Assistants	6,984	7,491	8,017	8,655	3.6

[1]Excludes those who had earned their doctorates from foreign universities.

[2]Includes medical schools and other branches of the university which may not grant Ph.D. degrees and hence are not included above under Ph.D.-granting schools.

NOTE: Estimates reported in the first four columns of this table are derived from a sample survey and are subject to sampling errors of less than 10 percent of the reported estimates, unless otherwise indicated. Growth percentages (last column) which are based on survey estimates with sampling errors of 10 percent or more are reported in parentheses. See Appendix G for a description of the formula used to calculate approximate sampling errors.

SOURCE: National Research Council, Survey of Doctorate Recipients and Survey of Earned Doctorates and National Science Foundation, Survey of Graduate Science Student Support and Postdoctorals.

Engineers at Ph.D.-Granting Schools

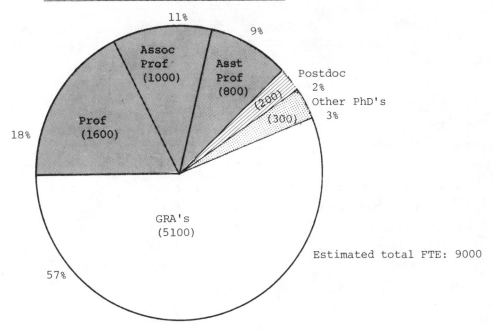

Engineers at Major Research Universities (Including Professional Schools)

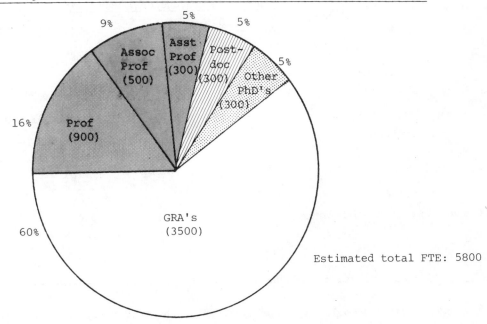

FIGURE 6.9 Distribution of estimated full-time equivalent research personnel employed in academia in engineering, 1979. FTE estimates are based on the average fraction of time each group devoted to research activities. Estimates for major research universities include those employed in medical schools and other branches of the university which may not grant Ph.D. degrees. From National Research Council, Survey of Doctorate Recipients and Survey of Earned Doctorates and National Science Foundation, Survey of Graduate Science Student Support and Postdoctorals.

Table 6.15

ESTIMATED NUMBER OF FACULTY, POSTDOCTORALS, AND GRADUATE STUDENTS
IN PH.D.-GRANTING AND MAJOR RESEARCH UNIVERSITIES, 1973-79

Agricultural Scientists at Ph.D.-Granting Schools

	1973	1975	1977	1979	6-year annual growth(%)
Total Ph.D. Staff[1]	5,743	7,217	7,218	7,127	3.7
Faculty Positions	5,296	6,584	6,613	6,357	3.1
Professor	2,732	3,244	3,314	3,496	4.2
Associate Professor	1,540	1,829	1,873	1,857	3.2
Asst. Prof./Instructor	1,024	1,511	1,426	1,004	(-0.2)
Nonfaculty Positions	447	633	605	770	(9.5)
Postdoctorals	166	249	187	185	(1.8)
Other Staff	281	384	418	585	(13.0)
Graduate Research Assistants	4,066	5,018	5,471	5,902	6.4

Agricultural Scientists at Major Research Institutions
(Including Professional Schools)[2]

	1973	1975	1977	1979	6-year annual growth(%)
Total Ph.D. Staff[1]	3,346	4,123	4,051	4,159	3.7
Faculty Positions	3,046	3,579	3,683	3,604	2.8
Professor	1,588	1,817	1,893	1,991	3.8
Associate Professor	871	1,016	934	1,129	(4.4)
Asst. Prof./Instructor	587	746	856	484	(-3.2)
Nonfaculty Positions	300	544	368	555	(10.8)
Postdoctorals	106	191	67	108	(0.3)
Other Staff	194	353	301	447	(14.9)
Graduate Research Assistants	2,715	3,145	3,417	3,587	4.8

[1] Excludes those who had earned their doctorates from foreign universities.

[2] Includes medical schools and other branches of the university which may not grant Ph.D. degrees and hence are not included above under Ph.D.-granting schools.

NOTE: Estimates reported in the first four columns of this table are derived from a sample survey and are subject to sampling errors of less than 10 percent of the reported estimates, unless otherwise indicated. Growth percentages (last column) which are based on survey estimates with sampling errors of 10 percent or more are reported in parentheses. See Appendix G for a description of the formula used to calculate approximate sampling errors.

SOURCE: National Research Council, Survey of Doctorate Recipients and Survey of Earned Doctorates and National Science Foundation, Survey of Graduate Science Student Support and Postdoctorals.

Agricultural Scientists at Ph.D.-Granting Schools

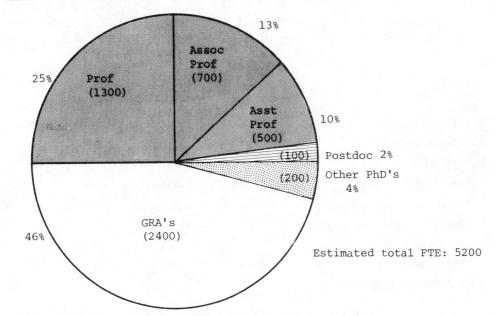

Estimated total FTE: 5200

Agricultural Scientists at Major Research Universities
(Including Professional Schools)

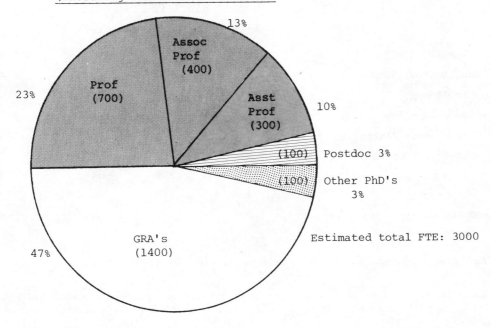

Estimated total FTE: 3000

FIGURE 6.10 Distribution of estimated full-time equivalent research personnel employed in academia in agricultural sciences, 1979. FTE estimates are based on the average fraction of time each group devoted to research activities. Estimates for major research universities include those employed in medical schools and other branches of the university which may not grant Ph.D. degrees. From National Research Council, Survey of Doctorate Recipients and Survey of Earned Doctorates and National Science Foundation, Survey of Graduate Science Student Support and Postdoctorals.

Table 6.16

ESTIMATED NUMBER OF FACULTY, POSTDOCTORALS, AND GRADUATE STUDENTS IN PH.D.-GRANTING AND MAJOR RESEARCH UNIVERSITIES, 1973-79

Psychologists at Ph.D.-Granting Schools

	1973	1975	1977	1979	6-year annual growth(%)
Total Ph.D. Staff[1]	8,109	9,035	9,053	8,751	1.3
Faculty Positions	7,308	8,029	7,918	7,429	0.3
Professor	2,739	3,141	3,161	3,261	3.0
Associate Professor	2,165	2,441	2,309	2,061	-0.8
Asst. Prof./Instructor	2,404	2,447	2,448	2,107	-2.2
Nonfaculty Positions	801	1,006	1,135	1,322	8.7
Postdoctorals	221	325	369	218	(-0.2)
Other Staff	580	681	766	1,104	(11.3)
Graduate Research Assistants	1,935	2,210	2,285	2,502	4.4

Psychologists at Major Research Universities (Including Professional Schools)[2]

	1973	1975	1977	1979	6-year annual growth(%)
Total Ph.D. Staff[1]	3,973	4,442	4,591	4,720	2.9
Faculty Positions	3,396	3,708	3,723	3,604	1.0
Professor	1,371	1,538	1,491	1,518	1.7
Associate Professor	964	1,192	972	818	(-2.7)
Asst. Prof./Instructor	1,061	978	1,260	1,268	3.0
Nonfaculty Positions	577	734	868	1,116	(11.6)
Postdoctorals	168	304	462	277	(8.7)
Other Staff	409	430	406	839	(12.7)
Graduate Research Assistants	797	922	864	974	3.4

[1] Excludes those who had earned their doctorates from foreign universities.

[2] Includes medical schools and other branches of the university which may not grant Ph.D. degrees and hence are not included above under Ph.D.-granting schools.

NOTE: Estimates reported in the first four columns of this table are derived from a sample survey and are subject to sampling errors of less than 10 percent of the reported estimates, unless otherwise indicated. Growth percentages (last column) which are based on survey estimates with sampling errors of 10 percent or more are reported in parentheses. See Appendix G for a description of the formula used to calculate approximate sampling errors.

SOURCE: National Research Council, Survey of Doctorate Recipients and Survey of Earned Doctorates and National Science Foundation, Survey of Graduate Science Student Support and Postdoctorals.

Psychologists at Ph.D.-Granting Schools

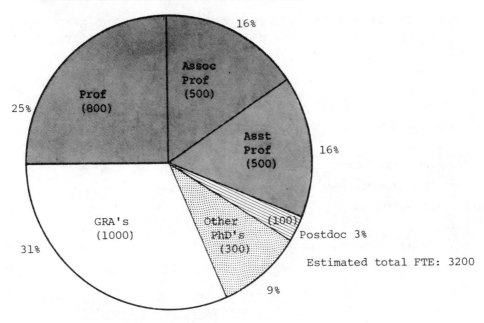

Psychologists at Major Research Universities (Including Professional Schools)

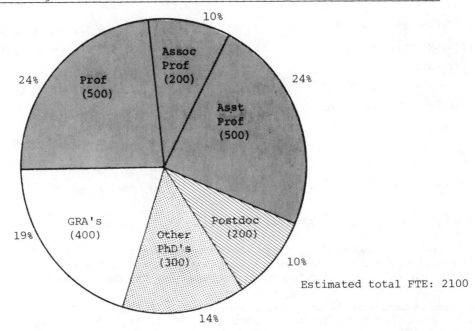

FIGURE 6.11 Distribution of estimated full-time equivalent research personnel employed in academia in psychology, 1979. FTE estimates are based on the average fraction of time each group devoted to research activities. Estimates for major research universities include those employed in medical schools and other branches of the university which may not grant Ph.D. degrees. From National Research Council, Survey of Doctorate Recipients and Survey of Earned Doctorates and National Science Foundation, Survey of Graduate Science Student Support and Postdoctorals.

Table 6.17

ESTIMATED NUMBER OF FACULTY, POSTDOCTORALS, AND GRADUATE STUDENTS
IN PH.D.-GRANTING AND MAJOR RESEARCH UNIVERSITIES, 1973-79

Social Scientists at Ph.D.-Granting Schools					6-year annual growth(%)
	1973	1975	1977	1979	
Total Ph.D. Staff[1]	13,399	15,510	18,522	19,837	6.8
Faculty Positions	12,720	14,635	17,504	18,363	6.3
Professor	5,249	5,701	6,656	7,230	5.5
Associate Professor	3,429	4,042	5,095	4,764	5.6
Asst. Prof./Instructor	4,042	4,892	5,753	6,369	7.9
Nonfaculty Positions	679	875	1,018	1,474	13.8
Postdoctorals	220	161	357	333	(7.2)
Other Staff	459	714	661	1,141	(16.4)
Graduate Research Assistants[2]	3,309	4,136	4,180	4,733	6.1

Social Scientists at Major Research Universities (Including Professional Schools)[3]					6-year annual growth(%)
	1973	1975	1977	1979	
Total Ph.D. Staff[1]	5,954	6,657	8,111	8,637	6.4
Faculty Positions	5,551	6,051	7,271	7,675	5.5
Professor	2,547	2,778	3,073	3,390	4.9
Associate Professor	1,386	1,449	1,957	1,638	2.8
Asst. Prof./Instructor	1,618	1,824	2,241	2,647	8.5
Nonfaculty Positions	403	606	840	962	(15.6)
Postdoctorals	152	134	312	328	(13.7)
Other Staff	251	472	528	634	(16.7)
Graduate Research Assistants[2]	1,766	2,080	2,092	2,398	5.2

[1]Excludes those who had earned their doctorates from foreign universities.

[2]Estimates of the number of graduate research assistants in 1973 in the biosciences and social sciences are based on an incomplete response to the Survey of Graduate Science Student Support and Postdoctorals that year and may be underestimated.

[3]Includes medical schools and other branches of the university which may not grant Ph.D. degrees and hence are not included above under Ph.D.-granting schools.

NOTE: Estimates reported in the first four columns of this table are derived from a sample survey and are subject to sampling errors of less than 10 percent of the reported estimates, unless otherwise indicated. Growth percentages (last column) which are based on survey estimates with sampling errors of 10 percent or more are reported in parentheses. See Appendix G for a description of the formula used to calculate approximate sampling errors.

SOURCE: National Research Council, Survey of Doctorate Recipients and Survey of Earned Doctorates and National Science Foundation, Survey of Graduate Science Student Support and Postdoctorals.

223

Social Scientists at Ph.D.-Granting Schools

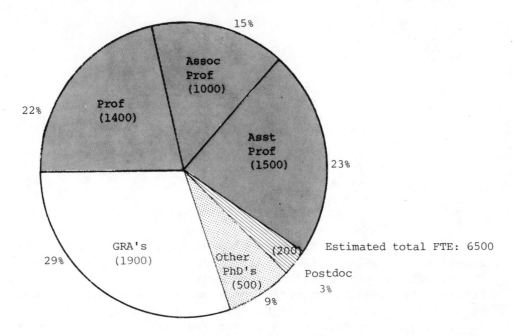

Social Scientists at Major Research Universities (Including Professional Schools)

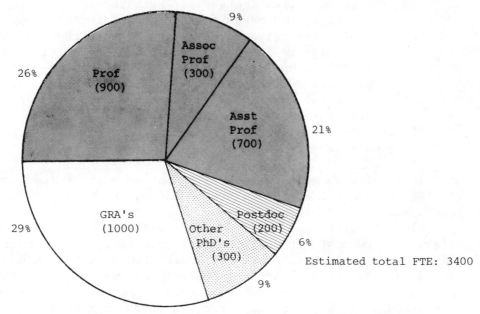

FIGURE 6.12 Distribution of estimated full-time equivalent research
personnel employed in academia in social sciences, 1979. FTE estimates are based on the average fraction of time each group devoted to
research activities. Estimates for major research universities
include those employed in medical schools and other branches of the
university which may not grant Ph.D. degrees. From National Research
Council, Survey of Doctorate Recipients and Survey of Earned Doctorates and National Science Foundation, Survey of Graduate Science
Student Support and Postdoctorals.

7. FINDINGS AND RECOMMENDATIONS

Summary of Findings

Postdoctorals continue to play an important role in the nation's research enterprise. At the same time the postdoctoral appointment has proven to be an invaluable mechanism for strengthening and confirming the research potential of a young investigator. Nevertheless, some serious concerns have arisen regarding the present and future role of postdoctorals in the research community, and it is these concerns that we address in this chapter:

(1) the lack of prestige and research independence in postdoctoral appointments for the most talented young people;
(2) the mismatch between the important role that postdoctorals play in the nation's research enterprise and the lack of opportunities that they find for subsequent career opportunities in research;
(3) the lack of recognized status of postdoctoral appointments in the academic community; and
(4) the underutilization of women and members of minority groups in scientific research.

In this chapter we summarize our findings on each of these points. Findings on many other issues are contained in Chapters 3-6 of this report and are summarized in Figure 7.1.

(1) In all science and engineering fields except mathematics, relatively few postdoctorals, however promising, are given full independence to determine the basic directions of the research effort. Most depend for their stipend or salary, as well as their research support, on a particular research group or mentor and have only as much freedom in choosing the direction of their research as the group or mentor will give them. In the majority of cases the scope of the research is rather narrowly delineated by the mentor, although there are significant exceptions in certain fields and for certain mentors. There are also very few programs of postdoctoral support that offer attractive financial rewards or other distinquishing characteristics that would set them apart as prestigious and desirable for the most promising young investigators.

224

(2) Postdoctorals have played an increasingly important part in enhancing research productivity, particularly in the academic sector. In physics, chemistry, and the biosciences they constitute an estimated 16 percent, 22 percent, and 18 percent, respectively, of the full-time equivalent research personnel in Ph.D.-granting universities.[1] In other fields their numbers are smaller, but by no means insignificant. Because they bring with them fresh ideas and new techniques, their importance to research is even greater than the numbers suggest. From the survey data and comments we received from department chairmen and university deans, it is evident that a decline in the numbers or quality of postdoctoral investigators could seriously damage the research effort in those institutions.

Although there is no evidence of such a decline as yet, there is some cause for concern. In recent years many more young scientists have been taking postdoctoral appointments than will find careers in academic research. This shortage of career opportunities is due, in part, to a lack of growth in research support in recent years. The frustrations of those unable to obtain the faculty positions to which they had aspired are apparent in the commments we received from recent graduates.[2] While some industrial and government laboratories look for candidates with postdoctoral experience, most do not set a premium on it. Although the majority of the postdoctorals surveyed who had taken jobs outside the academic sector indicated that their postdoctoral experience had contributed to their professional advancement in some way,[3] a significant fraction (at least 15 percent in every field) had serious reservations about the value of this experience in helping them acquire their position in industry or government.[4]

What has developed is a holding pattern for a sizable number in the postdoctoral ranks. Fifteen percent or more of the FY1978 Ph.D. recipients surveyed indicated that they had taken postdoctoral appointments because they could not find other employment they desired.[5] Of the FY1972 graduates who had taken postdoctoral appointments, approximately one-third had prolonged their appointments for this same reason.[6] In the biosciences and physics, moreover, as many as one-fourth of the postdoctorals have continued their apprenticeships for longer than 3 years.

The demand for postdoctorals is determined primarily by the level of research activity in the universities. When there are few alternative employment opportunities, the demand can be met out of the available supply, even when postdoctoral stipends are low. This has been the situation in some fields during most of the 1970's. But the

---

[1] See Figures 6.3, 6.4, and 6.5 in Chapter 6.
[2] A summary of the comments received is given in Chapter 5.
[3] See Table 5.12 in Chapter 5.
[4] See Table 5.11 in Chapter 5.
[5] See Table 4.1 in Chapter 4.
[6] See Table 4.5 in Chapter 4.

low stipends and the lack of long-term career opportunities requiring
postdoctoral experience make for a fragile balance between supply and
demand. Should more permanent employment opportunities open up, the
postdoctoral holding pattern would disappear, and the supply of
postdoctoral investigators would become inadequate for the demand,
with troubling consequences for the vitality of research. In some
fields this imbalance could be further exacerbated by a decline in the
number of graduate students completing the work for the doctorate.
Thus in chemistry, physics, and engineering, a decrease during the
past decade in doctoral candidates and an increase in opportunities outside academia[7] have resulted in a decline in the total
numbers seeking postdoctoral positions and a perceived shortage of
postdoctorals in relation to research needs. Without the influx of
foreign postdoctorals this shortage would be even greater.[8]

(3) We have found a lack of concern on the part of most universities for the well-being of their postdoctorals as an identifiable
group. It is unfortunate that most universities have extended the
tradition of "hands off" in the principal investigator's conduct of
research projects to a passive disregard for the postdoctoral
population. While this lack of concern has had a justifiable basis,
it is time for universities to pay more attention to this group,
particularly in view of the large population of individuals involved
in postdoctoral apprenticeships and the increasing portions of their
lives spent in this phase of their careers. Few universities assume
any responsibility for shaping or even monitoring the character of the
postdoctoral experience or for ensuring its quality. This is in sharp
contrast to the attitude toward undergraduate and graduate students.
In many large departments we visited no one even knew the number of
postdoctorals present. The terms and conditions of postdoctoral
appointments in universities are set almost entirely by individual
senior investigators and by outside funding sources. Much more
unified administration of postdoctoral programs was found in federally
funded research and development centers and other government
laboratories.

Whether they had taken postdoctoral appointments by choice or as
a last resort, whether they considered the experience valuable or not,
a significant fraction--in some fields a majority--of postdoctorals
deplore many of the conditions of their appointments. Stipends are a
particularly troublesome aspect. In 1979 the median 12-month stipend
paid to postdoctorals at academic institutions who had received their
doctorates the previous year fell short by $8,000 (more than 40
percent) of the salary of other graduates in their cohort who held

[7]These trends are discussed at some length in Chapter 3.
[8]The importance of foreign postdoctorals' contribution to the
research effort in U.S. universities is discussed in Chapter 6.

faculty positions.[9] The disparity between postdoctoral stipends and
industrial salaries was even greater.

It should be remembered that the scientist who takes a postdoctoral appointment for 2 years before seeking a permanent position is
likely to be more than 30 years old before he or she begins to earn an
income befitting his or her ability or training. Moreover, postdoctoral experience is found to contribute little or nothing in terms of
subsequent income. In many fields the income of those who have held
postdoctoral appointments continues to lag behind the income of those
who have not.[10] At a time when the difficulty of getting established in an academic career is already a deterrent to many prospec-
tive scholars, the lack of freedom and meager income of the postdoctoral is a further deterrent to taking a postdoctoral appointment.

(4) The committee found no difference in the way women and men
approach postdoctoral education. Women and men Ph.D. recipients are
equally likely to take postdoctoral appointments, give the same
reasons for doing so, hold appointments for roughly the same length of
time, and express the same opinion of the value of their postdoctoral
experience in contributing to their professional advancement and
helping them to find subsequent employment.[11] The difference is in
their progress afterwards. Women postdoctorals are more likely than
their male counterparts to pursue academic careers, but the men
entering academic employment are more likely to get faculty appointments and are more quickly given tenure. Women with postdoctoral
experience are paid less than their male counterparts in all fields,
whether employed in academia or elsewhere. It is clear that for a
variety of reasons many women scientists with postdoctoral experience
are being sidetracked to positions in which they are unable to use
their skills to the fullest.

The proportion of minority graduates taking postdoctoral appointments is significantly smaller than the proportion of other Ph.D.
recipients.[12] Both the discouragingly low level of postdoctoral
stipends and the availability of other higher-paying and more
promising career opportunities are absolute deterrents to many
minority students considering postdoctoral appointments. The fact
that few minority students pursue postdoctoral education reduces the
number developing their creative skills to the fullest, and the number
competing for the most challenging research positions in the universities and elsewhere. Efforts like the Postdoctoral Fellowship Program
for Minorities, which has been recently established by the Ford
Foundation, are needed to encourage more minority Ph.D. recipients to
engage in advanced training in research.

---

[9]See Table 5.3 in Chapter 5.
[10]See Table 4.4 and Table 4.9 in Chapter 4.
[11]See Tables 5.6, 5.8, and 5.9 and Figure 5.4 in Chapter 5.
[12]See Table 5.5 in Chapter 5.

Important Differences Among Fields

Early in this study the committee recognized important distinctions in the traditional roles of postdoctoral education in the various fields of science and engineering. Perhaps the most obvious of these lies in the reported shortage of candidates for engineering faculty openings, on the one hand, and the overall decline in new faculty hires in most science fields, on the other. In the course of our study we have examined a variety of factors and found major differences between sciences and engineering, as well as among the individual science disciplines. A detailed elucidation and interpretation of the differences among fields are presented in Chapters 3-6 of this report, but Figure 7.1 highlights a few of these. For example, a large majority of doctorate recipients planning careers in academic research in physics, chemistry, and the biosciences are expected to have held one or more postdoctoral appointments, while in other areas a much smaller fraction are expected to take such appointments. The committee found significant differences, as well, in the average length of postdoctoral tenure in each field and in the types of career opportunities available. Also noted were considerable variations in the postdoctoral stipend levels and sources of support, the postdoctoral fraction of all academic research personnel, and the foreign participation in postdoctoral appointments in U.S. universities. The variations in each of these factors are represented in Figure 7.1.

Recommendations

NATIONAL POSTDOCTORAL FELLOWSHIPS. One of the primary concerns of our committee is whether the most talented doctoral scientists and engineers are identified and induced to enter careers in research. The postdoctoral fellowship that provides the awardee with an opportunity to carry out his or her own research program under a chosen mentor remains a most effective mechanism for accomplishing these goals. However, during the past decade the postdoctoral appointment has been increasingly used to provide temporary support for those unable to obtain faculty and other research positions--to the point that such appointments no longer serve as an effective means for identifying the most talented investigators nor do they provide the postdoctorals with the independence necessary for them to develop their research potential fully. We believe that the concept of the original fellowship program[13] of the National Research Council remains valid, but existing federal fellowship programs fall short of meeting these goals. We therefore recommend the reestablishment of a

[13]A description of this program may be found in Chapter 2 and in National Research Council (1969), pp. 16-21.

FIGURE 7.1 Highlights of Committee Findings in Each Field

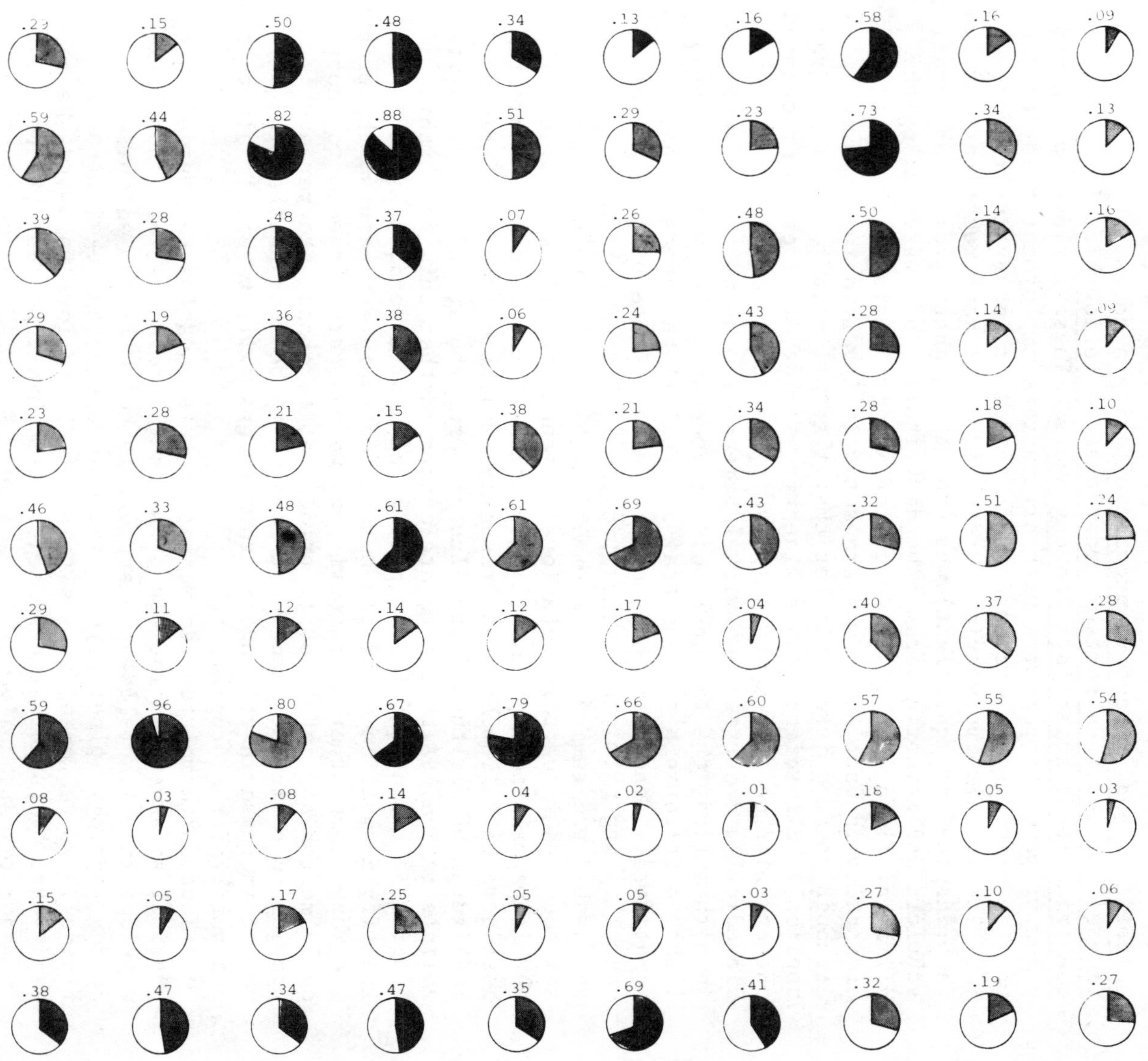

	All Fields	Math Sci	Physics	Chem	Earth Sci	Engin	Agric Sci	Biosci	Psych	Soc Sci
(1) Proportion of recent Ph.D. recipients taking postdoctoral appointments (Ch. IV)	.29	.15	.50	.48	.34	.13	.16	.58	.16	.09
(2) Proportion of assistant professors recently hired in major research universities who had held postdoctoral appointments (Ch. IV)	.59	.44	.82	.88	.51	.29	.23	.73	.34	.13
(3) Proportion of postdoctorals holding appointments longer than two years (Ch. IV)	.39	.28	.48	.37	.07	.26	.48	.50	.14	.16
(4) Proportion of postdoctorals prolonging appointment because job not available (Ch. IV)	.29	.19	.36	.38	.06	.24	.43	.28	.14	.09
(5) Proportion of former postdoctorals employed in major research universities (Ch. IV)	.23	.28	.21	.15	.38	.21	.34	.28	.18	.10
(6) Proportion of Ph.D. labor force employed outside academia (Ch. III)	.46	.33	.48	.61	.61	.69	.43	.32	.51	.24
(7) Proportion of postdoctorals supported by federal fellowships/ traineeships (Ch. V)	.29	.11	.12	.14	.12	.17	.04	.40	.37	.28
(8) Average annual postdoctoral stipend as proportion of salaries of other academic staff in cohort (Ch. V)	.59	.96	.80	.67	.79	.66	.60	.57	.55	.54
(9) Postdoctoral proportion of total research personnel in major research universities (Ch. VI)	.08	.03	.08	.14	.04	.02	.01	.16	.05	.03
(10) Postdoctoral proportion of FTE research personnel in major research universities (Ch. VI)	.15	.05	.17	.25	.05	.05	.03	.27	.10	.06
(11) Proportion of postdoctorals in U.S. universities who are foreign citizens (Ch. VI)	.38	.47	.34	.47	.35	.69	.41	.32	.19	.27

229

<u>competitive and attractive program offering a modest number of</u>
<u>federally supported, portable postdoctoral fellowships for specially</u>
<u>qualified young scientists and engineers.</u> These fellowships should
offer stipends competitive with alternative employment salaries and
provide some research expense funds to foster innovative research.

The fellowships should be reserved for recent recipients of the
Ph.D. degree (or equivalent) who show the highest promise as creative
scholars and investigators. The distribution of awards among the
different fields should be determined on the basis of the total number
of faculty in each field who are actively involved in research.
Although the committee believes that the rationale for this program
applies to all science and engineering fields, it does not recommend
the establishment of a new fellowship program in mathematics or in
biomedical and certain behavioral science fields at the present time.
In mathematics, the National Science Foundation has recently established a fellowship program that may fulfill the needs we have
identified. Consideration should be given to the possibility of
consolidating this mathematics program with the postdoctoral
fellowship program we are recommending here. In the biomedical
sciences and in certain behavioral science disciplines (e.g.,
physiological and experimental psychology), large-scale support of
postdoctoral fellowships is presently available from the National
Institutes of Health and the Alcohol, Drug Abuse, and Mental Health
Administration. Although we are concerned that this fellowship
program,[14] because of its magnitude and low stipend, does not
identify a small cadre of the most talented investigators, the program
does have some other characteristics we advocate--freedom to choose
one's mentor and, at least in principle, to choose the research
problem to be investigated. It remains to be seen whether the very
recent increase in stipends in this program will favorably alter the
character of the program.

Thus our committee recommends that fellowships be awarded in the
physical sciences, engineering, the social sciences, and those life
sciences in which fellowship support is not already adequate (e.g.,
botany, zoology, plant physiology, entomology, and agricultural
fields). We recommend that a total of 250 fellowship awards be made
each year. This number represents less than 1 percent of the faculty
in major research universities and only 2 percent of the doctoral
cohort graduating in these fields.

---

[14]The fellowship program was established by the National Research
Service Award Act in 1974. Under the act another committee of the
National Research Council has been mandated to investigate the needs
for research personnel in the biomedical and behavioral sciences and
make recommendations regarding federal predoctoral and postdoctoral
support. For this committee's most recent recommendations, see
National Research Council (1980), Chapter 1.

The stipends accompanying these awards should be comparable (on a 12-month basis) to the average starting salary paid to an assistant professor in the same field. Thus the annual stipend in 1980-81 should range, depending on the field, between $21,000 and $24,000--roughly 50 percent higher than mean stipends for postdoctorals now.

In order to stimulate these creative young scientists and engineers to initiate their own programs of research, the committee further recommends that some nominal funding for research expenses (including institutional costs) be made available and distributed according to need. Typical seed grants accompanying these fellowships might range between some stated minimum (perhaps $3,000) and maximum amounts (perhaps $20,000).

The committee recommends that the fellowships be tenable at institutions of the recipients' own choosing. Appointments might be held at universities in the United States or abroad, at nonprofit institutions or government laboratories, or at laboratories in the private sector. Candidates should be required to provide study plans that would be evaluated strictly on their own merit. The fellowships should generally carry an award for no more than 2 years, with renewal for a third year permitted only if warranted by special circumstances.

While the program we recommend provides several innovative features (i.e., higher stipends and some research support), it must be emphasized that the program is expected to cost less than $18 million per year to implement--a small price to pay for ensuring excellence of research. Of this sum, approximately one-third which is designated for research expenses might be provided from existing research budgets. The remaining $12 million for stipends should come from new appropriations.

POSTDOCTORAL FELLOWSHIPS FOR MINORITY SCIENTISTS AND ENGINEERS. While recognizing that there may be some difficulty in identifying individuals who belong to underrepresented minority groups, the committee believes that it is important to stimulate more young minority scientists and engineers to pursue careers in academic research. The committee recommends that a similar program of 50 postdoctoral fellowships a year be established expressly for minority Ph.D. recipients to encourage a larger number of those belonging to underrepresented minority groups to pursue postdoctoral training. These fellowships should be awarded without regard to faculty or student numbers in all areas of science and engineering--including mathematics and the biomedical fields as well as the physical sciences, engineering, the behavioral sciences, and other life sciences. The number of awards in each field should depend on the quality of the candidates. Otherwise this program should exactly resemble the program previously described. A minority scientist or engineer should be permitted to compete for either program or both.

It is anticipated that these 50 additional awards, along with a small number of minority fellowships supported by the Ford Founda-

tion,[15] will bring the fraction of minority Ph.D. recipients taking
postdoctoral appointments approximately in line with that for other
graduates. Furthermore, our committee is hopeful that other programs
designed to attract minority students into science and engineering
fields at earlier stages of education will substantially increase the
numbers of minority Ph.D. recipients. If this occurs, the number of
postdoctoral fellowships offered should be adjusted accordingly.

UNIVERSITIES' RESPONSIBILITY FOR POSTDOCTORALS AND DOCTORAL RESEARCH
STAFF. University administrators and faculty mentors must take full
responsibility for the character and quality of postdoctoral experience. They view the quality of their graduate and undergraduate
educational programs to be of prime importance. They regard the
quality and effectiveness of their faculties and research programs in
a similar light. Yet often they pay little attention to the role of
their institution in postdoctoral education. In spite of the large
contributions of postdoctorals to research, on many campuses they are
not fully members of the academic community. Many among this group
will be the future leaders of academic science. The fact that
postdoctorals usually do not take courses for credit, receive no
degrees, and do not pay tuition does not imply that universities
should ignore them. Our committee found much concern on the part of
both faculty and postdoctorals regarding the lack of status and
privileges afforded to postdoctoral appointees and other nonfaculty
doctoral research staff in universities.

We recommend that every university with sizable numbers of
nonfaculty research personnel establish a standing committee on
postdoctorals and other nonfaculty doctoral research staff. This
committee should review the situations of postdoctorals and other
nonfaculty research personnel on its campus and recommend university
policies regarding these groups. Among its primary concerns should be
the conditions of their appointments--including the minimum stipend or
salary levels, duration of appointments, status within the university
commmunity, availability of career counseling, and subsequent employment of those completing appointments. In departments in which there
are all too few faculty openings, serious consideration must be given
to developing a viable, alternative career track for talented young
young investigators.[16] To accomplish this goal may require a
reassessment of existing university personnel systems.

---

[15]A total of 35 fellowship awards were made this past spring. The
majority of those were in the humanities and social science fields.
[16]In an earlier report our committee examined several different approaches universities have taken to provide career opportunities for
nonfaculty staff. See National Research Council (1978).

The standing committee should also compile basic information that might be used in the formulation of university policy regarding postdoctoral and other research staff appointments. It is anticipated that the standing committees of different institutions will compare policy procedures and that out of such interactions will come a more active regard for postdoctorals and other doctoral research personnel in universities in the country.

MONITORING THE CAREER PATTERNS OF YOUNG INVESTIGATORS. The report of our committee follows more than 10 years after the last major study[17] of postdoctorals in science and engineering. If there is one lesson to be learned from our efforts, it is that many changes have occurred during the past decade, and that the entire postdoctoral institution is in a state of transition. Perhaps the most conspicuous changes have involved the size of the postdoctoral population and the role its members play in research. In our study we have collected volumes of original data that served as the basis for the committee's recommendations. Nevertheless, many uncertainties remain about the future role of young investigators. For instance, what impact will the expected decline in faculty hiring have on the numbers and caliber of students pursuing careers in science? To what extent will new federal programs influence the availability of academic research positions for those completing postdoctoral training? Will the trend to careers outside the academic sector accelerate, and if so, what impact will it have on academic research? How will the continuing boom in the electronics industry and the anticipated expansion in research in the areas of energy, defense, and genetic engineering, for example, influence the education and employment opportunities for young scientists and engineers?

These and many other questions cannot be answered with any certainty on the basis of past experience. During the next two decades we can expect many surprises as the scientific community adjusts to a rapidly changing milieu in universities and research institutions outside the academic sector. A continual monitoring of the entire research enterprise, but especially of the fragile postdoctoral component, is required to ensure that federal and university administrators have adequate information on which to base their policy decisions. At the present time the National Science Foundation sponsors several data collection activities that provide relevant information on research funding, graduate enrollments, doctoral awards, and science and engineering employment. Missing, however, is detailed information on the different career paths open to young investigators and the factors that influence their career choices.

---

[17]The last major report on postdoctoral education in the United States, entitled The Invisible University, was published by the National Research Council in 1969.

Monitoring the career patterns of postdoctorals and other young scientists and engineers is essential in order to keep abreast of quantitative and qualitative changes in the research workforce. Accordingly, we recommend that the National Science Foundation expand its longitudinal data-gathering activities to include a survey which specifically focusses on career decisions of young scientists and engineers, and publish a biennial series of reports that deal with the changing career patterns and utilization of postdoctorals and other groups of young investigators.

The availability of detailed, longitudinal data on the early careers of scientists and engineers would be valuable, in particular, to studies concerned with the utilization of women. As shown in Chapter 5, we have found women with postdoctoral experience to lag far behind their male colleagues--in terms of both salary level and faculty status. Information on the career choices of young women and men should help us understand the factors contributing to these differences and the extent to which these differences may or may not be narrowing. The survey recommended here would also provide much-needed information on issues pertaining to nonfaculty doctoral research staff positions in universities. In an earlier report[18] our committee examined the characteristics and employment situations of scientists and engineers holding such positions. We concluded that this is an important and rapidly expanding group within the academic research community. Whether or not nonfaculty academic research positions will present a viable career option for talented young scientists unable to secure faculty appointments will depend on the availability of research support and on the universities' recognition of those holding such positions.

In the preceding chapters findings are presented coveriing a broad range of issues concerned with the importance of postdoctorals to the research effort and with the utility of postdoctoral experience to the young scientist or engineer pursuing a career in research. From the findings of this study it is clear that the purpose and meaning of postdoctoral education has changed significantly during the past decade. Beyond the specific recommendations given above, the committee believes that the entire postdoctoral institution must regularly be reexamined by federal and university policymakers alike. We trust that this report will prove to be a primary resource to policymakers examining the role their university or agency plays in postdoctoral education.

References

National Research Council. The Invisible University. Washington, D.C.: National Academy of Sciences, 1969.

---

[18]National Research Council (1978).

_____. Nonfaculty Doctoral Research Staff in Science and Engineering in the United States. Washington, D.C.: National Academy of Sciences, 1978.

_____. Personnel Needs and Training for Biomedical and Behavioral Research. Washington, D.C.: National Academy of Sciences, 1980.

APPENDIXES

LETTER TO UNIVERSITY DEANS AND DEPARTMENT CHAIRMEN

NATIONAL RESEARCH COUNCIL
COMMISSION ON HUMAN RESOURCES

2101 Constitution Avenue   Washington, D. C. 20418

COMMITTEE ON THE STUDY OF   December 16, 1977
POSTDOCTORALS AND DOCTORAL RESEARCH STAFF

Dear

The National Research Council has appointed a committee to study the
policy implications of the changing role of postdoctorals and doctoral
research staff in higher education and research in the United States.
During the last decade, in the face of reduced numbers of faculty openings,
there has been a marked increase in the number of younger scholars taking
temporary postdoctoral appointments. There also appears to have been an
increase in the number of individuals holding nonfaculty research appointments on a continuing basis. We believe that the enlarged role of nonfaculty
research appointments in the universities needs to be assessed in the light
of perceived benefits and needs.

As a first step in the study, we are writing to a number of people in
different institutions and fields who we believe can help us put the situation in perspective. A list of some questions that particularly interest us
is enclosed. We would be grateful for your comments on two or three of the
questions in this list which you consider to be the most important issues
facing the postdoctoral and doctoral research staff at your institution.
Our working definitions of "postdoctoral" and of "doctoral research staff"
are given on an attached sheet.

We are wary of our own preconception; your views, with those of others,
will be important to us in shaping the study. We are especially concerned
to identify issues that bear on institutional and national policy or on professional practice. If there are other questions you think we should consider,
we would appreciate your suggestions. Please also send us any document your
institution may have prepared which bears on the subject. Individual comments
will not be identified in the Committee report.

We will greatly appreciate an early reply.

Sincerely yours,

Lee Grodzins, Chairman
Committee on Postdoctorals
   and Doctoral Research Staff

*The National Research Council is the principal operating agency of the National Academy of Sciences and the National Academy of Engineering
to serve government and other organizations*

QUESTIONS BEING CONSIDERED BY THE COMMITTEE
ON POSTDOCTORALS AND DOCTORAL RESEARCH STAFF

(1) What is the contribution of postdoctorals and of doctoral research
     staff, respectively, to the research effort of their host departments
     and laboratories? What would be the effect of a significant change
     in their number or quality?

(2) What is the influence of postdoctorals and of doctoral research staff
     on undergraduate and graduate education?

(3) From the point of view of the individual scholar, has there been any
     change in the desirability of taking a postdoctoral appointment, of
     taking a doctoral research staff position? How long should an indi-
     vidual hold these appointments?

(4) Are host institutions giving sufficient attention to their responsi-
     bilities towards postdoctorals, towards doctoral research staff? Are
     new, perhaps more formal, arrangements needed to make the most of their
     presence--for the benefit of the individuals themselves, their host
     departments and institutions, or the nation's research effort?

(5) Can a postdoctoral appointment which is supported with research funds
     serve the scholarly needs of the holder as effectively as an appointment
     (e.g., a fellowship or traineeship) which is expressly funded to support
     postdoctoral study? Is there an optimum mix of funding mechanisms?

(6) What view should one take of foreign postdoctorals? Are there too many
     of them or too few? How many take permanent positions in this country
     following their postdoctoral work?

(7) Have postdoctoral appointments helped minorities and women to fulfill
     their promise as research scholars?

(8) Is time spent as a postdoctoral an asset or a liability to a young
     scientist who will be making his career in industry or a government
     laboratory?

241

RECIPIENTS OF THE LETTER TO UNIVERSITIES

UNIVERSITY OF ARIZONA

 Graduate School (Dean)

 Department of Chemistry (Chairman)

 Department of Optical Sciences (Chairman)

 Department of Geosciences (Chairman)

 Department of Plant Sciences (Chairman)

BRANDEIS UNIVERSITY

 Graduate School (Dean)

 Department of Chemistry (Chairman)

 Department of Biochemistry (Chairman)

 Institute for Photobiology of Cells and Organelles (Chairman)

 Department of Sociology (Chairman)

BROWN UNIVERSITY

 Graduate School (Dean)

 Department of Engineering (Chairman)

 Department of Chemistry (Chairman)

 Department of Physics (Chairman)

 Department of Biological and Medical Science (Dean)

UNIVERSITY OF CALIFORNIA - BERKELEY

 Graduate School (Dean)

 Department of Electrical Engineering and Computer Science (Chairman)

 Department of Materials Science and Engineering (Chairman)

 Department of Chemistry (Dean)

 Department of Physics (Chairman)

 Department of Statistics (Chairman)

 Department of Physiology and Anatomy (Chairman)

 Department of Anthropology (Chairperson)

 Department of Sociology (Chairman)

UNIVERSITY OF CALIFORNIA - LOS ANGELES

Graduate School (Dean)

Department of Chemistry (Chairman)

Department of Physics (Chairman)

Department of Geology (Chairman)

Department of Geochemistry (Chairman)

Department of Economics (Chairman)

School of Medicine (Dean)

Department of Microbiology and Immunology (Chairman)

UNIVERSITY OF CALIFORNIA - SAN DIEGO

Office of Graduate Studies (Dean)

Department of Chemistry (Chairman)

Department of Biology (Chairman)

Department of Psychology (Chairman)

UNIVERSITY OF CALIFORNIA - SAN FRANCISCO

School of Medicine (Dean)

Department of Biochemistry and Biophysics (Chairman)

Department of Microbiology (Chairman)

Department of Physiology (Chairman)

CALIFORNIA INSTITUTE OF TECHNOLOGY

Graduate School (Dean)

Department of Chemical Engineering (Chairman)

Department of Environmental Engineering Science (Chairman)

Department of Astronomy (Chairman)

Department of Chemistry (Chairman)

Department of Physics (Chairman)

Department of Geology (Chairman)

Department of Applied Mathematics (Chairman)

CARNEGIE-MELLON UNIVERSITY

Office of Graduate Studies (Dean)

Department of Chemical Engineering (Chairman)

Department of Physics (Chairman)

Department of Computer Science (Chairman)

UNIVERSITY OF CHICAGO

    Graduate School (Dean)

    Department of Chemistry (Chairman)

    Department of Physics (Chairman)

    Department of Geophysical Sciences (Chairman)

    Department of Biochemistry (Chairman)

    Department of Biophysics and Theoretical Biology (Chairman)

    Department of Pharmacological and Physiological Sciences (Chairman)

    Department of Economics (Chairman)

UNIVERSITY OF COLORADO

    Graduate School (Dean)

    Department of Physics and Astrophysics (Chairman)

    School of Medicine (Dean)

    Department of Biophysics and Genetics (Chairman)

    Department of Microbiology (Chairman)

    Department of Pharmacology (Chairman)

COLORADO STATE UNIVERSITY

    Graduate School (Dean)

    Department of Chemistry (Chairman)

    Department of Range Science (Chairman)

    Department of Radiology (Chairman)

    Department of Physiology and Biophysics (Chairman)

COLUMBIA UNIVERSITY

    Office of Graduate Faculties (Associate Dean)

    Department of Chemistry (Chairman)

    Department of Physics (Chairman)

    Department of Geological Sciences (Chairman)

    College of Physicians and Surgeons (Dean)

    Department of Pathology (Chairman)

CORNELL UNIVERSITY

    Graduate School (Dean)

    Department of Astronomy

CORNELL UNIVERSITY (continued)

      Department of Chemistry (Chairman)

      Department of Physics (Chairman)

      Department of Agronomy (Chairman)

      Department of Biochemistry (Chairman)

DUKE UNIVERSITY

      Graduate School (Vice Provost)

      Department of Zoology (Chairman)

      Department of Psychology (Chairman)

      School of Medicine (Dean)

      Department of Physiology and Pharmacology (Chairman)

GEORGETOWN UNIVERSITY

      Graduate School (Dean)

      Department of Chemistry (Chairman)

      School of Medicine (Associate Dean for Academic Affairs)

      Department of Physiology (Chairman)

GEORGE WASHINGTON UNIVERSITY

      Graduate School (Dean)

      Department of Civil and Environmental Engineering (Chairman)

      School of Medicine and Health Sciences (Vice President)

      Department of Child Health and Development (Chairman)

HARVARD UNIVERSITY

      Graduate School (Acting Dean)

      Department of Chemistry (Chairman)

      Department of Physics (Chairman)

      Department of Mathematics (Chairman)

      Department of Biology (Chairman)

      Department of Nutrition (Chairman)

      Department of Sociology (Chairman)

      School of Medicine (Dean)

      Department of Biological Chemistry (Chairman)

      Department of Neuropathology (Chairman)

UNIVERSITY OF ILLINOIS - URBANA

Graduate School (Dean)

Department of Civil Engineering (Chairman)

Department of Chemistry (Chairman)

Department of Physics (Chairman)

Department of Agronomy (Chairman)

INDIANA UNIVERSITY - BLOOMINGTON

Graduate School (Acting Dean)

Department of Chemistry (Chairman)

Department of Plant Science (Chairman)

Department of Zoology (Chairman)

JOHNS HOPKINS UNIVERSITY

Office of Graduate Studies (Dean)

Department of Chemistry (Chairman)

Department of Physics (Chairman)

Department of Biology (Chairman)

Department of Anthropology (Chairman)

Department of Social Relations (Chairman)

School of Medicine (Dean)

Department of Pharmacology and Experimental Therapeutics (Chairman)

UNIVERSITY OF MARYLAND - COLLEGE PARK

Graduate School (Dean)

Department of Physics and Astronomy (Chairman)

Department of Chemistry (Chairman)

UNIVERSITY OF MASSACHUSETTS - AMHERST

Graduate School (Acting Dean)

Department of Polymer Science and Engineering (Chairman)

Department of Chemistry (Chairman)

Department of Physics (Chairman)

Department of Computer and Information Science (Chairman)

MASSACHUSETTS INSTITUTE OF TECHNOLOGY

Graduate School (Dean)

Department of Electrical Engineering and Computer Science (Chairman)

Department of Chemistry (Chairman)

Department of Earth and Planetary Science (Chairman)

Department of Mathematics (Chairman)

Department of Nutrition and Food Science (Chairman)

Department of Psychology (Chairman)

Department of Linguistics (Chairman)

UNIVERSITY OF MICHIGAN

Rackham School of Graduate Studies (Dean)

Department of Chemistry (Chairman)

Department of Physics (Chairman)

Medical School (Dean)

Department of Biological Chemistry (Chairman)

Department of Human Genetics (Chairman)

MICHIGAN STATE UNIVERSITY

Graduate School (Dean)

Department of Chemistry (Chairman)

Department of Physics (Chairman)

Department of Crop and Soil Science (Chairman)

Department of Biochemistry (Chairman)

Department of Microbiology (Chairman)

UNIVERSITY OF MINNESOTA

Graduate School (Dean)

Department of Mechanical Engineering (Chairman)

Department of Chemistry (Chairman)

Department of Physics (Chairman)

Department of Biochemistry (Chairman)

Department of Psychology (Chairman)

Minneapolis Medical School (Dean)

Department of Microbiology (Chairman)

NEW YORK UNIVERSITY

    Graduate School (Dean)

    Department of Chemistry (Chairman)

    Department of Physics (Chairman)

    Department of Mathematics (Chairman)

    School of Medicine (Chairman)

    Department of Pathology (Chairman)

UNIVERSITY OF NORTH CAROLINA - CHAPEL HILL

    Graduate School (Dean)

    Department of Chemistry (Chairman)

    Department of Physics (Chairman)

    Department of Biostatistics (Chairman)

NORTHWESTERN UNIVERSITY

    Graduate School (Dean)

    Department of Materials Science (Chairman)

    Department of Biological Sciences (Chairman)

    Department of Psychology (Chairman)

OHIO STATE UNIVERSITY

    Graduate School (Dean)

    Department of Metallurgical Engineering (Chairman)

    Department of Chemistry (Chairman)

    Department of Physics (Chairman)

UNIVERSITY OF PITTSBURGH

    Graduate School (Dean)

    Department of Chemistry (Chairman)

    Department of Physics and Astronomy (Chairman)

    Department of Computer Science (Chairman)

    Department of Life Sciences (Chairman)

PRINCETON UNIVERSITY

    Graduate School (Dean)

    Department of Aerospace and Mechanical Engineering (Chairman)

PRINCETON UNIVERSITY (continued)

    Department of Chemistry (Chairman)

    Department of Physics (Chairman)

    Department of Mathematics (Chairman)

    Department of Psychology (Chairman)

    Department of Economics (Chairman)

    Department of Sociology (Chairman)

PURDUE UNIVERSITY

    Graduate School (Dean)

    Department of Chemical Engineering (Chairman)

    Department of Chemistry (Chairman)

    Department of Physics (Chairman)

    Department of Biochemistry (Chairman)

    Department of Biological Sciences (Chairman)

RICE UNIVERSITY

    Graduate School (Dean)

    Department of Chemical Engineering (Chairman)

    Department of Chemistry (Chairman)

    Department of Space Physics and Astronomy (Chairman)

UNIVERSITY OF ROCHESTER

    Office of Graduate Studies (Dean)

    Department of Chemistry (Chairman)

    Department of Physics and Astronomy (Chairman)

    Department of Psychology (Chairman)

    School of Medicine (Chairman)

    Department of Radiation Biology and Biophysics (Chairman)

ROCKEFELLER UNIVERSITY

    Graduate School (Dean)

    Department of Cellular Biology (Chairman)

    Department of Physiological Psychology (Chairman)

    Department of Experimental Psychology (Chairman)

STANFORD UNIVERSITY

Graduate School (Dean)

Department of Electrical Engineering (Chairman)

Department of Chemistry (Chairman)

Department of Physics (Chairman)

Department of Computer Science (Chairman)

Department of Biological Sciences (Chairman)

Department of Sociology (Chairman)

School of Medicine (Dean)

Department of Biochemistry (Chairman)

Department of Genetics (Chairman)

Department of Pathology (Chairman)

UNIVERSITY OF SOUTHERN CALIFORNIA

Graduate School (Dean)

Department of Electrical Engineering (Chairman)

Department of Chemistry (Chairman)

SUNY - COLLEGE OF ENVIRONMENTAL SCIENCE AND FORESTRY

Office of Academic Affairs (Dean)

Department of Paper Science and Engineering (Chairman)

Department of Managerial Science and Policy (Chairman)

Department of Chemistry (Chairman)

TEXAS A&M UNIVERSITY

Graduate School (Dean)

Department of Chemistry (Chairman)

Department of Oceanography (Chairman)

Department of Entomology (Chairman)

UNIVERSITY OF TEXAS - AUSTIN

Graduate School (Dean)

Department of Astronomy (Chairman)

Department of Chemistry (Chairman)

Department of Physics (Chairman)

Department of Zoology (Chairman)

UNIVERSITY OF UTAH

  Graduate School (Dean)

  Department of Chemistry (Chairman)

  Department of Physics (Chairman)

  Department of Biology (Chairman)

  College of Medicine (Chairman)

  Department of Biochemistry (Chairman)

WASHINGTON UNIVERSITY

  School of Medicine (Dean)

  Department of Anatomy and Neurobiology (Chairman)

  Department of Biochemistry (Chairman)

  Department of Microbiology and Immunology (Chairman)

  Department of Pathology (Chairman)

UNIVERSITY OF WASHINGTON

  Graduate School (Dean)

  Department of Chemistry (Chairman)

  Department of Physics (Chairman)

  Department of Mathematics (Chairman)

  Department of Forest Resources (Chairman)

  Department of Zoology (Chairman)

  Department of Speech and Hearing Science (Chairman)

  School of Medicine (Dean)

  Department of Bioengineering (Chairman)

  Department of Biochemistry (Chairman)

  Department of Genetics (Chairman)

UNIVERSITY OF WISCONSIN - MADISON

  Graduate School (Dean)

  Department of Chemistry (Chairman)

  Department of Physics (Chairman)

  Department of Meat and Animal Science (Chairman)

  Department of Biochemistry (Chairman)

  Department of Entomology (Chairman)

UNIVERSITY OF WISCONSIN - MADISON (continued)

Medical School (Dean)

Department of Physiological Chemistry (Chairman)

Laboratory of Genetics (Chairman)

YALE UNIVERSITY

Graduate School (Dean)

Department of Engineering and Applied Science (Chairman)

Department of Chemistry (Chairman)

Department of Physics (Chairman)

Department of Economics (Chairman)

School of Medicine (Dean)

Department of Molecular Biophysics and Biochemistry (Chairman)

Department of Pharmacology (Chairman)

NATIONAL RESEARCH COUNCIL
COMMISSION ON HUMAN RESOURCES

2101 Constitution Avenue   Washington, D. C. 20418

COMMITTEE ON THE STUDY OF
POSTDOCTORALS AND DOCTORAL RESEARCH STAFF

February 21, 1978

Lee Grodzins, *Chairman*
Massachusetts Institute of
Technology

Richard D. Anderson
Louisiana State University

Frederick E. Balderston
University of California
Berkeley, California

Kenneth E. Clark
University of Rochester

Gerhart Friedlander
Brookhaven National Laboratory

Herbert Friedman
Naval Research Laboratory

John C. Hancock
Purdue University

Henry A. Hill
Riverside Research Laboratory,
Inc.

Donald F. Hornig
Harvard School of Public Health

Shirley Ann Jackson
Bell Laboratories

Ernest S. Kuh
University of California
Berkeley, California

William F. Miller
Stanford University

Nicholas C. Mullins
Indiana University

Thomas A. Reichert
Carnegie-Mellon University

Helen R. Whiteley
University of Washington

The National Research Council has appointed a committee to study the policy implications of the changing role of postdoctorals and doctoral research staff in higher education and research in the United States. The study is funded by the National Science Foundation and the National Aeronautics and Space Administration. During the last decade, in the face of reduced numbers of faculty openings, there has been a marked increase in the number of younger scholars taking temporary postdoctoral appointments. There also appears to have been an increase in the number of individuals holding nonfaculty research appointments on a continuing basis. We believe that the enlarged role of nonfaculty research appointments in the universities needs to be assessed in the light of perceived benefits and needs.

As a first step in the study, we are writing to a number of people in different institutions and fields who we believe can help us put the situation in perspective. A list of some questions that particularly interest us is enclosed. We would be grateful for your comments on two or three of the questions in this list which you consider to be the most important issues facing the postdoctoral and doctoral research staff at your institution. Our working definitions of "postdoctoral" and of "doctoral research staff" are given on an attached sheet.

We are wary of our own preconceptions; your views, with those of others, will be important to us in shaping the study. We are especially concerned to identify issues that bear on institutional and national policy or on professional practice. If there are other questions you think we should consider, we would appreciate your suggestions. Please also send us any document your institution may have prepared which bears on the subject. Individual comments will not be identified in the Committee report.

We will greatly appreciate an early reply.

Sincerely yours,

Lee Grodzins, Chairman

The National Research Council is the principal operating agency of the National Academy of Sciences and the National Academy of Engineering to serve government and other organizations

RECIPIENTS OF THE LETTER TO GOVERNMENT LABORATORIES

Dr. John C. Dusterberry
Research Assistant to the Director
Mail Stop 200-10
Ames Research Center
Moffett Field, CA 94035

Dr. Eldon E. Kordes
Dryden Flight Research Center
Edwards, CA 93523

Mr. George Abid
Assistant to the Director of Science
Code 600
Goddard Space Flight Center
Greenbelt, MD 20771

Dr. Robert Jastrow
Director, GISS
2880 Broadway
Goddard Institute for Space Studies
New York, NY 10025

Dr. James King
180-403
4800 Oak Grove Drive
Jet Propulsion Laboratory
Pasadena, CA 91103

Ms. Mary F. Cook
University Programs Coordinator
Bldg. 30, Room L214-A
Code BA-12
Johnson Space Center
Houston, TX 77058

Mr. John J. Cox, Head
Staffing & Special Programs Branch
Mail Stop 308
Langley Research Center
Hampton, VA 23365

Mr. Robert P. Allen
Chief, Manpower Programs
NASA - Lewis Research Center
21000 Brookpark Road
Cleveland, OH 44135

Dr. George C. Bucher
Deputy Associate Director for Science
DS30, Bldg. 4200
Marshall Space Flight Center
Huntsville, AL 35812

Mr. Philip F. Ryan
Employee Development Officer
NASA - Wallops Flight Center
Wallops Island, VA 23337

Dr. Richard Taschek,
Associate Director for Research
Los Alamos Scientific Laboratory
University of California
Los Alamos, New Mexico 87545

Dr. Andrew Sessler, Director
Lawrence Berkeley Laboratory
University of California
Berkeley, California 94720

Dr. Robert S. Hansen, Director
Ames Laboratory ERDA
Iowa State University of
   Science and Technology
Ames, Iowa 50010

Dr. Robert G. Sachs, Director
Argonne National Laboratory
University of Chicago and
   Argonne University Assn.
Argonne, Illinois 60439

Dr. Herman Postina, Director
Oak Ridge National Laboratories
Oak Ridge, Tennessee 37830

Dr. Gus Dorough, Associate Director
Lawrence Livermore Laboratory
Livermore, California 94550

QUESTIONS BEING CONSIDERED BY THE COMMITTEE
ON POSTDOCTORALS AND DOCTORAL RESEARCH STAFF

(1) What is the contribution of postdoctorals and of doctoral research
     staff, respectively, to the research effort of their host departments
     and laboratories? What would be the effect of a significant change
     in their number or quality?

(2) From the point of view of the individual scholar, has there been any
     change in the desirability of taking a postdoctoral appointment, of
     taking a doctoral research staff position? How long should an indi-
     vidual hold these appointments?

(3) Are host institutions giving sufficient attention to their responsi-
     bilities towards postdoctorals, towards doctoral research staff? Are
     new, perhaps more formal, arrangements needed to make the most of their
     presence--for the benefit of the individuals themselves, their host
     departments and institutions, or the nation's research effort?

(4) Can a postdoctoral appointment which is supported with research funds
     serve the scholarly needs of the holder as effectively as an appointment
     (e.g., a fellowship or traineeship) which is expressly funded to support
     postdoctoral study? Is there an optimum mix of funding mechanisms?

(5) What view should one take of foreign postdoctorals? Are there too many
     of them or too few? How many take permanent positions in this country
     following their postdoctoral work?

(6) Have postdoctoral appointments helped minorities and women to fulfill
     their promise as research scholars?

(7) Is time spent as a postdoctoral an asset or a liability to a young
     scientist who will be making his career in industry or a government
     laboratory?

LETTER TO INDUSTRIAL LABORATORY ADMINISTRATORS

NATIONAL RESEARCH COUNCIL
COMMISSION ON HUMAN RESOURCES

2101 Constitution Avenue   Washington, D. C. 20418

COMMITTEE ON THE STUDY OF
POSTDOCTORALS AND DOCTORAL RESEARCH STAFF

Lee Grodzins, *Chairman*
Massachusetts Institute of
Technology

Richard D. Anderson
Louisiana State University

Frederick E. Balderston
University of California
Berkeley, California

Kenneth E. Clark
University of Rochester

Gerhart Friedlander
Brookhaven National Laboratory

Herbert Friedman
Naval Research Laboratory

John C. Hancock
Purdue University

Henry A. Hill
Riverside Research Laboratory,
Inc.

Donald F. Hornig
Harvard School of Public Health

Shirley Ann Jackson
Bell Laboratories

Ernest S. Kuh
University of California
Berkeley, California

William F. Miller
Stanford University

Nicholas C. Mullins
Indiana University

Thomas A. Reichert
Carnegie-Mellon University

Helen R. Whiteley
University of Washington

Feburary 21, 1978

During the last decade an increasing number of young Ph.D.'s have been taking temporary postdoctoral appointments to continue their education and experience in research. Most of these appointments have been in the university setting, but some have been in government and industry laboratories. In the face of reduced faculty openings, there has also been an increase in the number of doctoral scientists and engineers taking nonfaculty research staff positions in the universities on a longer-term basis.

The National Research Council has appointed a committee to study the implications of these developments for the health of higher education and research. The study is funded by the National Science Foundation and the National Aeronautics and Space Administration. As a first step, we are writing to a number of people in the universities, government, and industry who we believe can help us put the situation in perspective.

We are particularly interested in the significance of these developments for industry. While a large proportion of Ph.D.'s are prolonging their research experience in academia, many will ultimately seek employment in industry. Indeed, because of the shortage of permanent jobs in academia, the number of Ph.D. scientists and engineers seeking jobs in industry is likely to grow. At the same time, the increasing complexity of industrial technology and the increasingly stringent demands placed on industry by customers, government, and society at large may be creating a new need in industry for Ph.D.'s with advanced training and a record of accomplishment.

A list of questions that concern us is enclosed. Also enclosed is our working definition of "postdoctoral" and of university-employed "doctoral research staff". We would be grateful for your response to the questions as they relate to your particular firm. We are wary of our own preconceptions, and if there are other questions you think we should consider, we would appreciate your comments. We are especially concerned to identify issues that call for action by the universities, by employers, or by interested agencies in government.

Page 2
February 21, 1978

    We will greatly appreciate an early reply. Respondents and their
organizations will not be identified in the Committee report.

                    Sincerely yours,

                    Lee Grodzins, Chairman

QUESTIONS BEING CONSIDERED BY THE COMMITTEE
ON POSTDOCTORALS AND DOCTORAL RESEARCH STAFF

1. What are the disciplines and specialties in which your firm hires Ph.D.'s?

2. Approximately what proportion of your recently hired Ph.D.'s (last two years) have had postdoctoral training in research?

3. For what activities (e.g., research, design, production engineering, etc.) does your firm hire Ph.D.'s? Are postdoctorals hired for the same activities as new Ph.D.'s?

4. In general, is time spent as a postdoctoral an asset or a liability to a young Ph.D. scientist or engineer who will be making his career in your firm? Are there situations in which your firm prefers postdoctorals (or others with extended research experience) to new Ph.D.'s?

5. Are former postdoctorals offered a higher starting salary than new Ph.D.'s? How do their salaries compare over the long run?

6. In some disciplines (notably engineering) a high proportion of new Ph.D.'s and postdoctorals are foreign, without permanent visas. To what extent is your firm interested in employing them? What are your views on the government regulations controlling their employment?

7. Some firms and government laboratories offer postdoctoral appointments resembling the postdoctoral appointments in the universities. Is your firm doing this, or thinking of doing it? If so, how large a program is involved?

RECIPIENTS OF THE LETTER TO INDUSTRIAL LABORATORIES

AIR PRODUCTS AND CHEMICALS, INC.
P.O. Box 538
Allentown, PA 18105

AVCO CORPORATION
1275 King Street
Greenwich, CT 06830

THE B. F. GOODRICH COMPANY
9921 Brecksville Road
Brecksville, OH 44141

BAXTER LABORATORIES, INC.
6301 Lincoln Avenue
Morton Grove, IL 60053

BECHTEL CORPORATION
50 Beale Street
San Francisco, CA 94105

BELL LABORATORIES
600 Mountain Avenue
Murray Hill, NJ 07974

THE COCA-COLA COMPANY
P. O. Drawer 1734
Atlanta, GA 30301

CONSOLIDATED EDISON COMPANY
    OF NEW YORK, INC.
4 Irving Place
New York, NY 10003

CONTROL DATA CORPORATION
4201 North Lexington Avenue
Arden Hills, MN 55112

DOW CHEMICAL U.S.A.
Barstow Building
2020 Dow Center
Midland, MI 48640

EASTMAN KODAK COMPANY
1669 Lake Avenue
Rochester, NY 14650

E. I. DU PONT DE NEMOURS &
    COMPANY, INC.
Experimental Station
Wilmington, DE 19898

EXXON CORPORATION
1251 Avenue of the Americas
New York, NY 10020

GENERAL ELECTRIC COMPANY
Schenectady, NY 12301

GENERAL FOODS CORPORATION
White Plains, NY 10602

GENERAL MOTORS CORPORATION
Warren, MI 48090

GULF SCIENCE AND TECHNOLOGY COMPANY
Gulf Building
Pittsburgh, PA 15230

HONEYWELL, INC.
2701 Fourth Avenue, South
Minneapolis, MN 55408

HUGHES RESEARCH LABORATORIES
3011 S. Malibu Canyon Road
Malibu, CA 94265

INTERNATIONAL BUSINESS MACHINES
    CORPORATION
P. O. Box 218
Yorktown Heights, NY 10598

KAISER ALUMINUM & CHEMICAL CORPORATION
300 Lakeside Drive
Oakland, CA 94643

ARTHUR D. LITTLE, INC.
Acorn Park
Cambridge, MA 02140

LOCKHEED AIRCRAFT CORPORATION
Burbank, CA 91520

MERCK & COMPANY, INC.
Rahway, NJ 07065

MINE SAFETY APPLIANCES COMPANY
201 North Braddock Avenue
Pittsburgh, PA 15208

THE PROCTER & GAMBLE COMPANY
Ivorydale Technical Center
Cincinnati, OH 45217

THE RAND CORPORATION
1700 Main Street
Santa Monica, CA 90406

ROCKWELL INTERNATIONAL
2230 East Imperial Highway
El Segundo, CA 90245

SHELL DEVELOPMENT COMPANY
One Shell Plaza
P. O. Box 2463
Houston, TX 77001

STANDARD OIL COMPANY OF AMERICA
225 Bush Street
San Francisco, CA 94104

3M COMPANY
3M Center
St. Paul, MN 55101

UNION CARBIDE CORPORATION
270 Park Avenue
New York, NY 10017

WESTINGHOUSE RESEARCH LABORATORIES
Beulch Road
Pittsburgh, PA 15235

WEYERHAEUSER COMPANY
Tacoma, WA 98401

XEROX CORPORATION
3180 Porter Drive
Palo Alto, CA 94305

APPENDIX B

UNIVERSITIES AND LABORATORIES VISITED BY COMMITTEE

BROOKHAVEN NATIONAL LABORATORY - March 5, 1980

 Scientific Personnel Office (Head/Assistant Director of Laboratory)

 Biology Department (Chairman)

 Biology Department (two research associates)

 Chemistry Department (Chairman)

 Chemistry Department (two research associates)

 Department of Energy and Environment (Chairman)

 Department of Energy and Environment (three research associates)

 Physics Department (Chairman and a senior staff member)

 Physics Department (two research associates)

NATIONAL INSTITUTE FOR ARTHRITIS - February 14, 1980

 Division of Molecular Biology (Section Head)

 Division of Molecular Biology (Senior Postdoctoral)

INSTITUTE FOR DEFENSE - February 14, 1980

 Personnel Office (Director)

 Science and Technology Division (two senior and two junior staff members)

 Systems Evaluation Division (two staff members)

EXXON RESEARCH AND ENGINEERING COMPANY - February 1, 1980

 Engineering Technology Department (General Manager)

MERCK, SHARP & DOME RESEARCH LABORATORIES - February 1, 1980

 Personnel Division (Director)

 Research Scientists (three staff members in organic chemistry, immunology, and biochemistry)

BELL LABORATORIES - January 31, 1980

 Basic Research Division (senior staff member)

 Chemical Physics Division (Director)

 Material Sciences Division (Director)

STANFORD UNIVERSITY   -   <u>March 13-14, 1978</u>

    Department of Computer Sciences (faculty and graduate students)

    Department of Electrical Engineering (one professor, one postdoc, two
       graduate students)

    Department of Sociology (faculty, five postdocs, four graduate students)

UNIVERSITY OF CALIFORNIA, DAVIS   -   <u>March 9, 1978</u>

    Department of Agricultural Engineering (faculty and graduate students)

    Graduate Division (Dean)

PURDUE UNIVERSITY   -   <u>March 2, 1978</u>

    Department of Biological Sciences (Chairman and faculty)

    Department of Biological Sciences (three graduate students and two
      postdocs)

    School of Chemical Engineering (Chairman and faculty)

    School of Chemical Engineering (two graduate students and two postdocs)

    Department of Chemistry (professor)

    Department of Chemistry (two postdocs and one graduate student)

UNIVERSITY OF WASHINGTON, SEATTLE   -   <u>February 27-28, 1978</u>

    Department of Bioengineering (two research assistant professors, three
      postdocs, and one graduate student)

    College of Forest Resources (Dean and faculty)

    College of Forest Resources (two research assistant professors and one
      research associate)

    Medical School (Associate Dean)

    Department of Oceanography (faculty)

    Department of Oceanography (five postdocs)

    Department of Physiology and Biophysics (faculty)

    Department of Physiology and Biophysics (four graduate students, three
      postdocs, and one research assistant professor)

INDIANA UNIVERSITY   -   <u>February 24, 1978</u>

    Department of Biology (Chairman and Associate Chairman)

    Department of Biology (five postdocs)

    Graduate School (Dean and Associate Dean)

    Department of Psychology (faculty)

    Department of Psychology (three postdocs and two graduate students)

CHILDREN'S HOSPITAL   -   January 24, 1978

    Child Health and Development Unit (Head)

UNIVERSITY OF MARYLAND   -   January 23, 1978

    Department of Physics (faculty)

    Department of Physics (one research associate, one postdoc, and two
        graduate students)

M.I.T.   -   January 20, 1978; January 18-19, 1978

    Department of Electrical Engineering (faculty)

    Department of Nutrition and Food Sciences (faculty)

    Department of Nutrition and Food Sciences (two research associates, one D.D.S.,
        and three graduate students)

    Provost

    Department of Psychology (Chairman, four postdocs)

    School of Science (Dean)

HARVARD   -   January 17-19, 1978

    Department of Biology (Chairman and faculty)

    Department of Biology (one postdoc, four graduate students)

    Department of Mathematics (Chairman)

    Department of Mathematics (five Benjamin Pierce Assistant Professors)

    Department of Physics (Chairman, faculty, and two postdocs)

    School of Public Health (faculty)

    School of Public Health (three postdocs and three graduate students)

NATIONAL SCIENCE FOUNDATION   -   January 13, 1978

    Committee on the Role of NSF in Basic Research (Executive Secretary)

NAVAL RESEARCH LABORATORY   -   January 13, 1978

    Chemistry and Physics Sections (faculty)

    Chemistry and Physics Sections (fourteen NRC postdocs)

GEORGE WASHINGTON UNIVERSITY   -   January 10, 1978

    Medical School (Vice President for Medical Affairs, Dean for Student Affairs)

NATIONAL SCIENCE FOUNDATION - December 7, 1977; December 2, 1977

Chemistry Research Section (Section Head, six staff members)

Earth Sciences Research Section (Director)

Physics Research Section (Program Director)

EXAMPLES OF QUESTIONS ASKED
UNIVERSITY FACULTY/ADMINISTRATORS

Definitions

(1) What different titles do your postdocs hold? Do their responsibilities differ?

(2) Have any of your postdocs been out of graduate (medical) school longer than three years? longer than six years? What were their previous positions?

(3) What other doctoral research staff do you have that are not considered faculty? Do their responsibilities differ from the postdocs'?

(4) How long are doctoral research staff expected to remain in these positions?

(5) Is there a formal or informal research track parallel to the faculty tenure track?

Contribution to Research

(1) What do you consider a desirable mix of faculty, postdocs, other doctoral staff, and graduate students working on a research project?

(2) Could some of the faculty or graduate students be replaced by postdocs and other doctoral research staff? What effect would this have on the cost and productivity of your research?

(3) What effect would reducing the number of postdocs and other doctoral staff have on your research?

(4) What unique contributions do postdocs and other doctoral staff make to the research project (e.g., training permanent staff in specialized techniques, providing cross-fertilization of ideas among fields or laboratories)?

(5) What fraction of the total intellectual input in a research project does the postdoc provide?

(6) If only the most able half of the postdoctoral group were retained, would it have a significant impact on the department's research productivity?

Contribution to Educational Programs

(1) Should postdocs be given any formal teaching responsibilities? To what extent?

(2) Would it be possible to establish a dual position of postdoc and lecturer? Has this been tried?

(3) What contributions, other than formal teaching, do postdocs and doctoral research staff make to your program of graduate and undergraduate education (e.g., "substitute" teaching, assistance in the lab)?

Training for Research Careers

(1) In recruiting new faculty do you require postdoc experience? How much?

(2) Do you discourage postdocs from remaining in your department more than two or three years? Why?

(3) How frequently have your postdocs or doctoral research staff moved into permanent positions in your department? What is your policy in this regard?

(4) Do you consider it desirable or undesirable for a Ph.D. to continue in the same department for his postdoc appointment? Why?

Institutional/Department Policies

(1) Who has the responsibility for reviewing appointments to postdoctoral positions?

(2) What status does the postdoc hold? What benefits does he/she receive? Is he/she given adequate space, etc.?

(3) Should more formal policies concerning postdoctoral appointments be established by the institution?

Support Mechanisms

(1) Approximately what fraction of the total support for postdocs in your department comes from federal fellowships, training grants, and research grants/contracts? What other sources of support are available?

(2) Which of these mechanisms is most effective in terms of the productivity and cost of research? Which in terms of providing training needs?

(3) What would you consider to be the optimum mix of funding mechanisms?

Foreign Postdocs

(1) What fraction of your postdocs are from foreign countries? How many of these received doctorates from U.S. universities?

(2) What visa status do the foreign postdocs hold? Do they remain in this country after completing their appointments?

(3) How are the foreign postdocs supported? Are they taking positions that might otherwise be held by U.S. citizens?

(4) What unique contributions does the foreign postdoc make?

(5) Should the number of foreign postdocs be increased or reduced?

Women and Minorities

(1) Is the postdoctoral appointment an advantage or a hindrance to a woman or minority scientist planning a research career?

(2) Have you encountered difficulty in recruiting women and minority scientists for postdoctoral appointments? If so, what are the major reasons for this (e.g., age, economic considerations)?

(3) How successful have these groups been in finding permanent positions after the postdoctoral?

Nonacademic Sector

(1) Is postdoctoral training an asset or a liability to the graduate planning a career in research outside the academic sector? Has this situation changed in recent years?

(2) To what extent are postdoctoral appointments in government and industrial labs used to recruit permanent staff? What other unique purposes do these appointments serve (e.g., strengthen the research program)?

(3) What types of positions do postdocs in government and industrial labs take after completing their appointments?

Future of Academic Research

(1) In the face of reduced numbers of faculty openings in the next fifteen years, what possible solutions do you see to maintain the vitality of academic research (e.g., longer-term postdoctoral appointments, visiting assistant professors, incentives for early retirement)?

EXAMPLES OF QUESTIONS ASKED
POSTDOCTORALS/GRADUATE STUDENTS

(1) Did you have a realistic picture of the supply-demand situation in your field before entering graduate school? If not, would this information have influenced your career choice?

(2) What was your primary motivation for taking a postdoctoral appointment? What alternative employment possibilities did you consider? How many had to pay back significant loans for graduate education?

(3) Are you satisfied with your current responsibilities? What improvements, if any, would you make? How much teaching do you do? How much freedom do you have in research? What benefits do you receive? What is your tax status? To what extent are you left out of the mainstream? Is this an advantage or disadvantage?

(4) What are your future career prospects like? To what extent is it possible to convert a postdoctoral appointment into a permanent faculty position in the same department? How do you feel about a career in industry or government? a career in teaching? What process do you use to find a job?

(5) In light of the shortage of tenured positions in academia, would you consider taking a five to ten year appointment? What other solutions to the shortage of permanent academic appointments do you see?

EXAMPLES OF QUESTIONS ASKED
INDUSTRIAL/GOVERNMENT MANAGERS

1. What are the disciplines and specialties in which your firm or agency
    hires Ph.D.'s or postdoctorals? Do you prefer postdoctorals in some
    disciplines?

2. Approximately what proportion of the Ph.D.'s hired in recent years (last
    two years) have had postdoctoral training?

3. What are the activities (e.g., basic research, applied research, design,
    analysis, consulting, etc.) for which you hire Ph.D.'s? Are postdoctorals
    hired for the same activities?

4. What qualities do you look for in a Ph.D. and/or postdoctoral candidate?

5. In general, is postdoctoral experience viewed as an asset or liability?
    Are there situations in which your firm prefers postdoctorals (or others
    with extended academic experience) over new Ph.D.'s?

6. Are postdoctorals offered a higher starting salary than new Ph.D.'s?
    How do the salaries of postdoctorals and Ph.D.'s compare over the long run?

7. What mobility do Ph.D.'s have in your organization? What are the activities
    and responsibilities to which they may move? Do you perceive a difference
    in the mobility (or adaptability) of Ph.D.'s and postdoctorals?

8. In some disciplines (notably engineering) a high proportion of new Ph.D.'s
    and postdoctorals are foreign citizens without permanent visas, while the
    supply of United States Ph.D. graduates has declined. What are your poli-
    cies or practices with regard to hiring foreign Ph.D.'s or postdoctorals?

9. Does your firm or agency itself offer temporary postdoctoral appointments?
    What are your motives in doing so? If you do not offer such appointments,
    is it possible you will do so in the future (or is the idea impracticable
    in your case)?

10. What stipends are paid to those holding such appointments? What are their
    responsibilities?

11. What are the career prospects like for these postdoctorals? Are they
    eligible for permanent positions within the laboratory.

APPENDIX C

OMB No. 99-S79002
Approval expires
December 31, 1979

SURVEY OF SCIENCE AND ENGINEERING DEPARTMENT CHAIRMEN
CONDUCTED BY THE NATIONAL RESEARCH COUNCIL WITH THE SUPPORT OF THE NATIONAL SCIENCE FOUNDATION

THE ACCOMPANYING LETTER requests your assistance in this survey of science and engineering departments.
PLEASE READ the instructions carefully and answer by printing your reply or entering an 'X' in the appropriate box.
PLEASE COMMENT on any questions which you think require fuller explanation.
PLEASE RETURN the completed form in the enclosed envelope to the Commission on Human Resources, JH 638, National Research Council, 2101 Constitution Avenue, N.W., Washington, D.C. 20418.

If you have any questions about the survey, please call Porter E. Coggeshall collect at (202) 389-6552.

NOTE: This information is solicited under the authority of the National Science Foundation Act of 1950, as amended. All information you provide will be treated as confidential and used for statistical purposes only. Information will be released only in the form of statistical summaries or in a form which does not identify information about any particular person. Your response is entirely voluntary and your failure to provide some or all of the requested information will in no way adversely affect you.

DEFINITION: POSTDOCTORAL APPOINTMENT means a temporary appointment, the primary purpose of which is to provide for continued education or experience in research usually, though not necessarily, under the supervision of a senior mentor. *Include only those appointments held by individuals with Ph.D. degrees or equivalent research doctorates.*

1. **Based on the above definition, how many individuals currently (as of April 1979) hold full-time postdoctoral appointments in your department?** _____   (8-9)

2. **How many of these postdoctoral appointees**

   a. **have held appointments in your department for longer than two years?** _____   (10-11)

   b. **earned their doctoral degrees from your department?** _____   (12-13)

   c. **earned their doctoral degrees from foreign universities?** _____   (14-15)

3. **How many of the postdoctoral appointees in your department are PRIMARILY supported by each of the following sources?**

	Number supported	
U.S. federal research grants or contracts	_____	(16-17)
U.S. federal fellowships or training grants	_____	(18-19)
Nonfederal U.S. nationally awarded fellowships	_____	(20-21)
University or state funds	_____	(22-23)
Sources from outside the U.S.	_____	(24-25)
Personal resources (e.g., loans, family income, etc.)	_____	(26-27)
Other sources, please specify below:		
_____	_____	(28-29)
Unknown	_____	(30-31)
(Column total should match your answer to question 1 above) Total	_____	(32-33)

269

4. What is the average starting stipend (excluding dependency allowances) for full-time postdoctoral appointees in your department who have just completed their graduate training? $_____ per year   (34-36)

5. What portion of the postdoctoral appointments in your department are reviewed

    a. by the chairman or departmental administrator?

        1 ☐ All   2 ☐ Most   3 ☐ Few   4 ☐ None (37)

    b. by the university or school administration?

        1 ☐ All   2 ☐ Most   3 ☐ Few   4 ☐ None (38)

6. Are postdoctoral appointees permitted to assume primary responsibility for teaching one or more courses?

    1 ☐ Yes   2 ☐ No (39)

    If YES, how many postdoctoral appointees are teaching one or more courses this semester? _____ (40-41)

7. In the next four years approximately how many students do you expect will earn Ph.D. degrees (or equivalent research doctorates) from your department?

	Academic year			
	1978-79	1979-80	1980-81	1981-82
Number of Ph.D. degrees expected to be awarded:	_____ (42-43)	_____ (44-45)	_____ (46-47)	_____ (48-49)

8. How many of the 1978-79 Ph.D. recipients included above do you expect will take (or already have accepted) postdoctoral appointments? _____ (50-51)

9. In terms of their research performance while in graduate training, how do you compare recent Ph.D. recipients from your department who have taken postdoctoral appointments with those who did not take postdoctorals?

    Those who took postdoctorals were: 1 ☐ Generally of higher caliber
                                 2 ☐ About the same
                                 3 ☐ Generally of lower caliber (52)

10. How many in each of the personnel groups below are engaged in research in your department (as of April 1979)? Include only full-time personnel who devote a significant fraction (approximately one-fourth or more) of their time to research activities. Exclude personnel with joint appointments in other departments unless they devote the *majority* of their time to activities in your department.

Full-time personnel involved in some (> 25%) research	Number of individuals
Faculty	_____ (53-54)
Postdoctoral appointees (as defined on page 1)	_____ (55-56)
Other doctoral staff (e.g., research scientists)	_____ (57-58)
Graduate research assistants	_____ (59-60)
Nondoctoral staff (e.g., technicians)	_____ (61-62)

11. a. How many of the faculty researchers included above are mentors or sponsors of postdoctoral appointees? _____ (63-64)

    b. How many of the "other doctoral staff" included above are mentors or sponsors of postdoctoral appointees? _____ (65-66)

12. a. **Considering the totality of the current research effort in your department, rate the contributions made by each of the personnel groups below to the OVERALL PRODUCTIVITY OF A RESEARCH PROJECT. Use the following scale:**

1 = essential	3 = unimportant
2 = important	4 = cannot determine

Contribution made by   Rating of contribution

   Faculty   _____ (67)

   Postdoctoral appointees (as defined on page 1)   _____ (68)

   Other doctoral staff (e.g., research scientists)   _____ (69)

   Graduate research assistants   _____ (70)

   Nondoctoral staff (e.g., technicians)   _____ (71)

b. **Using the same scale (above), rate the contributions of POSTDOCTORAL APPOINTEES (only) to each of the following aspects of the research project:**

                                       Rating of contribution

   Determining the basic directions of the research project   _____ (72)

   Intellectual vigor of the research effort   _____ (73)

   Infusion of new research techniques   _____ (74)

   Publication of research findings   _____ (75)

   Training of graduate students   _____ (76)

Additional comments: _____

_____

_____

_____

                                                                                 (77)

13. **Of the last five assistant professors hired in your department, how many had at any time in the past held postdoctoral appointments?**   _____ (8)

14. **How would you characterize the job market for individuals who have completed postdoctoral appointments in the last year and were seeking positions in academic research?**

   1 ☐ Many more positions available than candidates
   2 ☐ Approximately the same number of each
   3 ☐ Many more candidates available than positions
   4 ☐ Uncertain   (9)

15. **Of the total full-time postdoctoral appointees in your department (see Question 1), how many are foreign citizens (including those on either permanent or temporary visas)?**   _____ (10-11)

> NOTE: If you have no foreign postdoctoral appointees in your department, you have completed the survey. Thank you.
>
> If you DO HAVE one or more foreign postdoctoral appointees in your department, please answer the questions on page 4.

16. How many of these foreign postdoctorals

    a. are primarily supported by sources not generally available to U.S. citizens? _____ (12-13)

    b. are primarily supported by U.S. federal research grants and contracts? _____ (14-15)

    c. hold appointments for which U.S. citizens had also been considered as candidates? _____ (16-17)

    d. do you expect will return home after completing their appointments in your department? _____ (18-19)

17. Which of the following BEST describes the reasons for appointing foreign postdoctorals in your department? (*Check only one.*)

    1 ☐ Because foreign applicants were better qualified than U.S. candidates
    2 ☐ To utilize special skills or training of these foreign scientists
    3 ☐ Because no qualified U.S. citizens were available to take postdoctoral appointments
    4 ☐ Other reason, specify _____ (20)

18. Based on recent experience with foreign postdoctoral appointees in your department, in general how do you compare the contributions of this group with U.S. postdoctoral appointees?

In terms of:		Foreign group is better	About the same	U.S. group is better
Overall productivity of research	(21)	1 ☐	2 ☐	3 ☐
Determining the basic directions of the research project	(22)	1 ☐	2 ☐	3 ☐
Intellectual vigor of the research effort	(23)	1 ☐	2 ☐	3 ☐
Infusion of new research techniques	(24)	1 ☐	2 ☐	3 ☐
Publication of research findings	(25)	1 ☐	2 ☐	3 ☐
Training of graduate students	(26)	1 ☐	2 ☐	3 ☐

Additional comments: _____
_____
_____
_____ (27)

19. We would like to follow-up a sample of foreign citizens who currently hold postdoctoral appointments in U.S. universities. Would you kindly list the names of all the foreign citizens on postdoctorals in your department and the date they started?

Names of foreign postdoctoral appointees   Starting month and year

(28-29)

THANK YOU FOR YOUR COOPERATION

NATIONAL RESEARCH COUNCIL
COMMISSION ON HUMAN RESOURCES

2101 Constitution Avenue   Washington, D. C. 20418

COMMITTEE ON THE STUDY OF
POSTDOCTORALS AND DOCTORAL RESEARCH STAFF

Lee Grodzins, *Chairman*
Massachusetts Institute of
Technology

Richard D. Anderson
Louisiana State University

Frederick E. Balderston
University of California
Berkeley, California

Kenneth E. Clark
University of Rochester

Gerhart Friedlander
Brookhaven National Laboratory

Herbert Friedman
Naval Research Laboratory

John C. Hancock
Purdue University

Donald F. Hornig
Harvard School of Public Health

Shirley Ann Jackson
Bell Laboratories

Ernest S. Kuh
University of California
Berkeley, California

William F. Miller
. Stanford University

Nicholas C. Mullins
Indiana University

Thomas A. Reichert
Carnegie-Mellon University

Helen R. Whiteley
University of Washington

April 20, 1979

Dear Colleague:

The National Research Council has appointed a committee to study the policy implications of the changing role of postdoctorals and other doctoral research staff in science and engineering. During the last decade, in the face of reduced numbers of faculty openings, increasing numbers of young scientists and engineers have taken postdoctorals and other types of positions in universities and colleges as well as outside the academic setting. The accompanying survey requests information on the numbers of postdoctorals, faculty researchers, and other research staff in your department and the contributions of these groups to the research effort. The last section of the questionnaire focuses on the contributions of foreign citizens holding postdoctoral appointments.

The survey is sponsored by the National Science Foundation, but the survey records will be retained in the National Research Council. All information you provide is to be used for purposes of statistical description only and its confidentiality will be protected.

The survey results will provide a basis for the Committee's recommendations regarding federal and institutional policies. The success of this survey depends on your cooperation. Please return the completed questionnaire as soon as possible in the enclosed envelope. Thank you for your prompt assistance.

Sincerely,

Lee Grodzins
Chairman

The National Research Council is the principal operating agency of the National Academy of Sciences and the National Academy of Engineering to serve government and other organizations

* SURVEY OF SCIENCE AND ENGINEERING DEPARTMENT CHAIRMEN
* QUESTION 1

	SURVEY TOTAL RESP DEPTS		NUMBER OF POSTDOCS IN DEPARTMENT					
			1-2	3-4	5-6	7-8	9-10	>10
ALL DEPARTMENTS	H	650 1601	28.7	23.7	12.2	7.4	7.2	20.7
DEPARTMENTAL FIELD	H							
MATHEMATICAL SCI	H	22 28	50.0	17.9	14.3	3.6		14.3
PHYSICS	H	86 152	27.0	21.1	11.2	9.9	3.9	27.0
CHEMISTRY	H	82 162	9.9	14.2	9.3	7.4	4.9	54.3
EARTH SCIENCES	H	49 67	47.8	22.4	19.4	6.0		4.5
ENGINEERING	H	85 205	39.5	29.3	12.7	7.8	3.9	6.8
AGRICULTURAL SCIENCES	H	38 65	44.6	33.8	1.5	13.8	6.2	
BIOSCIENCES-GRADUATE SCH	H	104 372	26.1	23.1	12.6	6.7	12.9	18.5
BIOSCIENCES-MEDICAL SCH	H	105 430	22.1	25.3	12.3	8.1	8.8	23.3
PSYCHOLOGY	H	45 62	38.7	29.0	14.5	1.6	4.8	11.3
SOCIAL SCIENCES	H	34 58	53.4	17.2	19.0			10.3
DEPARTMENT WITHIN	H							
PRIVATE INSTITUTION	H	262 558	26.2	18.8	12.9	6.6	6.6	28.9
PUBLIC INSTITUTION	H	388 1043	30.1	26.4	11.9	7.8	7.5	16.4
DEPARTMENT WITH	H							
FIVE OR MORE POSTDOCS	H	280 761			25.8	15.5	15.1	43.6
FEWER THAN FIVE POSTDOCS	H	370 840	54.8	45.2				

* SURVEY OF SCIENCE AND ENGINEERING DEPARTMENT CHAIRMEN
* QUESTION 2

| | | TOTAL | | HELD APPT >2 YEARS | | PHD IN SAME DEPT | | PHD FROM FOREIGN DEPT | |
		DEPTS RESP	POST-DOCS	N	%	N	%	N	%
ALL DEPARTMENTS	H	647	12051	2830	23.5	1189	9.9	3640	30.2
	H								
DEPARTMENTAL FIELD	H								
MATHEMATICAL SCI	H	21	157	19	12.1	22	14.0	35	22.3
PHYSICS	H	86	1283	369	28.8	199	15.5	294	22.9
CHEMISTRY	H	82	2649	537	20.3	242	9.1	1085	41.0
EARTH SCIENCES	H	49	245	46	18.8	56	22.9	64	26.1
ENGINEERING	H	84	914	135	14.8	202	22.1	397	43.4
AGRICULTURAL SCIENCES	H	38	222	52	23.4	24	10.8	47	21.2
BIOSCIENCES-GRADUATE SCH	H	104	2887	674	23.3	221	7.7	719	24.9
BIOSCIENCES-MEDICAL SCH	H	104	3220	930	28.9	163	5.1	914	28.4
PSYCHOLOGY	H	45	273	44	16.1	31	11.4	45	16.5
SOCIAL SCIENCES	H	34	201	24	11.9	29	14.4	40	19.9
	H								
DEPARTMENT WITHIN	H								
PRIVATE INSTITUTION	H	261	4740	1040	21.9	486	10.3	1422	30.0
PUBLIC INSTITUTION	H	386	7311	1790	24.5	703	9.6	2218	30.3
	H								
DEPARTMENT WITH	H								
FIVE OR MORE POSTDOCS	H	280	10071	2370	23.5	862	8.6	3164	31.4
FEWER THAN FIVE POSTDOCS	H	367	1980	460	23.2	327	16.5	476	24.0

275

* SURVEY OF SCIENCE AND ENGINEERING DEPARTMENT CHAIRMEN
* QUESTION 3

PRIMARY SOURCE OF SUPPORT FOR APPOINTMENT

		DEPTS	TOTAL POST-RESP DOCS	FEDL RSRCH GRANT	FEDL FELL/ TRNEE	OTHER FELL	UNIV/ STATE FUNDS	FRGN SRCE	OWN RSRCE	OTHER	UNKN
ALL DEPARTMENTS	H	644	12051	61.6	17.0	4.2	7.0	4.4	.7	4.8	.5
	H										
DEPARTMENTAL FIELD	H										
MATHEMATICAL SCI	H	21	157	37.2	1.9	.6	45.5	9.6	1.9	.6	2.6
PHYSICS	H	86	1283	86.0	.5	.3	9.0	2.6		1.6	
CHEMISTRY	H	80	2645	72.5	5.0	3.0	4.6	3.6	.5	10.6	.2
EARTH SCIENCES	H	49	245	83.7	3.3	1.6	5.3	4.1		1.6	.4
ENGINEERING	H	85	914	74.6	2.8	.9	5.5	8.1	.7	6.0	1.4
AGRICULTURAL SCIENCES	H	38	222	53.2	4.1	.5	23.9	6.3		8.6	3.6
BIOSCIENCES-GRADUATE SCH	H	103	2887	60.1	22.4	5.3	5.5	3.8	.7	2.7	.6
BIOSCIENCES-MEDICAL SCH	H	103	3220	46.1	31.8	7.5	7.0	3.5	.7	3.3	
PSYCHOLOGY	H	45	273	30.0	41.4	3.7	6.6	11.7	4.0	1.8	.7
SOCIAL SCIENCES	H	34	201	15.9	42.8	5.0	7.0	16.4	4.0	5.0	4.0
	H										
DEPARTMENT WITHIN	H										
PRIVATE INSTITUTION	H	260	4740	60.7	20.2	5.4	4.5	4.8	.8	3.3	.4
PUBLIC INSTITUTION	H	384	7311	62.2	15.0	3.5	8.6	4.2	.6	5.8	.5
	H										
DEPARTMENT WITH	H										
FIVE OR MORE POSTDOCS	H	277	10071	61.8	17.4	4.8	6.0	4.2	.6	4.8	.5
FEWER THAN FIVE POSTDOCS	H	367	1980	60.3	15.0	1.6	11.9	5.2	1.0	4.8	.2

276

AVERAGE STARTING STIPEND

	SURVEY RESP	TOTAL DEPTS	<$10K	$10K-10999	$11K-11999	$12K-12999	$13K-13999	$14K-14999	$15K-15999	$16K-16999	>$17K
ALL DEPARTMENTS H	603	1601	4.0	26.5	14.6	21.6	9.8	8.1	6.5	4.5	4.5
H											
DEPARTMENTAL FIELD H											
MATHEMATICAL SCI H	18	28		4.2	8.3	12.5	12.5	4.2	20.8	16.7	20.8
PHYSICS H	81	152			9.0	17.2	28.3	29.7	5.7	6.2	
CHEMISTRY H	80	162	15.0	34.4	26.3	21.3	2.5	.6			
EARTH SCIENCES H	44	67		1.7	1.7	10.3	22.4	24.1	19.0	8.6	12.1
ENGINEERING H	81	205	5.1	4.1	2.1	21.0	7.7	13.8	13.3	15.9	16.9
AGRICULTURAL SCIENCES H	36	65		3.2	11.3	30.6	8.1	12.9	16.1	8.1	9.7
BIOSCIENCES-GRADUATE SCH H	98	372	5.4	34.3	16.3	24.0	6.9	5.1	4.6	.9	2.6
BIOSCIENCES-MEDICAL SCH H	100	430	.7	41.0	19.9	23.3	8.7	1.9	2.9	.7	.7
PSYCHOLOGY H	40	62	3.6	50.0	5.4	19.6	10.7	3.6		7.1	
SOCIAL SCIENCES H	25	58	4.7	34.9	18.6	14.0			9.3	7.0	11.6
H											
DEPARTMENT WITHIN H											
PRIVATE INSTITUTION H	245	558	3.1	32.3	13.0	20.1	9.4	9.0	7.1	3.3	2.9
PUBLIC INSTITUTION H	358	1043	4.5	23.4	15.4	22.4	10.0	7.6	6.2	5.1	5.4
H											
DEPARTMENT WITH H											
FIVE OR MORE POSTDOCS H	268	761	4.3	34.8	17.9	17.9	9.8	6.0	3.9	2.6	2.7
FEWER THAN FIVE POSTDOCS H	335	840	3.6	18.6	11.3	25.1	9.8	10.1	9.0	6.2	6.2

* SURVEY OF SCIENCE AND ENGINEERING DEPARTMENT CHAIRMEN
* QUESTION 5

		SURVEY TOTAL		PORTION OF POSTDOC APPOINTMENTS REVIEWED BY DEPT CHAIRMEN				PORTION OF POSTDOC APPOINTMENTS REVIEWED BY UNIVERSITY ADMIN			
		RESP	DEPTS	ALL	MOST	FEW	NONE	ALL	MOST	FEW	NONE
ALL DEPARTMENTS	H	646	1601	58.2	11.7	12.5	17.5	43.2	3.5	7.1	46.2
	H										
DEPARTMENTAL FIELD	H										
MATHEMATICAL SCI	H	21	28	77.8	7.4		14.8	43.5		4.3	52.2
PHYSICS	H	85	152	59.3	11.3	12.0	17.3	47.2	.7	10.4	41.7
CHEMISTRY	H	81	162	39.1	6.2	23.6	31.1	32.5	1.9	11.7	53.9
EARTH SCIENCES	H	49	67	73.1	6.0	4.5	16.4	59.4			40.6
ENGINEERING	H	85	205	71.2	6.3	7.8	14.6	55.9	4.6	11.3	28.2
AGRICULTURAL SCIENCES	H	38	65	72.3	16.9	6.2	4.6	45.2	11.3	12.9	30.6
BIOSCIENCES-GRADUATE SCH	H	104	372	56.7	5.4	16.9	21.0	47.2	3.6	5.0	44.2
BIOSCIENCES-MEDICAL SCH	H	105	430	53.3	24.0	11.2	11.6	31.4	4.6	3.9	60.1
PSYCHOLOGY	H	45	62	62.9	8.1	4.8	24.2	43.1	3.4	3.4	50.0
SOCIAL SCIENCES	H	33	58	61.4	3.5	12.3	22.8	57.9		14.0	28.1
	H										
DEPARTMENT WITHIN	H										
PRIVATE INSTITUTION	H	260	558	64.0	13.8	6.3	15.8	46.2	4.7	6.6	42.4
PUBLIC INSTITUTION	H	386	1043	55.1	10.6	15.9	18.5	41.6	2.9	7.3	48.3
	H										
DEPARTMENT WITH	H										
FIVE OR MORE POSTDOCS	H	279	761	53.8	10.3	15.5	20.4	43.0	1.7	8.7	46.5
FEWER THAN FIVE POSTDOCS	H	367	840	62.2	13.0	9.8	15.0	43.3	5.2	5.5	46.0

278

	SURVEY TOTAL RESP DEPTS		PCSTDOCS PERMITTED TO TEACH	ONE OR MORE PCSTDOCS TEACHING
ALL DEPARTMENTS H	643	1601	27.2	14.9
H				
DEPARTMENTAL FIELD H				
MATHEMATICAL SCI H	21	28	59.3	40.7
PHYSICS H	83	152	41.2	26.4
CHEMISTRY H	82	162	27.2	11.1
EARTH SCIENCES H	49	67	25.4	16.4
ENGINEERING H	85	205	43.9	34.1
AGRICULTURAL SCIENCES H	37	65	25.4	14.3
BIOSCIENCES-GRADUATE SCH H	103	372	19.6	6.0
BIOSCIENCES-MEDICAL SCH H	104	430	12.5	6.4
PSYCHOLOGY H	45	62	67.7	25.8
SOCIAL SCIENCES H	34	58	34.5	22.4
H				
DEPARTMENT WITHIN H				
PRIVATE INSTITUTION H	258	558	23.3	14.4
PUBLIC INSTITUTION H	385	1043	29.2	15.2
H				
DEPARTMENT WITH H				
FIVE OR MORE PCSTDOCS H	277	761	26.1	16.5
FEWER THAN FIVE PCSTDOCS H	366	840	28.1	13.4

279

* SURVEY OF SCIENCE AND ENGINEERING DEPARTMENT CHAIRMEN
* QUESTION 7

| | | SURVEY RESP | TOTAL DEPTS | PhD'S TO BE AWARDED IN | | | | 4 YR PROJECTED GROWTH |
				78-79	79-80	80-81	81-82	
ALL DEPARTMENTS	H	645	1601	9188	10124	10029	10030	109.2
DEPARTMENTAL FIELD								
MATHEMATICAL SCI	H	22	28	195	177	182	169	86.7
PHYSICS	H	86	152	897	991	880	884	98.6
CHEMISTRY	H	81	162	1641	1763	1755	1790	109.1
EARTH SCIENCES	H	48	67	281	326	315	329	117.1
ENGINEERING	H	85	205	1469	1618	1592	1642	111.8
AGRICULTURAL SCIENCES	H	38	65	373	472	459	482	129.2
BIOSCIENCES—GRADUATE SCH	H	103	372	2015	2247	2250	2202	109.3
BIOSCIENCES—MEDICAL SCH	H	104	430	1122	1271	1356	1319	117.6
PSYCHOLOGY	H	44	62	779	814	803	759	97.4
SOCIAL SCIENCES	H	34	58	416	445	437	454	109.1
DEPARTMENT WITHIN	H							
PRIVATE INSTITUTION	H	260	558	3233	3540	3366	3405	105.3
PUBLIC INSTITUTION	H	385	1043	5955	6584	6663	6625	111.3
DEPARTMENT WITH	H							
FIVE OR MORE POSTDOCS	H	277	761	5876	6285	6150	6020	102.5
FEWER THAN FIVE POSTDOCS	H	368	840	3312	3839	3879	4010	121.1

* SURVEY OF SCIENCE AND ENGINEERING DEPARTMENT CHAIRMEN
* QUESTION 8

		DEPTS RESP	78-79 PHD'S	TAKING POSTDOCS
ALL DEPARTMENTS	H	603	9188	39.3
	H			
DEPARTMENTAL FIELD	H			
MATHEMATICAL SCI	H	22	155	25.1
PHYSICS	H	79	897	46.4
CHEMISTRY	H	76	1641	40.3
EARTH SCIENCES	H	44	281	37.7
ENGINEERING	H	79	1465	13.4
AGRICULTURAL SCIENCES	H	34	373	14.2
BIOSCIENCES-GRADUATE SCH	H	99	2015	53.0
BIOSCIENCES-MEDICAL SCH	H	97	1122	79.4
PSYCHOLOGY	H	41	779	15.4
SOCIAL SCIENCES	H	32	416	11.8
	H			
DEPARTMENT WITHIN	H			
PRIVATE INSTITUTION	H	243	3233	43.2
PUBLIC INSTITUTION	H	360	5955	37.2
	H			
DEPARTMENT WITH	H			
FIVE OR MORE POSTDOCS	H	262	5876	44.2
FEWER THAN FIVE POSTDOCS	H	341	3312	30.6

	SURVEY RESP	TOTAL DEPTS	POSTDOCS COMPARED WITH OTHER GRADUATES		
			BETTER QUALIFIED	SAME	LESS QUALIFIED
ALL DEPARTMENTS	536	1601	39.3	56.7	4.0
DEPARTMENTAL FIELD					
MATHEMATICAL SCI	18	28	45.8	54.2	
PHYSICS	74	152	33.6	64.9	1.5
CHEMISTRY	71	162	45.1	54.9	
EARTH SCIENCES	39	67	35.8	64.2	
ENGINEERING	70	205	26.3	61.7	12.0
AGRICULTURAL SCIENCES	32	65	10.9	69.1	20.0
BIOSCIENCES-GRADUATE SCH	91	372	39.2	58.0	2.8
BIOSCIENCES-MEDICAL SCH	74	430	57.0	41.3	1.6
PSYCHOLOGY	42	62	22.4	74.1	3.4
SOCIAL SCIENCES	25	58	23.3	69.8	7.0
DEPARTMENT WITHIN					
PRIVATE INSTITUTION	228	558	41.6	55.3	3.2
PUBLIC INSTITUTION	308	1043	38.0	57.5	4.5
DEPARTMENT WITH					
FIVE OR MORE POSTDOCS	240	761	43.4	53.4	3.2
FEWER THAN FIVE POSTDOCS	296	840	35.4	59.8	4.8

* SURVEY OF SCIENCE AND ENGINEERING DEPARTMENT CHAIRMEN
* QUESTION 10

FULL-TIME RESEARCH PERSONNEL

	TOTAL DEPTS	RSRCH RESP STAFF	FACULTY N	%	POSTDOCS N	%	OTHER PHDS N	%	GRAD RA'S N	%	OTHER STAFF N	%
ALL DEPARTMENTS	645	91617	27223	29.7	12051	13.2	3171	3.5	33405	36.5	15767	17.2
DEPARTMENTAL FIELD												
MATHEMATICAL SCI	21	1488	738	49.6	157	10.6	91	6.1	397	26.7	105	7.1
PHYSICS	86	9382	3177	33.9	1283	13.7	427	4.6	3134	33.4	1361	14.5
CHEMISTRY	81	13114	3266	24.9	2649	20.2	236	1.8	6035	46.0	928	7.1
EARTH SCIENCES	49	3567	939	26.3	245	6.9	209	5.9	1648	46.2	526	14.7
ENGINEERING	85	12523	3469	27.7	914	7.3	263	2.1	6924	55.3	953	7.6
AGRICULTURAL SCIENCES	38	5372	1508	28.1	222	4.1	158	2.9	2125	39.6	1359	25.3
BIOSCIENCES-GRADUATE SCH	103	22641	6707	29.6	2887	12.8	759	3.4	7573	33.4	4715	20.8
BIOSCIENCES-MEDICAL SCH	105	18463	5197	28.1	3220	17.4	736	4.0	3924	21.3	5386	29.2
PSYCHOLOGY	45	3512	1461	41.6	273	7.8	248	7.1	1163	33.1	367	10.4
SOCIAL SCIENCES	32	1555	761	48.9	201	12.9	44	2.8	482	31.0	67	4.3
DEPARTMENT WITHIN												
PRIVATE INSTITUTION	259	29529	8421	28.5	4740	16.1	1394	4.7	10136	34.3	4838	16.4
PUBLIC INSTITUTION	386	62088	18802	30.3	7311	11.8	1777	2.9	23269	37.5	10929	17.6
DEPARTMENT WITH												
FIVE OR MORE POSTDOCS	277	56418	15191	26.9	10071	17.9	2257	4.0	19652	34.8	9247	16.4
FEWER THAN FIVE POSTDOCS	368	35199	12032	34.2	1980	5.6	914	2.6	13753	39.1	6520	18.5

283

* SURVEY CF SCIENCE ANC ENGINEERING DEPARTMENT CHAIRMEN
* QUESTICN 11

		DEPTS RESP	TOTAL FACULTY	POSTDOC MENTORS N	%	TOTAL NONFACULTY	POSTDOC MENTORS N	%
ALL DEPARTMENTS	H	630	27223	7841	28.8	3171	112	3.5
	H							
CEPARTMENTAL FIELD	H							
MATHEMATICAL SCI	H	19	738	110	14.9	91	4	4.4
PHYSICS	H	85	3177	952	30.0	427	21	4.9
CHEMISTRY	H	81	3266	1301	39.8	236	17	7.2
EARTH SCIENCES	H	48	939	217	23.1	209	6	2.9
ENGINEERING	H	82	3469	715	20.6	263	3	1.1
AGRICULTURAL SCIENCES	H	37	1508	181	12.0	158	3	1.9
BIOSCIENCES-GRADUATE SCH	H	103	6707	1944	29.0	759	15	2.0
BIOSCIENCES-MEDICAL SCH	H	102	5197	2095	40.3	736	20	2.7
PSYCHOLOGY	H	43	1461	208	14.2	248	23	9.3
SOCIAL SCIENCES	H	30	761	118	15.5	44		
	H							
DEPARTMENT WITHIN	H							
PRIVATE INSTITUTION	H	252	8421	3066	36.4	1394	42	3.0
PUBLIC INSTITUTION	H	378	18802	4775	25.4	1777	70	3.9
	H							
DEPARTMENT WITH	H							
FIVE OR MORE PCSTDCCS	H	275	15191	5729	37.7	2257	84	3.7
FEWER THAN FIVE POSTDOCS	H	355	12032	2112	17.6	914	28	3.1

* SURVEY OF SCIENCE AND ENGINEERING DEPARTMENT CHAIRMEN
* QUESTICN 12A1

		SURVEY RESP	TOTAL DEPTS	FACULTY CONTRIBUTION TO RESEARCH EFFCRT				
				ESSE-NTIAL	IMPC-RTANT	UNIM-PORT-ANT	NCNE IN DEPT	CAN'T DETER-MINE
ALL DEPARTMENTS	H	647	1601	94.7	2.6	.4	.9	1.4
	H							
DEPARTMENTAL FIELD	H							
MATHEMATICAL SCI	H	21	28	88.9			3.7	7.4
PHYSICS	H	86	152	96.7	1.3			2.0
CHEMISTRY	H	81	162	96.9	3.1			
EARTH SCIENCES	H	49	67	89.6	6.0			4.5
ENGINEERING	H	85	2C5	98.0				2.0
AGRICULTURAL SCIENCES	H	38	65	96.9	3.1			
BIOSCIENCES-GRADUATE SCH	H	104	372	95.2	3.2	1.3		.3
BIOSCIENCES-MEDICAL SCH	H	105	430	94.2	3.5		1.2	1.2
PSYCHOLOGY	H	45	62	91.9			4.8	3.2
SOCIAL SCIENCES	H	33	58	80.4	1.8	3.6	8.9	5.4
	H							
DEPARTMENT WITHIN	H							
PRIVATE INSTITUTICN	H	261	558	95.5	1.3		1.3	2.0
PUBLIC INSTITUTION	H	386	1043	94.2	3.3	.7	.7	1.2
	H							
DEPARTMENT WITH	H							
FIVE OR MORE PCSTDCCS	H	278	761	95.5	2.2	.7	.4	1.2
FEWER THAN FIVE PCSTDOCS	H	369	840	93.9	2.9	.2	1.3	1.7

	SURVEY RESP	TOTAL DEPTS	POSTDOC CONTRIBUTION TO RESEARCH EFFORT			
			ESSE-NTIAL	IMPO-RTANT	UNIM-PORT-ANT	CAN'T DETER-MINE
ALL DEPARTMENTS	H	647	16C1	34.4	60.5	1.6	3.4

		SURVEY RESP	TOTAL DEPTS	ESSE-NTIAL	IMPO-RTANT	UNIM-PORT-ANT	CAN'T DETER-MINE
DEPARTMENTAL FIELD	H						
MATHEMATICAL SCI	H	21	28	40.7	40.7	3.7	14.8
PHYSICS	H	86	152	37.5	58.6		3.9
CHEMISTRY	H	81	162	35.2	62.9	.6	1.3
EARTH SCIENCES	H	45	67	34.3	59.7	1.5	4.5
ENGINEERING	H	85	2C5	25.9	66.8		7.3
AGRICULTURAL SCIENCES	H	38	65	9.2	84.6	3.1	3.1
BIOSCIENCES-GRADUATE SCH	H	104	372	31.7	65.6	2.4	.3
BIOSCIENCES-MEDICAL SCH	H	105	430	46.3	51.9		1.9
PSYCHOLOGY	H	45	62	24.2	62.9	4.8	8.1
SOCIAL SCIENCES	H	33	58	19.6	48.2	16.1	16.1
DEPARTMENT WITHIN	H						
PRIVATE INSTITUTION	H	261	558	41.0	54.0	1.4	3.6
PUBLIC INSTITUTION	H	386	1043	30.9	64.0	1.7	3.4
DEPARTMENT WITH	H						
FIVE OR MORE POSTDOCS	H	278	761	43.9	54.0	.9	1.2
FEWER THAN FIVE POSTDOCS	H	369	840	25.9	66.4	2.3	5.5

* SURVEY OF SCIENCE AND ENGINEERING DEPARTMENT CHAIRMEN
* QUESTION 12A3

	SURVEY RESP	TOTAL DEPTS	OTHER PHD'S CONTRIBUTION TO RESEARCH EFFORT				
			ESSENTIAL	IMPORTANT	UNIMPORTANT	NONE IN DEPT	CAN'T DETERMINE
ALL DEPARTMENTS	647	1601	15.0	25.3	2.3	54.7	2.7
DEPARTMENTAL FIELD							
MATHEMATICAL SCI	21	28	14.8	18.5		59.3	7.4
PHYSICS	86	152	15.8	32.2	1.3	46.1	4.6
CHEMISTRY	81	162	3.1	27.0	6.3	54.7	8.8
EARTH SCIENCES	49	67	17.9	29.9		49.3	3.0
ENGINEERING	85	205	10.7	17.6	2.4	67.3	2.0
AGRICULTURAL SCIENCES	38	65	20.0	15.4	1.5	60.0	3.1
BIOSCIENCES-GRADUATE SCH	104	372	22.8	26.1	1.1	49.2	.8
BIOSCIENCES-MEDICAL SCH	105	430	13.5	29.3	2.3	53.7	1.2
PSYCHOLOGY	45	62	14.5	17.7	3.2	58.1	6.5
SOCIAL SCIENCES	33	58	14.3	10.7	3.6	71.4	
DEPARTMENT WITHIN							
PRIVATE INSTITUTION	261	558	16.9	27.7	2.5	50.0	2.9
PUBLIC INSTITUTION	386	1043	14.1	24.0	2.1	57.3	2.6
DEPARTMENT WITH							
FIVE OR MORE POSTDOCS	278	761	17.7	31.1	2.8	44.7	3.7
FEWER THAN FIVE POSTDOCS	369	840	12.6	20.0	1.8	63.8	1.8

* SURVEY OF SCIENCE AND ENGINEERING DEPARTMENT CHAIRMEN
* QUESTION 12A4

		SURVEY RESP	TOTAL DEPTS	GRAD RA'S CONTRIBUTION TO RESEARCH EFFORT				
				ESSE-NTIAL	IMPO-RTANT	UNIM-PORT ANT	NONE IN DEPT	CAN'T DETER-MINE
ALL DEPARTMENTS	H	647	1601	31.2	53.0	1.5	10.6	3.7
	H							
DEPARTMENTAL FIELD	H							
MATHEMATICAL SCI	H	21	28	7.4	55.6	3.7	25.9	7.4
PHYSICS	H	86	152	31.6	55.3	.7	9.9	2.6
CHEMISTRY	H	81	162	45.9	47.2	1.3	5.7	
EARTH SCIENCES	H	49	67	29.9	58.2	3.0	6.0	3.0
ENGINEERING	H	85	205	62.0	27.8	.5	6.8	2.9
AGRICULTURAL SCIENCES	H	38	65	46.2	44.6	3.1	6.2	
BIOSCIENCES-GRADUATE SCH	H	104	372	30.4	6C.8	1.3	3.8	3.8
BIOSCIENCES-MEDICAL SCH	H	105	43C	15.1	59.3	1.9	17.9	5.8
PSYCHOLOGY	H	45	62	22.6	58.1		12.9	6.5
SOCIAL SCIENCES	H	33	58	10.7	51.8	3.6	30.4	3.6
	H							
DEPARTMENT WITHIN	H							
PRIVATE INSTITUTICN	H	261	558	27.3	52.5	2.2	14.0	4.0
PUBLIC INSTITUTION	H	386	1043	33.3	53.2	1.2	8.8	3.6
	H							
DEPARTMENT WITH	H							
FIVE OR MCRE POSTDOCS	H	278	761	30.2	54.8	1.3	10.8	2.9
FEWER THAN FIVE POSTDOCS	H	369	840	32.2	51.4	1.7	10.4	4.4

* SURVEY OF SCIENCE AND ENGINEERING DEPARTMENT CHAIRMEN
* QUESTION 12A5

		SURVEY RESP	TOTAL DEPTS	OTHER STAFF'S CONTRIBUTION TO RESEARCH EFFORT				
				ESSE-NTIAL	IMPO-RTANT	UNIM-PORT-ANT	NONE IN DEPT	CAN'T DETER-MINE
ALL DEPARTMENTS	H	647	1601	26.5	50.4	2.4	15.6	5.1
	H							
DEPARTMENTAL FIELD	H							
MATHEMATICAL SCI	H	21	28	3.7	18.5	7.4	55.6	14.8
PHYSICS	H	86	152	21.1	45.4	2.0	27.6	3.9
CHEMISTRY	H	81	162	18.2	49.7	5.7	19.5	6.9
EARTH SCIENCES	H	49	67	26.9	44.8	4.5	14.9	9.0
ENGINEERING	H	85	205	27.8	47.8	2.9	16.1	5.4
AGRICULTURAL SCIENCES	H	38	65	52.3	40.0		7.7	
BIOSCIENCES-GRADUATE SCH	H	104	372	21.5	60.2	1.1	10.8	6.5
BIOSCIENCES-MEDICAL SCH	H	105	430	35.1	55.3	1.2	6.0	2.3
PSYCHOLOGY	H	45	62	17.7	48.4	1.6	21.0	11.3
SOCIAL SCIENCES	H	33	58	17.9	8.9	8.9	60.7	3.6
	H							
DEPARTMENT WITHIN	H							
PRIVATE INSTITUTION	H	261	558	25.9	46.2	4.3	18.2	5.4
PUBLIC INSTITUTION	H	386	1043	26.9	52.6	1.3	14.2	4.9
	H							
DEPARTMENT WITH	H							
FIVE OR MORE POSTDOCS	H	278	761	24.6	53.6	2.4	14.6	4.9
FEWER THAN FIVE POSTDOCS	H	369	840	28.2	47.6	2.4	16.6	5.2

* SURVEY OF SCIENCE AND ENGINEERING DEPARTMENT CHAIRMEN
* QUESTION 12B1

POSTDOC CONTRIBUTION IN DETERMINING BASIC DIRECTIONS OF RESEARCH PROJECT

		SURVEY RESP	TOTAL DEPTS	ESSE- NTIAL	IMPO- RTANT	UNIM- PORT- ANT	CAN'T DETER- MINE
ALL DEPARTMENTS	H	624	1601	6.9	62.5	26.1	4.5
	H						
DEPARTMENTAL FIELD	H						
MATHEMATICAL SCI	H	19	28	12.0	36.0	28.0	24.0
PHYSICS	H	84	152	2.0	53.0	36.2	8.7
CHEMISTRY	H	79	162		74.8	21.9	3.2
EARTH SCIENCES	H	48	67	9.1	68.2	19.7	3.0
ENGINEERING	H	81	205	5.1	51.0	40.3	3.6
AGRICULTURAL SCIENCES	H	37	65	12.5	53.1	25.0	9.4
BIOSCIENCES-GRADUATE SCH	H	102	372	12.8	64.2	23.0	
BIOSCIENCES-MEDICAL SCH	H	103	430	3.3	68.0	24.2	4.5
PSYCHOLOGY	H	44	62	9.8	63.9	13.1	13.1
SOCIAL SCIENCES	H	27	58	22.2	53.3	15.6	8.9
	H						
DEPARTMENT WITHIN	H						
PRIVATE INSTITUTION	H	246	558	7.0	66.9	22.8	3.4
PUBLIC INSTITUTION	H	378	1043	6.9	60.2	27.8	5.1
	H						
DEPARTMENT WITH	H						
FIVE OR MORE POSTDOCS	H	270	761	6.1	67.0	22.6	4.3
FEWER THAN FIVE POSTDOCS	H	354	840	7.6	58.4	29.3	4.7

* SURVEY OF SCIENCE AND ENGINEERING DEPARTMENT CHAIRMEN
* QUESTION 12B2

POSTDOC CONTRIBUTION TO INTELLECTUAL VIGOR OF THE RESEARCH EFFORT

		SURVEY RESP	TOTAL DEPTS	ESSENTIAL	IMPORTANT	UNIMPORTANT	CAN'T DETERMINE
ALL DEPARTMENTS	H	624	1601	35.2	60.4	1.9	2.5
	H						
DEPARTMENTAL FIELD	H						
MATHEMATICAL SCI	H	19	28	44.0	48.0		8.0
PHYSICS	H	84	152	33.6	62.4		4.0
CHEMISTRY	H	79	162	32.9	65.2	.6	1.3
EARTH SCIENCES	H	48	67	30.3	69.7		
ENGINEERING	H	81	205	29.1	64.3	3.6	3.1
AGRICULTURAL SCIENCES	H	37	65	35.9	54.7	6.3	3.1
BIOSCIENCES-GRADUATE SCH	H	102	372	29.0	66.9	2.7	1.4
BIOSCIENCES-MEDICAL SCH	H	103	430	45.3	53.8		.9
PSYCHOLOGY	H	44	62	24.6	59.0	6.6	9.8
SOCIAL SCIENCES	H	27	58	46.7	33.3	8.9	11.1
	H						
DEPARTMENT WITHIN	H						
PRIVATE INSTITUTION	H	246	558	41.2	54.4	1.9	2.4
PUBLIC INSTITUTION	H	378	1043	32.0	63.6	2.0	2.5
	H						
DEPARTMENT WITH	H						
FIVE OR MORE POSTDOCS	H	270	761	37.9	59.9	.5	1.6
FEWER THAN FIVE POSTDOCS	H	354	840	32.7	60.9	3.2	3.2

* SURVEY OF SCIENCE AND ENGINEERING DEPARTMENT CHAIRMEN
* QUESTION 12B3

	SURVEY RESP	TOTAL DEPTS	POSTDOC CONTRIBUTION TO INFUSION OF NEW RESEARCH TECHNIQUES			
			ESSE-NTIAL	IMPO-RTANT	UNIM-PORT-ANT	CAN'T DETER-MINE
ALL DEPARTMENTS	624	1601	24.3	64.4	7.4	3.9
DEPARTMENTAL FIELD						
MATHEMATICAL SCI	19	28	16.0	48.0	20.0	16.0
PHYSICS	84	152	24.8	59.1	8.1	8.1
CHEMISTRY	79	162	25.2	69.7	1.9	3.2
EARTH SCIENCES	48	67	30.3	60.6	9.1	
ENGINEERING	81	205	19.9	67.3	12.8	
AGRICULTURAL SCIENCES	37	65	26.6	57.8	6.3	9.4
BIOSCIENCES-GRADUATE SCH	102	372	28.7	63.1	6.3	1.9
BIOSCIENCES-MEDICAL SCH	103	430	21.3	70.4	5.5	2.8
PSYCHOLOGY	44	62	21.3	57.4	13.1	8.2
SOCIAL SCIENCES	27	58	28.9	37.8	11.1	22.2
DEPARTMENT WITHIN						
PRIVATE INSTITUTION	246	558	24.5	64.4	6.8	4.3
PUBLIC INSTITUTION	378	1043	24.3	64.3	7.7	3.7
DEPARTMENT WITH						
FIVE OR MORE POSTDOCS	270	761	26.0	67.4	3.4	3.3
FEWER THAN FIVE POSTDOCS	354	840	22.9	61.6	10.9	4.6

292

	SURVEY RESP	TOTAL DEPTS	ESSENTIAL	IMPORTANT	UNIMPORTANT	CAN'T DETERMINE
			\- POSTDOC CONTRIBUTION TO PUBLICATION OF RESEARCH FINDINGS -			
ALL DEPARTMENTS	624	1601	21.5	68.8	6.4	3.3
DEPARTMENTAL FIELD						
MATHEMATICAL SCI	19	28	20.0	48.0	12.0	20.0
PHYSICS	84	152	19.5	73.2	7.4	
CHEMISTRY	79	162	14.8	78.1	5.8	1.3
EARTH SCIENCES	48	67	33.3	56.1	10.6	
ENGINEERING	81	205	25.5	64.3	10.2	
AGRICULTURAL SCIENCES	37	65	21.9	70.3	4.7	3.1
BIOSCIENCES-GRADUATE SCH	102	372	17.8	76.0	5.5	.8
BIOSCIENCES-MEDICAL SCH	103	430	26.5	63.0	7.1	3.3
PSYCHOLOGY	44	62	9.8	75.4	4.9	9.8
SOCIAL SCIENCES	27	58	15.6	57.8	8.9	17.8
DEPARTMENT WITHIN						
PRIVATE INSTITUTION	246	558	22.8	66.9	7.2	3.2
PUBLIC INSTITUTION	378	1043	20.8	69.8	6.0	3.3
DEPARTMENT WITH						
FIVE OR MORE POSTDOCS	270	761	22.7	71.9	3.4	2.0
FEWER THAN FIVE POSTDOCS	354	840	20.4	66.1	9.1	4.4

293

		SURVEY RESP	TOTAL DEPTS	PCSTDOC CONTRIBUTION TO TRAINING OF GRADUATE STUDENTS			
				ESSE-NTIAL	IMPC-RTANT	UNIM-PORT-ANT	CAN'T DETER-MINE
ALL DEPARTMENTS	H	624	1601	4.7	56.1	32.2	7.0
	H						
DEPARTMENTAL FIELD	H						
MATHEMATICAL SCI	H	19	28		36.0	56.0	8.0
PHYSICS	H	84	152	6.0	59.7	23.5	10.7
CHEMISTRY	H	79	162	5.8	74.2	14.8	5.2
EARTH SCIENCES	H	48	67	7.6	54.5	37.9	
ENGINEERING	H	81	205	9.7	43.9	37.2	9.2
AGRICULTURAL SCIENCES	H	37	65	6.3	42.2	35.9	15.6
BIOSCIENCES-GRADUATE SCH	H	102	372	2.2	60.7	34.2	3.0
BIOSCIENCES-MEDICAL SCH	H	103	430	3.1	57.6	32.5	6.9
PSYCHOLOGY	H	44	62	3.3	57.4	31.1	8.2
SOCIAL SCIENCES	H	27	58	8.9	15.6	55.6	20.0
	H						
DEPARTMENT WITHIN	H						
PRIVATE INSTITUTION	H	246	558	4.3	57.3	31.3	7.2
PUBLIC INSTITUTION	H	378	1043	4.9	55.5	32.7	6.9
	H						
DEPARTMENT WITH	H						
FIVE OR MORE POSTDOCS	H	270	761	3.3	65.8	25.5	5.4
FEWER THAN FIVE POSTDOCS	H	354	840	6.0	47.4	38.3	8.4

* SURVEY CF SCIENCE ANC ENGINEERING DEPARTMENT CHAIRMEN
* QUESTICN 13

		SURVEY RESP	TOTAL DEPTS	NUMBER OF LAST FIVE FACULTY HIRED WITH PCSTDOCS					
				0	1	2	3	4	5
ALL DEPARTMENTS	H	629	16C1	12.4	14.1	10.9	11.5	13.4	37.7
	H								
DEPARTMENTAL FIELD	H								
MATHEMATICAL SCI	H	20	28	32.0	28.0	8.0	8.0	8.0	16.0
PHYSICS	H	85	152	2.7	4.7	10.1	11.4	20.8	50.3
CHEMISTRY	H	79	162		3.9	3.9	9.7	24.5	58.1
EARTH SCIENCES	H	46	67	14.3	20.6	20.6	7.9	25.4	11.1
ENGINEERING	H	82	205	39.6	29.4	12.7	5.1	10.7	2.5
AGRICULTURAL SCIENCES	H	38	65	43.1	27.7	20.0	1.5	7.7	
BIOSCIENCES-GRADUATE SCH	H	103	372	6.8	13.6	16.1	22.3	10.1	31.1
BIOSCIENCES-MEDICAL SCH	H	101	430	.7	5.3	2.7	9.2	13.6	68.4
PSYCHCLOGY	H	44	62	13.1	39.3	27.9	8.2	1.6	9.8
SOCIAL SCIENCES	H	31	58	53.8	25.0	15.4	5.8		
	H								
CEPARTMENT WITHIN	H								
PRIVATE INSTITUTION	H	251	558	9.1	13.9	10.2	8.9	12.9	45.0
PUBLIC INSTITUTION	H	378	1043	14.0	14.2	11.3	12.9	13.6	34.C
	H								
DEPARTMENT WITH	H								
FIVE OR MORE PCSTDCCS	H	270	761	5.9	10.3	6.2	8.1	18.3	51.3
FEWER THAN FIVE POSTDOCS	H	359	840	18.2	17.5	15.2	14.6	9.0	25.5

295

* SURVEY OF SCIENCE AND ENGINEERING DEPARTMENT CHAIRMEN
* QUESTION 14

	SURVEY RESP	TOTAL DEPTS	JOB MARKET FOR RECENT POSTDOCS			
			MORE POSITIONS THAN CANDIDATES	ABOUT THE SAME	MORE CANDIDATES THAN POSITIONS	UNCERTAIN
ALL DEPARTMENTS	632	1601	16.0	31.3	39.0	13.6
DEPARTMENTAL FIELD						
MATHEMATICAL SCI	20	28	34.6	38.5	19.2	7.7
PHYSICS	83	152	9.4	24.2	47.7	18.8
CHEMISTRY	77	162	9.9	30.3	49.3	10.5
EARTH SCIENCES	48	67	16.7	42.4	27.3	13.6
ENGINEERING	84	205	43.1	25.2	18.8	12.9
AGRICULTURAL SCIENCES	38	65	21.5	36.9	23.1	18.5
BIOSCIENCES-GRADUATE SCH	104	372	11.6	34.9	41.4	12.1
BIOSCIENCES-MEDICAL SCH	101	430	12.0	33.3	42.5	12.2
PSYCHOLOGY	44	62	6.6	29.5	50.8	13.1
SOCIAL SCIENCES	33	58	7.1	16.1	48.2	28.6
DEPARTMENT WITHIN						
PRIVATE INSTITUTION	252	558	16.9	32.8	37.6	12.7
PUBLIC INSTITUTION	380	1043	15.6	30.5	39.8	14.1
DEPARTMENT WITH						
FIVE OR MORE POSTDOCS	270	761	11.3	31.3	48.0	9.4
FEWER THAN FIVE POSTDOCS	362	840	20.3	31.3	30.9	17.4

NUMBER OF FOREIGN PCSTDOCS

	SURVEY RESP	TOTAL DEPTS	NONE	1-2	3-4	5-6	7-8	9-10	>10
ALL DEPARTMENTS H	639	1601	27.5	38.1	13.1	7.0	5.9	3.0	5.4
H									
DEPARTMENTAL FIELD H									
MATHEMATICAL SCI H	22	28	28.6	46.4	10.7		3.6		10.7
PHYSICS H	85	152	25.3	35.3	14.7	8.7	10.0	2.7	3.3
CHEMISTRY H	80	162	5.1	28.0	8.3	10.2	15.3	9.6	23.6
EARTH SCIENCES H	48	67	39.4	42.4	15.2	1.5		1.5	
ENGINEERING H	85	205	6.8	57.6	14.6	7.8	7.3		5.9
AGRICULTURAL SCIENCES H	38	65	41.5	35.4	13.8	4.6	4.6		
BIOSCIENCES-GRADUATE SCH H	102	372	27.9	37.7	14.5	6.6	7.9	4.6	.8
BIOSCIENCES-MEDICAL SCH H	101	430	33.0	35.2	14.8	8.5		2.4	6.1
PSYCHOLOGY H	45	62	74.2	14.5	4.8	1.6	4.8		
SOCIAL SCIENCES H	33	58	46.4	46.4	3.6		3.6		
H									
DEPARTMENT WITHIN H									
PRIVATE INSTITUTION H	257	558	21.5	42.5	9.6	6.3	9.4	3.9	7.0
PUBLIC INSTITUTION H	382	1043	30.7	35.8	15.1	7.3	4.0	2.5	4.6
H									
DEPARTMENT WITH H									
FIVE OR MORE PCSTDOCS H	275	761	8.2	26.0	21.1	14.6	12.3	6.3	11.4
FEWER THAN FIVE PCSTDOCS H	364	840	45.0	49.0	6.0				

297

QUESTION 16

	DEPTS RESP	TOTAL FRGN POST-DOCS	SUPPORTED BY SOURCES UNAVAIL. TO U.S. CITIZENS N	%	SUPPORTED BY U.S., FEDL RSRCH GRANT & CONTRACT N	%	HELD APPOINTMENT FOR WHICH THERE WERE U.S. CANDIDATES N	%	RETURN HOME AFTER APPOINTMENT N	%
ALL DEPARTMENTS	443	4608	578	12.5	3260	70.7	3137	68.1	2755	59.8
DEPARTMENTAL FIELD										
MATHEMATICAL SCI	16	74	16	21.6	29	39.2	50	67.6	40	54.1
PHYSICS	62	434	31	7.1	353	81.3	365	84.1	230	53.0
CHEMISTRY	71	1258	83	6.6	977	77.7	1065	84.7	809	64.3
EARTH SCIENCES	29	85	7	8.2	69	81.2	54	63.5	41	48.2
ENGINEERING	79	629	71	11.3	471	74.9	336	53.4	340	54.1
AGRICULTURAL SCIENCES	22	91	20	22.0	49	53.8	36	39.6	63	69.2
BIOSCIENCES-GRADUATE SCH	70	922	122	13.2	656	71.1	557	60.4	494	53.6
BIOSCIENCES-MEDICAL SCH	65	1010	163	16.1	632	62.6	655	64.9	651	64.5
PSYCHOLOGY	13	51	30	58.8	11	21.6	7	13.7	44	86.3
SOCIAL SCIENCES	16	54	35	64.8	13	24.1	12	22.2	43	79.6
DEPARTMENT WITHIN										
PRIVATE INSTITUTION	191	1827	244	13.4	1304	71.4	1186	64.9	1075	58.8
PUBLIC INSTITUTION	252	2781	334	12.0	1956	70.3	1951	70.2	1680	60.4
DEPARTMENT WITH										
FIVE OR MORE POSTDOCS	247	3929	479	12.2	2795	71.1	2745	69.9	2391	60.9
FEWER THAN FIVE POSTDOCS	196	679	99	14.6	465	68.5	392	57.7	364	53.6

298

* SURVEY OF SCIENCE AND ENGINEERING DEPARTMENT CHAIRMEN
* QUESTION 18.1

| | SURVEY RESP | TOTAL DEPTS | FOREIGN & U.S. POSTDOCS COMPARED IN TERMS OF OVERALL PRODUCTIVITY OF RESEARCH | | | |
			FRGN BETTER	ABOUT SAME	U.S. BETTER	UNCERTAIN
ALL DEPARTMENTS	382	1136	14.8	77.2	7.9	.2
DEPARTMENTAL FIELD						
MATHEMATICAL SCI	13	20	5.9	94.1		
PHYSICS	55	112	9.1	85.9	5.1	
CHEMISTRY	68	149	16.5	73.4	10.1	
EARTH SCIENCES	27	40	20.0	74.3	5.7	
ENGINEERING	56	191	8.3	87.1	4.5	
AGRICULTURAL SCIENCES	19	38	9.4	75.0	15.6	
BIOSCIENCES—GRADUATE SCH	64	264	11.2	73.7	15.1	
BIOSCIENCES—MEDICAL SCH	61	276	22.6	74.2	3.2	
PSYCHOLOGY	9	16	33.3	41.7	8.3	16.7
SOCIAL SCIENCES	10	30	11.1	88.9		
DEPARTMENT WITHIN						
PRIVATE INSTITUTION	163	427	15.6	80.2	3.6	.6
PUBLIC INSTITUTION	219	709	14.3	75.4	10.3	
DEPARTMENT WITH						
FIVE OR MORE POSTDOCS	221	684	17.2	77.5	5.1	.3
FEWER THAN FIVE POSTDOCS	161	452	10.7	76.7	12.6	

299

* SURVEY CF SCIENCE ANC ENGINEERING DEPARTMENT CHAIRMEN
* QUESTICN 18.2

FCREIGN & U.S. POSTDOCS COMPARED IN TERMS OF
DETERMINING BASIC DIRECTIONS CF RESEARCH PROJECT

	SURVEY TOTAL RESP DEPTS		FRGN ABCUT U.S. BETTER	SAME	BETTER	UNCERTAIN
ALL DEPARTMENTS	382	1136	2.9	73.2	22.7	1.1
DEPARTMENTAL FIELD						
MATHEMATICAL SCI	13	20		88.2		11.8
PHYSICS	55	112	4.0	71.7	22.2	2.0
CHEMISTRY	68	149		68.3	29.5	2.2
EARTH SCIENCES	27	40	5.7	74.3	17.1	2.9
ENGINEERING	56	151	4.5	62.1	31.8	1.5
AGRICULTURAL SCIENCES	19	38		43.8	56.3	
BIOSCIENCES—GRADUATE SCH	64	264	1.3	73.7	24.6	.4
BIOSCIENCES—MEDICAL SCH	61	276	4.0	84.9	11.1	
PSYCHCLGY	9	16	25.0	58.3	16.7	
SUCIAL SCIENCES	10	30		77.8	22.2	
DEPARTMENT WITHIN						
PRIVATE INSTITUTION	163	427	2.8	79.1	16.5	1.7
PUBLIC INSTITUTION	219	709	3.0	65.8	26.4	.8
DEPARTMENT WITH						
FIVE OR MORE PCSTDCCS	221	684	2.8	78.4	18.1	.7
FEWER THAN FIVE PCSTDOCS	161	452	3.1	64.3	30.6	2.0

* SURVEY OF SCIENCE AND ENGINEERING DEPARTMENT CHAIRMEN
* QUESTION 18.3

FOREIGN & U.S. POSTDOCS COMPARED IN TERMS OF
INTELLECTUAL VIGOR OF THE RESEARCH EFFORT

	SURVEY RESP	TOTAL DEPTS	FRGN ABOUT U.S. BETTER	SAME	U.S. BETTER	UNCERTAIN
ALL DEPARTMENTS	382	1136	9.9	77.4	12.4	.3
DEPARTMENTAL FIELD						
MATHEMATICAL SCI	13	20	5.9	94.1		
PHYSICS	55	112	11.1	77.8	9.1	2.0
CHEMISTRY	68	149	7.2	77.0	15.8	
EARTH SCIENCES	27	40	11.4	80.0	5.7	2.9
ENGINEERING	56	191	7.6	87.1	5.3	
AGRICULTURAL SCIENCES	19	38	18.8	56.3	25.0	
BIOSCIENCES-GRADUATE SCH	64	264	.4	78.9	20.7	
BIOSCIENCES-MEDICAL SCH	61	276	18.7	71.8	9.5	
PSYCHOLOGY	9	16	33.3	66.7		
SOCIAL SCIENCES	10	30	11.1	88.9		
DEPARTMENT WITHIN						
PRIVATE INSTITUTION	163	427	13.4	77.9	8.4	.3
PUBLIC INSTITUTION	219	709	7.9	77.0	14.8	.3
DEPARTMENT WITH						
FIVE OR MORE POSTDOCS	221	684	9.8	80.6	9.5	.2
FEWER THAN FIVE POSTDOCS	161	452	10.1	71.9	17.4	.6

FOREIGN & U.S. POSTDOCS COMPARED IN TERMS OF
INFUSION OF NEW RESEARCH TECHNIQUES

	SURVEY RESP	TOTAL DEPTS	FRGN BETTER	ABOUT SAME	U.S. BETTER	UNCERTAIN
ALL DEPARTMENTS	382	1136	8.0	70.8	20.4	.9
DEPARTMENTAL FIELD						
MATHEMATICAL SCI	13	2C		88.2		11.8
PHYSICS	55	112	5.1	67.7	25.3	2.0
CHEMISTRY	68	149	8.6	66.9	24.5	
EARTH SCIENCES	27	40	14.3	65.7	17.1	2.9
ENGINEERING	56	191	2.3	75.0	20.5	2.3
AGRICULTURAL SCIENCES	19	38		75.0	25.0	
BIOSCIENCES-GRADUATE SCH	64	264	10.3	70.3	19.0	.4
BIOSCIENCES-MEDICAL SCH	61	276	9.1	71.0	19.8	
PSYCHOLOGY	9	16	25.0	66.7	8.3	
SOCIAL SCIENCES	10	30	11.1	77.8	11.1	
DEPARTMENT WITHIN						
PRIVATE INSTITUTION	163	427	9.8	77.4	11.7	1.1
PUBLIC INSTITUTION	219	709	6.9	66.9	25.4	.8
DEPARTMENT WITH						
FIVE OR MORE POSTDOCS	221	684	7.8	72.4	19.6	.2
FEWER THAN FIVE POSTDOCS	161	452	8.1	68.0	21.6	2.2

* SURVEY OF SCIENCE AND ENGINEERING DEPARTMENT CHAIRMEN
* QUESTION 18.5

FOREIGN & U.S. POSTDOCS COMPARED IN TERMS OF PUBLICATION OF RESEARCH FINDINGS

	SURVEY RESP	TOTAL DEPTS	FRGN BETTER	ABOUT SAME	U.S. BETTER	UNCERTAIN
ALL DEPARTMENTS	382	1136	6.5	73.6	18.8	1.1
DEPARTMENTAL FIELD						
MATHEMATICAL SCI	13	20	5.9	88.2	5.9	
PHYSICS	55	112	3.0	87.9	7.1	2.0
CHEMISTRY	68	149		75.5	24.5	
EARTH SCIENCES	27	40	20.0	68.6	8.6	2.9
ENGINEERING	56	191	9.8	72.0	15.9	2.3
AGRICULTURAL SCIENCES	19	38	12.5	56.3	31.3	
BIOSCIENCES-GRADUATE SCH	64	264	5.2	69.4	23.3	2.2
BIOSCIENCES-MEDICAL SCH	61	276	7.1	73.4	19.4	
PSYCHOLOGY	9	16	25.0	75.0		
SOCIAL SCIENCES	10	30	11.1	72.2	16.7	
DEPARTMENT WITHIN						
PRIVATE INSTITUTION	163	427	4.7	74.9	20.1	.3
PUBLIC INSTITUTION	219	709	7.5	72.8	18.0	1.6
DEPARTMENT WITH						
FIVE OR MORE POSTDOCS	221	684	4.9	80.1	14.9	.2
FEWER THAN FIVE POSTDOCS	161	452	9.3	62.4	25.6	2.8

FOREIGN & U.S. POSTDOCS COMPARED IN TERMS OF TRAINING OF GRADUATE STUDENTS

	SURVEY RESP	TOTAL DEPTS		FRGN BETTER	ABOUT SAME	US BETTER	UNCERTAIN
ALL DEPARTMENTS	382	1136	H	1.2	51.1	39.2	8.5
DEPARTMENTAL FIELD			H				
MATHEMATICAL SCI	13	20	H		64.7	5.9	29.4
PHYSICS	55	112	H		52.5	36.4	11.1
CHEMISTRY	68	149	H	1.4	42.4	50.4	5.8
EARTH SCIENCES	27	40	H		68.6	20.0	11.4
ENGINEERING	56	151	H		46.2	51.5	2.3
AGRICULTURAL SCIENCES	19	38	H	6.3	40.6	43.8	9.4
BIOSCIENCES—GRADUATE SCH	64	264	H	2.2	56.5	39.2	2.2
BIOSCIENCES—MEDICAL SCH	61	276	H		49.2	34.1	16.7
PSYCHOLOGY	9	16	H	25.0	50.0	16.7	8.3
SOCIAL SCIENCES	10	30	H		77.8	22.2	
			H				
DEPARTMENT WITHIN			H				
PRIVATE INSTITUTION	163	427	H	.8	52.0	34.9	12.3
PUBLIC INSTITUTION	219	709	H	1.5	50.7	41.6	6.2
			H				
DEPARTMENT WITH			H				
FIVE OR MORE POSTDOCS	221	684	H	1.3	54.9	34.6	9.2
FEWER THAN FIVE POSTDOCS	161	452	H	1.1	44.7	46.9	7.3

* RATIO OF NUMBER OF POSTDOCS IN THE DEPARTMENT TO NUMBER OF PHD'S AWARDED
* IN 1978-1979

	SURVEY RESP	TOTAL DEPTS	POSTDOC/PHD RATIO GREATER THAN					NO PHD'S
			2/1	1/1	1/2	1/4	0	
ALL DEPARTMENTS	590	1601	25.6	24.8	23.1	16.7	9.8	8.0
DEPARTMENTAL FIELD								
MATHEMATICAL SCI	21	28	3.7	7.4	40.7	25.9	22.2	3.7
PHYSICS	79	152	19.9	44.0	21.3	10.6	4.3	7.8
CHEMISTRY	72	162	31.7	38.6	15.9	11.0	2.8	5.7
EARTH SCIENCES	43	67	10.5	19.3	36.8	24.6	8.8	8.8
ENGINEERING	81	205	6.6	15.8	38.3	21.4	17.9	4.6
AGRICULTURAL SCIENCES	34	65	1.8	8.8	38.6	31.6	19.3	10.5
BIOSCIENCES-GRADUATE SCH	97	372	21.1	26.9	27.4	18.0	6.6	5.7
BIOSCIENCES-MEDICAL SCH	89	430	53.2	24.2	11.8	8.6	2.2	11.8
PSYCHOLOGY	43	62	6.8	6.8	8.5	30.5	47.5	1.7
SOCIAL SCIENCES	31	58	3.8	11.3	18.9	34.0	32.1	9.4
DEPARTMENT WITHIN								
PRIVATE INSTITUTION	238	558	29.5	24.7	20.9	14.7	10.2	9.2
PUBLIC INSTITUTION	352	1043	23.6	24.8	24.3	17.7	9.6	7.3
DEPARTMENT WITH								
FIVE OR MORE POSTDOCS	268	761	45.6	31.7	16.2	4.8	1.7	3.2
FEWER THAN FIVE POSTDOCS	322	840	5.9	18.0	30.0	28.3	17.8	12.7

305

* FRACTION OF TOTAL POSTDOCS IN THE DEPARTMENT WHO ARE FOREIGN

	SURVEY RESP	TOTAL DEPTS	FOREIGN POSTDOC FRACTION				NC FRGN PDOCS
			=1	>1/2	>1/4	>0	
ALL DEPARTMENTS	639	1601	12.8	16.8	29.6	13.2	27.5
DEPARTMENTAL FIELD							
MATHEMATICAL SCI	22	28	21.4	17.9	25.0	7.1	28.6
PHYSICS	85	152	8.0	14.7	37.3	14.7	25.3
CHEMISTRY	80	162	3.8	41.4	41.4	8.3	5.1
EARTH SCIENCES	48	67	16.7	10.6	24.2	9.1	39.4
ENGINEERING	85	205	38.0	27.8	22.9	4.4	6.8
AGRICULTURAL SCIENCES	38	65	20.0	10.8	18.5	9.2	41.5
BIOSCIENCES-GRADUATE SCH	102	372	10.4	14.5	29.2	18.0	27.9
BIOSCIENCES-MEDICAL SCH	101	430	6.1	8.7	35.2	17.0	33.0
PSYCHOLOGY	45	62	9.7	9.7	6.5	9.7	74.2
SOCIAL SCIENCES	33	58	21.4	10.7	8.9	12.5	46.4
DEPARTMENT WITHIN							
PRIVATE INSTITUTION	257	558	12.5	18.0	32.2	15.8	21.5
PUBLIC INSTITUTION	382	1043	13.0	16.2	28.3	11.8	30.7
DEPARTMENT WITH							
FIVE OR MORE POSTDOCS	275	761	2.6	27.7	39.9	21.7	8.2
FEWER THAN FIVE POSTDOCS	364	840	22.1	7.1	20.3	5.5	45.0

306

APPENDIX D

1972 Ph.D. Recipients

OMB No. 99-S79002
Approval expires
December 31, 1979

SURVEY OF SCIENTISTS AND ENGINEERS

CONDUCTED BY THE NATIONAL RESEARCH COUNCIL WITH THE SUPPORT OF THE NATIONAL SCIENCE FOUNDATION AND THE NATIONAL INSTITUTES OF HEALTH

THE ACCOMPANYING LETTER requests your assistance in this survey of scientists and engineers.

PLEASE READ the instructions carefully and answer by printing your reply or entering an 'X' in the appropriate box.

PLEASE COMMENT on any questions which you think require fuller explanation.

PLEASE RETURN the completed form in the enclosed envelope to the Commission on Human Resources, JH 638, National Research Council, 2101 Constitution Avenue, N.W., Washington, D.C. 20418

NOTE: This information is solicited under the authority of the National Science Foundation Act of 1950, as amended. All information you provide will be treated as confidential and used for statistical purposes only. Information will be released only in the form of statistical summaries or in a form which does not identify information about any particular person. Your response is entirely voluntary and your failure to provide some or all of the requested information will in no way adversely affect you.

DEFINITION: POSTDOCTORAL APPOINTMENT means a temporary appointment, the primary purpose of which is to provide for continued education or experience in research usually, though not necessarily, under the supervision of a senior mentor. Included are appointments in government and industrial laboratories which resemble in their character and objectives postdoctoral appointments in universities. Excluded are appointments in residency training programs in the health professions.

EMPLOYMENT

INSTRUCTIONS: Please answer questions 1 through 9 with respect to your PRINCIPAL employment or postdoctoral appointment AS OF APRIL 1979.

1. Which BEST describes your employment status? (*Check only one.*)   (8)

1 ☐ Full-time postdoctoral appointment (as defined above)

2 ☐ Part-time postdoctoral appointment (as defined above)

3 ☐ Full-time employed (other than postdoctoral appointment)

4 ☐ Part-time employed (other than postdoctoral appointment)

5 ☐ Unemployed and seeking employment

6 ☐ Unemployed and NOT seeking employment

7 ☐ Student (other than postdoctoral appointment)

8 ☐ Other status, please specify _____

NOTE: If you checked items 5, 6, or 7 above, please skip to question 10 on page 3.

2. What is the name and location of your employer or postdoctoral affiliation?   (9-14)

Name of Institution/Organization	*City*	*State*

3. Which category below BEST describes the type of organization of your employer/postdoctoral affiliation? (*Check only one.*)

1 ☐ University or 4-year college (other than items 2 and 6 below)

2 ☐ Medical school or other health professional school (including university-affiliated teaching hospital)

3 ☐ 2-year college or technical school

4 ☐ Elementary or secondary school

5 ☐ Other educational institution, please specify _____

6 ☐ FFRDC laboratory (i.e., federally funded research and development centers such as Brookhaven, Lincoln, Los Alamos, Oak Ridge, etc.)

7 ☐ Federal government (including military)

8 ☐ State or local government

9 ☐ Business or industry

10 ☐ Hospital or clinic (other than those included above)

11 ☐ Nonprofit organization (other than those included above)

12 ☐ Self-employed

13 ☐ Other type of employer, please specify _____

(15-16)

307

4. If affiliated with an INSTITUTION OF HIGHER EDUCATION (*items 1, 2, or 3 in Question 3*),

   a. What is the title of your position? _____ (17)

   b. Which category BEST describes the type of position you hold? (*Check only one.*)

      1 ☐ Faculty
      2 ☐ Postdoctoral appointment (as defined on page 1)
      3 ☐ Other nonfaculty research staff
      4 ☐ Other nonfaculty teaching staff
      5 ☐ Other, please specify _____ (18)

   c. Are you primarily employed in a research unit OUTSIDE the traditional academic/departmental structure?

      1 ☐ Yes   2 ☐ No (19)

   d. Is your position considered to be in a tenure track?

      1 ☐ Yes   2 ☐ No (20)

   e. If YES, do you have tenure?

      1 ☐ Yes   2 ☐ No (21)

5. Approximately what percent of the time associated with your principal employment (as of April 1979) do you devote to each of the following activities?

   a. Basic research (including supervision of students engaged in research) _____ % (22)

   b. Applied research and development (including supervision of students engaged in research) _____ % (24)

   c. Classroom teaching (not involving research supervision) _____ % (26)

   d. Administration/management _____ % (28)

   e. Consulting _____ % (30)

   f. Professional service (other than consulting) _____ % (32)

   g. Other, please specify _____ _____ % (34)

                                                       100 %

6. If your activities include research, which of the following federal agencies, if any, support the research in which you are engaged? (*Check all that apply.*)

      1 ☐ No federal support for research
      2 ☐ ADAMHA (National Institute of Mental Health, National Institute on Alcohol and Alcoholism, and National Institute on Drug Abuse)
      3 ☐ Department of Defense
      4 ☐ Department of Energy
      5 ☐ National Aeronautics and Space Administration
      6 ☐ National Institutes of Health
      7 ☐ National Science Foundation
      8 ☐ Other federal agency, please specify _____ (36-43)

7. From the enclosed list of specialty areas on the reverse side of the covering letter, select the areas most closely related to your employment or postdoctoral appointment, and enter their titles and 3-digit codes below. Write in your specialty if it is not on the list.

	Title of employment specialty	3-digit code	
Most closely related field:	_____	_____	(44-46)
Other fields (if applicable):	_____	_____	(47-49)
	_____	_____	(50-52)
	_____	_____	(53-55)

8. What is the BASIC ANNUAL SALARY* associated with your principal employment? If you hold a postdoctoral appointment (as defined on page 1) and receive a stipend, include the stipend plus personal allowances.

$ _____ per calendar year (11-12 months)   OR $ _____ per academic year (9-10 months)
　　(56-58)　　　　　　　　　　　　　　　　　　　　　　　　　　　　(59-61)

*Include your salary before deductions for income tax, social security, retirement, etc., but do NOT include bonuses, overtime, summer teaching, consulting, or other payment for professional work.

9. Which of the following BEST describes your immediate career plans? (Check only one.)

1 ☐ Not actively seeking new position
2 ☐ Actively seeking new position because present position terminates shortly

3 ☐ Actively seeking new position because of dissatisfaction with present position
4 ☐ Other, please specify _____
　　　　　　　　　　　　　　　　　　　　(62)

EMPLOYMENT HISTORY

10. Did you take a postdoctoral appointment (as defined on page 1) within a year after receiving your doctoral degree?

1 ☐ Yes   2 ☐ No   (63)

a. If YES, what were the reasons for taking your FIRST postdoctoral appointment? (Check all that apply and CIRCLE the most important ONE.)

1 ☐ To obtain additional research experience in your doctoral field
2 ☐ To work with a particular scientist or research group
3 ☐ To switch into a different field of research

4 ☐ Couldn't obtain type of employment position you wanted
5 ☐ Other reason, please specify _____
　　_____
　　　　　　　　　　　　　　(64-68)

b. If NO, what were the reasons for not taking a postdoctoral appointment? (Check all that apply and CIRCLE the most important ONE.)

1 ☐ Couldn't obtain postdoctoral appointment
2 ☐ Felt that a postdoctoral would be of little or no benefit in terms of your career aspirations
3 ☐ More promising career opportunities were available

4 ☐ Postdoctoral salaries too low compared with other employment opportunities
5 ☐ Other reason, please specify _____
　　_____
　　　　　　　　　　　　　　(69-73)

11. If you DID take a postdoctoral appointment within a year after receiving your doctoral degree,

a. what was the PRIMARY source of support for your FIRST postdoctoral appointment? (Check only one.)

1 ☐ Federal research grant or contract
2 ☐ Federal fellowship or training grant
3 ☐ Nonfederal nationally awarded fellowship
4 ☐ University or state funds (including teaching asst.)

5 ☐ Personal resources (e.g., loans, family income, etc.)
6 ☐ Other source, please specify below:
　　_____
　　　　　　　　　　　　　　(74)

b. to what extent did LIMITATIONS in geographic mobility influence your decision to take your FIRST postdoctoral appointment?

1 ☐ Important consideration
2 ☐ Incidental consideration
3 ☐ Not a consideration   (75)

c. did you prolong the length of time you held postdoctoral appointment(s) because of difficulty in finding other employment you wanted?

1 ☐ Yes   2 ☐ No   (76)

12. With respect to ALL postdoctoral appointments you have held (or now hold),

a. under how many different mentors have you held postdoctoral appointments? _____ (8)

b. how many TOTAL months have you held postdoctoral appointments? _____ (9-10)

c. how important were your postdoctoral appointments in enabling you to ATTAIN your present positions?

1 ☐ Essential qualification
2 ☐ Helpful, but not essential

3 ☐ Made no difference
4 ☐ Cannot determine   (11)

d. to what extent has your experience on postdoctoral appointments contributed to your professional advancement?

1 ☐ Extremely valuable
2 ☐ Useful

3 ☐ Not useful
4 ☐ Cannot determine   (12)

13. Since receiving your doctoral degree, have you held any UNIVERSITY RESEARCH POSITIONS which were considered neither faculty nor postdoctoral appointments?

1 ☐ Yes   2 ☐ No   (13)

If YES, how many TOTAL months have you held these university research positions (include the months you have spent in your present position if applicable)? _____ (14-15)

14. How many articles in refereed journals or books have you had published? _____ _____
                                                                          Articles   Books
                                                                          (16-17)   (18-19)

Of how many were you the principal author? _____ _____
                                           Articles   Books
                                           (20-21)   (22-23)

15. a. If you are currently (as of April 1979) involved in a research project in a university, how many individuals (including yourself) are working on the projects? Please provide the number of individuals in each of the personnel groups below and rate the contributions made by each group to the OVERALL PRODUCTIVITY OF THE RESEARCH EFFORT. In rating the contributions, use the following scale:

1 = essential   3 = not important
2 = important   4 = cannot determine

Personnel Group	Number of individuals	Rating of contribution
Faculty	_____ (24-25)	_____ (26)
Postdoctoral appointees (as defined on page 1)	_____ (27-28)	_____ (29)
Other doctoral staff (e.g., research scientists)	_____ (30-31)	_____ (32)
Graduate research assistants	_____ (33-34)	_____ (35)
Nondoctoral staff (e.g., technicians)	_____ (36-37)	_____ (38)

b. Using the same scale (above), rate the contributions of POSTDOCTORAL APPOINTEES (only) to each of the following aspects of the research project:

	Rating of contribution
Determining the basic directions of the research project	_____ (39)
Intellectual vigor of the research effort	_____ (40)
Infusion of new research techniques	_____ (41)
Publication of research findings	_____ (42)
Training of graduate students	_____ (43)

16. Racial or ethnic group (Check all that apply.)

0 ☐ American Indian or Alaskan Native . . . any of the original peoples of North America, and who maintain cultural identification through tribal affiliation or community recognition.

1 ☐ Asian or Pacific Islander . . . . . . any of the original peoples of the Far East, Southeast Asia, the Indian Subcontinent, or the Pacific Islands. This area includes, for example, China, Japan, Korea, the Philippine Islands, and Samoa.

2 ☐ Black, not of Hispanic Origin . . . . . any of the black racial groups of Africa.

3 ☐ White, not of Hispanic Origin . . . . . any of the original peoples of Europe, North Africa, or the Middle East.

4 ☐ Hispanic . . . . Mexican, Puerto Rican, Central or South American, or other Spanish culture or
(44-48)   origins, regardless of race.

17. Do you have any additional comments on the advantages and disadvantages of postdoctoral appointments in your particular field?

_____

_____

_____

(49)

THANK YOU FOR YOUR COOPERATION

LIST OF EMPLOYMENT SPECIALTY AREAS (to be used for question 7)

MATHEMATICS

000 · Algebra
010 · Analysis & Functional Analysis
020 · Geometry
030 · Logic
040 · Number Theory
052 · Probability
055 · Math Statistics (see also 544, 670, 725, 727)
060 · Topology
082 · Operations Research (see also 478)
085 · Applied Mathematics
089 · Combinatorics & Finite Mathematics
091 · Physical Mathematics
098 · Mathematics, General
099 · Mathematics, Other*

COMPUTER SCIENCES

071 · Theory
072 · Software Systems
073 · Hardware Systems
074 · Intelligent Systems
079 · Computer Sciences, Other* (see also 437, 476)

PHYSICS & ASTRONOMY

101 · Astronomy
102 · Astrophysics
110 · Atomic & Molecular Physics
120 · Electromagnetism
130 · Mechanics
132 · Acoustics
134 · Fluids
135 · Plasma Physics
136 · Optics
138 · Thermal Physics
140 · Elementary Particles
150 · Nuclear Structure
160 · Solid State
198 · Physics, General
199 · Physics, Other*

CHEMISTRY

200 · Analytical
210 · Inorganic
215 · Synthetic Inorganic & Organometallic
220 · Organic
225 · Synthetic Organic & Natural Products
230 · Nuclear
240 · Physical
245 · Quantum
250 · Theoretical
255 · Structural
260 · Agricultural & Food
265 · Thermodynamics & Material Properties
270 · Pharmaceutical
275 · Polymers
280 · Biochemistry (see also 540)
285 · Chemical Dynamics
298 · Chemistry, General
299 · Chemistry, Other*

EARTH, ENVIRONMENTAL, AND MARINE SCIENCES

301 · Mineralogy, Petrology
305 · Geochemistry
310 · Stratigraphy, Sedimentation
320 · Paleontology
330 · Structural Geology
341 · Geophysics (Solid Earth)
350 · Geomorph. & Glacial Geology
391 · Applied Geol., Geol. Engr. & Econ. Geol.
395 · Fuel Tech. & Petrol. Engr. (see also 479)
360 · Hydrology & Water Resources
370 · Oceanography
397 · Marine Sciences, Other*
381 · Atmospheric Physics & Chemistry
382 · Atmospheric Dynamics
383 · Atmospheric Sciences, Other*
388 · Environmental Sciences, General (see also 480, 528)
389 · Environmental Sciences, Other*
398 · Earth Sciences, General
399 · Earth Sciences, Other*

ENGINEERING

400 · Aeronautical & Astronautical
410 · Agricultural
415 · Biomedical
420 · Civil
430 · Chemical
435 · Ceramic
437 · Computer
440 · Electrical
445 · Electronics
450 · Industrial & Manufacturing
455 · Nuclear
460 · Engineering Physics
470 · Mechanical
475 · Metallurgy & Phys. Met. Engr.
476 · Systems Design & Systems Science (see also 072, 073, 074)
478 · Operations Research (see also 082)
479 · Fuel Technology & Petrol. Engr. (see also 395)
480 · Sanitary & Environmental
486 · Mining
497 · Materials Science
498 · Engineering, General
499 · Engineering, Other*

AGRICULTURAL SCIENCES

500 · Agronomy
501 · Agricultural Economics
502 · Animal Husbandry
503 · Food Science & Technology (see also 573)
504 · Fish & Wildlife
505 · Forestry
506 · Horticulture
507 · Soils & Soil Science
510 · Animal Science & Animal Nutrition
511 · Phytopathology
518 · Agriculture, General
519 · Agriculture, Other*

MEDICAL SCIENCES

520 · Medicine & Surgery
522 · Public Health & Epidemiology
523 · Veterinary Medicine
524 · Hospital Administration
526 · Nursing
527 · Parasitology
528 · Environmental Health
534 · Pathology
536 · Pharmacology
537 · Pharmacy
538 · Medical Sciences, General
539 · Medical Sciences, Other*

BIOLOGICAL SCIENCES

540 · Biochemistry (see also 280)
542 · Biophysics
543 · Biomathematics
544 · Biometrics and Biostatistics (see also 055, 670, 725, 727)
545 · Anatomy
546 · Cytology
547 · Embryology
548 · Immunology
550 · Botany
560 · Ecology
562 · Hydrobiology
564 · Microbiology & Bacteriology
566 · Physiology, Animal
567 · Physiology, Plant
569 · Zoology
570 · Genetics
571 · Entomology
572 · Molecular Biology
573 · Food Science & Technology (see also 503)
574 · Behavior/Ethology
576 · Nutrition & Dietetics
578 · Biological Sciences, General
579 · Biological Sciences, Other*

PSYCHOLOGY

600 · Clinical
610 · Counseling & Guidance
620 · Developmental & Gerontological
630 · Education
635 · School Psychology
641 · Experimental
642 · Comparative
643 · Physiological
650 · Industrial & Personnel
660 · Personality
670 · Psychometrics (see also 055, 544, 725, 727)
680 · Social
698 · Psychology, General
699 · Psychology, Other*

SOCIAL SCIENCES

700 · Anthropology
703 · Archeology
708 · Communications*
709 · Linguistics
710 · Sociology
720 · Economics (see also 501)
725 · Econometrics (see also 055, 544, 670, 727)
727 · Social Statistics (see also 055, 544, 670, 725)
740 · Geography
745 · Area Studies*
751 · Political Science
752 · Public Administration
755 · International Relations
770 · Urban & Regional Planning
775 · History & Philosophy of Science
798 · Social Sciences, General
799 · Social Sciences, Other*

ARTS & HUMANITIES

841 · Fine & Applied Arts (including Music, Speech, Drama, etc.)
842 · History
843 · Philosophy, Religion, Theology
845 · Languages & Literature
846 · Other Arts and Humanities*

EDUCATION & OTHER PROFESSIONAL FIELDS

938 · Education

882 · Business Administration
883 · Home Economics
884 · Journalism
885 · Speech and Hearing Sciences
886 · Law, Jurisprudence
887 · Social Work
891 · Library & Archival Science
898 · Professional Field, Other*

899 · OTHER FIELDS*

*Identify the specific field in the space on the questionnaire.

312

NATIONAL RESEARCH COUNCIL
COMMISSION ON HUMAN RESOURCES

2101 Constitution Avenue   Washington, D. C. 20418

COMMITTEE ON THE STUDY OF
POSTDOCTORALS AND DOCTORAL RESEARCH STAFF

Lee Grodzins, *Chairman*
Massachusetts Institute of
Technology

Richard D. Anderson
Louisiana State University

Frederick E. Balderston
University of California
Berkeley, California

Kenneth E. Clark
University of Rochester

Gerhart Friedlander
Brookhaven National Laboratory

Herbert Friedman
Naval Research Laboratory

John C. Hancock
Purdue University

Donald F. Hornig
Harvard School of Public Health

Shirley Ann Jackson
Bell Laboratories

Ernest S. Kuh
University of California
Berkeley, California

William F. Miller
Stanford University

Nicholas C. Mullins
Indiana University

Thomas A. Reichert
Carnegie-Mellon University

Helen R. Whiteley
University of Washington

April 20, 1979

Dear Colleague:

The National Research Council has appointed a committee to study the policy implications of the changing role of postdoctorals and other doctoral research staff in science and engineering. During the last decade, in the face of reduced numbers of faculty openings, increasing numbers of young scientists and engineers have taken postdoctorals and other types of positions in universities and colleges as well as outside the academic setting. The accompanying survey is designed to furnish information on the changing employment patterns in each field and the implications for individual careers and for the national research effort.

The survey is sponsored by the National Science Foundation and the National Institutes of Health, but the survey records will be retained in the National Research Council. All information you provide is to be used for purposes of statistical description only and its confidentiality will be protected.

The survey results will provide a basis for the Committee's recommendations regarding federal and institutional policies. The success of this survey depends on your cooperation. Please return the completed questionnaire as soon as possible in the enclosed envelope. Thank you for your prompt assistance.

Sincerely,

Lee Grodzins
Chairman

NOTE: List of specialty areas to be used for survey question 7 is on the reverse side of this page.

The National Research Council is the principal operating agency of the National Academy of Sciences and the National Academy of Engineering to serve government and other organizations

* SURVEY OF 1972 PHD RECIPIENTS
* QUESTION 1

CURRENT EMPLOYMENT STATUS

	SURVEY RESP	TOTAL PHD'S	F-T POSTDOC	F-T EMPL	P-T PDOC	P-T EMPL	SEEK EMPL	OTHER
ALL 1972 PHD RECIPIENTS	3589	15275	1.5	93.2	.1	2.7	1.2	1.3
PHD FIELD								
MATHEMATICAL SCI	171	1021	.4	94.7		2.9	.3	1.7
PHYSICS	619	1264	1.8	93.9	.4	2.0	.3	1.6
CHEMISTRY	319	1610	2.0	94.3	.2	1.4	.9	1.1
EARTH SCI	126	480		94.8		3.5	.4	1.3
ENGINEERING	224	2357	.3	96.4			2.2	1.2
AGRICULTURAL SCI	115	630	1.4	95.7		2.9		
BIOSCIENCES	1372	3234	3.4	90.0	.2	2.2	1.8	2.4
PSYCHOLOGY	390	2117	1.1	88.4		7.4	1.4	1.7
SOCIAL SCIENCES	253	2562	.7	95.6		2.8	1.0	
POSTDOCTORAL EXPERIENCE								
SOME	1586	4315	5.2	88.8	.4	2.2	1.7	1.7
NONE	2003	10960		94.9		2.9	1.0	1.2
SEX								
MEN	2915	13479	1.3	95.0	.1	1.8	1.1	.8
WOMEN	674	1796	2.5	79.8	.3	9.4	2.4	5.6
RACIAL GROUP								
WHITE	3404	14559	1.4	93.2	.1	2.7	1.3	1.3
OTHER	185	716	3.2	92.7	.3	2.1	.6	1.1

313

* SURVEY OF 1972 PHD RECIPIENTS
* QUESTION 3

EMPLOYER OR POSTDOCTORAL AFFILIATION

	SURVEY RESP	TOTAL EMPL PHD'S	EDUCATIONAL INSTITUTION				GOVERNMENT			OTHER SECTORS				
			UNIV/ COLL	MED SCHL	JR COLL	OTHER EDUC	FFRDC	FEDL GOVT	OTHER GOVT	BUSN	HOSP/ CLNIC	NON-PRUFT	SELF EMPL	OTHER
ALL 1972 PHD RECIPIENTS	3431	14883	42.9	9.5	2.2	1.2	2.6	10.5	2.8	20.8	1.7	3.1	2.7	
PHD FIELD														
MATHEMATICAL SCI	165	1001	63.0	3.8	2.1		1.4	8.9	.1	19.7		.8	.2	
PHYSICS	597	1240	32.5	4.4	4.0	.7	14.3	14.5	.5	24.7	1.1	1.9	1.4	
CHEMISTRY	307	1577	21.7	4.2	4.2	.4	2.4	7.2	3.3	50.4	1.6	3.9	.6	
EARTH SCI	122	472	51.9	1.7	1.7	.2	4.5	20.7	2.4	16.7		1.9		
ENGINEERING	219	2277	28.6	3.5			3.6	15.4	1.2	46.6	.1	.4	.4	
AGRICULTURAL SCI	114	630	60.8	1.1	2.7			11.1	4.8	18.2		1.3		
BIOSCIENCES	1290	3099	32.1	28.9	2.4	.7	1.4	11.6	2.5	11.4	2.5	4.3	2.1	.1
PSYCHOLOGY	371	2051	37.5	10.3	2.7	5.5	.6	7.5	8.1	3.5	5.5	6.4	12.5	
SOCIAL SCIENCES	246	2536	77.1	2.5	1.4	1.0		6.0	1.8	4.7	.6	3.4	1.6	
POSTDOCTORAL EXPERIENCE														
SOME	1512	4169	33.8	18.9	1.0	.3	4.7	9.4	1.2	23.6	2.0	3.8	1.3	.1
NONE	1919	10714	46.4	5.8	2.7	1.5	1.8	10.9	3.4	19.7	1.5	2.8	3.3	
SEX														
MEN	2831	13230	42.8	8.6	1.8	1.0	2.9	10.9	2.7	22.6	1.4	2.9	2.4	
WOMEN	600	1653	43.7	16.4	5.3	2.3	.7	7.6	3.8	6.7	3.8	4.6	5.2	
RACIAL GROUP														
WHITE	3252	14179	42.5	9.2	2.3	1.2	2.7	10.5	2.9	21.1	1.7	3.2	2.7	
OTHER	179	704	50.9	15.5	.3		1.5	9.8	.9	14.6	1.6	1.9	3.0	

314

* SURVEY OF 1972 PHD RECIPIENTS
* QUESTION 4

POSITION IN UNIVERSITY

| | SURVEY RESP | TOTAL PHD'S IN ACAD | --FACULTY-- | | ------NONFACULTY------ | | | | PERCENT EMPLOYED OUTSIDE DEPARTMENT |
| | | | TENURE | NO TENR | POST-DOCS | RSRCH STAFF | TEACH STAFF | OTHER STAFF | |

	SURVEY RESP	TOTAL PHD'S IN ACAD	TENURE	NO TENR	POST-DOCS	RSRCH STAFF	TEACH STAFF	OTHER STAFF	PERCENT EMPLOYED OUTSIDE DEPARTMENT
ALL 1972 PHD RECIPIENTS H	1892	8207	56.3	32.8	2.4	4.2	.5	3.9	6.8
H									
PHD FIELD									
MATHEMATICAL SCI H	111	690	76.8	20.7	.6			1.9	.4
PHYSICS H	246	508	42.5	37.2	5.2	10.9	1.2	3.0	14.3
CHEMISTRY H	103	478	45.4	40.8	5.0	2.4	1.3	5.0	9.0
EARTH SCI H	62	252	68.9	21.9		9.2			10.0
ENGINEERING H	73	722	59.2	28.3	.4	8.1		4.0	5.0
AGRICULTURAL SCI H	73	406	67.5	22.7	2.2	.2		7.4	15.3
BIOSCIENCES H	837	1964	38.6	48.5	4.5	4.9	1.0	2.5	7.6
PSYCHOLOGY H	195	1133	50.5	36.2	2.0	5.1	.5	5.8	7.1
SOCIAL SCIENCES H	192	2054	70.2	22.1	.8	2.2		4.7	4.5
H									
POSTDOCTORAL EXPERIENCE H									
SOME H	865	2226	29.9	53.0	8.6	5.5	.6	2.4	11.9
NONE H	1027	5981	66.3	25.1		3.7	.4	4.5	4.9
H									
SEX									
MEN H	1489	7097	59.0	31.3	2.0	3.9	.4	3.4	6.9
WOMEN H	403	1110	39.0	42.1	4.4	6.4	1.0	7.2	6.5
H									
RACIAL GROUP									
WHITE H	1769	7756	56.6	32.2	2.2	4.4	.5	4.1	6.9
OTHER H	123	451	50.6	41.9	4.5	1.8	.7	.7	5.3

315

	SURVEY RESP	TOTAL EMPL PHD'S	MEAN PERCENT TIME DEVOTED TO						
			BASIC RSRCH	APPL RSRCH	TEACH	ADMIN	CON-SULT	PROF SERV	OTHER
ALL 1972 PHD RECIPIENTS	3378	14883	18.7	18.6	24.0	20.5	5.7	9.8	2.9
PHD FIELD									
MATHEMATICAL SCI	162	1001	17.2	12.4	40.2	12.7	7.9	7.4	2.1
PHYSICS	593	1240	21.2	27.4	18.4	17.1	4.2	8.1	3.6
CHEMISTRY	298	1577	21.8	27.7	14.7	22.3	2.8	7.9	2.7
EARTH SCI	121	472	23.0	17.3	23.1	26.1	4.6	3.7	2.1
ENGINEERING	211	2277	6.6	31.3	13.4	27.6	7.8	9.3	4.0
AGRICULTURAL SCI	112	630	8.2	31.5	19.5	19.3	3.7	10.3	7.6
BIOSCIENCES	1270	3099	34.2	11.6	23.9	16.7	3.7	7.7	2.4
PSYCHOLOGY	368	2051	10.4	12.6	20.8	19.0	9.5	24.4	3.4
SOCIAL SCIENCES	243	2536	16.3	10.6	38.9	22.9	5.3	4.7	1.2
POSTDOCTORAL EXPERIENCE									
SOME	1487	4169	35.8	19.4	17.2	14.7	3.4	6.9	2.5
NONE	1891	10714	12.2	18.3	26.5	22.6	6.5	10.8	3.0
SEX									
MEN	2787	13230	18.2	19.7	23.3	21.0	5.7	9.3	2.8
WOMEN	591	1653	22.5	10.2	28.9	16.1	5.2	13.4	3.6
RACIAL GROUP									
WHITE	3203	14179	18.4	18.6	23.9	20.6	5.6	9.9	2.9
OTHER	175	704	25.0	18.2	25.7	17.3	6.1	6.0	1.8

* SURVEY OF 1972 PHD RECIPIENTS
* QUESTION 6

	SURVEY RESP	TOTAL PHD'S DOING SOME RSRCH	SOME FEDL SUPT	NO FEDL SUPT	FEDERAL SUPPORT FOR RESEARCH FROM						
					ADAMHA	DOD	DOE	NASA	NIH	NSF	OTHER AGENCY
ALL 1972 PHD RECIPIENTS	2648	11774	52.6	47.4	2.2	9.4	7.3	3.6	14.2	11.2	18.1
PHD FIELD											
MATHEMATICAL SCI	118	773	46.0	54.0	.3	11.5	5.7	.7	3.0	27.2	6.0
PHYSICS	469	984	72.6	27.4		24.4	28.1	13.2	6.7	16.8	5.8
CHEMISTRY	221	1234	42.4	57.6	.2	9.0	8.2	2.7	15.5	9.8	13.4
EARTH SCI	100	392	83.2	16.8		7.3	15.2	10.8		38.2	32.5
ENGINEERING	170	1782	58.0	42.0		24.7	12.2	9.5	7.1	10.9	16.7
AGRICULTURAL SCI	83	493	52.9	47.1			4.7	1.6	.4	4.7	52.9
BIOSCIENCES	1058	2589	62.2	37.8	2.2	3.7	3.7	.8	37.0	9.8	16.0
PSYCHOLOGY	233	1423	40.2	59.8	10.7	4.9	1.6	.8	15.0	3.8	16.0
SOCIAL SCIENCES	196	2104	36.8	63.2	2.1	1.4	.3		3.2	7.1	25.4
POSTDOCTORAL EXPERIENCE											
SOME	1288	3655	65.7	34.3	2.5	10.2	9.7	5.1	28.2	15.7	13.3
NONE	1360	8119	46.5	53.5	2.1	9.0	6.1	2.9	7.6	9.2	20.2
SEX											
MEN	2235	10570	52.7	47.3	2.0	10.1	7.8	3.9	13.2	11.6	18.1
WOMEN	413	1204	51.3	48.7	4.0	2.7	2.3	1.2	22.6	8.1	17.5
RACIAL GROUP											
WHITE	2497	11169	52.0	48.0	2.1	9.0	7.2	3.6	13.7	11.3	18.2
OTHER	151	605	62.1	37.9	3.5	16.8	7.9	3.2	22.3	10.4	15.8

317

* SURVEY OF 1972 PHD RECIPIENTS
* QUESTION 7

FIELD OF EMPLOYMENT OR POSTDOCTORAL

	SURVEY RESP	TOTAL EMPL PHD'S	MATH	PHYS	CHEM	EARTH SCI	ENGIN	AGRI SCI	BIO SCI	PSYCH	SOCIAL SCI	NON SCI
ALL 1972 PHD RECIPIENTS	3379	14883	9.6	5.4	8.4	5.7	14.0	4.4	21.7	11.8	12.6	6.3
PHD FIELD												
MATHEMATICAL SCI	161	1001	87.0		.4		5.5		3.9		.2	3.0
PHYSICS	590	1240	7.0	52.7	.8	7.6	18.3	.4	7.2		.5	5.5
CHEMISTRY	301	1577	3.2	2.1	70.1	3.1	5.0	.8	10.2		.4	5.2
EARTH SCI	118	472		.2		93.0	.9	.9	1.3	.4	.4	2.8
ENGINEERING	217	2277	10.4	4.4	.3	4.0	72.1		4.5		.2	4.2
AGRICULTURAL SCI	112	630			1.5	2.4	1.1	80.8	11.4		1.1	1.6
BIOSCIENCES	1273	3099	.6	.5	3.9	3.6	.6	2.8	84.6	.8	.6	2.1
PSYCHOLOGY	365	2051	1.5	.3		.1	.7	.2	4.3	83.3	2.8	6.9
SOCIAL SCIENCES	242	2536	5.3			1.6	.7	1.5	1.7	1.2	70.8	17.2
POSTDOCTORAL EXPERIENCE												
SOME	1493	4169	5.2	9.7	18.3	5.1	6.5	2.3	39.6	5.6	5.4	2.3
NONE	1886	10714	11.3	3.8	4.6	5.9	16.9	5.3	14.7	14.3	15.4	7.9
SEX												
MEN	2787	13230	10.3	6.0	8.7	6.1	15.6	4.9	20.3	10.2	12.0	6.1
WOMEN	592	1653	4.3	1.1	6.6	2.0	1.7	.6	32.9	25.0	17.8	8.0
RACIAL GROUP												
WHITE	3205	14179	9.7	5.4	8.3	5.5	14.0	4.5	21.3	11.9	12.8	6.5
OTHER	174	704	7.0	5.3	10.5	9.3	15.1	2.0	28.7	10.7	9.1	2.3

* SURVEY OF 1972 PHD RECIPIENTS
* QUESTION 8C

	SURVEY RESP	TOTAL F-T EMPL	SALARY RANGE OF FULL-TIME EMPLOYED										MEDIAN SALARY
			<$18K	$18K -20K	$20K -22K	$22K -24K	$24K -26K	$26K -28K	$28K -30K	$30K -32K	$32K -34K	>$34K	
ALL 1972 PHD RECIPIENTS	3053	13419	4.3	5.8	8.7	13.1	13.9	9.8	9.6	9.2	6.5	19.0	$26,750
PHD FIELD													
MATHEMATICAL SCI	147	892	4.6	8.2	11.5	22.6	13.2	9.1	9.0	2.6	4.8	14.3	24,400
PHYSICS	540	1108	5.2	7.2	9.2	8.9	12.5	10.6	10.3	12.7	8.0	15.3	27,000
CHEMISTRY	274	1424	5.8	4.4	5.1	10.5	13.5	10.9	12.0	14.3	7.7	15.9	27,800
EARTH SCI	115	444	3.8	3.4	13.1	14.4	13.3	9.9	3.6	9.5	4.5	24.5	26,000
ENGINEERING	206	2203	.1	1.6	1.5	5.1	9.4	5.8	10.9	12.7	13.4	39.5	32,000
AGRICULTURAL SCI	105	580	6.4	3.3	8.8	14.8	18.4	15.2	6.6	8.4	4.1	14.0	25,250
BIOSCIENCES	1134	2697	7.2	7.3	10.3	14.2	16.1	11.3	8.1	8.1	4.4	13.1	25,000
PSYCHOLOGY	309	1768	3.2	5.1	11.5	13.4	18.4	9.9	10.0	9.6	5.1	13.7	25,400
SOCIAL SCIENCES	223	2303	4.0	9.0	11.2	18.8	12.4	9.6	10.2	4.7	3.8	16.3	25,350
POSTDOCTORAL EXPERIENCE													
SOME	1317	3639	5.9	6.3	12.8	11.3	15.1	12.8	10.7	9.9	4.8	10.4	25,450
NONE	1736	9780	3.7	5.6	7.1	13.8	13.5	8.7	9.2	8.9	7.2	22.2	27,000
SEX													
MEN	2564	12079	3.7	5.0	8.5	13.1	13.7	9.9	9.5	9.6	6.9	20.2	26,850
WOMEN	489	1340	9.9	13.1	9.8	14.0	16.3	8.8	10.8	5.7	3.1	8.7	24,350
RACIAL GROUP													
WHITE	2896	12795	4.3	5.9	8.8	12.8	13.9	9.8	9.4	9.5	6.4	19.2	26,750
OTHER	157	624	5.3	4.5	4.6	19.7	13.8	9.8	13.8	3.5	9.3	15.7	26,000

319

IMMEDIATE CAREER PLANS

	SURVEY RESP	TOTAL EMPL PHD'S	NO CHANGE	JOB ENDS SCON	SEEK NEW JOB	OTHER
ALL 1972 PHD RECIPIENTS	3365	14883	81.1	3.8	12.6	2.5
PHD FIELD						
MATHEMATICAL SCI	162	1001	82.2	2.8	13.3	1.7
PHYSICS	587	1240	83.1	2.4	11.9	2.6
CHEMISTRY	300	1577	80.1	2.6	14.9	2.4
EARTH SCI	118	472	93.7	.4	5.5	.4
ENGINEERING	216	2277	87.4	1.3	9.9	1.4
AGRICULTURAL SCI	113	630	88.7	1.4	8.2	1.6
BIOSCIENCES	1267	3099	77.9	5.3	13.5	3.3
PSYCHOLOGY	362	2051	74.3	6.9	14.8	4.0
SOCIAL SCIENCES	240	2536	79.7	4.8	13.0	2.5
POSTDOCTORAL EXPERIENCE						
SOME	1483	4169	77.5	5.7	13.5	3.3
NONE	1882	10714	82.5	3.0	12.2	2.3
SEX						
MEN	2779	13230	81.6	3.3	13.0	2.2
WOMEN	586	1653	76.8	8.1	9.4	5.7
RACIAL GROUP						
WHITE	3194	14179	81.3	3.7	12.5	2.5
OTHER	171	704	77.5	5.4	13.6	3.5

* SURVEY OF 1972 PHD RECIPIENTS
* QUESTION 10

	SURVEY RESP	TOTAL PHD'S	REASON FOR TAKING POSTDOC						REASON FOR NOT TAKING POSTDOC					
			TOTAL TAKING POSTDOC APPT	ADDED RSRCH EXPER	WORK WITH MENTR	SWTCH FIELD	NO EMPL	OTHER OR UNKN	TOTAL NOT TAKING POSTDOC	APPT NOT AVAIL	APPT NOT USEFL	BETTR OFFER	STIPND TOO LOW	OTHER OR UNKN
ALL 1972 PHD RECIPIENTS	3559	15275	28.1	11.9	4.4	3.3	7.2	1.2	71.9	2.6	16.2	35.0	6.4	11.8
PHD FIELD														
MATHEMATICAL SCI	168	1021	14.3	7.0	2.4	1.2	3.8		85.7	7.3	25.0	32.9	2.5	18.0
PHYSICS	616	1264	44.8	19.5	6.4	4.5	13.0	1.4	55.2	4.8	14.0	23.4	4.8	8.3
CHEMISTRY	317	1610	59.6	19.7	8.1	8.0	22.2	1.6	40.4	2.2	11.1	18.1	3.5	5.5
EARTH SCI	125	480	23.0	15.2	3.8	.2	3.2	.6	77.0	2.3	15.2	47.5	7.6	4.4
ENGINEERING	222	2357	10.9	3.8	1.7	.3	5.1		89.1	2.2	27.1	36.0	8.4	15.5
AGRICULTURAL SCI	114	630	12.7	4.2	1.9	.3	5.9	.3	87.3	1.4	21.7	49.1	5.3	11.2
BIOSCIENCES	1364	3234	50.4	25.9	8.9	7.4	6.8	1.4	49.6	1.4	8.7	23.6	5.0	10.8
PSYCHOLOGY	385	2117	14.4	5.4	2.9	2.1	.9	3.1	85.6	3.4	18.3	41.4	10.8	11.7
SOCIAL SCIENCES	248	2562	9.1	1.7	.7	.7	4.8	1.1	90.9	1.9	13.5	54.5	6.7	14.3
POSTDOCTORAL EXPERIENCE														
SOME	1586	4315	98.5	41.8	15.6	11.7	25.2	4.4	1.5	.1	.2	.4	.1	.6
NONE	1973	10960							100.0	3.6	22.6	48.7	8.9	16.2
SEX														
MEN	2893	13479	28.0	11.5	4.4	3.3	7.7	1.1	72.0	2.5	16.8	35.1	6.8	10.7
WOMEN	666	1796	28.3	15.0	4.6	3.4	3.3	2.0	71.7	3.7	11.5	34.0	3.0	19.4
RACIAL GROUP														
WHITE	3375	14559	27.8	11.7	4.4	3.1	7.4	1.2	72.2	2.5	16.6	34.8	6.5	11.8
OTHER	184	716	32.7	15.5	5.5	8.7	2.0	1.1	67.3	4.8	9.1	37.9	3.8	11.7

	SURVEY RESP	TOTAL PHD'S WHO TOOK POSTDOC	FEDL RSRCH FUNDS	FEDL FEL/ TRNEE	OTHER NATL FEL	UNIV OR STATE	PER- SONAL	OTHER
ALL 1972 PHD RECIPIENTS	1551	4251	39.0	28.1	7.7	13.2	.7	11.3
PHD FIELD								
MATHEMATICAL SCI	41	144	19.4	8.3	.7	50.7		20.8
PHYSICS	306	563	58.1	16.0	2.0	11.2	.5	12.3
CHEMISTRY	184	952	43.4	23.0	5.1	15.3		13.1
EARTH SCI	49	109	66.1	12.8	3.7	4.6		12.8
ENGINEERING	68	256	38.6	11.4	12.6	16.9	.8	19.7
AGRICULTURAL SCI	34	79	65.8	3.8	3.8	10.1		16.5
BIOSCIENCES	722	1617	34.3	39.3	12.3	6.0	.9	7.2
PSYCHOLOGY	109	303	17.7	58.7	2.3	15.0	2.0	4.3
SOCIAL SCIENCES	38	228	24.7	5.9	9.6	35.2	2.3	22.4
POSTDOCTORAL EXPERIENCE								
SOME	1551	4251	39.0	28.1	7.7	13.2	.7	11.3
NONE								
SEX								
MEN	1294	3750	40.1	26.5	7.4	13.4	.8	11.8
WOMEN	257	501	30.5	40.4	9.9	11.1	.2	7.9
RACIAL GROUP								
WHITE	1461	4017	39.1	27.7	7.6	13.3	.7	11.7
OTHER	90	234	37.8	35.7	10.4	10.4	.9	4.8

SOURCE OF SUPPORT FOR FIRST POSTDOC

322

	TOTAL SURVEY RESP	PHD'S WHO TOOK POSTDOC	GEOGRAPHIC LIMITATIONS		
			IMPORT FACTOR	INCIDENTAL FACTOR	NOT A FACTOR
ALL 1972 PHD RECIPIENTS	1549	4251	18.7	15.3	66.0
PHD FIELD					
MATHEMATICAL SCI	41	144	9.7	4.2	86.1
PHYSICS	305	563	14.6	18.5	66.8
CHEMISTRY	183	952	14.3	18.2	67.5
EARTH SCI	49	109	7.3	18.3	74.3
ENGINEERING	67	256	10.3	15.5	74.2
AGRICULTURAL SCI	34	79	20.3	10.1	69.6
BIOSCIENCES	720	1617	25.5	13.9	60.6
PSYCHOLOGY	111	303	27.7	21.5	50.8
SOCIAL SCIENCES	39	228	7.0	5.3	87.7
POSTDOCTORAL EXPERIENCE					
SOME	1549	4251	18.7	15.3	66.0
NONE					
SEX					
MEN	1292	3750	13.5	15.7	70.7
WOMEN	257	501	57.7	12.3	30.0
RACIAL GROUP					
WHITE	1460	4017	18.6	15.4	66.0
OTHER	89	234	20.3	15.0	64.8

323

	SURVEY RESP	TOTAL PHD'S WHO TOOK POSTDOC	PROLONGED POSTDOC APPTS BECAUSE NO JOB
ALL 1972 PHD RECIPIENTS	1537	4251	28.6
PHD FIELD			
MATHEMATICAL SCI	41	144	18.8
PHYSICS	302	563	36.2
CHEMISTRY	184	952	38.3
EARTH SCI	49	109	6.4
ENGINEERING	68	256	24.0
AGRICULTURAL SCI	33	79	42.9
BIOSCIENCES	712	1617	28.0
PSYCHOLOGY	110	303	13.6
SOCIAL SCIENCES	38	228	9.4
POSTDOCTORAL EXPERIENCE			
SOME	1537	4251	28.6
NONE			
SEX			
MEN	1284	3750	28.4
WOMEN	253	501	29.8
RACIAL GROUP			
WHITE	1449	4017	28.8
OTHER	88	234	24.0

	SURVEY RESP	TOTAL PHD'S WITH SOME POSTDOC	NUMBER OF DIFFERENT MENTORS			
			0	1	2	>3
ALL 1972 PHD RECIPIENTS H	1641	4666	3.5	66.9	24.4	5.1
H						
PHD FIELD H						
MATHEMATICAL SCI H	44	183	5.6	69.1	25.3	
PHYSICS H	320	601	2.2	65.1	28.4	4.4
CHEMISTRY H	192	980	.7	69.2	26.0	4.1
EARTH SCI H	50	117	7.8	89.6	2.6	
ENGINEERING H	71	259	10.4	67.6	20.8	1.2
AGRICULTURAL SCI H	34	79		60.8	34.2	5.1
BIOSCIENCES H	765	1702	.3	64.9	26.7	8.1
PSYCHOLOGY H	113	343		73.3	23.1	3.6
SOCIAL SCIENCES H	52	402	23.3	60.8	12.5	3.5
H						
POSTDOCTORAL EXPERIENCE H						
SOME H	1554	4245	2.2	66.8	25.4	5.6
NONE H	87	421	16.6	68.4	14.5	.5
H						
SEX H						
MEN H	1353	4026	3.5	67.9	23.9	4.6
WOMEN H	288	640	3.5	60.6	27.7	8.2
H						
RACIAL GROUP H						
WHITE H	1544	4417	3.7	66.8	24.4	5.1
OTHER H	97	249	1.6	68.7	24.9	4.8

SURVEY OF 1972 PHD RECIPIENTS
QUESTION 12B

	SURVEY RESP	TOTAL PHD'S WITH SOME POSTDOC	TOTAL MONTHS ON POSTDOC						
			<12	12-23	24-35	36-47	48-59	60-71	>72
ALL 1972 PHD RECIPIENTS	1656	4666	16.4	28.4	26.0	16.9	5.8	2.9	3.6
PHD FIELD									
MATHEMATICAL SCI	46	183	27.3	24.6	27.3	15.3	5.5		
PHYSICS	323	601	12.1	23.3	27.1	17.1	10.0	4.3	6.0
CHEMISTRY	192	980	12.6	34.3	25.9	19.4	4.3	1.4	2.1
EARTH SCI	51	117	13.7	46.2	36.8	2.6	.9		
ENGINEERING	71	259	18.9	45.9	16.2	13.9	1.5	2.7	.8
AGRICULTURAL SCI	34	79	17.7	16.5	50.6	13.9	1.3		
BIOSCIENCES	768	1702	7.6	24.4	27.8	21.5	8.3	5.0	5.3
PSYCHOLOGY	118	343	23.3	40.5	25.1	5.5	2.3	.6	2.6
SOCIAL SCIENCES	53	402	57.7	16.4	14.9	8.2	.5		2.2
POSTDOCTORAL EXPERIENCE									
SOME	1569	4245	13.7	29.4	26.5	17.3	6.1	3.1	3.9
NONE	87	421	43.7	19.2	20.9	12.8	2.1	.7	.5
SEX									
MEN	1362	4026	16.3	27.7	26.7	17.2	5.6	2.7	3.8
WOMEN	294	640	17.2	33.0	21.6	14.8	7.0	4.1	2.3
RACIAL GROUP									
WHITE	1559	4417	16.8	28.1	26.4	16.5	5.8	3.0	3.5
OTHER	97	249	8.8	35.3	19.3	24.5	6.4	.4	5.2

326

* SURVEY OF 1972 PHD RECIPIENTS
* QUESTION 12C

	SURVEY RESP	TOTAL PHD'S WITH SOME POSTDOC	POSTDOCTORAL IMPORTANCE FOR ATTAINING POSITION			
			ESSEN	HELP-FUL	NO DIFF	CAN'T DETER
ALL 1972 PHD RECIPIENTS	1634	4666	36.9	34.4	23.2	5.5
PHD FIELD						
MATHEMATICAL SCI	46	183	29.5	37.2	22.4	10.9
PHYSICS	321	601	39.3	30.8	26.6	3.3
CHEMISTRY	190	980	35.7	41.9	17.7	4.7
EARTH SCI	51	117	28.2	54.7	10.3	6.8
ENGINEERING	71	259	10.8	42.5	45.9	.8
AGRICULTURAL SCI	34	79	13.9	41.8	26.6	17.7
BIOSCIENCES	756	1702	48.8	28.0	17.0	6.2
PSYCHOLOGY	114	343	35.3	40.8	16.6	7.3
SOCIAL SCIENCES	51	402	14.7	28.8	52.2	4.4
POSTDOCTORAL EXPERIENCE						
SOME	1551	4245	38.0	35.7	21.2	5.1
NONE	83	421	26.3	20.7	43.4	9.5
SEX						
MEN	1354	4026	36.8	34.8	23.8	4.6
WOMEN	280	640	38.0	31.3	19.2	11.5
RACIAL GROUP						
WHITE	1537	4417	36.4	34.5	23.6	5.5
OTHER	97	249	46.6	32.5	14.9	6.0

327

* SURVEY OF 1972 PHD RECIPIENTS
* QUESTION 12D

	SURVEY RESP	TOTAL PHD'S WITH SOME POSTDOC	POSTDOCTORAL IMPORTANCE FOR PROF ADVANCEMENT			
			EXTR VALU	USE-FUL	NOT USE-FUL	CAN'T DETER
ALL 1972 PHD RECIPIENTS	1645	4666	44.0	35.8	12.5	7.7
PHD FIELD						
MATHEMATICAL SCI	46	183	48.6	31.1	9.3	10.9
PHYSICS	322	601	42.6	31.1	21.2	5.2
CHEMISTRY	191	980	39.5	38.7	12.7	9.2
EARTH SCI	51	117	40.2	45.3	10.3	4.3
ENGINEERING	71	259	14.3	64.1	8.9	12.7
AGRICULTURAL SCI	34	79	46.8	32.9	15.2	5.1
BIOSCIENCES	761	1702	53.5	28.0	12.1	6.4
PSYCHOLOGY	116	343	52.7	37.9	5.6	3.8
SOCIAL SCIENCES	53	402	27.4	48.8	10.9	12.9
POSTDOCTORAL EXPERIENCE						
SOME	1559	4245	44.9	35.3	12.5	7.4
NONE	86	421	35.3	41.1	13.1	10.5
SEX						
MEN	1358	4026	44.1	36.3	12.9	6.7
WOMEN	287	640	43.3	32.5	10.5	13.7
RACIAL GROUP						
WHITE	1548	4417	43.7	35.8	12.9	7.6
OTHER	97	249	49.4	35.3	6.8	8.4

328

* SURVEY OF 1972 PHD RECIPIENTS
* QUESTION 13

	SURVEY RESP	TOTAL PHD'S	HELD DOCTORAL RSRCH STAFF POSITION N	%	TOTAL MONTHS <12	12-23	24-35	36-47	>48
ALL 1972 PHD RECIPIENTS	3447	15275	1720	12.2	24.5	26.0	15.9	10.9	22.7
PHD FIELD									
MATHEMATICAL SCI	163	1021	72	8.4	36.1	47.2	16.7		
PHYSICS	596	1264	183	16.0	29.0	32.8	8.7	6.6	23.0
CHEMISTRY	303	1610	110	7.2	15.5	20.9	29.1	26.4	8.2
EARTH SCI	123	480	76	16.2	26.3	23.7		.4	50.0
ENGINEERING	215	2357	252	11.5	15.5	36.5	25.0		22.6
AGRICULTURAL SCI	108	630	23	3.9		56.5		8.7	34.8
BIOSCIENCES	1323	3234	493	16.5	21.3	23.9	15.4	13.0	26.4
PSYCHOLOGY	377	2117	196	9.6	36.7	13.8	11.2	19.9	18.4
SOCIAL SCIENCES	239	2562	315	13.5	28.3	19.7	16.8	13.0	22.2
POSTDOCTORAL EXPERIENCE									
SOME	1564	4315	566	13.6	18.0	29.3	17.3	13.6	21.7
NONE	1883	10960	1154	11.6	27.6	24.4	15.3	9.6	23.1
SEX									
MEN	2796	13479	1462	11.7	23.5	25.4	16.0	12.1	23.0
WOMEN	651	1796	258	15.9	29.8	29.5	15.5	4.3	20.9
RACIAL GROUP									
WHITE	3267	14559	1597	11.8	24.8	25.2	16.6	10.3	23.1
OTHER	180	716	123	19.2	20.3	35.8	7.3	19.5	17.1

329

	SURVEY RESP	TOTAL PHD'S	HAVE PUBLISHED SOME ARTICLES %	HAVE PUBLISHED SOME BOOKS %	PRINCIPAL AUTHOR OF SOME ARTICLES %	PRINCIPAL AUTHOR OF SOME BOOKS %
ALL 1972 PHD RECIPIENTS H	3482	15275	87.7	24.0	80.6	17.0
H						
PHD FIELD						
MATHEMATICAL SCI H	166	1021	79.5	17.0	74.8	14.0
PHYSICS H	603	1264	91.2	14.1	85.4	11.3
CHEMISTRY H	309	1610	94.8	19.1	71.4	13.3
EARTH SCI H	123	480	91.0	20.6	89.5	16.3
ENGINEERING H	216	2357	88.9	10.1	83.7	7.1
AGRICULTURAL SCI H	110	630	88.5	16.3	84.7	13.3
BIOSCIENCES H	1336	3234	95.6	31.0	91.2	21.1
PSYCHOLOGY H	374	2117	76.7	24.0	67.2	15.4
SOCIAL SCIENCES H	245	2562	82.3	41.1	78.8	29.7
H						
POSTDOCTORAL EXPERIENCE H						
SOME H	1572	4315	96.9	27.0	89.0	18.5
NONE H	1910	10960	84.0	22.8	77.2	16.4
H						
SEX H						
MEN H	2837	13479	88.1	23.3	81.4	16.6
WOMEN H	645	1796	85.2	29.8	74.6	20.0
H						
RACIAL GROUP H						
WHITE H	3299	14559	87.5	23.5	80.3	16.7
OTHER H	183	716	92.4	34.6	88.0	23.9

	TOTAL SURVEY RESP	RSRCH STAFF	FULL-TIME RESEARCH PERSONNEL FACULTY N	%	POSTDOCS N	%	OTHER PHDS N	%	GRAD RA'S N	%	OTHER STAFF N	%
ALL 1972 PHD RECIPIENTS	1451	29357	10339	35.2	1451	4.9	1732	5.9	8287	28.2	7548	25.7
PHD FIELD												
MATHEMATICAL SCI	58	1134	630	55.6	102	9.0	88	7.8	123	10.8	191	16.8
PHYSICS	195	2967	839	28.3	262	8.8	387	13.0	662	22.3	817	27.5
CHEMISTRY	70	1609	416	25.9	183	11.4	46	2.9	670	41.6	294	18.3
EARTH SCI	61	1620	519	32.0	20	1.2	101	6.2	588	36.3	392	24.2
ENGINEERING	65	3585	1024	28.6	101	2.8	193	5.4	1381	38.5	886	24.7
AGRICULTURAL SCI	54	1756	642	36.6	10	.6	64	3.6	658	37.5	382	21.8
BIOSCIENCES	716	9251	3002	32.5	670	7.2	422	4.6	2182	23.6	2975	32.2
PSYCHOLOGY	139	3705	1631	44.0	90	2.4	215	5.8	922	24.9	847	22.9
SOCIAL SCIENCES	93	3730	1636	43.9	13	.3	216	5.8	1101	29.5	764	20.5
POSTDOCTORAL EXPERIENCE												
SOME	782	11186	3317	29.7	1032	9.2	671	6.0	3115	27.8	3051	27.3
NONE	669	18171	7022	38.6	419	2.3	1061	5.8	5172	28.5	4497	24.7
SEX												
MEN	1185	25799	9201	35.7	1253	4.9	1606	6.2	7399	28.7	6340	24.6
WOMEN	266	3558	1138	32.0	198	5.6	126	3.5	888	25.0	1208	34.0
RACIAL GROUP												
WHITE	1346	26437	9195	34.8	1271	4.8	1563	5.9	7699	29.1	6709	25.4
OTHER	105	2920	1144	39.2	180	6.2	169	5.8	588	20.1	839	28.7

331

	SURVEY RESP	EST TOTAL	FACULTY CONTRIBUTION TO RESEARCH EFFORT			
			ESSENTIAL	IMPORTANT	UNIMPORTANT	NONE IN DEPT
ALL 1972 PHD RECIPIENTS	1451	5436	72.7	14.4	2.4	8.9
PHD FIELD						
MATHEMATICAL SCI	58	314	88.5	10.8		.6
PHYSICS	195	387	73.4	16.5	2.8	5.4
CHEMISTRY	70	332	75.3	8.1	4.2	10.2
EARTH SCI	61	230	78.3	10.9		10.9
ENGINEERING	65	534	67.6	6.7	9.9	10.1
AGRICULTURAL SCI	54	298	60.7	21.1	2.7	15.4
BIOSCIENCES	716	1619	70.7	17.4	2.0	8.8
PSYCHOLOGY	139	742	68.2	19.1	1.5	10.2
SOCIAL SCIENCES	93	980	78.4	11.1		8.3
POSTDOCTORAL EXPERIENCE						
SOME	782	1914	73.8	13.3	2.7	9.2
NONE	669	3522	72.1	14.9	2.2	8.7
SEX						
MEN	1185	4814	73.4	13.9	2.5	9.0
WOMEN	266	622	67.7	18.3	1.8	7.7
RACIAL GROUP						
WHITE	1346	5102	72.7	14.2	2.3	9.2
OTHER	105	334	72.5	16.5	3.6	4.2

	SURVEY RESP	EST TOTAL	POSTDOC CONTRIBUTION TO RESEARCH EFFORT			
			ESSE- NTIAL	IMPO- RTANT	UNIM- PCRT- ANT	NONE IN DEPT
ALL 1972 PHD RECIPIENTS	1451	5436	7.9	6.1	1.2	84.1
PHD FIELD						
MATHEMATICAL SCI	58	314	3.5	5.4		90.4
PHYSICS	195	387	18.1	10.9	1.0	68.0
CHEMISTRY	70	332	21.7	13.0		64.5
EARTH SCI	61	230	2.6	2.6	.9	93.0
ENGINEERING	65	534	5.4	1.5	4.9	87.8
AGRICULTURAL SCI	54	298	3.4			96.6
BIOSCIENCES	716	1619	13.0	10.4	1.3	74.4
PSYCHOLOGY	139	742	2.6	5.3	1.8	90.4
SOCIAL SCIENCES	93	980	.2	1.1		98.7
POSTDOCTORAL EXPERIENCE						
SOME	782	1914	18.1	12.4	2.5	66.2
NONE	669	3522	2.4	2.8	.5	93.9
SEX						
MEN	1185	4814	7.9	5.9	1.3	84.3
WOMEN	266	622	8.0	8.0	.5	83.0
RACIAL GROUP						
WHITE	1346	5102	7.5	5.9	1.0	84.9
OTHER	105	334	13.5	9.9	4.2	71.9

* SURVEY OF 1972 PHD RECIPIENTS
* QUESTION 15A3

	SURVEY RESP	EST TOTAL	OTHER PH'DS CONTRIBUTION TO RESEARCH EFFORT			
			ESSENTIAL	IMPORTANT	UNIMPORTANT	NONE IN DEPT
ALL 1972 PHD RECIPIENTS	1451	5436	8.9	5.9	.7	84.3
PHD FIELD						
MATHEMATICAL SCI	58	314	8.0	4.1		87.9
PHYSICS	195	387	23.0	8.0	.5	67.4
CHEMISTRY	70	332	3.0	7.2		89.8
EARTH SCI	61	230	12.2	5.2	3.5	79.1
ENGINEERING	65	534	11.8	6.6	.6	81.1
AGRICULTURAL SCI	54	298	13.1	.3	2.7	83.9
BIOSCIENCES	716	1619	7.0	7.5	1.1	84.2
PSYCHOLOGY	139	742	7.0	6.5		86.5
SOCIAL SCIENCES	93	980	6.8	3.5		89.7
POSTDOCTORAL EXPERIENCE						
SOME	782	1914	12.6	5.4	.7	80.9
NONE	669	3522	6.9	6.1	.7	86.2
SEX						
MEN	1185	4814	9.0	6.0	.8	84.2
WOMEN	266	622	8.7	5.0	.2	85.7
RACIAL GROUP						
WHITE	1346	5102	8.9	5.6	.7	84.7
OTHER	105	334	10.2	10.2	.9	78.7

334

* SURVEY OF 1972 PHD RECIPIENTS
* QUESTION 15A4

	SURVEY RESP	EST TOTAL	GRAD RA'S CONTRIBUTION TO RESEARCH EFFORT			
			ESSE-NTIAL	IMPO-RTANT	UNIM-PCRT-IN ANT	NONE PCRT-IN DEPT
ALL 1972 PHD RECIPIENTS	1451	5436	21.5	30.0	2.4	45.5
PHD FIELD						
MATHEMATICAL SCI	58	314	4.1	8.3	6.4	81.2
PHYSICS	195	387	16.0	33.9	3.6	43.4
CHEMISTRY	70	332	35.8	14.5	1.2	46.1
EARTH SCI	61	230	27.4	37.8		33.5
ENGINEERING	65	534	28.5	46.6	.4	24.5
AGRICULTURAL SCI	54	298	43.6	25.8	2.7	27.9
BIOSCIENCES	716	1619	20.4	29.6	2.0	47.3
PSYCHOLOGY	139	742	17.8	37.2	1.1	43.7
SOCIAL SCIENCES	93	980	17.1	26.1	4.0	52.8
POSTDOCTORAL EXPERIENCE						
SOME	782	1914	21.3	29.2	3.0	45.3
NONE	669	3522	21.7	30.4	2.0	45.6
SEX						
MEN	1185	4814	22.1	29.5	2.1	45.6
WOMEN	266	622	16.9	33.8	4.3	44.5
RACIAL GROUP						
WHITE	1346	5102	22.0	29.1	2.5	45.8
OTHER	105	334	13.8	43.4	.6	41.0

335

POSTDOC CONTRIBUTION IN DETERMINING
BASIC DIRECTIONS OF RESEARCH PROJECT

	SURVEY RESP	EST TOTAL	ESSE- NTIAL	IMPO- RTANT	UNIM- PCRT- ANT	CAN'T DETER- MINE
ALL 1972 PHD RECIPIENTS H	359	966	16.9	46.4	34.1	2.7
H						
PHD FIELD H						
MATHEMATICAL SCI H	6	30		90.0	10.0	
PHYSICS H	68	128	24.2	39.1	34.4	2.3
CHEMISTRY H	33	142	15.5	52.8	26.1	5.6
EARTH SCI H	7	18	11.1	33.3	55.6	
ENGINEERING H	9	65		49.2	47.7	3.1
AGRICULTURAL SCI H	8	35	20.0	34.3	45.7	
BIOSCIENCES H	206	447	14.8	47.2	35.1	2.9
PSYCHOLOGY H	20	88	39.8	39.8	20.5	
SOCIAL SCIENCES H	2	13		100.0		
H						
POSTDOCTORAL EXPERIENCE H						
SOME H	288	720	19.0	48.2	29.7	3.1
NONE H	71	246	10.6	41.1	46.7	1.6
H						
SEX H						
MEN H	302	850	15.9	47.1	34.2	2.8
WOMEN H	57	116	24.1	41.4	32.8	1.7
H						
RACIAL GROUP H						
WHITE H	322	851	17.4	47.1	32.4	3.1
OTHER H	37	115	13.0	40.9	46.1	

336

* SURVEY OF 1972 PHD RECIPIENTS
* QUESTION 15B2

	SURVEY RESP	EST TOTAL	POSTDOC CONTRIBUTION TO INTELLECTUAL VIGOR OF THE RESEARCH EFFORT			
			ESSE-NTIAL	IMPO-RTANT	UNIM-PORT-ANT	CAN'T DETER-MINE
ALL 1972 PHD RECIPIENTS	359	966	38.1	54.0	5.7	2.2
PHD FIELD						
MATHEMATICAL SCI	6	30	6.7	86.7	6.7	
PHYSICS	68	128	35.2	57.8	4.7	2.3
CHEMISTRY	33	142	47.2	52.8		
EARTH SCI	7	18	22.2	77.8		
ENGINEERING	9	65	46.2	47.7	3.1	3.1
AGRICULTURAL SCI	8	35	31.4	48.6		20.0
BIOSCIENCES	206	447	39.4	51.5	7.2	2.0
PSYCHOLOGY	20	88	37.5	47.7	14.8	
SOCIAL SCIENCES	2	13		100.0		
POSTDOCTORAL EXPERIENCE						
SOME	288	720	44.7	49.9	4.0	1.4
NONE	71	246	18.7	66.3	10.6	4.5
SEX						
MEN	302	850	36.6	55.3	5.6	2.5
WOMEN	57	116	49.1	44.8	6.0	
RACIAL GROUP						
WHITE	322	851	37.1	55.8	4.6	2.5
OTHER	37	115	45.2	40.9	13.9	

337

	SURVEY RESP	EST TOTAL	POSTDOC CONTRIBUTION TO INFUSION OF NEW RESEARCH TECHNIQUES			
			ESSE-NTIAL	IMPO-RTANT	UNIM-PCKT-ANT	CAN'T DETER-MINE
ALL 1972 PHD RECIPIENTS	359	966	36.1	44.1	14.5	5.3
PHD FIELD						
MATHEMATICAL SCI	6	30	43.3	56.7		
PHYSICS	68	128	23.4	50.8	22.7	3.1
CHEMISTRY	33	142	35.9	52.8	7.0	4.2
EARTH SCI	7	18	22.2	33.3	33.3	11.1
ENGINEERING	9	65	43.1	49.2	4.6	3.1
AGRICULTURAL SCI	8	35	57.1	22.9		20.0
BIOSCIENCES	206	447	36.9	42.1	17.2	3.8
PSYCHOLOGY	20	88	40.9	39.8	17.0	2.3
SOCIAL SCIENCES	2	13	15.4			84.6
POSTDOCTORAL EXPERIENCE						
SOME	288	720	40.1	42.4	13.5	4.0
NONE	71	246	24.4	49.2	17.5	8.9
SEX						
MEN	302	850	34.8	46.9	13.8	4.5
WOMEN	57	116	45.7	23.3	19.8	11.2
RACIAL GROUP						
WHITE	322	851	38.5	43.8	13.3	4.3
OTHER	37	115	18.3	46.1	23.5	12.2

338

* SURVEY OF 1972 PHD RECIPIENTS
* QUESTION 1584

	SURVEY RESP	EST TOTAL	POSTDOC CONTRIBUTION TO PUBLICATION OF RESEARCH FINDINGS			
			ESSE-NTIAL	IMPO-RTANT	UNIM-PORT-ANT	CAN'T DETER-MINE
ALL 1972 PHD RECIPIENTS	359	966	26.8	54.0	13.4	5.8
PHD FIELD						
MATHEMATICAL SCI	6	30				
PHYSICS	68	128	28.1	56.3	10.9	4.7
CHEMISTRY	33	142	36.6	41.5	17.6	4.2
EARTH SCI	7	18	22.2	55.6	22.2	
ENGINEERING	9	65	3.1	90.8	3.1	3.1
AGRICULTURAL SCI	8	35	22.9	57.1		20.0
BIOSCIENCES	206	447	27.3	53.7	13.9	5.1
PSYCHOLOGY	20	88	37.5	38.6	22.7	1.1
SOCIAL SCIENCES	2	13	15.4			84.6
POSTDOCTORAL EXPERIENCE						
SOME	288	720	30.1	53.6	12.2	4.0
NONE	71	246	17.1	55.3	16.7	11.0
SEX						
MEN	302	850	26.1	55.1	13.8	5.1
WOMEN	57	116	31.9	46.6	10.3	11.2
RACIAL GROUP						
WHITE	322	851	26.4	56.1	12.5	5.1
OTHER	37	115	29.6	39.1	20.0	11.3

339

	SURVEY RESP	EST TOTAL	POSTDOC CONTRIBUTION TO TRAINING OF GRADUATE STUDENTS			
			ESSE-NTIAL	IMPO-RTANT	UNIM-PORT-ANT	CAN'T DETER-MINE
ALL 1972 PHD RECIPIENTS	359	966	5.3	40.2	35.6	18.9
PHD FIELD						
MATHEMATICAL SCI	6	30		6.7	40.0	53.3
PHYSICS	68	128	3.1	51.6	28.1	17.2
CHEMISTRY	33	142	5.6	52.1	23.9	18.3
EARTH SCI	7	18	11.1	55.6	22.2	11.1
ENGINEERING	9	65		44.6	49.2	6.2
AGRICULTURAL SCI	8	35		11.4	45.7	42.9
BIOSCIENCES	206	447	7.6	39.1	32.9	20.4
PSYCHOLOGY	20	88	3.4	29.5	59.1	8.0
SOCIAL SCIENCES	2	13		15.4	84.6	
POSTDOCTORAL EXPERIENCE						
SOME	288	720	5.4	44.2	30.8	19.6
NONE	71	246	4.9	28.5	49.6	17.1
SEX						
MEN	302	850	4.4	41.4	34.0	20.2
WOMEN	57	116	12.1	31.0	47.4	9.5
RACIAL GROUP						
WHITE	322	851	5.5	41.6	33.5	19.4
OTHER	37	115	3.5	29.6	51.3	15.7

1978 Ph.D. Recipients

OMB No. 99-S79002
Approval expires
December 31, 1979

SURVEY OF SCIENTISTS AND ENGINEERS

CONDUCTED BY THE NATIONAL RESEARCH COUNCIL WITH THE SUPPORT OF THE NATIONAL SCIENCE FOUNDATION AND THE NATIONAL INSTITUTES OF HEALTH

THE ACCOMPANYING LETTER requests your assistance in this survey of scientists and engineers.

PLEASE READ the instructions carefully and answer by printing your reply or entering an 'X' in the appropriate box.

PLEASE COMMENT on any questions which you think require fuller explanation.

PLEASE RETURN the completed form in the enclosed envelope to the Commission on Human Resources, JH 638, National Research Council, 2101 Constitution Avenue, N.W., Washington, D.C. 20418

NOTE: This information is solicited under the authority of the National Science Foundation Act of 1950, as amended. All information you provide will be treated as confidential and used for statistical purposes only. Information will be released only in the form of statistical summaries or in a form which does not identify information about any particular person. Your response is entirely voluntary and your failure to provide some or all of the requested information will in no way adversely affect you.

DEFINITION: POSTDOCTORAL APPOINTMENT means a temporary appointment, the primary purpose of which is to provide for continued education or experience in research usually, though not necessarily, under the supervision of a senior mentor. Included are appointments in government and industrial laboratories which resemble in their character and objectives postdoctoral appointments in universities. Excluded are appointments in residency training programs in the health professions.

EMPLOYMENT

INSTRUCTIONS: Please answer questions 1 through 9 with respect to your PRINCIPAL employment or postdoctoral appointment AS OF APRIL 1979.

1. Which BEST describes your employment status? *(Check only one.)* (8)

1 ☐ Full-time postdoctoral appointment (as defined above)
2 ☐ Part-time postdoctoral appointment (as defined above)
3 ☐ Full-time employed (other than postdoctoral appointment)
4 ☐ Part-time employed (other than postdoctoral appointment)
5 ☐ Unemployed and seeking employment

6 ☐ Unemployed and NOT seeking employment
7 ☐ Student (other than postdoctoral appointment)
8 ☐ Other status, please specify _____

NOTE: If you checked items 5, 6, or 7 above, please skip to question 10 on page 3.

2. What is the name and location of your employer or postdoctoral affiliation? (9-14)

_____   _____   _____
Name of Institution/Organization   *City*   *State*

3. Which category below BEST describes the type of organization of your employer/postdoctoral affiliation? *(Check only one.)*

1 ☐ University or 4-year college (other than items 2 and 6 below)
2 ☐ Medical school or other health professional school (including university-affiliated teaching hospital)
3 ☐ 2-year college or technical school
4 ☐ Elementary or secondary school
5 ☐ Other educational institution, please specify _____

6 ☐ FFRDC laboratory (i.e., federally funded research and development centers such as Brookhaven, Lincoln, Los Alamos, Oak Ridge, etc.)

7 ☐ Federal government (including military)
8 ☐ State or local government
9 ☐ Business or industry
10 ☐ Hospital or clinic (other than those included above)
11 ☐ Nonprofit organization (other than those included above)
12 ☐ Self-employed
13 ☐ Other type of employer, please specify _____

(15-16)

341

4. If affiliated with an INSTITUTION OF HIGHER EDUCATION (*items 1, 2, or 3 in Question 3*),

   a. What is the title of your position? _____ (17)

   b. Which category BEST describes the type of position you hold? (*Check only one.*)

     1 ☐ Faculty
     2 ☐ Postdoctoral appointment (as defined on page 1)
     3 ☐ Other nonfaculty research staff
     4 ☐ Other nonfaculty teaching staff
     5 ☐ Other, please specify _____ (18)

   c. Are you primarily employed in a research unit OUTSIDE the traditional academic/departmental structure?

     1 ☐ Yes   2 ☐ No (19)

   d. Is your position considered to be in a tenure track?

     1 ☐ Yes   2 ☐ No (20)

   e. If YES, do you have tenure?

     1 ☐ Yes   2 ☐ No (21)

5. Approximately what percent of the time associated with your principal employment (as of April 1979) do you devote to each of the following activities?

   a. Basic research (including supervision of students engaged in research) _____ % (22)

   b. Applied research and development (including supervision of students engaged in research) _____ % (24)

   c. Classroom teaching (not involving research supervision) _____ % (26)

   d. Administration/management _____ % (28)

   e. Consulting _____ % (30)

   f. Professional service (other than consulting) _____ % (32)

   g. Other, please specify _____ _____ % (34)

                                                                  100 %

6. If your activities include research, which of the following federal agencies, if any, support the research in which you are engaged? (*Check all that apply.*)

   1 ☐ No federal support for research
   2 ☐ ADAMHA (National Institute of Mental Health, National Institute on Alcohol and Alcoholism, and National Institute on Drug Abuse)
   3 ☐ Department of Defense
   4 ☐ Department of Energy
   5 ☐ National Aeronautics and Space Administration
   6 ☐ National Institutes of Health
   7 ☐ National Science Foundation
   8 ☐ Other federal agency, please specify _____ (36-43)

7. From the enclosed list of specialty areas on the reverse side of the covering letter, select the areas most closely related to your employment or postdoctoral appointment, and enter their titles and 3-digit codes below. Write in your specialty if it is not on the list.

	Title of employment specialty	3-digit code	
Most closely related field:	_____	_____	(44-46)
Other fields (if applicable):	_____	_____	(47-49)
	_____	_____	(50-52)
	_____	_____	(53-55)

8. What is the BASIC ANNUAL SALARY* associated with your principal employment? If you hold a postdoctoral appointment (as defined on page 1) and receive a stipend, include the stipend plus personal allowances.

$ _____ per calendar year (11-12 months)   *OR* $_____ per academic year (9-10 months)
   (56-58)   (59-61)

*Include your salary before deductions for income tax, social security, retirement, etc., but do NOT include bonuses, overtime, summer teaching, consulting, or other payment for professional work.

9. Which of the following BEST describes your immediate career plans? *(Check only one.)*

1 ☐ Not actively seeking new position
2 ☐ Actively seeking new position because present position terminates shortly

3 ☐ Actively seeking new position because of dissatisfaction with present position
4 ☐ Other, please specify _____
                                                              (62)

EMPLOYMENT HISTORY

10. Did you take a postdoctoral appointment (as defined on page 1) within a year after receiving your doctoral degree?

1 ☐ Yes   2 ☐ No   (63)

a. If YES, what were the reasons for taking your FIRST postdoctoral appointment? *(Check all that apply and CIRCLE the most important ONE.)*

1 ☐ To obtain additional research experience in your doctoral field
2 ☐ To work with a particular scientist or research group
3 ☐ To switch into a different field of research

4 ☐ Couldn't obtain type of employment position you wanted
5 ☐ Other reason, please specify _____
                                                              (64-68)

b. If NO, what were the reasons for not taking a postdoctoral appointment? *(Check all that apply and CIRCLE the most important ONE.)*

1 ☐ Couldn't obtain postdoctoral appointment
2 ☐ Felt that a postdoctoral would be of little or no benefit in terms of your career aspirations
3 ☐ More promising career opportunities were available

4 ☐ Postdoctoral salaries too low compared with other employment opportunities
5 ☐ Other reason, please specify _____
                                                              (69-73)

11. If you DID take a postdoctoral appointment within a year after receiving your doctoral degree,

a. what was the PRIMARY source of support for your FIRST postdoctoral appointment? *(Check only one.)*

1 ☐ Federal research grant or contract
2 ☐ Federal fellowship or training grant
3 ☐ Nonfederal nationally awarded fellowship
4 ☐ University or state funds (including teaching asst.)

5 ☐ Personal resources (e.g., loans, family income, etc.)
6 ☐ Other source, please specify below:
_____
                                                              (74)

b. to what extent did LIMITATIONS in geographic mobility influence your decision to take your FIRST postdoctoral appointment?

1 ☐ Important consideration   2 ☐ Incidental consideration   3 ☐ Not a consideration   (75)

c. did you prolong the length of time you held postdoctoral appointment(s) because of difficulty in finding other employment you wanted?   1 ☐ Yes   2 ☐ No   (76)

12. If you are currently (as of April 1979) involved in a research project in a university, how many individuals (including yourself) are working on the project? Please provide the number of individuals in each of the personnel groups below and rate the contributions made by each group to the OVERALL PRODUCTIVITY OF THE RESEARCH EFFORT. In rating the contributions, use the following scale:

1 = essential   2 = important   3 = not important   4 = cannot determine

Personnel Group	Number of individuals	Rating of contribution
Faculty	_____ (8-9)	____
Postdoctoral appointees (as defined on page 1)	_____ (11-12)	____
Other doctoral staff (e.g., research scientists)	_____ (14-15)	____
Graduate research assistants	_____ (17-18)	____
Nondoctoral staff (e.g., technicians)	_____ (20-21)	____

344

13. Using the same scale (as in question 12), rate the contributions of POSTDOCTORAL APPOINTEES (only) to each of the following aspects of the research project:

Rating of contribution

Determining the basic directions of the research project _____ (23)

Intellectual vigor of the research effort _____ (24)

Infusion of new research techniques _____ (25)

Publication of research findings _____ (26)

Training of graduate students _____ (27)

14. At the time you received your doctoral degree, what employment options did you consider? Indicate below the number of job inquiries you made and the number of offers you received in each employment category.

Type of position	Number of inquiries made		Number of offers received	
Educational Institutions (other than FFRDC laboratories)				
Faculty	_____	(28-29)	_____	(30)
Postdoctoral appointment (as defined on page 1)	_____	(31-32)	_____	(33)
Other nonfaculty staff	_____	(34-35)	_____	(36)
FFRDC Laboratories				
Postdoctoral appointment (as defined on page 1)	_____	(37-38)	_____	(39)
Other research staff	_____	(40-41)	_____	(42)
Other position	_____	(43-44)	_____	(45)
Industry or Business				
Postdoctoral appointment (as defined on page 1)	_____	(46-47)	_____	(48)
Other research staff	_____	(49-50)	_____	(51)
Other position	_____	(52-53)	_____	(54)
Federal, State, or Local Government				
Postdoctoral appointment (as defined on page 1)	_____	(55-56)	_____	(57)
Other research staff	_____	(58-59)	_____	(60)
Other position	_____	(61-62)	_____	(63)
Other Positions (please specify)				
_____	_____	(64-65)	_____	(66)
_____	_____	(67-68)	_____	(69)
_____	_____	(70-71)	_____	(72)

15. Do you have any additional comments on the advantages and disadvantages of postdoctoral appointments in your particular field?

_____

_____

_____

_____

(73)

THANK YOU FOR YOUR COOPERATION

LIST OF EMPLOYMENT SPECIALTY AREAS (to be used for question 7)

MATHEMATICS

000 - Algebra
010 - Analysis & Functional Analysis
020 - Geometry
030 - Logic
040 - Number Theory
052 - Probability
055 - Math Statistics (see also 544, 670, 725, 727)
060 - Topology
082 - Operations Research (see also 478)
085 - Applied Mathematics
089 - Combinatorics & Finite Mathematics
091 - Physical Mathematics
098 - Mathematics, General
099 - Mathematics, Other*

COMPUTER SCIENCES

071 - Theory
072 - Software Systems
073 - Hardware Systems
074 - Intelligent Systems
079 - Computer Sciences, Other* (see also 437, 476)

PHYSICS & ASTRONOMY

101 - Astronomy
102 - Astrophysics
110 - Atomic & Molecular Physics
120 - Electromagnetism
130 - Mechanics
132 - Acoustics
134 - Fluids
135 - Plasma Physics
136 - Optics
138 - Thermal Physics
140 - Elementary Particles
150 - Nuclear Structure
160 - Solid State
198 - Physics, General
199 - Physics, Other*

CHEMISTRY

200 - Analytical
210 - Inorganic
215 - Synthetic Inorganic & Organometallic
220 - Organic
225 - Synthetic Organic & Natural Products
230 - Nuclear
240 - Physical
245 - Quantum
250 - Theoretical
255 - Structural
260 - Agricultural & Food
265 - Thermodynamics & Material Properties
270 - Pharmaceutical
275 - Polymers
280 - Biochemistry (see also 540)
285 - Chemical Dynamics
298 - Chemistry, General
299 - Chemistry, Other*

EARTH, ENVIRONMENTAL, AND MARINE SCIENCES

301 - Mineralogy, Petrology
305 - Geochemistry
310 - Stratigraphy, Sedimentation
320 - Paleontology
330 - Structural Geology
341 - Geophysics (Solid Earth)
350 - Geomorph. & Glacial Geology
391 - Applied Geol., Geol. Engr. & Econ. Geol.
395 - Fuel Tech. & Petrol. Engr. (see also 479)
360 - Hydrology & Water Resources
370 - Oceanography
397 - Marine Sciences, Other*
381 - Atmospheric Physics & Chemistry
382 - Atmospheric Dynamics
383 - Atmospheric Sciences, Other*
388 - Environmental Sciences, General (see also 480, 528)
389 - Environmental Sciences, Other*
398 - Earth Sciences, General
399 - Earth Sciences, Other*

ENGINEERING

400 - Aeronautical & Astronautical
410 - Agricultural
415 - Biomedical
420 - Civil
430 - Chemical
435 - Ceramic
437 - Computer
440 - Electrical
445 - Electronics
450 - Industrial & Manufacturing
455 - Nuclear
460 - Engineering Physics
470 - Mechanical
475 - Metallurgy & Phys. Met. Engr.
476 - Systems Design & Systems Science (see also 072, 073, 074)
478 - Operations Research (see also 082)
479 - Fuel Technology & Petrol. Engr. (see also 395)
480 - Sanitary & Environmental
486 - Mining
497 - Materials Science
498 - Engineering, General
499 - Engineering, Other*

AGRICULTURAL SCIENCES

500 - Agronomy
501 - Agricultural Economics
502 - Animal Husbandry
503 - Food Science & Technology (see also 573)
504 - Fish & Wildlife
505 - Forestry
506 - Horticulture
507 - Soils & Soil Science
510 - Animal Science & Animal Nutrition
511 - Phytopathology
518 - Agriculture, General
519 - Agriculture, Other*

MEDICAL SCIENCES

520 - Medicine & Surgery
522 - Public Health & Epidemiology
523 - Veterinary Medicine
524 - Hospital Administration
526 - Nursing
527 - Parasitology
528 - Environmental Health
534 - Pathology
536 - Pharmacology
537 - Pharmacy
538 - Medical Sciences, General
539 - Medical Sciences, Other*

BIOLOGICAL SCIENCES

540 - Biochemistry (see also 280)
542 - Biophysics
543 - Biomathematics
544 - Biometrics and Biostatistics (see also 055, 670, 725, 727)
545 - Anatomy
546 - Cytology
547 - Embryology
548 - Immunology
550 - Botany
560 - Ecology
562 - Hydrobiology
564 - Microbiology & Bacteriology
566 - Physiology, Animal
567 - Physiology, Plant
569 - Zoology
570 - Genetics
571 - Entomology
572 - Molecular Biology
573 - Food Science & Technology (see also 503)
574 - Behavior/Ethology
576 - Nutrition & Dietetics
578 - Biological Sciences, General
579 - Biological Sciences, Other*

PSYCHOLOGY

600 - Clinical
610 - Counseling & Guidance
620 - Developmental & Gerontological
630 - Education
635 - School Psychology
641 - Experimental
642 - Comparative
643 - Physiological
650 - Industrial & Personnel
660 - Personality
670 - Psychometrics (see also 055, 544, 725, 727)
680 - Social
698 - Psychology, General
699 - Psychology, Other*

SOCIAL SCIENCES

700 - Anthropology
703 - Archeology
708 - Communications*
709 - Linguistics
710 - Sociology
720 - Economics (see also 501)
725 - Econometrics (see also 055, 544, 670, 727)
727 - Social Statistics (see also 055, 544, 670, 725)
740 - Geography
745 - Area Studies*
751 - Political Science
752 - Public Administration
755 - International Relations
770 - Urban & Regional Planning
775 - History & Philosophy of Science
798 - Social Sciences, General
799 - Social Sciences, Other*

ARTS & HUMANITIES

841 - Fine & Applied Arts (including Music, Speech, Drama, etc.)
842 - History
843 - Philosophy, Religion, Theology
845 - Languages & Literature
846 - Other Arts and Humanities*

EDUCATION & OTHER PROFESSIONAL FIELDS

938 - Education

882 - Business Administration
883 - Home Economics
884 - Journalism
885 - Speech and Hearing Sciences
886 - Law, Jurisprudence
887 - Social Work
891 - Library & Archival Science
898 - Professional Field, Other*

899 - OTHER FIELDS*

*Identify the specific field in the space on the questionnaire.

NATIONAL RESEARCH COUNCIL
COMMISSION ON HUMAN RESOURCES

2101 Constitution Avenue   Washington, D. C. 20418

COMMITTEE ON THE STUDY OF
POSTDOCTORALS AND DOCTORAL RESEARCH STAFF

Lee Grodzins, *Chairman*
Massachusetts Institute of
Technology

Richard D. Anderson
Louisiana State University

Frederick E. Balderston
University of California
Berkeley, California

Kenneth E. Clark
University of Rochester

Gerhart Friedlander
Brookhaven National Laboratory

Herbert Friedman
Naval Research Laboratory

John C. Hancock
Purdue University

Donald F. Hornig
Harvard School of Public Health

Shirley Ann Jackson
Bell Laboratories

Ernest S. Kuh
University of California
Berkeley, California

William F. Miller
Stanford University

Nicholas C. Mullins
Indiana University

Thomas A. Reichert
Carnegie-Mellon University

Helen R. Whiteley
University of Washington

April 20, 1979

Dear Colleague:

The National Research Council has appointed a committee to study the policy implications of the changing role of postdoctorals and other doctoral research staff in science and engineering. During the last decade, in the face of reduced numbers of faculty openings, increasing numbers of young scientists and engineers have taken postdoctorals and other types of positions in universities and colleges as well as outside the academic setting. The accompanying survey is designed to furnish information on the changing employment patterns in each field and the implications for individual careers and for the national research effort.

The survey is sponsored by the National Science Foundation and the National Institutes of Health, but the survey records will be retained in the National Research Council. All information you provide is to be used for purposes of statistical description only and its confidentiality will be protected.

The survey results will provide a basis for the Committee's recommendations regarding federal and institutional policies. The success of this survey depends on your cooperation. Please return the completed questionnaire as soon as possible in the enclosed envelope. Thank you for your prompt assistance.

Sincerely,

Lee Grodzins
Chairman

NOTE: List of specialty areas to be used for survey question 7 is on the reverse side of this page.

The National Research Council is the principal operating agency of the National Academy of Sciences and the National Academy of Engineering to serve government and other organizations

* SURVEY OF 1978 PHD RECIPIENTS
* QUESTION 1

	SURVEY RESP	TOTAL PHD'S	CURRENT EMPLOYMENT STATUS F-T POSTDOC	F-T EMPL	P-T PDOC	P-T EMPL	SEEK EMPL	OTHER
ALL 1978 PHD RECIPIENTS	4110	14062	21.1	71.4	.9	3.7	1.3	1.6
PHD FIELD								
MATHEMATICAL SCI	177	710	9.9	84.2	.6	3.5	1.5	.3
PHYSICS	521	788	37.1	56.9	1.8	2.3	1.3	.8
CHEMISTRY	249	1189	32.9	62.9		.8	2.2	1.2
EARTH SCI	189	523	18.4	74.0	1.1	4.8	1.1	.6
ENGINEERING	261	1310	6.2	92.9	.1	.2	.2	.5
AGRICULTURAL SCI	153	625	8.0	89.4		2.4		.2
BIOSCIENCES	1765	3286	47.9	43.4	1.4	2.1	1.5	3.8
PSYCHOLOGY	519	2888	11.4	78.5	.3	6.6	1.9	1.3
SOCIAL SCIENCES	276	2743	3.1	87.1	1.9	5.9	.8	1.3
POSTDOCTORAL EXPERIENCE								
SOME	1979	4176	71.0	22.3	3.1	1.7	.7	1.1
NONE	2131	9886		92.1		4.5	1.5	.9
SEX								
MEN	2989	11031	21.3	74.0	.8	2.1	.9	.9
WOMEN	1121	3031	20.4	61.9	1.4	9.4	2.6	4.3
RACIAL GROUP								
WHITE	3639	13197	21.5	71.0	.9	3.6	1.2	1.7
OTHER	471	865	14.8	77.0	.9	4.4	2.0	.9

347

EMPLOYER OR POSTDOCTORAL AFFILIATION

	SURVEY RESP	TOTAL EMPL PHD'S	EDUCATIONAL INSTITUTION				GOVERNMENT			BUSN	HOSP CLNIC	NON-PROFT	OTHER SECTORS	
			UNIV/ COLL	MED SCHL	JR COLL	OTHER EDUC	FFRDC	FEDL GOVT	OTHER GOVT				SELF EMPL	OTHER
ALL 1978 PHD RECIPIENTS	3905	13651	42.1	11.8	1.2	1.6	2.9	8.8	5.3	16.6	3.8	4.4	1.5	.1
PHD FIELD														
MATHEMATICAL SCI	169	697	66.8	.9	1.5	1.3	5.6	2.8	1.2	18.9		.9	.3	
PHYSICS	508	772	38.7	.9	1.2		15.2	10.4	.7	29.4	.7	2.5		.4
CHEMISTRY	232	1149	36.6	3.7	.5		2.9	7.4	1.3	45.2	1.2	1.1		
EARTH SCI	184	514	43.8		.8	1.9	5.3	12.6	3.3	27.6		4.3	.4	
ENGINEERING	254	1302	32.1	2.9			3.5	13.4	1.3	40.0	.2	6.1	.5	
AGRICULTURAL SCI	151	624	49.5	.8	.2	.3	2.8	16.2	3.2	21.9		2.8	.8	1.5
BIOSCIENCES	1651	3112	33.6	35.0	.8	.4	2.5	8.8	2.9	7.8	2.4	4.9	.6	.3
PSYCHOLOGY	491	2795	26.8	11.2	2.1	5.1	.1	6.3	14.4	7.8	15.3	6.4	4.5	
SOCIAL SCIENCES	265	2686	67.5	3.8	1.7	1.4	1.3	8.0	5.7	4.9		4.2	1.5	
POSTDOCTORAL EXPERIENCE														
SOME	1932	4101	44.8	26.0	.5	.2	4.4	7.4	1.7	7.1	2.2	5.2	.4	.1
NONE	1973	9550	40.9	5.6	1.5	2.1	2.3	9.3	6.9	20.7	4.5	4.1	1.9	.2
SEX														
MEN	2871	10828	41.7	10.3	1.0	1.4	3.3	9.7	5.1	18.6	3.3	4.3	1.2	.2
WOMEN	1034	2823	43.6	17.2	1.8	2.1	1.5	5.1	6.2	9.2	6.0	4.8	2.6	
RACIAL GROUP														
WHITE	3452	12811	42.3	11.9	1.1	1.6	2.9	8.7	5.3	16.3	3.9	4.5	1.4	.2
OTHER	453	840	39.3	9.1	1.7	1.6	3.6	8.9	5.5	21.6	2.5	3.5	2.6	

* SURVEY OF 1978 PHD RECIPIENTS
* QUESTION 4

	SURVEY RESP	TOTAL PHD'S IN ACAD	POSITION IN UNIVERSITY						PERCENT EMPLOYED OUTSIDE DEPARTMENT
			--FACULTY--			------NONFACULTY------			
			TENURE	NO TENR	POST-DOCS	RSRCH STAFF	TEACH STAFF	OTHER STAFF	
ALL 1978 PHD RECIPIENTS	2325	7638	4.3	53.5	32.7	5.3	1.0	3.3	11.5
PHD FIELD									
MATHEMATICAL SCI	121	482	4.4	80.0	13.3	2.3			6.5
PHYSICS	220	313	4.8	21.4	63.9	4.8	3.5	1.6	16.9
CHEMISTRY	116	462		28.1	68.8	1.7	.4	.9	9.1
EARTH SCI	87	239	7.2	51.9	30.6	9.4	.9		17.9
ENGINEERING	93	450	.4	72.6	11.8	11.1		4.0	12.9
AGRICULTURAL SCI	92	313	3.6	62.8	16.2	6.5	.3	10.7	13.9
BIOSCIENCES	1153	2157	2.6	29.8	59.8	4.0	.4	3.4	7.4
PSYCHOLOGY	246	1249	2.2	59.7	24.2	3.1	4.0	6.7	9.6
SOCIAL SCIENCES	197	1973	8.9	75.2	6.6	7.4	.1	1.8	16.3
POSTDOCTORAL EXPERIENCE									
SOME	1404	2915	.6	12.7	83.3	2.5	.3	.5	14.2
NONE	921	4723	6.7	79.9		7.0	1.4	5.0	9.7
SEX									
MEN	1658	5823	4.2	53.8	33.6	5.3	.8	2.3	11.5
WOMEN	667	1815	4.6	52.6	29.9	5.0	1.5	6.4	11.2
RACIAL GROUP									
WHITE	2102	7208	4.0	53.4	33.1	5.2	1.0	3.2	11.4
OTHER	223	430	9.0	55.1	25.7	6.1	.7	3.4	12.4

349

	SURVEY RESP	TOTAL EMPL PHD'S	MEAN PERCENT TIME DEVOTED TO						
			BASIC RSRCH	APPL RSRCH	TEACH	ADMIN	CON-SULT	PROF SERV	OTHER
ALL 1978 PHD RECIPIENTS	3843	13651	31.4	20.9	17.4	10.8	5.5	11.2	2.7
PHD FIELD									
MATHEMATICAL SCI	163	697	22.5	14.5	40.2	6.3	5.1	9.6	1.8
PHYSICS	499	772	45.3	29.9	10.1	7.0	1.9	4.1	1.6
CHEMISTRY	230	1149	43.9	34.6	7.7	7.3	0.6	3.5	2.3
EARTH SCI	182	514	37.2	24.8	15.1	9.8	6.2	4.4	2.5
ENGINEERING	248	1302	14.9	41.8	15.0	16.6	4.6	4.9	2.0
AGRICULTURAL SCI	149	624	18.4	39.9	8.1	13.6	2.6	9.0	8.3
BIOSCIENCES	1626	3112	58.0	12.4	12.4	7.8	2.5	5.0	1.8
PSYCHOLOGY	486	2795	13.2	13.1	12.2	11.9	12.3	33.9	3.2
SOCIAL SCIENCES	260	2686	22.4	16.8	33.2	13.3	6.2	5.4	2.8
POSTDOCTORAL EXPERIENCE									
SOME	1918	4101	67.7	15.4	6.6	3.7	2.0	3.4	1.3
NONE	1925	9550	16.0	23.3	22.1	13.8	7.0	14.6	3.2
SEX									
MEN	2825	10828	31.9	22.4	16.8	11.0	5.6	10.0	2.4
WOMEN	1018	2823	29.8	15.3	19.8	10.0	5.2	16.1	3.8
RACIAL GROUP									
WHITE	3400	12811	32.0	20.7	17.4	10.7	5.5	11.2	2.6
OTHER	443	840	23.1	24.6	18.3	12.2	6.1	12.4	3.3

350

* SURVEY OF 1978 PHD RECIPIENTS
* QUESTION 6

	SURVEY RESP	TOTAL PHD'S DOING SOME RSRCH	SOME FEDL SUPT	NO FEDL SUPT	FEDERAL SUPPORT FOR RESEARCH FROM						
					ADAMHA	DOD	DOE	NASA	NIH	NSF	OTHER AGENCY
ALL 1978 PHD RECIPIENTS	3226	11024	53.1	46.9	3.0	7.3	6.5	2.7	19.6	10.9	14.6
PHD FIELD											
MATHEMATICAL SCI	134	580	36.0	64.0		14.6	8.2	.2	3.4	11.2	6.7
PHYSICS	446	695	78.2	21.8		24.1	28.6	14.0	3.3	28.6	7.1
CHEMISTRY	200	1063	46.6	53.4	.7	4.3	9.5	1.3	21.3	15.9	4.9
EARTH SCI	166	466	58.7	41.3		7.2	10.9	7.2	.9	20.4	25.0
ENGINEERING	206	1112	58.6	41.4	.1	20.9	15.5	7.7	7.3	14.0	14.0
AGRICULTURAL SCI	122	508	54.7	45.3		3.1	3.9	1.9	2.1	1.6	47.3
BIOSCIENCES	1439	2770	72.6	27.4	2.7	3.0	3.7	.5	51.9	10.8	11.4
PSYCHOLOGY	305	1722	39.7	60.3	8.8	6.3	.2	1.0	14.8	3.3	10.0
SOCIAL SCIENCES	208	2108	32.2	67.8	5.1	1.6	.3	.8	4.1	6.5	21.5
POSTDOCTORAL EXPERIENCE											
SOME	1807	3875	82.1	17.9	4.8	5.7	8.8	3.5	45.6	20.3	11.4
NONE	1419	7149	36.9	63.1	2.1	8.3	5.2	2.2	5.0	5.6	16.3
SEX											
MEN	2434	8889	53.0	47.0	2.1	8.5	7.3	2.9	17.9	11.7	14.6
WOMEN	792	2135	53.6	46.4	7.0	2.4	2.8	1.7	26.8	7.3	14.3
RACIAL GROUP											
WHITE	2892	10370	53.3	46.7	3.0	7.3	6.4	2.7	19.7	11.2	14.6
OTHER	334	654	49.2	50.8	3.7	8.6	7.0	2.7	16.8	5.2	14.3

* SURVEY OF 1978 PHD RECIPIENTS
* QUESTION 7

	SURVEY RESP	TOTAL EMPL PHD'S	FIELD OF EMPLOYMENT OR POSTDOCTORAL									
			MATH	PHYS	CHEM	EARTH SCI	ENGIN	AGRI SCI	BIO SCI	PSYCH	SOCIAL SCI	NON SCI
ALL 1978 PHD RECIPIENTS	3850	13651	6.5	5.0	8.5	4.7	9.2	4.2	23.5	18.9	15.4	4.2
PHD FIELD												
MATHEMATICAL SCI	167	697	86.5			1.3	4.7		2.2		1.2	4.0
PHYSICS	501	772	6.3	73.1	1.3	3.4	10.8		2.2		.5	2.1
CHEMISTRY	229	1149	.8	3.2	87.3	1.8	1.4	.2	5.3		.1	
EARTH SCI	182	514	.4	.6	1.6	85.4	1.6		7.9		1.0	1.6
ENGINEERING	247	1302	7.3	5.2	.2	4.8	78.1	1.2	1.6		.1	1.5
AGRICULTURAL SCI	148	624			.7	2.0	2.8	80.0	13.2		.3	1.0
BIOSCIENCES	1630	3112	.5	.4		2.0	.5	1.9	88.8	.3	.4	.9
PSYCHOLOGY	487	2795	.5		4.3		.2		4.1	88.4	1.8	5.0
SOCIAL SCIENCES	259	2686	3.8			.1	2.4	.2	3.2	3.2	75.1	12.1
POSTDOCTORAL EXPERIENCE												
SOME	1914	4101	3.3	8.9	14.0	5.6	3.2	2.2	47.9	11.2	3.1	.7
NONE	1936	9550	7.9	3.3	6.1	4.3	11.7	5.0	12.9	22.3	20.7	5.7
SEX												
MEN	2826	10828	6.8	6.0	9.7	5.3	11.3	5.1	21.4	15.7	14.9	3.8
WOMEN	1024	2823	5.1	1.2	4.0	2.4	1.2	.6	31.5	31.2	17.3	5.5
RACIAL GROUP												
WHITE	3404	12811	6.5	5.2	8.5	4.8	8.9	4.1	23.7	19.0	15.3	4.0
OTHER	446	840	5.9	2.7	9.3	3.3	12.9	5.3	20.6	17.5	16.4	6.2

	SURVEY RESP	TOTAL F-T EMPL	SALARY RANGE OF FULL-TIME EMPLOYED										MEDIAN SALARY
			<$18K	$18K-20K	$20K-22K	$22K-24K	$24K-26K	$26K-28K	$28K-30K	$30K-32K	$32K-34K	>$34K	
ALL 1978 PHD RECIPIENTS	2153	9474	18.6	18.4	15.1	14.2	11.8	8.5	3.3	3.4	2.2	4.4	$21,300
PHD FIELD													
MATHEMATICAL SCI	124	547	36.4	27.1	9.9	8.2	9.1	2.4	3.1	1.8	1.3	.7	18,900
PHYSICS	263	413	15.0	8.2	12.3	14.0	17.9	14.3	7.7	5.1	.7	4.6	23,950
CHEMISTRY	122	711	9.8	6.9	11.5	21.4	26.2	18.0	5.8	.3	.1		23,950
EARTH SCI	120	364	15.1	17.3	19.5	18.7	8.5	5.8	7.7	2.2		5.2	21,600
ENGINEERING	196	1128	3.2	2.5	5.4	17.8	17.6	18.1	6.9	11.6	5.9	11.0	26,050
AGRICULTURAL SCI	109	508	3.7	23.8	24.8	20.1	7.5	7.3	3.7	2.4	1.8	4.9	21,050
BIOSCIENCES	687	1334	28.3	17.8	15.1	9.1	12.7	6.2	3.4	3.2	1.4	2.7	20,000
PSYCHOLOGY	329	2178	22.9	23.9	18.8	15.6	7.6	2.4	1.1	2.3	1.6	3.9	20,000
SOCIAL SCIENCES	203	2291	19.5	23.7	16.5	11.4	8.9	8.9	1.2	2.0	3.1	4.8	20,850
POSTDOCTORAL EXPERIENCE													
SOME	386	878	22.0	15.8	15.7	18.5	11.3	6.8	3.9	1.0	.9	4.1	21,000
NONE	1767	8596	18.3	18.7	15.1	13.8	11.9	8.6	3.2	3.7	2.3	4.5	21,300
SEX													
MEN	1599	7699	15.2	17.5	15.4	14.9	13.0	9.3	3.3	3.8	2.4	5.2	22,000
WOMEN	554	1775	33.4	22.5	13.9	11.0	6.8	4.7	3.4	1.6	1.4	1.3	19,000
RACIAL GROUP													
WHITE	1821	8857	19.1	18.6	15.1	14.2	11.7	8.5	3.0	3.2	2.2	4.4	21,150
OTHER	332	617	11.2	15.6	15.4	14.6	13.1	7.8	7.8	7.3	2.4	4.9	22,650

353

* SURVEY OF 1978 PHD RECIPIENTS
* QUESTION 8B

STIPEND RANGE OF FULL-TIME POSTDOCS

	SURVEY RESP	TOTAL F-T POST-DOCS	<$10K	$10K -12K	$12K -14K	$14K -16K	$16K -18K	$18K -20K	$20K -22K	>$22K	MEDIAN STIPEND
ALL 1978 PHD RECIPIENTS H	1434	2925	3.6	42.7	23.4	12.7	6.9	7.6	1.3	1.8	$12,000
H											
PHD FIELD											
MATHEMATICAL SCI H	25	70	4.3	18.6	1.4	11.4	15.7	35.7	2.9	10.0	17,050
PHYSICS H	206	289		4.2	27.3	26.6	16.6	19.0	4.8	1.4	15,000
CHEMISTRY H	98	387	15.5	33.6	35.9	3.6	4.1	6.7		.5	11,950
EARTH SCI H	46	96		6.3	26.0	36.5	7.3	24.0			14,900
ENGINEERING H	39	81		17.3	9.9	25.9	25.9	17.3		2.5	15,050
AGRICULTURAL SCI H	29	50		32.0	38.0	24.0	4.0		2.0		12,000
BIOSCIENCES H	846	1545	1.3	52.8	23.5	11.8	5.6	3.4	1.0	.7	11,500
PSYCHOLOGY H	112	324	5.9	61.7	13.6	5.9	2.5	2.5		8.0	10,450
SOCIAL SCIENCES H	33	83	3.6	51.8	8.4	3.6	2.4	22.9	4.8	2.4	11,050
H											
POSTDOCTORAL EXPERIENCE H											
SOME H	1434	2925	3.6	42.7	23.4	12.7	6.9	7.6	1.3	1.8	12,000
NONE H											
H											
SEX											
MEN H	1084	2315	3.7	39.1	24.3	13.6	7.9	7.8	1.4	2.2	12,000
WOMEN H	350	610	3.1	56.4	20.0	9.3	3.1	6.7	.7	.7	11,050
H											
RACIAL GROUP											
WHITE H	1359	2800	3.8	42.5	23.4	12.8	6.8	7.7	1.2	1.9	12,000
OTHER H	75	125		47.2	24.8	9.6	9.6	5.6	2.4	.8	12,000

* SURVEY OF 1978 PHD RECIPIENTS
* QUESTION 9

IMMEDIATE CAREER PLANS

	SURVEY RESP	TOTAL EMPL PHD'S	NO CHANGE	JOB ENDS SOON	SEEK NEW JOB	OTHER
ALL 1978 PHD RECIPIENTS	3850	13651	66.2	14.7	15.0	4.1
PHD FIELD						
MATHEMATICAL SCI	169	697	71.1	18.6	7.3	3.1
PHYSICS	496	772	65.4	21.8	10.4	2.4
CHEMISTRY	228	1149	68.2	21.7	8.2	1.9
EARTH SCI	182	514	69.6	13.0	15.2	2.2
ENGINEERING	250	1302	82.2	5.1	10.4	2.3
AGRICULTURAL SCI	149	624	79.3	8.3	11.9	.5
BIOSCIENCES	1624	3112	61.4	24.2	10.5	4.0
PSYCHOLOGY	491	2795	63.4	10.4	20.6	5.7
SOCIAL SCIENCES	261	2686	61.4	8.7	23.6	6.3
POSTDOCTORAL EXPERIENCE						
SOME	1909	4101	53.2	35.1	8.5	3.2
NONE	1941	9550	71.8	5.8	17.9	4.5
SEX						
MEN	2829	10828	66.3	14.7	15.4	3.7
WOMEN	1021	2823	66.1	14.6	13.6	5.7
RACIAL GROUP						
WHITE	3400	12811	66.4	14.9	14.6	4.1
OTHER	450	840	63.5	11.4	21.6	3.5

355

	SURVEY RESP	TOTAL PHD'S	REASON FOR TAKING POSTDOC						REASON FOR NOT TAKING POSTDOC					
			TOTAL TAKING POSTDOC APPT	ADDED RSRCH EXPER	WORK WITH MENTR	SWTCH FIELD	NO EMPL	OTHER OR UNKN	TOTAL NOT TAKING POSTDOC	APPT NOT AVAIL	APPT NOT USEFL	BETTR OFFER	STIPND TOO LOW	OTHER OR UNKN
ALL 1978 PHD RECIPIENTS	4081	14062	29.3	13.7	5.1	4.2	4.7	1.7	70.7	4.9	13.2	33.1	7.8	11.7
PHD FIELD														
MATHEMATICAL SCI	175	710	15.0	5.8	5.2	.1	2.8	1.0	85.0	12.0	19.0	35.0	6.1	12.9
PHYSICS	517	788	49.9	27.7	9.0	4.5	7.1	1.7	50.1	4.4	10.3	18.2	8.7	8.6
CHEMISTRY	249	1189	48.4	17.6	9.9	9.7	9.0	2.3	51.6	1.4	18.0	24.6	3.0	5.9
EARTH SCI	188	523	33.6	18.1	5.4	3.5	5.0	1.5	66.4	3.5	6.6	45.8	6.6	6.2
ENGINEERING	261	1310	13.4	5.7	2.9	1.2	3.4	.1	86.6	1.4	19.2	41.9	6.9	15.0
AGRICULTURAL SCI	150	625	15.9	6.8	1.6	.3	3.9	3.4	84.1	2.9	15.9	51.2	4.8	10.6
BIOSCIENCES	1750	3286	57.8	29.8	10.1	8.9	7.7	1.2	42.2	5.4	7.6	18.5	4.1	9.1
PSYCHOLOGY	517	2888	16.4	6.7	1.7	2.2	2.5	3.2	83.6	9.2	13.9	38.3	16.4	9.6
SOCIAL SCIENCES	274	2743	8.6	3.0	1.2	1.6	1.9	1.0	91.4		14.3	41.9	6.5	19.5
POSTDOCTORAL EXPERIENCE														
SOME	1977	4176	98.4	46.0	17.0	14.0	15.7	5.7	1.6	.2	.6	.6	.4	.4
NONE	2104	9886							100.0	6.9	18.8	47.0	10.9	16.4
SEX														
MEN	2971	11031	29.2	13.7	5.3	3.7	5.1	1.5	70.8	5.6	13.1	33.4	8.3	10.4
WOMEN	1110	3031	29.9	14.0	4.2	6.0	3.2	2.5	70.1	2.4	13.6	32.3	5.8	16.1
RACIAL GROUP														
WHITE	3614	13197	29.8	14.0	5.2	4.2	4.7	1.7	70.2	4.8	13.2	33.2	7.5	11.6
OTHER	467	865	22.2	8.8	2.8	4.0	4.6	2.1	77.8	6.8	13.6	32.8	11.5	13.1

* SURVEY OF 1978 PHD RECIPIENTS
* QUESTION 11A

	TOTAL PHD'S WHO		SOURCE OF SUPPORT FOR FIRST POSTDOC					
	SURVEY RESP	TOOK POSTDOC	FEDL RSRCH FUNDS	FEDL FEL/ TRNEE	OTHER NATL FEL	UNIV OR STATE	PER- SONAL	OTHER
ALL 1978 PHD RECIPIENTS	1947	4106	43.1	29.1	7.6	9.3	2.7	8.1
PHD FIELD								
MATHEMATICAL SCI	41	106	40.6	11.3	5.7	40.6		1.9
PHYSICS	278	389	74.0	11.6	3.1	5.7	1.0	4.6
CHEMISTRY	139	576	67.4	13.5	3.1	5.0		10.9
EARTH SCI	81	174	63.2	12.1	8.6	7.5		8.6
ENGINEERING	75	175	35.1	17.2	20.7	2.9	8.6	15.5
AGRICULTURAL SCI	51	99	48.5	4.0	4.0	20.2		23.2
BIOSCIENCES	1035	1880	34.7	40.5	10.7	7.2	.5	6.4
PSYCHOLOGY	175	471	24.5	37.5	1.1	17.9	6.8	12.2
SOCIAL SCIENCES	72	236	26.5	28.2	6.8	13.2	21.4	3.8
POSTDOCTORAL EXPERIENCE								
SOME	1947	4106	43.1	29.1	7.6	9.3	2.7	8.1
NONE								
SEX								
MEN	1459	3207	45.8	25.9	8.0	9.5	2.2	8.5
WOMEN	488	899	33.6	40.2	6.1	8.7	4.6	6.8
RACIAL GROUP								
WHITE	1841	3916	43.2	29.1	7.6	9.3	2.7	8.1
OTHER	106	190	41.0	28.7	8.5	9.6	3.2	9.0

	SURVEY RESP	TOTAL PHD'S WHO TOOK POSTDOC	GEOGRAPHIC LIMITATIONS		
			IMPORT FACTOR	INCIDENTAL FACTOR	NOT A FACTOR
ALL 1978 PHD RECIPIENTS	1940	4106	30.1	23.0	46.9
PHD FIELD					
MATHEMATICAL SCI	41	106	41.5	24.5	34.0
PHYSICS	277	389	24.2	22.9	52.8
CHEMISTRY	138	576	24.9	29.4	45.6
EARTH SCI	79	174	13.2	25.1	61.7
ENGINEERING	75	175	29.5	17.3	53.2
AGRICULTURAL SCI	51	99	22.2	22.2	55.6
BIOSCIENCES	1031	1880	28.7	22.8	48.6
PSYCHOLOGY	176	471	38.0	22.0	40.1
SOCIAL SCIENCES	72	236	59.0	13.7	27.4
POSTDOCTORAL EXPERIENCE					
SOME	1940	4106	30.1	23.0	46.9
NONE					
SEX					
MEN	1451	3207	24.3	25.0	50.7
WOMEN	489	899	50.7	15.8	33.4
RACIAL GROUP					
WHITE	1837	3916	30.1	23.1	46.8
OTHER	103	190	29.7	21.4	48.9

* SURVEY OF 1978 PHD RECIPIENTS
* QUESTION 11C

| | TOTAL PHD'S WHO TOOK POSTDOC | | PROLONGED POSTDOC APPTS BECAUSE NO JOB |
	SURVEY RESP	TOOK POSTDOC	
ALL 1978 PHD RECIPIENTS	1694	4106	21.2
PHD FIELD			
MATHEMATICAL SCI	39	106	2.1
PHYSICS	244	389	22.2
CHEMISTRY	129	576	13.4
EARTH SCI	76	174	29.3
ENGINEERING	72	175	17.6
AGRICULTURAL SCI	49	99	24.2
BIOSCIENCES	856	1880	25.3
PSYCHOLOGY	162	471	16.7
SOCIAL SCIENCES	67	236	21.6
POSTDOCTORAL EXPERIENCE			
SOME	1694	4106	21.2
NONE			
SEX			
MEN	1270	3207	21.5
WOMEN	424	899	20.2
RACIAL GROUP			
WHITE	1602	3916	21.2
OTHER	92	190	20.1

* SURVEY OF 1978 PHD RECIPIENTS
* QUESTION 12

	SURVEY RESP	TOTAL RSRCH STAFF	FULL-TIME RESEARCH PERSONNEL									
			FACULTY N	%	POSTDOCS N	%	OTHER PHDS N	%	GRAD RA'S N	%	OTHER STAFF N	%
ALL 1978 PHD RECIPIENTS	1970	29732	9264	31.2	4033	13.6	1879	6.3	6818	22.9	7738	26.0
PHD FIELD												
MATHEMATICAL SCI	62	1214	481	39.6	97	8.0	87	7.2	203	16.7	346	28.5
PHYSICS	202	2694	680	25.2	481	17.9	324	12.0	482	17.9	727	27.0
CHEMISTRY	102	2115	481	22.7	476	22.5	78	3.7	758	35.8	322	15.2
EARTH SCI	75	926	274	29.6	110	11.9	71	7.7	252	27.2	219	23.7
ENGINEERING	92	2341	675	28.8	80	3.4	207	8.8	855	36.5	524	22.4
AGRICULTURAL SCI	75	1149	468	40.7	69	6.0	35	3.0	254	22.1	323	28.1
BIOSCIENCES	1065	10721	3020	28.2	2259	21.1	543	5.1	1835	17.1	3064	28.6
PSYCHOLOGY	181	3989	1302	32.6	307	7.7	228	5.7	1011	25.3	1141	28.6
SOCIAL SCIENCES	116	4583	1883	41.1	154	3.4	306	6.7	1168	25.5	1072	23.4
POSTDOCTORAL EXPERIENCE												
SOME	1377	16451	4231	25.7	3886	23.6	1153	7.0	3142	19.1	4039	24.6
NONE	593	13281	5033	37.9	147	1.1	726	5.5	3676	27.7	3699	27.9
SEX												
MEN	1464	23390	7116	30.4	3240	13.9	1489	6.4	5630	24.1	5915	25.3
WOMEN	506	6342	2148	33.9	793	12.5	390	6.1	1188	18.7	1823	28.7
RACIAL GROUP												
WHITE	1805	28142	8737	31.0	3864	13.7	1751	6.2	6513	23.1	7277	25.9
OTHER	165	1590	527	33.1	169	10.6	128	8.1	305	19.2	461	29.0

* SURVEY OF 1978 PHD RECIPIENTS
* QUESTION 12.1

	SURVEY RESP	EST TOTAL	FACULTY CONTRIBUTION TO RESEARCH EFFORT			
			ESSE- NTIAL	IMPO- RTANT	UNIM- PORT- ANT	NONE IN DEPT
ALL 1978 PHD RECIPIENTS	1929	5555	66.2	22.0	4.1	7.6
PHD FIELD						
MATHEMATICAL SCI	61	231	73.6	18.6		7.8
PHYSICS	199	285	55.8	34.4	2.1	7.7
CHEMISTRY	100	421	65.8	25.2	7.6	1.4
EARTH SCI	75	187	62.6	18.7	9.1	9.6
ENGINEERING	90	445	77.8	10.8	.4	11.0
AGRICULTURAL SCI	74	238	55.0	31.5	2.5	10.9
BIOSCIENCES	1038	1933	56.2	30.5	6.0	7.3
PSYCHOLOGY	179	793	64.7	20.4	5.8	9.1
SOCIAL SCIENCES	113	1022	86.0	6.6	.5	6.9
POSTDOCTORAL EXPERIENCE						
SOME	1346	2745	54.3	31.7	6.3	7.7
NONE	583	2810	77.9	12.5	2.0	7.6
SEX						
MEN	1439	4422	66.9	21.9	4.1	7.1
WOMEN	490	1133	63.6	22.5	4.3	9.5
RACIAL GROUP						
WHITE	1768	5263	66.4	22.1	4.1	7.4
OTHER	161	292	62.7	20.9	4.1	12.3

361

	SURVEY RESP	EST TOTAL	POSTDOC CONTRIBUTION TO RESEARCH EFFORT			
			ESSE-NTIAL	IMPO-RTANT	UNIM-PORT-ANT	NONE IN DEPT
ALL 1978 PHD RECIPIENTS	1948	5660	29.6	8.7	1.1	60.5
PHD FIELD						
MATHEMATICAL SCI	61	232	7.8	8.6	.9	82.8
PHYSICS	199	285	49.8	22.5	.7	27.0
CHEMISTRY	100	420	45.7	16.9	.5	36.9
EARTH SCI	75	187	35.3	7.0		57.8
ENGINEERING	91	446	13.0	2.0		85.0
AGRICULTURAL SCI	75	246	16.3	4.1		79.7
BIOSCIENCES	1053	1959	47.0	13.1	2.3	37.6
PSYCHOLOGY	178	797	18.3	4.1	.5	77.0
SOCIAL SCIENCES	116	1088	8.5	1.7	.9	88.9
POSTDOCTORAL EXPERIENCE						
SOME	1355	2757	58.8	16.8	1.9	22.4
NONE	593	2903	1.9	1.1	.4	96.7
SEX						
MEN	1448	4509	28.8	8.8	1.2	61.2
WOMEN	500	1151	32.8	8.3	1.0	57.9
RACIAL GROUP						
WHITE	1785	5363	30.0	9.0	1.1	59.9
OTHER	163	297	22.2	4.4	2.7	70.7

	SURVEY RESP	EST TOTAL	OTHER PHD'S CONTRIBUTION TO RESEARCH EFFORT			
			ESSE-NTIAL	IMPO-RTANT	UNIM-PORT-ANT	NONE IN DEPT
ALL 1978 PHD RECIPIENTS	1954	5632	8.0	6.6	1.9	83.6
PHD FIELD						
MATHEMATICAL SCI	62	233	.9	7.7		91.4
PHYSICS	202	288	16.0	13.9	3.1	67.0
CHEMISTRY	100	420	4.8	6.0	1.7	87.6
EARTH SCI	75	187	11.8	13.9		74.3
ENGINEERING	92	447	8.3	10.5	.4	80.8
AGRICULTURAL SCI	75	246	5.7	2.8	.4	91.1
BIOSCIENCES	1055	1964	7.9	7.6	2.6	81.9
PSYCHOLOGY	178	792	8.7	6.2	.1	85.0
SOCIAL SCIENCES	115	1055	8.1	.8	3.2	88.0
POSTDOCTORAL EXPERIENCE						
SOME	1363	2764	8.9	8.4	2.3	80.4
NONE	591	2868	7.1	4.8	1.4	86.6
SEX						
MEN	1456	4490	7.6	7.0	1.7	83.7
WOMEN	498	1142	9.7	4.7	2.4	83.2
RACIAL GROUP						
WHITE	1789	5332	7.8	6.4	1.9	83.9
OTHER	165	300	12.0	8.7	.7	78.7

	SURVEY RESP	EST TOTAL	GRAD RA'S CONTRIBUTION TO RESEARCH EFFORT			
			ESSENTIAL	IMPORTANT	UNIMPORTANT	NONE DEPT
ALL 1978 PHD RECIPIENTS	1923	5577	15.2	27.0	7.0	50.8
PHD FIELD						
MATHEMATICAL SCI	62	233	9.4	12.0	1.7	76.8
PHYSICS	192	274	14.2	32.5	11.3	42.0
CHEMISTRY	95	408	20.1	27.0	7.1	45.8
EARTH SCI	74	182	11.0	33.5	2.2	53.3
ENGINEERING	92	447	33.6	23.9	7.4	35.1
AGRICULTURAL SCI	75	246	25.6	26.0	5.3	43.1
BIOSCIENCES	1043	1941	10.3	22.6	6.7	60.4
PSYCHOLOGY	177	795	18.5	36.5	3.3	41.8
SOCIAL SCIENCES	113	1051	12.1	30.3	11.3	46.3
POSTDOCTORAL EXPERIENCE						
SOME	1337	2715	11.2	24.9	7.6	56.4
NONE	586	2862	19.1	29.0	6.4	45.5
SEX						
MEN	1430	4436	14.7	27.1	7.1	51.1
WOMEN	493	1141	17.2	26.8	6.7	49.3
RACIAL GROUP						
WHITE	1766	5290	15.1	27.4	7.0	50.5
OTHER	157	287	18.1	18.8	6.3	56.8

* SURVEY OF 1978 PHD RECIPIENTS
* QUESTION 12.5

	SURVEY RESP	EST TOTAL	OTHER STAFF'S CONTRIBUTION TO RESEARCH EFFORT			
			ESSE- NTIAL	IMPO- RTANT	UNIM- PORT- ANT	NONE IN DEPT
ALL 1978 PHD RECIPIENTS	1928	5531	16.1	28.0	4.8	51.1
PHD FIELD						
MATHEMATICAL SCI	62	233	6.0	2.1	3.4	88.4
PHYSICS	195	280	20.7	18.9	1.4	58.9
CHEMISTRY	98	415	5.5	23.4	7.5	63.6
EARTH SCI	74	182	16.5	12.6	10.4	60.4
ENGINEERING	92	447	16.8	21.0	1.8	60.4
AGRICULTURAL SCI	74	238	40.3	27.7	5.5	26.5
BIOSCIENCES	1045	1940	20.1	37.8	7.4	34.6
PSYCHOLOGY	175	775	15.9	32.3	2.8	49.0
SOCIAL SCIENCES	113	1021	7.8	22.4	1.7	68.1
POSTDOCTORAL EXPERIENCE						
SOME	1347	2730	16.5	34.9	7.4	41.2
NONE	581	2801	15.6	21.3	2.3	60.7
SEX						
MEN	1434	4406	15.3	26.1	4.7	53.9
WOMEN	494	1125	19.1	35.8	5.1	40.0
RACIAL GROUP						
WHITE	1769	5238	15.7	28.2	4.9	51.3
OTHER	159	293	23.5	25.3	3.8	47.4

* SURVEY OF 1978 PHD RECIPIENTS
* QUESTION 13.1

POSTDOC CONTRIBUTION IN DETERMINING
BASIC DIRECTIONS OF RESEARCH PROJECT

		SURVEY RESP	EST TOTAL	ESSE- NTIAL	IMPO- RTANT	UNIM- PCRT- ANT	CAN'T DETER- MINE
ALL 1978 PHD RECIPIENTS	H	1279	2648	39.7	45.5	13.1	1.8
	H						
PHD FIELD							
MATHEMATICAL SCI	H	17	42	33.3	33.3	33.3	
PHYSICS	H	166	232	25.9	52.2	19.4	2.6
CHEMISTRY	H	86	344	26.5	59.0	14.0	.6
EARTH SCI	H	45	103	40.8	36.9	22.3	
ENGINEERING	H	39	91	37.4	57.1	5.5	
AGRICULTURAL SCI	H	32	56	26.8	58.9	7.1	7.1
BIOSCIENCES	H	777	1423	43.2	43.7	10.8	2.2
PSYCHOLOGY	H	80	224	50.9	35.7	12.9	.4
SOCIAL SCIENCES	H	37	133	48.9	30.8	18.8	1.5
	H						
POSTDOCTORAL EXPERIENCE	H						
SOME	H	1230	2500	40.2	46.0	12.3	1.5
NONE	H	49	148	31.1	36.5	26.4	6.1
	H						
SEX	H						
MEN	H	970	2107	38.9	46.5	12.9	1.7
WOMEN	H	309	541	42.7	41.4	13.9	2.0
	H						
RACIAL GROUP	H						
WHITE	H	1207	2528	39.4	45.6	13.6	1.5
OTHER	H	72	120	45.0	43.3	3.3	8.3

POSTDOC CONTRIBUTION TO INTELLECTUAL
VIGOR OF THE RESEARCH EFFORT

	SURVEY RESP	EST TOTAL	ESSE-NTIAL	IMPO-RTANT	UNIM-PORT-ANT	CAN'T DETER-MINE
ALL 1978 PHD RECIPIENTS	1279	2648	60.7	33.6	3.8	1.9
PHD FIELD						
MATHEMATICAL SCI	17	42	23.8	73.8		2.4
PHYSICS	166	232	49.1	44.0	4.7	2.2
CHEMISTRY	86	344	55.8	38.4	.3	5.5
EARTH SCI	45	103	61.2	29.1	9.7	
ENGINEERING	39	91	70.3	29.7		
AGRICULTURAL SCI	32	56	51.8	37.5	3.6	7.1
BIOSCIENCES	777	1423	62.3	32.7	3.9	1.1
PSYCHOLOGY	80	224	70.1	27.2	1.8	.9
SOCIAL SCIENCES	37	133	68.4	16.5	12.8	2.3
POSTDOCTORAL EXPERIENCE						
SOME	1230	2500	61.9	33.2	3.0	1.8
NONE	49	148	39.9	40.5	16.2	3.4
SEX						
MEN	970	2107	61.3	33.4	3.3	2.0
WOMEN	309	541	58.2	34.6	5.7	1.5
RACIAL GROUP						
WHITE	1207	2528	60.7	33.6	3.9	1.8
OTHER	72	120	60.8	35.0	.8	3.3

367

	SURVEY RESP	EST TOTAL	POSTDOC CONTRIBUTION TO INFUSION OF NEW RESEARCH TECHNIQUES			
			ESSENTIAL	IMPORTANT	UNIMPORTANT	CAN'T DETERMINE
ALL 1978 PHD RECIPIENTS	1279	2648	51.3	35.3	9.9	3.5
PHD FIELD						
MATHEMATICAL SCI	17	42	40.5	45.2	11.9	2.4
PHYSICS	166	232	38.4	44.8	11.6	5.2
CHEMISTRY	86	344	41.0	45.1	11.9	2.0
EARTH SCI	45	103	62.1	17.5	16.5	3.9
ENGINEERING	39	91	47.3	50.5	1.1	1.1
AGRICULTURAL SCI	32	56	51.8	35.7	5.4	7.1
BIOSCIENCES	777	1423	56.9	32.0	8.4	2.7
PSYCHOLOGY	80	224	58.5	22.3	12.1	7.1
SOCIAL SCIENCES	37	133	26.3	49.6	17.3	6.8
POSTDOCTORAL EXPERIENCE						
SOME	1230	2500	53.6	34.2	9.1	3.1
NONE	49	148	11.5	54.1	24.3	10.1
SEX						
MEN	970	2107	52.1	35.0	9.6	3.3
WOMEN	309	541	48.2	36.2	11.3	4.3
RACIAL GROUP						
WHITE	1207	2528	51.5	34.9	10.2	3.4
OTHER	72	120	47.5	42.5	3.3	6.7

POSTDOC CONTRIBUTION TO
PUBLICATION OF RESEARCH FINDINGS

	SURVEY RESP	EST TOTAL	ESSE-NTIAL	IMPO-RTANT	UNIM-PCRT-ANT	CAN'T DETER-MINE
ALL 1978 PHD RECIPIENTS	1279	2648	48.5	38.2	7.9	5.4
PHD FIELD						
MATHEMATICAL SCI	17	42	50.0	45.2	4.8	7.8
PHYSICS	166	232	41.8	43.5	6.9	7.8
CHEMISTRY	86	344	23.5	51.5	19.8	5.2
EARTH SCI	45	103	54.4	23.3	9.7	12.6
ENGINEERING	39	91	76.9	18.7	3.3	1.1
AGRICULTURAL SCI	32	56	30.4	64.3		5.4
BIOSCIENCES	777	1423	54.1	35.0	6.2	4.7
PSYCHOLOGY	80	224	53.1	33.9	7.1	5.8
SOCIAL SCIENCES	37	133	39.1	47.4	5.3	8.3
POSTDOCTORAL EXPERIENCE						
SOME	1230	2500	50.1	37.5	7.4	5.0
NONE	49	148	20.9	50.0	16.2	12.8
SEX						
MEN	970	2107	47.1	39.8	8.6	4.5
WOMEN	309	541	53.8	31.8	5.4	9.1
RACIAL GROUP						
WHITE	1207	2528	48.3	38.3	8.0	5.4
OTHER	72	120	50.8	36.7	6.7	5.8

* SURVEY OF 1978 PHD RECIPIENTS
* QUESTION 13.5

	SURVEY RESP	EST TOTAL	POSTDOC CONTRIBUTION TO TRAINING OF GRADUATE STUDENTS			
			ESSE-NTIAL	IMPO-RTANT	UNIM-PCRT-ANT	CAN'T DETER-MINE
ALL 1978 PHD RECIPIENTS	1279	2648	11.9	28.5	38.1	21.4
PHD FIELD						
MATHEMATICAL SCI	17	42		33.3	61.9	4.8
PHYSICS	166	232	12.5	28.4	36.6	22.4
CHEMISTRY	86	344	14.2	34.6	29.9	21.2
EARTH SCI	45	103	9.7	32.0	47.6	10.7
ENGINEERING	39	91	38.5	33.0	20.9	7.7
AGRICULTURAL SCI	32	56	14.3	32.1	41.1	12.5
BIOSCIENCES	777	1423	10.5	26.9	38.8	23.8
PSYCHOLOGY	80	224	7.1	30.8	36.6	25.4
SOCIAL SCIENCES	37	133	14.3	18.0	52.6	15.0
POSTDOCTORAL EXPERIENCE						
SOME	1230	2500	12.2	29.0	36.8	22.0
NONE	49	148	8.1	20.3	59.5	12.2
SEX						
MEN	970	2107	11.8	30.3	38.2	19.7
WOMEN	309	541	12.4	21.8	37.7	28.1
RACIAL GROUP						
WHITE	1207	2528	12.0	28.5	38.3	21.2
OTHER	72	120	10.8	29.2	34.2	25.8

* SURVEY OF 1978 PHD RECIPIENTS
* QUESTION 14A
* RATIO OF THE NUMBER OF PHD'S OFFERED FACULTY, POSTDOCTORAL, OR NONFACULTY
* POSITIONS IN UNIVERSITIES AND COLLEGES TO NUMBER SEEKING POSITIONS (X 100)

	SURVEY TOTAL RESP	PHD'S	FACULTY POSITION OFFER %	SEEK %	O/S RATIO	POSTDOCTORAL APPT OFFER %	SEEK %	O/S RATIO	NONFACULTY APPT OFFER %	SEEK %	O/S RATIO
ALL 1978 PHD RECIPIENTS	3657	14062	40.4	57.6	70.1	30.5	35.9	85.0	6.3	8.6	72.9
PHD FIELD											
MATHEMATICAL SCI	160	710	73.0	87.1	83.8	14.4	23.9	60.3	1.7	2.8	61.1
PHYSICS	483	788	17.1	39.8	43.1	48.0	58.6	82.0	4.5	7.1	63.5
CHEMISTRY	233	1189	13.4	26.2	51.0	54.2	53.6	101.0	1.6	2.3	68.0
EARTH SCI	172	523	39.6	71.6	55.3	36.4	42.1	86.5	2.5	3.8	66.7
ENGINEERING	226	1310	39.0	50.1	77.7	14.3	17.2	83.0	6.1	7.4	83.1
AGRICULTURAL SCI	135	625	44.4	81.6	54.4	24.9	29.4	84.8	9.9	10.4	94.6
BIOSCIENCES	1577	3286	29.4	44.7	65.8	60.4	66.0	91.5	4.2	6.7	63.3
PSYCHOLOGY	452	2888	38.6	59.0	65.5	15.0	23.0	65.1	11.7	10.8	69.5
SOCIAL SCIENCES	219	2743	67.6	80.4	84.2	4.7	8.2	57.3	7.1	8.4	84.7
POSTDOCTORAL EXPERIENCE											
SOME	1891	4176	16.2	37.2	43.5	78.1	80.6	96.8	3.1	4.5	69.5
NONE	1766	9886	51.6	67.1	76.9	8.4	15.1	55.6	7.7	10.5	73.6
SEX											
MEN	2681	11031	38.8	57.3	67.7	31.0	36.3	85.4	5.8	8.2	71.0
WOMEN	976	3031	46.3	58.8	78.7	28.6	34.1	83.6	7.9	10.0	78.8
RACIAL GROUP											
WHITE	3261	13197	40.4	57.7	70.0	31.0	36.2	85.5	6.3	8.6	74.2
OTHER	396	865	40.6	56.3	72.0	22.9	30.3	75.6	5.2	9.6	53.6

371

* SURVEY OF 1978 PHD RECIPIENTS
* QUESTION 14B
* RATIO OF THE NUMBER OF PHD'S OFFERED POSTDOCTORAL AND OTHER POSITIONS IN
* FFRDC LABORATORIES TO NUMBER SEEKING POSITIONS (X 100)

	SURVEY TOTAL RESP PHD'S	POSTDOCTORAL APPT OFFER %	SEEK %	O/S RATIO	OTHER POSITION OFFER %	SEEK %	O/S RATIO
ALL 1978 PHD RECIPIENTS	3657 14062	3.0	6.1	48.3	3.2	6.7	47.3
PHD FIELD							
MATHEMATICAL SCI	160 710	2.5	3.5	69.6	4.8	8.0	59.6
PHYSICS	483 788	16.0	28.0	57.4	11.9	28.4	42.0
CHEMISTRY	233 1189	4.2	9.1	46.5	2.8	8.5	33.3
EARTH SCI	172 523	3.2	7.6	41.7	5.9	11.6	50.9
ENGINEERING	226 1310	2.9	7.2	40.7	11.1	20.8	53.2
AGRICULTURAL SCI	135 625	.4	2.2	16.7	3.0	7.1	42.1
BIOSCIENCES	1577 3286	4.1	7.3	56.5	1.2	3.3	35.7
PSYCHOLOGY	452 2888	.6	2.0	28.0	.1	.2	50.0
SOCIAL SCIENCES	219 2743	.6	1.6	2.7	1.5	1.7	84.6
POSTDOCTORAL EXPERIENCE							
SOME	1891 4176	7.9	12.2	64.9	2.0	5.4	36.2
NONE	1766 9886	.6	3.3	19.5	3.7	7.2	51.1
SEX							
MEN	2681 11031	3.2	7.0	46.2	3.8	8.0	47.3
WOMEN	976 3031	1.9	2.8	67.6	.8	1.6	46.5
RACIAL GROUP							
WHITE	3261 13197	3.0	6.2	47.7	3.1	6.6	46.7
OTHER	396 865	2.6	4.3	61.3	4.5	8.1	55.2

* SURVEY OF 1978 PHD RECIPIENTS
* QUESTION 14C
* RATIO OF THE NUMBER OF PHD'S OFFERED POSTDOCTORAL AND OTHER POSITIONS IN
* IN INDUSTRY OR BUSINESS TO NUMBER SEEKING POSITIONS (x 100)

	SURVEY TOTAL RESP PHD'S		POSTDOCTORAL APPT			OTHER POSITION		
			OFFER %	SEEK %	O/S RATIO	OFFER %	SEEK %	O/S RATIO
ALL 1978 PHD RECIPIENTS	3657	14062	1.8	3.1	57.8	23.9	32.9	72.7
PHD FIELD								
MATHEMATICAL SCI	160	710	.3	3.1	10.0	27.0	36.8	73.3
PHYSICS	483	788	3.2	5.5	57.5	33.1	45.3	73.0
CHEMISTRY	233	1189	2.5	4.2	58.7	45.6	60.9	74.8
EARTH SCI	172	523	2.1	2.5	83.3	33.9	49.1	69.1
ENGINEERING	226	1310	1.9	3.3	59.5	60.0	66.1	90.8
AGRICULTURAL SCI	135	625		2.4		33.1	45.0	73.6
BIOSCIENCES	1577	3286	1.4	2.9	47.7	13.0	24.0	54.0
PSYCHOLOGY	452	2888	1.7	3.0	55.3	13.0	20.6	63.0
SOCIAL SCIENCES	219	2743	2.3	2.1	108.5	13.7	16.5	82.8
POSTDOCTORAL EXPERIENCE								
SOME	1891	4176	2.8	4.9	57.6	9.3	23.3	39.7
NONE	1766	9886	1.3	2.2	58.1	30.7	37.3	82.3
SEX								
MEN	2681	11031	1.6	2.9	53.3	26.8	36.4	73.7
WOMEN	976	3031	2.5	3.5	71.7	13.2	19.9	66.2
RACIAL GROUP								
WHITE	3261	13197	1.8	3.0	57.9	23.4	32.3	72.4
OTHER	396	865	1.8	3.2	56.5	31.8	41.4	76.8

* SURVEY OF 1978 PHD RECIPIENTS
* QUESTION 14D
* RATIO OF THE NUMBER OF PHD'S OFFERED POSTDOCTORAL AND OTHER POSITIONS IN
* FEDERAL, STATE, OR LOCAL GOVERNMENT TO NUMBER SEEKING POSITIONS (X 100)

	SURVEY RESP	TOTAL PHD'S	POSTDOCTORAL APPT			OTHER POSITION		
			OFFER %	SEEK %	O/S RATIO	OFFER %	SEEK %	O/S RATIO
ALL 1978 PHD RECIPIENTS	3657	14062	3.8	5.9	65.5	15.3	22.5	68.2
PHD FIELD								
MATHEMATICAL SCI	160	710	.5	.5	100.0	6.7	12.6	53.7
PHYSICS	483	788	5.5	9.1	60.6	6.6	13.7	48.0
CHEMISTRY	233	1189	5.5	7.4	74.1	3.6	10.4	34.5
EARTH SCI	172	523	5.9	13.5	43.8	17.9	27.8	64.4
ENGINEERING	226	1310	2.3	4.8	48.1	12.8	17.3	73.8
AGRICULTURAL SCI	135	625	.2	2.4	7.7	27.3	40.3	67.7
BIOSCIENCES	1577	3286	6.2	9.2	67.3	10.0	17.5	57.1
PSYCHOLOGY	452	2888	3.6	4.9	72.6	25.6	30.5	83.8
SOCIAL SCIENCES	219	2743	2.0	2.1	91.7	19.8	28.9	68.5
POSTDOCTORAL EXPERIENCE								
SOME	1891	4176	7.9	10.7	73.4	4.5	10.8	42.2
NONE	1766	9886	1.9	3.6	54.5	20.4	28.0	72.9
SEX								
MEN	2681	11031	3.8	5.9	64.7	15.4	22.7	67.9
WOMEN	976	3031	3.9	5.7	68.7	15.2	21.9	69.5
RACIAL GROUP								
WHITE	3261	13197	3.9	5.9	65.5	15.4	22.6	68.2
OTHER	396	865	3.1	4.6	66.7	14.4	21.1	68.2

* SURVEY OF 1978 PHD RECIPIENTS
* QUESTION 14E
* RATIO OF THE NUMBER OF PHD'S OFFERED POSITIONS IN OTHER SECTORS TO NUMBER
* SEEKING POSITIONS (x 100)

OTHER POSITION

	SURVEY RESP	TOTAL PHD'S	OFFER %	SEEK %	O/S RATIO
ALL 1978 PHD RECIPIENTS	3657	14062	7.8	8.9	87.7
PHD FIELD					
MATHEMATICAL SCI	160	710	.5	.8	60.0
PHYSICS	483	788	2.2	2.6	84.2
CHEMISTRY	233	1189	2.2	2.9	75.0
EARTH SCI	172	523	4.8	5.7	85.2
ENGINEERING	226	1310	1.9	2.2	84.0
AGRICULTURAL SCI	135	625	.4	2.2	16.7
BIOSCIENCES	1577	3286	4.1	4.6	88.9
PSYCHOLOGY	452	2888	22.3	25.2	88.4
SOCIAL SCIENCES	219	2743	8.2	8.8	93.0
POSTDOCTORAL EXPERIENCE					
SOME	1891	4176	4.4	5.6	79.1
NONE	1766	9886	9.3	10.4	89.9
SEX					
MEN	2681	11031	6.4	7.2	88.4
WOMEN	976	3031	12.9	14.9	86.5
RACIAL GROUP					
WHITE	3261	13197	7.9	9.0	87.7
OTHER	396	865	6.4	7.3	88.5

* SURVEY OF 1978 PHD RECIPIENTS
* QUESTION 14F
* RATIO OF THE NUMBER OF PHD'S OFFERED POSTDOCTORAL OR OTHER POSITIONS IN
* ALL SECTORS TO NUMBER SEEKING POSITIONS (X 100)

	SURVEY TOTAL RESP PHD'S	POSTDOCTORAL APPT			OTHER POSITION		
		OFFER %	SEEK %	O/S RATIO	OFFER %	SEEK %	O/S RATIO
ALL 1978 PHD RECIPIENTS	3657 14062	40.9	48.0	85.3	70.4	82.0	85.9
PHD FIELD							
MATHEMATICAL SCI	160 710	18.7	29.8	62.9	89.7	95.6	93.9
PHYSICS	483 788	62.3	71.5	87.1	56.7	72.8	77.8
CHEMISTRY	233 1189	61.2	61.6	99.4	61.5	78.0	78.8
EARTH SCI	172 523	45.7	55.2	82.8	74.3	89.7	82.9
ENGINEERING	226 1310	23.9	30.8	77.6	87.0	90.8	95.8
AGRICULTURAL SCI	135 625	34.9	39.6	88.3	79.9	95.0	84.1
BIOSCIENCES	1577 3286	67.8	74.4	91.0	45.8	60.6	75.5
PSYCHOLOGY	452 2888	31.4	42.7	73.5	78.7	89.0	88.4
SOCIAL SCIENCES	219 2743	15.5	19.8	78.1	85.1	94.0	90.6
POSTDOCTORAL EXPERIENCE							
SOME	1891 4176	88.2	89.8	98.2	30.2	55.2	54.8
NONE	1766 9886	19.0	28.6	66.4	89.1	94.5	94.3
SEX							
MEN	2681 11031	40.9	48.0	85.2	70.4	83.2	84.7
WOMEN	976 3031	41.0	47.9	85.4	70.5	77.8	90.6
RACIAL GROUP							
WHITE	3261 13197	41.5	48.4	85.8	70.1	81.8	85.7
OTHER	396 865	31.8	42.0	75.7	76.0	85.4	89.1

OMB No. 99-S79002

Approval expires
December 31, 1979

SURVEY OF FOREIGN SCIENTISTS AND ENGINEERS

CONDUCTED BY THE NATIONAL RESEARCH COUNCIL WITH THE SUPPORT OF THE NATIONAL SCIENCE FOUNDATION

THE ACCOMPANYING LETTER requests your assistance in this survey of foreign scientists and engineers.

PLEASE READ the instructions carefully and answer by printing your reply or entering an 'X' in the appropriate box.

PLEASE COMMENT on any questions which you think require fuller explanation.

PLEASE RETURN the completed form in the enclosed envelope to the Commission on Human Resources, JH 638, National Research Council, 2101 Constitution Avenue, N.W., Washington, D.C. 20418.

NOTE: This information is solicited under the authority of the National Science Foundation Act of 1950, as amended. All information you provide will be treated as confidential and used for statistical purposes only. Information will be released only in the form of statistical summaries or in a form which does not identify information about any particular person. Your response is entirely voluntary and your failure to provide some or all of the requested information will in no way adversely affect you.

Please provide the following background information about yourself.

---

1. Date of birth: _____ (8-12)
(Month)   (Day)   (Year)

2. Sex: 1 ☐ Male   2 ☐ Female (13)

3. Country of citizenship: _____ (14-15)

4. Type of visa:

1 ☐ Permanent resident visa (immigrant)
2 ☐ Student visa (F)
3 ☐ Temporary worker or trainee visa (H)
4 ☐ Exchange visitor visa (J)
5 ☐ Other, please specify _____ (16)

5. Marital status: 1 ☐ Married   2 ☐ Not married (including widowed, divorced) (17)

6. Number of dependents: _____ (Include any relatives receiving at least one-half of his or her support from you; do NOT include yourself.) (18)

7. Ph.D. degree (or equivalent research doctorate):

_____ (19) _____ (20-22) ☐☐☐ _____
Title of degree   Month and year granted   Field* (23-25)   Institution and location   (26-31)

Please provide the following information about the most recent postdoctoral appointment you have held in a United States university.

---

8. Starting and termination dates of postdoctoral appointment:

Starting date _____ (32-34)
(Month)   (Year)

Expected termination date _____ (35-37)
(Month)   (Year)

*See attached list of specialty field codes.

377

9. Position held immediately prior to the postdoctoral appointment:

Institution/organization and location   (38-43)

Field*   (44-46)   Months held   (47-48)

Type of position:
- 1 ☐ Graduate student
- 2 ☐ Postdoctoral appointee
- 3 ☐ Faculty member
- 4 ☐ Other university position

- 5 ☐ Position in industry
- 6 ☐ Position in government
- 7 ☐ Other position, please specify

_____ (49)

10. What were your reasons for taking a postdoctoral appointment at a United States university? *(Check all that apply and CIRCLE the most important ONE.)*

- 1 ☐ Couldn't obtain postdoctoral training you wanted in your native country
- 2 ☐ To work with a particular scientist or research group
- 3 ☐ To work in the United States
- 4 ☐ Couldn't obtain type of employment position you wanted in your native country

- 5 ☐ Other reason, please specify_____ (50-54)

11. How important do you consider a postdoctoral appointment at a United States university to be in enabling you to ATTAIN a research position in your native country?

- 1 ☐ Very important
- 2 ☐ Sometimes helpful
- 3 ☐ Not important
- 4 ☐ Cannot determine   (55)

12. Postdoctoral stipend (including personal allowances for dependents, etc.): $_____ per year   (56-58)

13. What has been the PRIMARY source of support for your postdoctoral appointment? *(Check only one.)*

- 1 ☐ U.S. federal research grant or contract
- 2 ☐ U.S. university or state funds (including teaching assistant)
- 3 ☐ Other U.S. sources, please specify _____

- 4 ☐ Funds from government *OUTSIDE* the United States
- 5 ☐ Funds from non-governmental sources *OUTSIDE* the United States

- 6 ☐ Personal resources (e.g., loans, family income, etc.)

- 7 ☐ Other sources, please specify_____ (59)

14. What are your employment plans after completing the postdoctoral appointment? *(Check any employment alternatives you have seriously considered and CIRCLE the ONE you PREFER.)*

- 1 ☐ Employment position OUTSIDE the United States

- 2 ☐ Another postdoctoral appointment at a United States university
- 3 ☐ Faculty position at a United States university
- 4 ☐ Other position at a United States university

- 5 ☐ Employment position in industry in the United States
- 6 ☐ Employment position in government in the United States
- 7 ☐ Other employment in the United States

- 8 ☐ Other, please specify _____ (60-67)

*See attached list of specialty field codes.

15. If there were no visa restrictions, what would be your long-term career plans? *(Check any career plans you are seriously considering and CIRCLE the ONE you PREFER.)*

1 ☐ Faculty or other position in a university OUTSIDE the United States
2 ☐ Employment position in industry OUTSIDE the United States
3 ☐ Employment position in government OUTSIDE the United States
4 ☐ Other employment OUTSIDE the United States, please specify_____

5 ☐ Faculty or other appointment at a United States university
6 ☐ Employment position in industry in the United States
7 ☐ Employment position in government in the United States
8 ☐ Other employment in the United States, please specify_____

9 ☐ Other, please specify _____ (68-76)

16. How many individuals (including yourself) work on the research project with which you have been involved? Please provide the number of individuals in each of the personnel groups below and rate the contributions made by each group to the OVERALL PRODUCTIVITY OF THE RESEARCH EFFORT. In rating the contributions, use the following scale:

1 = essential   3 = not important
2 = important   4 = cannot determine

Personnel Group	Number of individuals	Rating of contribution
Faculty	_____ (8-9)	_____ (10)
Postdoctoral appointees	_____ (11-12)	_____ (13)
Other doctoral staff (e.g., research scientists)	_____ (14-15)	_____ (16)
Graduate research assistants	_____ (17-18)	_____ (19)
Nondoctoral staff (e.g., technicians)	_____ (20-21)	_____ (22)

17. In general, how do you compare the contributions of the foreign postdoctoral appointees with other postdoctoral appointees in the department in which you have been working?

In terms of:		Foreign group is better	About the same	U.S. group is better
Overall productivity of research	(23)	1 ☐	2 ☐	3 ☐
Determining the basic directions of the research project	(24)	1 ☐	2 ☐	3 ☐
Intellectual vigor of the research effort	(25)	1 ☐	2 ☐	3 ☐
Infusion of new research techniques	(26)	1 ☐	2 ☐	3 ☐
Publication of research findings	(27)	1 ☐	2 ☐	3 ☐
Training of graduate students	(28)	1 ☐	2 ☐	3 ☐

Additional comments: _____
_____
_____ (29)

THANK YOU FOR YOUR COOPERATION

LIST OF EMPLOYMENT SPECIALTY AREAS (to be used for questions 7 and 9)

MATHEMATICS

- 000 - Algebra
- 010 - Analysis & Functional Analysis
- 020 - Geometry
- 030 - Logic
- 040 - Number Theory
- 052 - Probability
- 055 - Math Statistics (see also 544, 670, 725, 727)
- 060 - Topology
- 082 - Operations Research (see also 478)
- 085 - Applied Mathematics
- 089 - Combinatorics & Finite Mathematics
- 091 - Physical Mathematics
- 098 - Mathematics, General
- 099 - Mathematics, Other*

COMPUTER SCIENCES

- 071 - Theory
- 072 - Software Systems
- 073 - Hardware Systems
- 074 - Intelligent Systems
- 079 - Computer Sciences, Other* (see also 437, 476)

PHYSICS & ASTRONOMY

- 101 - Astronomy
- 102 - Astrophysics
- 110 - Atomic & Molecular Physics
- 120 - Electromagnetism
- 130 - Mechanics
- 132 - Acoustics
- 134 - Fluids
- 135 - Plasma Physics
- 136 - Optics
- 138 - Thermal Physics
- 140 - Elementary Particles
- 150 - Nuclear Structure
- 160 - Solid State
- 198 - Physics, General
- 199 - Physics, Other*

CHEMISTRY

- 200 - Analytical
- 210 - Inorganic
- 215 - Synthetic Inorganic & Organometallic
- 220 - Organic
- 225 - Synthetic Organic & Natural Products
- 230 - Nuclear
- 240 - Physical
- 245 - Quantum
- 250 - Theoretical
- 255 - Structural
- 260 - Agricultural & Food
- 265 - Thermodynamics & Material Properties
- 270 - Pharmaceutical
- 275 - Polymers
- 280 - Biochemistry (see also 540)
- 285 - Chemical Dynamics
- 298 - Chemistry, General
- 299 - Chemistry, Other*

EARTH, ENVIRONMENTAL, AND MARINE SCIENCES

- 301 - Mineralogy, Petrology
- 305 - Geochemistry
- 310 - Stratigraphy, Sedimentation
- 320 - Paleontology
- 330 - Structural Geology
- 341 - Geophysics (Solid Earth)
- 350 - Geomorph. & Glacial Geology
- 391 - Applied Geol., Geol. Engr. & Econ. Geol.
- 395 - Fuel Tech. & Petrol. Engr. (see also 479)
- 360 - Hydrology & Water Resources
- 370 - Oceanography
- 397 - Marine Sciences, Other*
- 381 - Atmospheric Physics & Chemistry
- 382 - Atmospheric Dynamics
- 383 - Atmospheric Sciences, Other*
- 388 - Environmental Sciences, General (see also 480, 528)
- 389 - Environmental Sciences, Other*
- 398 - Earth Sciences, General
- 399 - Earth Sciences, Other*

ENGINEERING

- 400 - Aeronautical & Astronautical
- 410 - Agricultural
- 415 - Biomedical
- 420 - Civil
- 430 - Chemical
- 435 - Ceramic
- 437 - Computer
- 440 - Electrical
- 445 - Electronics
- 450 - Industrial & Manufacturing
- 455 - Nuclear
- 460 - Engineering Physics
- 470 - Mechanical
- 475 - Metallurgy & Phys. Met. Engr.
- 476 - Systems Design & Systems Science (see also 072, 073, 074)
- 478 - Operations Research (see also 082)
- 479 - Fuel Technology & Petrol. Engr. (see also 395)
- 480 - Sanitary & Environmental
- 486 - Mining
- 497 - Materials Science
- 498 - Engineering, General
- 499 - Engineering, Other*

AGRICULTURAL SCIENCES

- 500 - Agronomy
- 501 - Agricultural Economics
- 502 - Animal Husbandry
- 503 - Food Science & Technology (see also 573)
- 504 - Fish & Wildlife
- 505 - Forestry
- 506 - Horticulture
- 507 - Soils & Soil Science
- 510 - Animal Science & Animal Nutrition
- 511 - Phytopathology
- 518 - Agriculture, General
- 519 - Agriculture, Other*

MEDICAL SCIENCES

- 520 - Medicine & Surgery
- 522 - Public Health & Epidemiology
- 523 - Veterinary Medicine
- 524 - Hospital Administration
- 526 - Nursing
- 527 - Parasitology
- 528 - Environmental Health
- 534 - Pathology
- 536 - Pharmacology
- 537 - Pharmacy
- 538 - Medical Sciences, General
- 539 - Medical Sciences, Other*

BIOLOGICAL SCIENCES

- 540 - Biochemistry (see also 280)
- 542 - Biophysics
- 543 - Biomathematics
- 544 - Biometrics and Biostatistics (see also 055, 670, 725, 727)
- 545 - Anatomy
- 546 - Cytology
- 547 - Embryology
- 548 - Immunology
- 550 - Botany
- 560 - Ecology
- 562 - Hydrobiology
- 564 - Microbiology & Bacteriology
- 566 - Physiology, Animal
- 567 - Physiology, Plant
- 569 - Zoology
- 570 - Genetics
- 571 - Entomology
- 572 - Molecular Biology
- 573 - Food Science & Technology (see also 503)
- 574 - Behavior/Ethology
- 576 - Nutrition & Dietetics
- 578 - Biological Sciences, General
- 579 - Biological Sciences, Other*

PSYCHOLOGY

- 600 - Clinical
- 610 - Counseling & Guidance
- 620 - Developmental & Gerontological
- 630 - Education
- 635 - School Psychology
- 641 - Experimental
- 642 - Comparative
- 643 - Physiological
- 650 - Industrial & Personnel
- 660 - Personality
- 670 - Psychometrics (see also 055, 544, 725, 727)
- 680 - Social
- 698 - Psychology, General
- 699 - Psychology, Other*

SOCIAL SCIENCES

- 700 - Anthropology
- 703 - Archeology
- 708 - Communications*
- 709 - Linguistics
- 710 - Sociology
- 720 - Economics (see also 501)
- 725 - Econometrics (see also 055, 544, 670, 727)
- 727 - Social Statistics (see also 055, 544, 670, 725)
- 740 - Geography
- 745 - Area Studies*
- 751 - Political Science
- 752 - Public Administration
- 755 - International Relations
- 770 - Urban & Regional Planning
- 775 - History & Philosophy of Science
- 798 - Social Sciences, General
- 799 - Social Sciences, Other*

ARTS & HUMANITIES

- 841 - Fine & Applied Arts (including Music, Speech, Drama, etc.)
- 842 - History
- 843 - Philosophy, Religion, Theology
- 845 - Languages & Literature
- 846 - Other Arts and Humanities*

EDUCATION & OTHER PROFESSIONAL FIELDS

- 938 - Education

- 882 - Business Administration
- 883 - Home Economics
- 884 - Journalism
- 885 - Speech and Hearing Sciences
- 886 - Law, Jurisprudence
- 887 - Social Work
- 891 - Library & Archival Science
- 898 - Professional Field, Other*

- 899 - OTHER FIELDS*

*Identify the specific field in the space on the questionnaire.

381

NATIONAL RESEARCH COUNCIL
COMMISSION ON HUMAN RESOURCES

2101 Constitution Avenue   Washington, D. C. 20418

**COMMITTEE ON THE STUDY OF
POSTDOCTORALS AND DOCTORAL RESEARCH STAFF**

Lee Grodzins, *Chairman*
Massachusetts Institute of
Technology

Richard D. Anderson
Louisiana State University

Frederick E. Balderston
University of California
Berkeley, California

Kenneth E. Clark
University of Rochester

Gerhart Friedlander
Brookhaven National Laboratory

Herbert Friedman
Naval Research Laboratory

John C. Hancock
Purdue University

Donald F. Hornig
Harvard School of Public Health

Shirley Ann Jackson
Bell Laboratories

Ernest S. Kuh
University of California
Berkeley, California

William F. Miller
Stanford University

Nicholas C. Mullins
Indiana University

Thomas A. Reichert
Carnegie-Mellon University

Helen R. Whiteley
University of Washington

September 1979

Dear Colleague:

The National Research Council has appointed a committee to study the policy implications of the changing role of postdoctorals and other doctoral research staff in science and engineering. During the last decade, in the face of reduced numbers of faculty openings, increasing numbers of young scientists and engineers have taken postdoctorals and other types of positions in universities and colleges as well as outside the academic setting. Of particular interest to the Committee are foreign citizens who have held postdoctoral appointments in United States universities. You have been included in a list of foreign postdoctorals provided by department chairmen. The accompanying survey requests information about your employment history and career plans.

The survey is sponsored by the National Science Foundation, but the survey records will be retained in the National Research Council. All information you provide is to be used for purposes of statistical description only and its confidentiality will be protected.

The survey results will provide a basis for the Committee's recommendations regarding federal and institutional policies. The success of this survey depends on your cooperation. Please return the completed questionnaire as soon as possible in the enclosed envelope. Thank you for your prompt assistance.

Sincerely,

Lee Grodzins
Chairman

* SURVEY OF FOREIGN SCIENTISTS AND ENGINEERS
* QUESTION 2

FIELD OF DOCTORATE		SURVEY RESP	TOTAL FRGN PDOCS	MALE	FEML
ALL SCIENCES & ENGR	H	520	523	88.5	11.5
PHYSICAL/MATH SCI	H	296	298	89.5	10.5
ENGINEERING	H	62	62	98.4	1.6
LIFE SCIENCES	H	146	147	84.9	15.1
SOCIAL SCI (INCL PSYCH)	H	8	8	62.5	37.5
UNKNOWN	H	8	8	62.5	37.5

* SURVEY OF FOREIGN SCIENTISTS AND ENGINEERS
* QUESTION 3

CCUNTRY OF CITIZENSHIP

FIELD OF DOCTORATE		SURVEY RESP	TOTAL FRGN PDOCS	CAN	MEX & CENTR AMER	SOUTH AMER	NTHRN EUR	CENTR EUR	EAST EUR	WEST EUR	EAST ASIA	WEST ASIA	AUSTR-ALASIA	AFRICA
ALL SCIENCES & ENGR	H	513	523	4.3	.2	2.1	14.4	6.2	4.3	7.2	28.1	25.3	5.8	1.9
PHYSICAL/MATH SCI	H	292	298	4.8	.3	1.4	14.4	6.5	5.8	8.6	25.3	26.0	5.1	1.7
ENGINEERING	H	61	62				9.8	4.9	3.3		41.0	31.1	6.6	3.3
LIFE SCIENCES	H	145	147	5.5		3.4	15.9	5.5	1.4	6.9	30.3	23.4	5.5	2.1
SOCIAL SCI (INCL PSYCH)	H	8	8				25.0	12.5	12.5	25.0			25.0	
UNKNOWN	H	7	8			28.6	14.3	14.3			14.3	14.3		

* SURVEY OF FOREIGN SCIENTISTS AND ENGINEERS
* QUESTION 4

		SURVEY RESP	TOTAL FRGN PDOCS	TYPE OF VISA				
				PERM RES	STUD-ENT	TEMP WORK	EXCH	OTHER
FIELD OF DOCTORATE								
ALL SCIENCES & ENGR	H	515	523	23.5	4.1	7.0	64.5	1.0
PHYSICAL/MATH SCI	H	296	298	19.9	4.1	8.8	66.2	1.0
ENGINEERING	H	61	62	32.8	8.2	6.6	50.8	1.6
LIFE SCIENCES	H	143	147	26.6	2.8	4.2	66.4	
SOCIAL SCI (INCL PSYCH)	H	8	8	50.0			37.5	12.5
UNKNOWN	H	7	8				100.0	

* SURVEY OF FOREIGN SCIENTISTS AND ENGINEERS
* QUESTION 5

FIELD OF DOCTORATE		SURVEY RESP	TOTAL FRGN PDOCS	MAR- RIED	NOT MAR- RIED
ALL SCIENCES & ENGR	H	522	523	71.8	28.2
PHYSICAL/MATH SCI	H	298	298	68.1	31.9
ENGINEERING	H	62	62	77.4	22.6
LIFE SCIENCES	H	147	147	78.2	21.8
SOCIAL SCI (INCL PSYCH)	H	8	8	62.5	37.5
UNKNOWN	H	7	8	57.1	42.9

* SURVEY OF FOREIGN SCIENTISTS AND ENGINEERS
* QUESTION 6

FIELD OF DOCTORATE		SURVEY RESP	TOTAL FRGN PDOCS	NUMBER OF DEPENDENTS					
				0	1	2	3	4	>4
ALL SCIENCES & ENGR	H	502	523	31.7	20.7	22.1	18.1	5.8	1.6
PHYSICAL/MATH SCI	H	288	298	34.7	20.5	21.2	17.4	4.9	1.4
ENGINEERING	H	59	62	18.6	27.1	30.5	18.6	3.4	1.7
LIFE SCIENCES	H	142	147	29.6	17.6	21.8	20.4	9.2	1.4
SOCIAL SCI (INCL PSYCH)	H	8	8	50.0	25.0	12.5	12.5		
UNKNOWN	H	5	8	40.0	40.0				20.0

* SURVEY OF FOREIGN SCIENTISTS AND ENGINEERS
* QUESTION 7A

		TOTAL	TITLE OF DEGREE		
					MD &
	SURVEY	FRGN	U.S.	FRGN	OTHER
FIELD OF DOCTORATE	RESP	PDOCS	PHD	PHD	PROF
ALL SCIENCES & ENGR	H	486	523	31.7	66.7	1.6
PHYSICAL/MATH SCI	H	278	298	29.1	70.9	
ENGINEERING	H	61	62	49.2	50.8	
LIFE SCIENCES	H	135	147	29.6	64.4	5.9
SOCIAL SCI (INCL PSYCH)	H	8	8	37.5	62.5	
UNKNOWN	H	4	8		100.0	

387

* SURVEY OF FOREIGN SCIENTISTS AND ENGINEERS
* QUESTION 78

FIELD OF DOCTORATE		SURVEY RESP	TOTAL FRGN PDOCS	CY OF DOCTORATE							
				PRE60	60-64	65-69	70-71	72-73	74-75	76-77	78-79
ALL SCIENCES & ENGR	H	483	523	.2	.8	4.1	3.3	8.7	15.9	31.3	35.6
PHYSICAL/MATH SCI	H	277	298	.4	1.4	4.7	2.9	7.9	14.8	31.4	36.5
ENGINEERING	H	60	62			1.7	3.3	13.3	6.7	30.0	45.0
LIFE SCIENCES	H	134	147			3.7	4.5	8.2	21.6	32.1	29.9
SOCIAL SCI (INCL PSYCH)	H	8	8					12.5	25.0	37.5	25.0
UNKNOWN	H	4	8			25.0			25.0		50.0

388

* SURVEY OF FOREIGN SCIENTISTS AND ENGINEERS
* QUESTION 8

FIELD OF DOCTORATE		SURVEY RESP	TOTAL FRGN PDOCS	LENGTH OF POSTDOCTORAL APPOINTMENT				
				1 YR OR LESS	2 YRS	3 YRS	4 YRS	MORE THAN 5 YRS
ALL SCIENCES & ENGR	H	461	523	37.7	43.4	15.4	2.6	.9
PHYSICAL/MATH SCI	H	269	298	42.4	40.5	14.5	2.6	
ENGINEERING	H	54	62	37.0	46.3	11.1	1.9	3.7
LIFE SCIENCES	H	125	147	27.2	48.0	20.0	3.2	1.6
SOCIAL SCI (INCL PSYCH)	H	6	8	33.3	50.0	16.7		
UNKNOWN	H	7	8	57.1	42.9			

389

* SURVEY OF FOREIGN SCIENTISTS AND ENGINEERS
* QUESTION 9

FIELD OF DOCTORATE		SURVEY RESP	TOTAL FRGN PDOCS	POSITION HELD PRIOR TO POSTDOC					
				GRAD STDT	POST DOC	FAC-ULTY POSIT	OTHER UNIV POSIT	INDUS POSIT	GOVT POSIT	OTHER
ALL SCIENCES & ENGR	H	500	523	39.2	24.0	21.0	4.8	2.2	5.2	3.6
PHYSICAL/MATH SCI	H	284	298	34.5	26.4	22.2	5.6	2.8	4.9	3.5
ENGINEERING	H	61	62	59.0	11.5	19.7		3.3	4.9	1.6
LIFE SCIENCES	H	141	147	39.7	25.5	18.4	5.0	.7	5.7	5.0
SOCIAL SCI (INCL PSYCH)	H	7	8	42.9		42.9	14.3			
UNKNOWN	H	7	8	42.9	28.6	14.3			14.3	

390

* SURVEY OF FOREIGN SCIENTISTS AND ENGINEERS
* QUESTION 9A

FIELD OF DOCTORATE		SURVEY RESP	TOTAL FRGN PDOCS	FIELD OF PRIOR POSITION			
				PHYS SCI & MATH	ENGIN	LIFE SCI & SCI	SOC SCI & PSYCH
ALL SCIENCES & ENGR	H	487	523	55.6	12.9	29.8	1.6
PHYSICAL/MATH SCI	H	276	298	95.7	2.2	2.2	
ENGINEERING	H	59	62	5.1	94.9		
LIFE SCIENCES	H	140	147	.7	.7	97.9	.7
SOCIAL SCI (INCL PSYCH)	H	7	8				100.0
UNKNOWN	H	5	8	60.0		40.0	

* SURVEY OF FOREIGN SCIENTISTS AND ENGINEERS
* QUESTION 10

REASON FOR TAKING POSTDOC AT U.S. UNIVERSITY

FIELD OF DOCTORATE		SURVEY RESP	TOTAL FRGN PDOCS	NO TRNG NATIVE CNTRY	WORK WITH MENTR	WORK IN U.S.	NO EMPL IN NATIVE CNTRY	OTHER REASON
ALL SCIENCES & ENGR	H	519	523	10.0	58.6	19.8	6.7	4.8
PHYSICAL/MATH SCI	H	296	298	10.5	57.4	19.6	7.8	4.7
ENGINEERING	H	62	62	4.8	50.0	30.6	9.7	4.8
LIFE SCIENCES	H	147	147	9.5	64.6	17.0	4.1	4.8
SOCIAL SCI (INCL PSYCH)	H	7	8	28.6	42.9	14.3		14.3
UNKNOWN	H	7	8	28.6	71.4			

392

* SURVEY OF FOREIGN SCIENTISTS AND ENGINEERS
* QUESTION 11

PCSTDOCTORAL IMPORTANCE FOR ATTAINING POSITION

FIELD OF DOCTORATE		SURVEY RESP	TOTAL FRGN PDOCS	VERY IMPRT	SCME- TIMES HELP	NOT IMPRT	CAN'T DETER
ALL SCIENCES & ENGR	H	516	523	32.4	44.0	9.7	14.0
PHYSICAL/MATH SCI	H	297	298	30.6	45.8	8.8	14.8
ENGINEERING	H	61	62	29.5	44.3	9.8	16.4
LIFE SCIENCES	H	144	147	38.9	38.9	11.1	11.1
SOCIAL SCI (INCL PSYCH)	H	7	8	14.3	57.1	14.3	14.3
UNKNOWN	H	7	8	14.3	57.1	14.3	14.3

393

* SURVEY OF FOREIGN SCIENTISTS AND ENGINEERS
* QUESTION 13

FIELD OF DOCTORATE		SURVEY RESP	TOTAL FRGN PDOCS	PRIMARY SOURCE OF SUPPORT FOR POSTDOC						
				U.S. RSRCH GRANT FUND	UNIV/ STATE FUND	OTHER U.S. SOURCE	FRGN GOVT FUNDS	OTHER FRGN FUNDS	PERS RSRC	OTHER SOURCE
ALL SCIENCES & ENGR	H	515	523	66.6	13.4	10.7	5.6	1.9	1.0	.8
PHYSICAL/MATH SCI	H	295	298	72.2	10.8	9.8	4.1	1.7	1.0	.3
ENGINEERING	H	60	62	66.7	15.0	15.0	1.7	1.7		
LIFE SCIENCES	H	147	147	57.1	19.0	10.9	9.5	2.0	.7	.7
SOCIAL SCI (INCL PSYCH)	H	7	8	28.6	14.3	14.3		14.3	14.3	28.6
UNKNOWN	H	6	8	66.7			33.3			

* SURVEY OF FOREIGN SCIENTISTS AND ENGINEERS
* QUESTION 14

EMPLOYMENT PLANS AFTER POSTDOCTORAL

FIELD OF DOCTORATE		SURVEY RESP	TOTAL FRGN PDOCS	EMPL OUT-SIDE U.S.	U.S. POST-DOC	U.S. FAC-ULTY POSIT	OTHER U.S. UNIV POSIT	U.S. INDUS POSIT	U.S. GOVT POSIT	OTHER U.S. EMPL	OTHER
ALL SCIENCES & ENGR	H	514	523	55.8	4.7	22.2	1.8	13.4	1.0	1.0	.2
PHYSICAL/MATH SCI	H	293	298	60.4	3.1	17.7	2.0	14.0	1.4	1.4	
ENGINEERING	H	60	62	35.0	3.3	30.0		30.0	1.7	1.7	
LIFE SCIENCES	H	147	147	55.1	6.8	27.9	2.0	6.8		.7	.7
SOCIAL SCI (INCL PSYCH)	H	7	8	42.9	28.6	28.6					
UNKNOWN	H	7	8	71.4	14.3	14.3					

* SURVEY OF FOREIGN SCIENTISTS AND ENGINEERS
* QUESTION 15

FIELD OF DOCTORATE		SURVEY RESP	TOTAL FRGN PDOCS	LONG-TERM CAREER PLANS								
				FRGN UNIV POSIT	FRGN INDUS POSIT	FRGN GOVT POSIT	OTHER FRGN EMPL	U.S. UNIV POSIT	U.S. INDUS POSIT	U.S. GOVT POSIT	OTHER U.S. EMPL	OTHER
ALL SCIENCES & ENGR	H	499	523	46.9	5.6	3.8	1.8	25.9	13.0	2.2	.2	.6
PHYSICAL/MATH SCI	H	287	298	46.7	8.0	3.5	2.8	22.0	14.3	2.1	.3	.3
ENGINEERING	H	60	62	31.7	6.7	3.3		30.0	23.3	5.0		
LIFE SCIENCES	H	139	147	53.2		4.3	.7	31.7	7.2	1.4		1.4
SOCIAL SCI (INCL PSYCH)	H	7	8	42.9		14.3		42.9				
UNKNOWN	H	6	8	66.7	16.7			16.7				

396

FIELD OF DOCTORATE		SURVEY RESP	TOTAL FRGN PDOCS	FACULTY CONTRIBUTION TO RESEARCH EFFORT				
				ESSE- NTIAL	IMPO- RTANT	UNIM- PORT- ANT	NONE IN DEPT	CAN'T DETER- MINE
ALL SCIENCES & ENGR	H	507	523	54.0	31.2	4.7	5.7	4.3
PHYSICAL/MATH SCI	H	289	298	54.3	30.4	5.2	5.5	4.5
ENGINEERING	H	62	62	54.8	27.4	3.2	3.2	11.3
LIFE SCIENCES	H	144	147	52.1	34.7	4.9	6.9	1.4
SOCIAL SCI (INCL PSYCH)	H	7	8	57.1	28.6		14.3	
UNKNOWN	H	5	8	80.0	20.0			

* SURVEY OF FOREIGN SCIENTISTS AND ENGINEERS
* QUESTION 16.2

FIELD OF DOCTORATE		SURVEY RESP	TOTAL FRGN PDOCS	POSTDOC CONTRIBUTION TO RESEARCH EFFORT			
				ESSE-NTIAL	IMPO-RTANT	UNIM-PORT-ANT	CAN'T DETER-MINE
ALL SCIENCES & ENGR	H	508	523	53.0	20.5	2.6	24.0
PHYSICAL/MATH SCI	H	290	298	52.8	24.5	2.4	20.3
ENGINEERING	H	62	62	58.1	12.9	3.2	25.8
LIFE SCIENCES	H	144	147	54.9	15.3	2.1	27.8
SOCIAL SCI (INCL PSYCH)	H	7	8	14.3	28.6	14.3	42.9
UNKNOWN	H	5	8		20.0		80.0

398

* SURVEY OF FOREIGN SCIENTISTS AND ENGINEERS
* QUESTION 16.3

FIELD OF DOCTORATE		SURVEY RESP	TOTAL FRGN PDOCS	OTHER PHD'S CONTRIBUTION TO RESEARCH EFFORT				
				ESSENTIAL	IMPORTANT	UNIMPORTANT	NONE IN DEPT	CAN'T DETERMINE
ALL SCIENCES & ENGR	H	507	523	5.9	8.3	3.0	82.2	.6
PHYSICAL/MATH SCI	H	289	298	6.6	8.0	3.1	81.7	.7
ENGINEERING	H	62	62	1.6	4.8	4.8	87.1	1.6
LIFE SCIENCES	H	144	147	4.9	11.1	2.1	81.9	
SOCIAL SCI (INCL PSYCH)	H	7	8	28.6			71.4	
UNKNOWN	H	5	8	20.0			80.0	

399

* SURVEY OF FOREIGN SCIENTISTS AND ENGINEERS
* QUESTION 16.4

GRAD RA'S CONTRIBUTION TO RESEARCH EFFORT

FIELD OF DOCTORATE		SURVEY RESP	TOTAL FRGN PDOCS	ESSE-NTIAL	IMPO-RTANT	UNIM-PORT-ANT	NONE IN DEPT	CAN'T DETER-MINE
ALL SCIENCES & ENGR	H	508	523	8.9	32.1	8.3	46.1	4.7
PHYSICAL/MATH SCI	H	290	298	10.3	32.4	9.7	42.1	5.5
ENGINEERING	H	62	62	9.7	37.1	6.5	43.5	3.2
LIFE SCIENCES	H	144	147	5.6	30.6	4.9	54.9	4.2
SOCIAL SCI (INCL PSYCH)	H	7	8	14.3	14.3	28.6	42.9	
UNKNOWN	H	5	8	20.0	20.0		60.0	

* SURVEY OF FOREIGN SCIENTISTS AND ENGINEERS
* QUESTION 16.5

FIELD OF DOCTORATE		SURVEY RESP	TOTAL FRGN PDOCS	OTHER STAFF'S CONTRIBUTION TO RESEARCH EFFORT				
				ESSE- NTIAL	IMPO- RTANT	UNIM- PORT- ANT	NONE IN DEPT	CAN'T DETER- MINE
ALL SCIENCES & ENGR	H	507	523	8.5	23.7	6.9	57.8	3.2
PHYSICAL/MATH SCI	H	289	298	6.6	17.0	5.5	68.5	2.4
ENGINEERING	H	62	62	11.3	22.6	3.2	59.7	3.2
LIFE SCIENCES	H	144	147	11.1	36.8	11.8	35.4	4.9
SOCIAL SCI (INCL PSYCH)	H	7	8		42.9		57.1	
UNKNOWN	H	5	8	20.0	20.0		60.0	

401

* SURVEY OF FOREIGN SCIENTISTS AND ENGINEERS
* QUESTION 17.1

FOREIGN POSTDOCS VERSUS U.S. POSTDOCS IN TERMS OF
OVERALL PRODUCTIVITY OF RESEARCH

FIELD OF DOCTORATE		SURVEY RESP	TOTAL FRGN PDOCS	FRGN GROUP BETTER	SAME	U.S. GROUP BETTER
ALL SCIENCES & ENGR	H	422	523	33.9	61.4	4.7
PHYSICAL/MATH SCI	H	242	298	33.5	62.0	4.5
ENGINEERING	H	49	62	49.0	46.9	4.1
LIFE SCIENCES	H	124	147	30.6	64.5	4.8
SOCIAL SCI (INCL PSYCH)	H	3	8		100.0	
UNKNOWN	H	4	8		75.0	25.0

402

FOREIGN POSTDOCS VERSUS U.S. POSTDOCS IN TERMS OF DETERMINING BASIC DIRECTIONS OF RESEARCH

FIELD OF DOCTORATE		SURVEY RESP	TOTAL FRGN PDOCS	FRGN GROUP BETTER	SAME	U.S. GROUP BETTER
ALL SCIENCES & ENGR	H	413	523	13.3	70.9	15.7
PHYSICAL/MATH SCI	H	237	298	12.7	72.2	15.2
ENGINEERING	H	48	62	27.1	58.3	14.6
LIFE SCIENCES	H	121	147	9.9	74.4	15.7
SOCIAL SCI (INCL PSYCH)	H	3	8		66.7	33.3
UNKNOWN	H	4	8		50.0	50.0

FOREIGN POSTDOCS VERSUS U.S. POSTDOCS IN TERMS OF
INTELLECTUAL VIGOR OF RESEARCH EFFORT

FIELD OF DOCTORATE		SURVEY RESP	TOTAL FRGN PDOCS	FRGN GROUP BETTER	SAME	U.S. GROUP BETTER
ALL SCIENCES & ENGR	H	411	523	30.4	64.2	5.4
PHYSICAL/MATH SCI	H	234	298	32.9	61.5	5.6
ENGINEERING	H	48	62	45.8	54.2	
LIFE SCIENCES	H	122	147	21.3	73.8	4.9
SOCIAL SCI (INCL PSYCH)	H	3	8		66.7	33.3
UNKNOWN	H	4	8		50.0	50.0

404

* SURVEY OF FOREIGN SCIENTISTS AND ENGINEERS
* QUESTION 17.4

FOREIGN POSTDOCS VERSUS U.S. POSTDOCS IN TERMS OF
INFUSION OF NEW RESEARCH TECHNIQUES

FIELD OF DOCTORATE		SURVEY RESP	TOTAL FRGN PDOCS	FRGN GROUP BETTER	SAME	U.S. GROUP BETTER
ALL SCIENCES & ENGR	H	411	523	18.7	63.3	18.0
PHYSICAL/MATH SCI	H	234	298	17.1	65.4	17.5
ENGINEERING	H	48	62	20.8	68.8	10.4
LIFE SCIENCES	H	122	147	20.5	59.0	20.5
SOCIAL SCI (INCL PSYCH)	H	3	8	33.3	33.3	33.3
UNKNOWN	H	4	8	25.0	25.0	50.0

405

* SURVEY OF FOREIGN SCIENTISTS AND ENGINEERS
* QUESTION 17.5

FOREIGN POSTDOCS VERSUS U.S. POSTDOCS IN TERMS OF
PUBLICATION OF RESEARCH FINDINGS

FIELD OF DOCTORATE		SURVEY RESP	TOTAL FRGN PDOCS	FRGN GROUP BETTER	SAME	U.S. GROUP BETTER
ALL SCIENCES & ENGR	H	411	523	16.3	57.7	26.0
PHYSICAL/MATH SCI	H	234	298	17.9	55.1	26.9
ENGINEERING	H	48	62	20.8	50.0	29.2
LIFE SCIENCES	H	122	147	12.3	63.9	23.8
SOCIAL SCI (INCL PSYCH)	H	3	8		66.7	33.3
UNKNOWN	H	4	8		100.0	

406

* SURVEY OF FOREIGN SCIENTISTS AND ENGINEERS
* Q17.6

FCREIGN PCSTDOCS VERSUS U.S. POSTDOCS IN TERMS OF
TRAINING OF GRADUATE STUDENTS

FIELD OF DOCTORATE		SURVEY RESP	TOTAL FRGN PDOCS	FRGN GROUP BETTER	SAME	U.S. GROUP BETTER
ALL SCIENCES & ENGR	H	399	523	13.5	50.6	35.8
PHYSICAL/MATH SCI	H	227	298	15.4	50.7	33.9
ENGINEERING	H	49	62	20.4	53.1	26.5
LIFE SCIENCES	H	116	147	6.9	50.9	42.2
SOCIAL SCI (INCL PSYCH)	H	3	8		66.7	33.3
UNKNOWN	H	4	8	25.0		75.0

407

APPENDIX G

SAMPLING ERROR ESTIMATES FOR SURVEY DATA

Most of the statistics presented in this report are ratios
of two weighted sums of responses to national surveys conducted
under the aegis of our committee. To assist the reader in
interpreting the statistics reported from the surveys of
FY1978 and FY1972 Ph.D. recipients and the survey of department
chairmen, approximate sampling errors have been calculated for
each survey. The sampling error is a measure of the precision
with which a statistic derived from a survey sample approximates
the true population parameter being estimated. On the assumption
that the sample statistic is normally distributed around the
true population parameter, a confidence interval can be established around the sample statistic. Under this assumption,
the probability that it lies within two sampling errors of the
actual parameter is about .95--and within three sampling errors,
about .99. For example, given a survey estimate of 50 percent
with a sampling error of 5 percent, we can infer that the
likelihood that the true population parameter is between 45 and
55 percent is .67. There is a .95 likelihood that it falls
between 40 and 60 percent, and .99 likelihood between 35 and
65 percent.

The sampling error estimates presented in the three tables
that follow were computed on the basis of a simple random design,
using the expression:

$$Se = \left[\frac{p(1-p)(N-n)}{n(N-1)} \right]^{\frac{1}{2}}$$

where

p = reported percentage
N = total population size
n = number of respondents

Each table gives approximate sampling errors associated with
alternative ranges of percentages that might be reported for
certain groups included in one of the surveys. Table G.1
provides sampling errors for types of departments frequently
examined in the committee's Survey of Chairmen of Science and
Engineering Departments. Tables G.2 and G.3 give sampling
errors for groups of scientists and engineers frequently
analyzed in the surveys of FY1972 and FY1978 Ph.D. recipients.
Sampling errors associated with other groups analyzed in this
study may be calculated using the above expression.

In addition to the three surveys mentioned above, two other
data sources are utilized extensively in this report: the
Survey of Earned Doctorates and the Survey of Doctorate Recipients (both conducted by the National Research Council).
The former survey compiles responses from all new Ph.D. recipients each year and consequently involves no sampling error.
The latter is a survey of an 8-20 percent sample of doctoral
scientists and engineers. A comprehensive description of
sampling errors associated with results from this survey is
given in National Research Council, Science, Engineering, and
Humanities Doctorates in the United States: 1979 Profile.

Table G.1

APPROXIMATE SAMPLING ERRORS ASSOCIATED WITH VARIOUS PERCENTAGES
REPORTED IN THE SURVEY OF CHAIRMEN OF SCIENCE AND ENGINEERING DEPARTMENTS

	Total Depts.	Survey Response[1]	Percentage Reported				
			1-10% or 90-99%	11-20% or 80-89%	21-30% or 70-79%	31-40% or 60-69%	41-50% or 50-59%
All Departments	1601	650	0-1%	1%	1%	1%	1-2%
Departmental Field							
Mathematical Sciences	28	22	1-3%	3-4%	4-5%	5%	5%
Physics	152	86	1-2%	2-3%	3%	3%	4%
Chemistry	162	82	1-2%	2-3%	3-4%	4%	4%
Earth Sciences	67	49	1-2%	2-3%	3%	3-4%	4%
Engineering	205	85	1-2%	3%	3-4%	4%	4%
Agricultural Sciences	65	38	1-3%	3-4%	4-5%	5%	5%
Biosciences - Grad Schls	372	104	1-3%	3%	3-4%	4%	4%
Biosciences - Med Schls	430	105	1-3%	3%	3-4%	4%	4%
Psychology	62	45	1-2%	2-3%	3-4%	4%	4%
Social Sciences	58	34	1-3%	3-4%	5%	5%	5-6%
Department Within							
Private Institution	558	262	0-1%	1-2%	2%	2%	2%
Public Institution	1043	388	0-1%	1-2%	2%	2%	2%
Department With							
Five or more postdocs	761	280	0-1%	1-2%	2%	2%	2%
Fewer than five postdocs	840	370	0-1%	1-2%	2%	2%	2%

[1]Number of respondents to a particular survey item may vary somewhat. More precise estimates of sampling error for any size group may be calculated using the expression given on the first page of Appendix G. Response numbers exclude departments which reported that they had no postdoctorals in 1979.

Table G.2

APPROXIMATE SAMPLING ERRORS ASSOCIATED WITH VARIOUS PERCENTAGES
REPORTED IN THE SURVEY OF SCIENTISTS AND ENGINEERS--FY1972 PH.D. RECIPIENTS

	Total FY1972 Ph.D.'s	Survey Response[1]	Percentage Reported				
			1-10% or 90-99%	11-20% or 80-89%	21-30% or 70-79%	31-40% or 60-69%	41-50% or 50-59%
All FY1972 Ph.D.'s	15275	3589	0-½%	0-1%	1%	1%	1%
Ph.D. Field							
Mathematical Sciences	1021	171	1-2%	2-3%	3%	3%	3%
Physics	1264	619	0-1%	1%	1%	1%	1%
Chemistry	1610	319	0-2%	2%	2%	2%	2-3%
Earth Sciences	480	126	1-2%	2-3%	3-4%	4%	4%
Engineering	2357	224	1-2%	2-3%	3%	3%	3%
Agricultural Sciences	630	115	1-3%	3%	3-4%	4%	4%
Biosciences	3234	1372	0-1%	1%	1%	1%	1%
Psychology	2117	390	0-1%	1-2%	2%	2%	2%
Social Sciences	2562	253	1-2%	2%	2-3%	3%	3%
Postdoctoral Experience							
Some	4315	1586	0-1%	1%	1%	1%	1%
None	10960	2003	0-1%	1%	1%	1%	1%
Sex							
Men	13479	2915	0-½%	1%	1%	1%	1%
Women	1796	674	0-1%	1%	1%	1%	1-2%
Racial Group							
White	14559	3404	0-½%	0-1%	1%	1%	1%
Other	716	185	1-2%	2-3%	3%	3%	3%

[1]Number of respondents to a particular survey item may vary somewhat. More precise estimates of sampling error for any size group may be calculated using the expression given on the first page of Appendix G. Response numbers exclude scientists and engineers who reported that they were employed outside the United States in 1979.

Table G.3

APPROXIMATE SAMPLING ERRORS ASSOCIATED WITH VARIOUS PERCENTAGES
REPORTED IN THE SURVEY OF SCIENTISTS AND ENGINEERS--FY1978 PH.D. RECIPIENTS

	Total FY1978 Ph.D.'s	Survey Response[1]	Percentage Reported				
			1-10% or 90-99%	11-20% or 80-89%	21-30% or 70-79%	31-40% or 60-69%	41-50% or 50-59%
All FY1978 Ph.D.'s	14062	4110	0-½%	0-1%	1%	1%	1%
Ph.D. Field							
Mathematical Sciences	710	177	1-2%	2-3%	3%	3%	3%
Physics	788	521	0-1%	1%	1%	1%	1%
Chemistry	1189	249	1-2%	2%	2-3%	3%	3%
Earth Sciences	523	189	1-2%	2%	2-3%	3%	3%
Engineering	1310	261	1-2%	2%	2-3%	3%	3%
Agricultural Sciences	625	153	1-2%	2-3%	3%	3%	3-4%
Biosciences	3286	1765	0-½%	1%	1%	1%	1%
Psychology	2888	519	0-1%	1-2%	2%	2%	2%
Social Sciences	2743	276	1-2%	2%	2-3%	3%	3%
Postdoctoral Experience							
Some	4176	1979	0-½%	1%	1%	1%	1%
None	9886	2131	0-1%	1%	1%	1%	1%
Sex							
Men	11031	2989	0-½%	0-1%	1%	1%	1%
Women	3031	1121	0-1%	1%	1%	1%	1%
Racial Group							
White	13197	3639	0-½%	0-1%	1%	1%	1%
Other	865	471	0-1%	1%	1%	1-2%	2%

[1]Number of respondents to a particular survey item may vary somewhat. More precise estimates of sampling error for any size group may be calculated using the expression given on the first page of Appendix G. Response numbers exclude scientists and engineers who reported that they were employed outside the United States in 1979.